IMPROVING READING COMPREHENSION

IMPROVING READING COMPREHENSION: RESEARCH-BASED PRINCIPLES AND PRACTICES

Joanne F. Carlisle and Melinda S. Rice

York Press, Inc.
Baltimore, Maryland

This book was manufactured in the United States of America
Typography by Type Shoppe II Productions Ltd.
Printing and binding by Data Reproductions Corporation
Cover design by Joseph Dieter, Jr.

Library of Congress Cataloging-in-Publication Data
Carlisle, Joanne.
    Improving reading comprehension : research-based principles and practices / Joanne F. Carlisle and Melinda S. Rice.
        p. cm.
    Includes bibliographical references and index.
    ISBN 0-912752-70-X
        1. Reading comprehension. I. Rice, Melinda S. II. Title.

LB1050.45 C34 2002
372.47--dc21   2002033141

CONTENTS

PREFACE

There are many signs that reading instruction has assumed center stage in the contemporary educational arena.

- A number of expert panels have been convened for the purpose of clarifying the knowledge base pertaining to the teaching of reading across the life-span and with diverse populations of children. The National Research Council sponsored *Preventing Reading Difficulties in Young Children* (Snow, Burns, and Griffin 1998). The National Institute of Child Health and Human Development supported the preparation of *Teaching Children to Read: An Evidence-Based Assessment of the Scientific Research Literature on Reading and Its Implications for Reading Instruction* (National Reading Panel 2000). The Office of Educational Research and Improvement, in conjunction with RAND, published *Reading for Understanding: Toward an R & D Program in Reading Comprehension*.
- Professional organizations (such as the American Federation of Teachers, the National Council of Teachers of English, and the International Reading Association) have redrafted literacy teaching standards and launched significant efforts to disseminate the knowledge bases specific to the teaching of reading (e.g., the publication of *Teaching Reading IS Rocket Science* by the American Federation of Teachers).
- The American Speech, Language, Hearing Association has issued a position statement identifying the important role of speech and language clinicians in advancing literacy learning.
- The Reading Excellence Act, and its successors, Reading First and Early Reading First (totaling more than $5 billion over the next five years) are federal initiatives dedicated to enhancing the professional development of educators and the implementation of effective programs of reading instruction.

What is fueling these efforts? There are a number of sources of impetus. While mathematics achievement has shown steady improvement over the last 30 years (as reported by the National Assessment of Educational Progress), reading achievement has stagnated and even declined for 12th graders. Despite the fact that US 4th graders place close to the top in international comparisons of reading achievement, US 11th graders now place close to the bottom on international comparisons of reading achievement, behind students from a number of developing countries. Furthermore, the 1992 National Adult Literacy Survey revealed that more than 20% of adults in the U.S. read at or below a fifth-grade level.

The significance of this finding is made more salient when juxtaposed with the demands for literacy in today's culture and economy. While historians are careful to remind us that our nation's literacy skills have increased dramatically in response to new requirements and opportunities (Stedman and Kaestle 1991), there is evidence that literacy levels have not kept pace with the increased expectations relative to: attending to multiple features of information in lengthy and complex displays, comparing, contrasting, and integrating information, and generating ideas based upon what has been read. As a consequence, there is evidence of a widening division of our society based largely on race and socioeconomic status. From 1980-1994, the gap in earnings between professionals and clerical workers has grown from 47 to 86%; the gap between white collar workers and skilled tradespeople has risen from 2 to 37%, and earnings for college educated males have increased by 10% while earnings for those with high school diplomas have declined by 9% (Kirsch et al. 1993).

In response to the disparities between the literacy profiles of high school graduates and contemporary societal needs and demands, there are increased pressures on educators to do more to advance literacy achievement. Goals 2000 raised curricular standards to levels that are more consistent with those in other societies, and there are increased calls for students to achieve competence in the "new literacies" including their capacity to navigate, interpret, coordinate, and critique multi-media web-based sources.

These demands on educators are all the more challenging considering the changing demographics of contemporary US classrooms. According to the 1990 US census data, 6.3 million, or 14%, of the school-aged population come from a home in which a language other than English is spoken. Of this number, about half are students identified as English-language learners; furthermore, 53% of English Language Learners are found in kindergarten through fourth grades (August and Hakuta 1997). Second-language acquisition is a complex process in which the speaker must develop grammatical rules for sentence production, the vocabulary and pragmatic skills necessary for cognitive tasks, and the social aspects of language that facilitate interpersonal communication. Adding to the complexity of this picture is the fact that 77% of students learning English as a Second Language are eligible for free- or reduced-cost lunch, as compared with 33% of their peers attending the same schools (August and Hakuta 1997).

Finally, reauthorization of the Individuals with Disabilities Education Act (IDEA) and the increased inclusion of students with disabilities in general education classes also contribute to changing classroom demographics. Between 1997 and 1999, 88% of children with speech and language difficulties were being served primarily in general education settings (Nathanson 2001). Hence, well-prepared teachers must not only have in-depth knowledge of subject matter and how to teach subject matter effectively, they must also understand the variations in students' acquisition and development of reading, and the concomitant instructional implications.

One prominent theme emerging across these various literatures is the power of good instruction to develop proficient readers and prevent reading problems. Research is finally informing our understanding of the dramatic effect that teachers can have on outcomes for students. For example, "Students whose teachers have received training in working with special populations outperform their peers by more than one grade level" (NCATE 2001, p. 3); furthermore, teachers who have high expectations of all their students hold their students to high standards, provide more instructional opportunities, and realize higher learning gains (Entwisle and Alexander 1988). And, despite the complexity described above for English Language Learners, the best predictor of the success these children will experience acquiring literacy is their access to effective reading instruction (Goldenberg and Gallimore 1991; Slavin and Madden 1995). A second theme emerging from research syntheses is that there is a significant knowledge base informing us about the features of solid reading instruction. Many aspects of the knowledge base are richly presented in this volume by Carlisle and Rice.

There are several features of the volume that I find particularly noteworthy. One is the prominence assigned to language and language development as foundational to understanding reading development and the teaching of reading comprehension. Wong Fillmore and Snow (2000) have called for teachers to receive systematic and intensive preparation in "educational linguistics," arguing that such a grounding would support teachers' undertakings overall, and in particular, their teaching of literacy skills. In this volume, Carlisle and Rice provide such a grounding, signaling and illustrating the role that word, sentence, text structure, and discourse knowledge play in promoting or impeding reading comprehension.

A second feature that distinguishes this volume is the border crossing in which the authors have engaged. It is not uncommon in volumes of this kind to find one of two discrete research literatures cited; one that appears in journals populated with the work of those who conduct research with identified students receiving special education services (e.g., Journal of Learning Disabilities, Learning Disabilities: Research and Practice) and the other that appears in general education reading literature (e.g., Reading Research Quarterly). The authors have deftly drawn across these two literatures presenting information characterizing the many sources of variation in the development of reading comprehension and offering a full complement of approaches to enhancing comprehension instruction for diverse learners.

A third feature is the close attention paid to the developmental issues that attend reading comprehension instruction. Across the life-span, the purposes, texts, and contexts associated with comprehension activity are expanding. These differences have important implications for educators as they choose materials, design activities, and assess learning.

Finally, the authors have achieved a rare—but enormously useful—blending of instructional principles with specific instructional practices. This is particularly important in an area as complex as reading comprehension instruction. In order for educators to make wise decisions about what practices to use, for which individuals, and toward what ends, they have to be equipped with the knowledge base informing these practices. To illustrate, strategy instruction in reading comprehension has had considerable currency, but, in our research (Palincsar, Stevens, and Gavelek 1989), we saw significant differences in instructional opportunities and outcomes when teachers approached strategy instruction as a means to an end; that is, the construction of meaning, than when they approached the teaching of strategies as an end in itself.

In summary, this is a timely and accessible volume. It offers an array of tools in an accessible manner to support educators in planning, enacting, and evaluating instruction designed to support diverse readers in the complex activity of learning from text.

Annemarie Sullivan Palincsar
Jean and Charles Walgreen Professor of Reading and Literacy
University of Michigan

REFERENCES

August, D., and Hakuta, K. 1997. *Improving Schooling for Language-minority Children: A Research Agenda.* National Research Council. Washington, DC: National Academy Press.

Entwisle, D. R., and Alexander, K. L. 1988. Factors affecting achievement test scores and marks of black and white first graders. *The Elementary School Journal* 88:449–71.

Goldenberg, C. N., and Gallimore, R. 1991. Local knowledge, research knowledge, and educational change: A case study of early [first grade] Spanish reading improvement. *Educational Researcher* 20 (8):2–14.

Kirsch, I. S., Jungeblut, A., Jenkins, L., and Kolstad, A. 1993. *Executive Summary of Adult Literacy in America: A First Look at the Results of the National Adult Literacy Survey.* Retrieved June 3, 2002 from http://nces.ed.gov//naal/resources/execsumm.asp

National Reading Panel. 2000. *Teaching Children to Read: An Evidence-Based Assessment of the Scientific Research Literature on Reading and its Implications for Reading Instruction.* Washington, DC: National Institute of Child Health and Human Development.

Palincsar, A. S., Stevens, D. D., and Gavelek, J. R. 1989. Collaborating with teachers in the interest of student collaboration. *International Journal of Research in Education* 13:41–53.

RAND. 2002. *Reading for Understanding: Toward an R & D Program in Reading Comprehension.* Santa Monica, CA: RAND.

Slavin, R. E., and Madden, N. 1995. *Effects of Success for All on the Achievement of English Language Learners.*

Snow, C. E., Burns, M. S., and Griffin, P., Eds. 1998. *Preventing Reading Difficulties in Young Children.* Washington, DC: National Academy Press.

Stedman, L. C., and Kaestle, C. E. 1991. Literacy and reading performance in the United States from 1880 to the present. *Reading Research Quarterly* 22:8–46.

Wong Fillmore, L., and Snow, C. E. 2000. What teachers need to know about language. A paper prepared for the US Department of Education.

1

Instruction in Reading Comprehension: Goals and Challenges

GETTING STARTED

✓ What are the comprehension requirements for adults in today's technological society?
✓ Are schools preparing students to meet these requirements?
✓ What factors must teachers keep in mind in designing or choosing methods to improve students' reading comprehension?
✓ Who teaches reading comprehension—reading teachers? content area teachers? special education teachers? Who *should be* teaching reading comprehension?

LITERACY IN A TECHNOLOGICALLY ADVANCED SOCIETY

Our schools are responsible for making sure that students acquire skills in reading and writing. As members of a literate society, children must be prepared to earn a living, continue their education to meet vocational goals, and participate in civic responsibilities. In recent years, businesses and industries have found that many of their workers are ill-prepared for the literacy requirements of the workplace. State and local educational agencies establish the school curriculum and requirements for graduation, but they may not make decisions about these matters with the literacy requirements of adult life in mind (Venezky 2000). According to Venezky, the chasm between adult literacy needs and school literacy instruction began in the 18th century and continues today. In schools, students read literature and textbooks that hold information about content areas such as history and science. In the world outside of school, adults must cope with a broader set of literacy requirements, both in terms of the types of texts they encounter and the ways that they interface with them. Schools do not have a national policy with regard to adult literacy. They do provide a free public education through twelfth grade, but simply providing an *opportunity* to learn to read and write has left a large portion of the adults in the US with only basic reading and writing skills.

In the general population, national reports indicate that between a third and a half of all adults have only very basic literacy skills (Kirsch et al. 1993). Thornburg, Hoffman, and Remeika (1991) reported that more than 23 million adults were functionally illiterate and that 13% of all teenagers joined this group annually. Reading a daily newspaper, a bus schedule, or the directions on packages of household products would be a challenge for these adolescents and adults. National reports indicate particularly weak literacy skills among ethnic minorities, individuals for whom English is not the native language, and students with learning disabilities (LD) (Kirsch et al. 1993). Students who struggle with reading and writing in high school are very likely to drop out of school. Their low-level literacy skills limit their employment opportunities. They can hold such jobs as food servers in the fast-food industry, and in these jobs they are often supported by technology. For example, as Milulecky (in Smith et al. 2000) has pointed out, a worker who cannot read can nonetheless push the picture of French fries on the cash register. He added:

> The low salaries of these jobs tend to subsidize the technology directing human effort or supplanting human thought. On the positive side, such jobs can temporarily support people who have gained little from our educational system. On the negative side, very little learned in such jobs is likely to support moving up to jobs in the middle skill level, and some (perhaps many) people will be trapped in jobs well below their ability level (p. 380).

Quality of life in a highly technological society, such as that of the US, is largely dependent on the level of literacy an individual achieves. As industries and businesses invest in more and more technological advances, greater demands for both print and computer literacy are placed on the employees. In their lives outside of the workplace, as well, adults need to be able to read and understand complex information in different types of written texts, such as directions to complete tax returns or instructions on the labels of over-the-counter medications. To function independently in the US today, adults may need not only a variety of reading and writing skills that are typically taught in schools but also experience with types of texts and literacy requirements that fall outside the "traditional" areas of instruction in schools. Some examples of workplace literacy are instructions for operating machinery or guidelines for handling crises (Kirsch et al. 1993; Smith et al. 2000).

Some experts in reading believe that effective instruction in reading and writing, combined with a focus on the development of critical thinking skills, will arm students adequately to meet the challenges of adult literacy. For example, Chall (1990) argued that, to be prepared for the literacy requirements of a modern technological society, high school students need to be able to read a variety of texts written in sophisticated and abstract language and requiring a range of background knowledge and critical thinking. While not specifying where adults acquire sophisticated workplace literacy, Kibby (in Smith et al. 2000) had this to say about the future:

> In most workplaces, doing the job well will require accessing numerous knowledge bases (e.g., texts, manuals, tables, tapes, videos, graphics); reading, viewing, and listening to information (e.g., facts, viewpoints, analyses, critiques, demonstrations); understanding, analyzing, synthesizing, and evaluating this information; and then distributing or applying it (p. 380).

In recent years, businesses and industries have made an effort to provide training through workplace literacy programs. Although such programs may play an important role in preparing adults for specific types of workplace literacy, schools should be doing a lot more than they currently are to assure that students are prepared for the literacy demands they will face after they finish high school. Kibby placed the burden on the middle and high schools to raise expectations for what students can do with texts and information, to increase the amount of reading and the difficulty of texts, and to provide adequate instruction. Dole commented succinctly, "the alarmingly high rates of illiteracy and low-level literacy in the U.S., as well as elsewhere, must change" (in Smith et al. p. 383).

THE CURRENT DRIVE TO IMPROVE NATIONAL LITERACY

At present, there is a national drive to raise the standards for literacy in US schools. One goal is for all children to learn to read by the end of third grade, so that they have the basic skills that are the foundation for developing higher-level literacy skills and learning in the content areas. The national focus on literacy is in response to continued reports of poor reading achievement at all ages in US schools. For example, results of the 1998 National Assessment of Educational Progress indicated that 69 percent of fourth graders are reading below the proficient level (NAEP 1999).

In 1994, President Clinton signed into law the Goals 2000: Educate America Act. Since that time, a number of prestigious national committees have been formed to determine how best to bring about higher levels of literacy of all children. The National Research Council's Committee on Prevention of Reading Difficulties in Children undertook an evaluation of empirical research on reading and related fields in order to summarize the current status of our understanding of early reading difficulties. They provided recommendations for practitioners as well as researchers in their published report, *Preventing Reading Difficulties in Young Children* (Snow, Burns, and Griffin 1998). At about the same time, a group of reading experts compiled a report of research on reading instruction; the Report of the National Reading Panel (NRP Report 2000), *Teaching Every Child to Read*, has generated an interest in implementing those instructional methods that have been found to be effective in classrooms. Most recently (January of 2002), President Bush signed into law the No Child Left Behind Act, a reform of the Elementary and Secondary Education Act; this legislation is noteworthy for its promise of comprehensive federal support for the improvement of reading in the early school years.

Other projects currently sponsored by national organizations are focused on the development of performance standards for English and language arts. Many school reform projects are underway to determine how best to improve reading instruction in elementary schools where a large percent of the children are underachieving in reading (e.g., Kame'enui, Simmons, and Coyne 2000; Saint-Laurent et al. 1998; Taylor and Pearson 2001). In recent years, federal support for school improvement projects and "high-stakes" assessments have both worked to hold schools and teachers more responsible for the reading achievement of their students than has been the case in the past.

It is all well and good to set high standards, but it is imperative that we also help teachers who are responsible for helping all the children in their classes reach these standards. General curricular goals are offered by state and local educational agencies and professional organizations. For example, a third-grade objective might be: "Students can make predictions of up-coming events in stories." However, teachers need practical guidelines and measures to take. How should they teach third graders so that all can read fluently and with comprehension? How can teachers prepare students at the secondary level for the literacy challenges of adult life, including those of the workplace? One step that can be taken to help teachers answer such questions is to strengthen the links between research and practice. Researchers and teachers need to work together to identify instructional methods that are effective.

Do we already know how to improve students' reading comprehension? In some respects, yes, but there is still a lot to be learned. Recently published overviews of the research literature indicate that many methods of comprehension instruction have been found to improve the reading performance of school-age students (e.g., Gersten et al. 2001; Swanson 1999). Still, the Report of the National Reading Panel (NRP 2000) indicated that we lack sufficient well-designed studies in many areas of comprehension instruction to provide a basis for determining "best practices." A thorough evaluation of what we know and do not know about effective comprehension instruction has been compiled by a committee of reading experts commissioned by the RAND Foundation (RAND 2002). Their report shows the many challenges we continue to face in selecting methods of instruction that are likely to improve our students' reading comprehension. It is fair to say that as a nation, we are experiencing a surge of interest in reading comprehension, and we hope teachers and school administrators will participate in the dialogue about ways to improve students' reading comprehension.

Access to information about effective methods continues to be a problem for teachers. Books, instructional systems, computer programs, and the like are often advertised as providing the "best" methods of reading instruction. How can teachers who are busy with their students for a full school day evaluate these products and the claims of their proponents? This is a daunting task. One solution is for teachers to form study groups or school-wide discussion groups to search for and evaluate instructional methods and products (Putnam and Borko 2000). At the same time, they can discuss curricular goals common to all subject areas and domain-specific goals, given their school population and educational philosophy, and in this way identify programs of instruction appropriate for different grade levels and content areas.

Because schools, classrooms, teaching styles, and content goals vary so widely, no one method of comprehension instruction will be ideal for every classroom. Teachers need options, but they also need knowledge to select wisely among the options that are available. They must consider how the responsibilities for literacy are shared across the content domains and for the duration of students' years in schools. Gone are the days when the collective belief was that reading was taught in the early elementary years. Today, all teachers need to see themselves as teachers of reading, whether they work with kindergartners or high-school students in physics or math.

Of course, teachers must plan their courses with the curriculum of the specific courses they are teaching in mind. Initially, this means establishing goals for the year and selecting instructional techniques and materials to meet these goals. At the same time, they need to determine how they will ensure that their students are understanding and learning the ideas and information in the course(s). Assessment of learning provides the basis for evaluation of the effectiveness of instruction. In this phase of their planning, teachers must consider the learning capabilities and problems of the children and the demands placed on the children by the reading and other learning materials.

A MODEL FOR PLANNING INSTRUCTION IN READING COMPREHENSION

For many years, educators did not consider it necessary to provide instruction in reading comprehension. Becoming literate entailed reading, discussing, and writing about great literature and works of history and science. With the advent of the "basal reader," publishers provided post-reading questions and discussion topics for teachers to use with each reading selection. These were intended to focus students' thinking about central ideas and information, but they were also useful for evaluating the students' comprehension. The 1980s saw basal readers replaced with literature-based reading programs, in keeping with the whole language philosophy. Not only were teachers left with the job of making up their own reading activities, but they also were discouraged from providing direct instruction in skills and strategies. In the mean time, however, through the 1980s and 1990s, researchers completed numerous investigations of the effectiveness of strategies. Interest in the value of specific comprehension methods (e.g., summarizing texts) was followed by the belief that students needed to (and could) learn multiple strategies (Paris, Wasik, and Turner 1991; Pressley 2000). The consensus among researchers is that we know quite a bit about methods of instruction in comprehension that can be used to improve students' reading and learning from written texts, but we know far less about how to help teachers select methods and use them effectively in different educational settings (Dole 2000).

It is a mistake to assume that having learned about various procedures or strategies to aid comprehension and learning, the teacher's job is done. A comprehensive plan is needed. The teacher needs to map out the curricular goals for a course, and then plans for units and specific lessons can be made. At this level, it is important to take into account factors that play a role in students' comprehension and learning. A model of reading comprehension adapted from Mosenthal (1984), who in turn adapted it from Jenkins (1979), is very useful for this purpose. Figure 1.1 provides a schematic diagram of this model, which we call the context pyramid. It shows that five factors interact and mutually influence student outcomes when reading in the classroom; these are the reader, the text, the setting, the task, and the situation organizer (e.g., the way the teacher has organized the lesson or learning activities). This model provides a framework for thinking about instruction throughout this book.

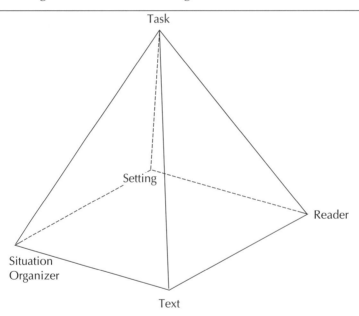

Figure 1.1   The context pyramid of reading comprehension, adapted from Mosenthal (1984)

Plans for teaching comprehension should include all five factors in the context pyramid. Let's take as an example a history teacher who spent part of her summer planning a course on American history for the eighth-grade class she would teach in the fall (the Setting). When school started, there were two students with learning disabilities and three students with limited proficiency in English in her class of 30 sixth graders. She knew that she would have to adjust her plans for particular lessons and assignments as the year went along because of the wide range of reading abilities in the group (the Reader factor). Now she is about to start the unit on the Civil War, and she is mindful of the fact that the textbook is laden with facts about the war. Although only one part of the unit involves reading and learning the information in the textbook, she needs to consider how best to structure her lessons and assignments so that her students will understand and retain information from the textbook. She decides that summarizing would be an appropriate technique for this purpose (the Task factor), as it would force students to concentrate on the main ideas. Having mastered these, she can have them reread the chapter to study the numerous events of the war (a second Task). She considers whether the students can learn to summarize effectively if she explains and models procedures for summarizing to the whole class and then asks students to practice writing summaries of passages on their own (Situation Organizer).

Thus, selection of methods to ensure students' comprehension is just one part of a more general decision-making process. The process includes consideration of the difficulty of the texts, the value of different tasks for different learning goals, and the capabilities and interests of the readers. Situation organizers can provide the teachers with options for varying the combinations of these other factors. In the example above, our history teacher might have used different tasks—for example, making maps of the movements of troops in the war or planning a reenactment of a central event in the war. But in what context will these tasks be most successfully carried out? Will students work best individually in the classroom, sharing their progress with the teacher and each other as they work? Or might they do better if she asked them to complete the tasks at home, thereby involving some of the parents? A third option that occurred to her was to have the students work with a peer or in a small group; this would provide a way for students with reading problems to learn cooperatively.

Over the course of the year, a teacher such as the one we have referred to above might teach a set of different strategies that students need to carry out different types of assignments and with different types of texts. Over time, students need to take some responsibility for using the reading strategies and study procedures they have been taught. But, like teachers, they need options to select amongst, depending on the task and situation organizer, as well as the challenges of the text. They need to learn to select methods for reading and learning that are appropriate, given their own strengths and weaknesses. Active involvement in making decisions and evaluating one's own comprehension is a crucial component in becoming a skilled reader. Interactive learning experiences may support the process, as is evident from situations in which students take part in activities that prompt them to evaluate the requirements of a given assignment and think about appropriate procedures to ensure good comprehension and learning (Vaughn, Gersten, and Chard 2000).

ISSUES OF THE CONTEXTS OF READING COMPREHENSION INSTRUCTION

The practice of grouping children for reading by ability fell into disfavor a number of years ago. Today, reading comprehension instruction is typically delivered to the whole class, and both the methods of instruction and the tasks students are asked to complete are uniform (Schumm, Moody, and Vaughn 2000). Students with diverse learning needs receive the same instruction, but not all students experience growth in reading achievement in this environment.

Between the late 1970s and the mid-1990s, students with LD often received instruction in reading in the resource room (Mastropieri et al. 1996). In that setting, comprehension interventions, delivered in small groups or one-to-one, often resulted in significant improvements in reading comprehension for students with learning disabilities (Mastropieri et al. 1996; Swanson 1999; Talbott, Lloyd, and Tankersley 1994). Most regular and special educators would probably still say that the most effective way to teach reading to a struggling reader is one-to-one. However, such an arrangement is often not practical. There aren't sufficient teachers, aides, or volunteer tutors to work individually with all of the children who have trouble learning to read. Even in resource settings, teachers are likely to work with large numbers of students at once. Not surprisingly, therefore, reading instruction is not always individualized—that is, the individual students' needs are not taken into account in selecting the goals and methods of instruction (Vaughn, Moody, and Schumm 1998). In today's educational climate, all students, even those with severe learning disabilities, are increasingly likely to receive most or all of their education in the general education classroom, although placement practices do differ from state to state and district to district within a state (McCleskey, Henry, and Axelrod 1999).

One argument for providing comprehension instruction in regular education settings, even when students attend pull-out programs (e.g., ESL), is the increased likelihood that students will learn strategies that are useful, given the demands of the curriculum. Furthermore, methods for understanding and learning from texts can be taught in relation to the types of tasks that students deal with on a daily basis. Content-area teachers are in a position to determine whether students are appropriately using strategies for understanding and learning, and they can help students adapt learning strategies as the tasks and texts change. Content-area courses also provide opportunities for practicing a *variety* of strategies for effective reading and studying, and without practice, strategies are unlikely to become part of the student's repertoire.

In recent school-based research projects, a concerted effort was made to help schools revise the curriculum and instructional methods in order to provide suitable learning environments for students with LD included in general education classrooms. Nonetheless, the gains in reading for students with LD were disappointing (Zigmond et al. 1995). Zigmond and Baker (1994) published a case study of a boy named Randy who spent fourth grade in a pull-out reading program and fifth grade in an inclusive classroom, in which a special educator assisted the regular educator in teaching reading and language arts to students with learning disabilities. Randy appeared to adjust well to the literacy curriculum of the fifth-grade class, and his teachers thought that he was making gains in reading. However, in both years, his performance on curriculum-based measures indicated very little growth in the accuracy and fluency of reading, far less growth than was typical for other students at his grade level in the same school.

The results of this study suggest that neither individualized study of reading (i.e., lots of independent seatwork in the resource room) nor participation in group literacy activities in the regular education classroom led to significant gains in reading. This study has an important message for teachers: accommodations that provide access to the regular curriculum (i.e., providing alternative ways for students to read texts and/or complete learning tasks) may not be sufficient to ensure growth of reading skills for children with severe reading problems. The modest gains made by poor readers in studies such as this one have prompted researchers and practitioners to look closely at the situation organization and other aspects of the context pyramid that might be adjusted to assure that struggling readers benefit from instruction in their regular classrooms.

Recent studies of effective instruction in regular education classes have shown that whole class teaching is not the best way to engage students in learning to monitor and control their own comprehension, particularly given the diversity of reading abilities and learning styles in most classrooms. Schumm, Moody, and Vaughn (2000) studied reading instruction and gains in achievement in third-grade classrooms with at least one student with a learning disability. They found that the teachers used primarily whole-group instruction, and no accommodations were made to help the students with limited reading skill. By end of year, students in the classes had made less than a year's gain in reading, and the students with LD made little or no gain.

There are a number of alternatives that teachers can consider. These include reading partners, small groups, and multiple grouping formats (Elbaum et al. 1999). Flexible grouping arrangements can be used throughout the school day. Thus, teachers might form relatively homogeneous groups for reading and discussing literature, but then reorganize the class into different groups for other language arts projects or instruction in other content areas (e.g., math). As we will discuss at later points in the book, small group instruction is one of several factors that contribute to improved reading achievement in elementary schools (Swanson 1999). Recent studies have shown that through participation in small groups, children learn to reflect on their own strategies and develop the language skills they need to talk about ideas in the books they read (Vaughn, Gersten, and Chard 2000).

There is a critical need to link assessment and decisions about the nature and content of reading instruction and to develop school-wide goals and plans for providing appropriate instruction to all children. Regular assessments provide a way to identify levels of need among students with comprehension problems and to evaluate the effectiveness of instructional designs for particular children (and indeed whole classes) on a timely basis.

In one school-improvement study (Kame'enui, Simmons, and Coyne 2000), for example, a premise was that instruction should be tailored to fit the unique needs of an individual school and should be implemented and sustained at the school-building level. The study of change in this school was intended to serve as a model of school-wide evaluation of reading instruction and achievement. The school collected normative data to identify children who fell into three levels of instructional need. The "intensive" students were seriously at risk based on low performance on one or more indicators of reading achievement. "Strategic" students had less acute problems but needed systematic intervention, whereas "Benchmark" students were on target on critical literacy skills. Because the children's reading skills were assessed regularly, the school had a feasible system in place to determine the extent and type of instruction in reading needed by each child. With this information in hand, the teacher could fine-tune instructional programs. Coordinating assessment and instruction in this manner appears to be an optimal condition for assuring that children have an opportunity to make steady progress toward developmentally appropriate goals in reading.

In school improvement studies, two important hallmarks of success are the involvement of the teachers in setting achievement goals for the students and the sense of shared responsibility for appropriate reading instruction across the curriculum (Kame'enui, Simmons, and Coyne 2000; Taylor and Pearson 2001). The partnerships that come from collective endeavors provide much-needed support for individual teachers as they struggle to meet the expectation that all children become skilled and competent readers. School plans should include all staff, including those who provide special services.

Some specialists in the field of learning disabilities have argued that students with severe reading disabilities need more intensive and more individualized instruction in reading than they can receive in regular education classrooms (Mather and Roberts 1994). The greater the gap between a student's reading skill development and that of his or her peers, the greater the likelihood that the student needs intensive and individualized instruction that is difficult to provide in a regular classroom setting. Nonetheless, just because instruction is one-to-one does not guarantee that the nature of the instruction is suitable, given the student's needs, or effective in improving his or her reading. Tutoring programs are not all effective for struggling readers (Elbaum et al. 2000). One shortcoming of some pull-out programs is that the students miss important lessons while they are out of the classroom, and at the same time the instruction they receive is not linked to other work they are doing in the classroom. One way to address this problem is through collaboration of the regular and special education teachers. It is necessary to coordinate reading instruction and literacy experiences for students who work on reading in both settings.

Ideally, both regular and special education teachers not only take the students' individual needs into account but also consider these in relation to the academic demands the students' currently face. Because reading comprehension involves thinking (integrating information, making inferences, drawing conclusions) and the use of appropriate strategies for comprehension monitoring and learning from text, students are not likely to retain information and strategies that they do not use. They also will reject reading strategies and study procedures that do not seem to pay off in terms of improvement in their reading or their ability to complete their assignments successfully. Techniques taught in isolated lessons without follow-through, whether in a pull-out setting or a regular classroom, may be a waste of time for both the teacher and the student.

PROVIDING TEACHERS WITH OPPORTUNITIES TO LEARN

Teachers have three ways to learn about instruction in reading comprehension in their area of education—through pre-service education, in-service education, and self-education. Surveys have found that teachers rate their pre-service education as only adequate (not good) in terms of providing them with knowledge of instructional methods in reading (Bauman et al. 2000). We would all agree that schools of education have a responsibility for providing teachers-in-training with sound knowledge of instructional methods in literacy. Nonetheless, without extensive experience in the classroom, many teachers-in-training are not in a position to learn all that they need to know to teach their students to read effectively. As a result, the second way to acquire knowledge about teaching—in-service education—plays a very important role in the continuing education of teachers. An additional reason for effectively designed and delivered in-service education is that teachers need help learning new methods or refining their understanding of tried-and-true methods. Apart from these two sources of professional knowledge, the main way teachers improve their knowledge base is through self-education. Studies of effective teachers have shown that they seek out opportunities to improve their knowledge and stay abreast of changes in their field; they are eager to find ways to do a better job teaching the children in their classes (Ashton 1984; Sparks 1988). They attend professional conferences and read journals or books; they may also form study groups within their schools.

All three ways teachers might learn about literacy instruction need to be developed, indeed exploited, so that teachers are more knowledgeable and therefore in a better position to make wise decisions about instructional methods and materials. In general, pre-service education does not appear to prepare teachers so that they can successfully address students' literacy needs (Anders, Hoffman, and Duffy 2000). Moats (1995) reported that "graduate-level teachers are typically undereducated for the very demanding task of teaching reading and spelling explicitly." Schools of education must improve their programs of teacher education with an eye toward including methods of literacy instruction for all appropriate degree programs. Individuals preparing to teach content-area courses, especially at the secondary level, might believe that someone should teach their students all they need to know to be effective readers before they take high school courses in such areas as science. This is a misconception. In all of the content areas, teachers need to consider what students need to be able to do to understand and learn from written texts in their domain.

Along with the obligation of schools of education to improve their course work on literacy, primary and secondary schools must find more effective ways to provide continuing education for their teachers. The problem of providing an adequate knowledge base for teachers through both teacher education and in-service programs certainly needs further study (Anders, Hoffman, and Duffy 2000; Dole 2000; Vaughn, Moody, and Schumm 1998). Then, too, teachers need to understand the importance of self-education. Teachers must value improvement in their understanding of the processes and problems of becoming literate and of methods in their area of teaching that are known to be effective.

The task of teaching reading effectively to diverse groups of children is a daunting one to many teachers. In a survey of general education teachers, Coates (1989) found that only about 13% agreed with the statement that, given an effective set of techniques, it would be possible both to raise the achievement levels of the entire class and to meet the educational needs of special-needs children. Nonetheless, in the present political climate, educators are increasingly held responsible for making sure that students reach the advanced levels of literacy they need to function in our society. Regular and special educators must learn to share their knowledge and work together to achieve the goal of helping all children become proficient readers. Getting the job done well requires that school administrators, too, appreciate the need for leadership and support of their teachers' efforts to learn more about literacy instruction and develop school-wide programs to improve their students' literacy.

Despite the availability of research reports such as the National Reading Panel Report, a continuing problem for teachers is access to information about reading comprehension and explanations of research-supported approaches to reading instruction that they can interpret with their students in mind. If teachers understand the purpose and benefits of different methods of instruction, they have a basis for making informed decisions about practices they might use in their classrooms. In addition, teachers need sufficient knowledge of instructional methods so that they can keep abreast of current debates that might affect their decisions about instructional programs and methods.

Our book has been written with exactly these goals in mind. We imagine our audience to be pre-service teachers, experienced teachers who would like to learn more about reading instruction, and graduate students interested in reading and reading difficulties. The book is organized so that teachers at various school levels can find chapters on topics relevant to their needs. Our particular focus is on students who are struggling readers. Often, but not always, the methods that have been shown to work well for normally achieving readers are also those that are effective for students who are poor readers. We have tried to provide sufficient description of methods so that readers can make at least a preliminary evaluation of their usefulness in different educational contexts. It was not feasible to provide detailed explanations of instructional methods (the "how-to" information teachers rely on), but we do provide references so that an interested reader will know where to go to get more information.

There are also limitations as to what research studies really tell practitioners. From the results of many studies, we learn that the odds are a method will work for a particular type of child (e.g., age, reading ability) under particular conditions. Moreover, a statistically significant result doesn't necessarily mean all children who participated in that study benefited from it. Until a technique has been tested in many studies on children of different ages with different ability levels under a variety of different conditions and compared with various competing techniques, there is very little we can truly say about the relative effectiveness of a given instructional method. There are very few comprehension methods that meet such a rigorous standard.

It is also rare that teachers can replicate study conditions in their classrooms. A teacher attempting to extend research to practice is likely to find it necessary to make adaptations in some aspects of the methodology. With this problem in mind, we hope we can at least model some of the thought processes involved in extending research to practice. We encourage teachers to ask themselves how a general approach might be adjusted to fit the constraints imposed by different situations. Put another way, good teaching at its core is research, a continual process of forming and testing hypotheses.

It is our belief that recipes for instructional methods are not enough—teachers deserve to (indeed, need to) understand issues and problems that may affect their decisions about instructional methods. Thus, we have made an effort to engage our readers in thinking about issues and applications. In particular, we have raised questions for discussion and included case studies and classroom scenarios in the final chapter to provoke reflection and debate. These might help teachers think through decisions about curriculum, methods of instruction, and the progress of the children in their classes. We hope teachers are able to relate the ideas and information in this book to their daily lives in the educational arena.

REFERENCES

Anders, P. L., Hoffman, J. V., and Duffy, G. G. 2000. Teaching teachers to teach reading: Paradigm shifts, persistent problems, and challenges. In *Handbook of Reading Research*, Vol. 3. M. L. Kamil, P. B. Mosenthal, P. D. Pearson, and R. Barr (Eds.), (pp. 719–42). Mahwah, NJ: Lawrence Erlbaum.

Ashton, P. 1984. Teacher efficacy: A motivational paradigm for effective teacher education. *Journal of Teacher Education*, 35:28–32.

Baumann, J. F., Hoffman, J. V., Duffy-Hester, A. M., and Ro, J. M. 2000. The First R yesterday and today: U.S. elementary reading instruction practices reported by teachers and administrators. *Reading Research Quarterly*, 35:338–77.

Chall, J. 1990. Policy implications of literacy definitions. In *Toward Defining Literacy*, R. L. Venezky, D. A. Wagner, and B. S. Ciliberti (Eds.), (pp. 54–62). Newark, DE: International Reading Association.

Coates, R. D. 1989. The regular education initiative and opinions of regular classroom teachers. *Journal of Learning Disabilities*, 22:532–36.

Dole, J. A. 2000. Explicit and implicit instruction in comprehension. In *Reading for Meaning: Fostering Comprehension in the Middle Grades*, B. M. Taylor, M. F. Graves, and P. van den Broek (Eds.), (pp. 52–69). Newark, DE: International Reading Assoc.

Elbaum, B., Vaughn, S., Hughes, M., and Moody, S. W. 2000. How effective are one-to-one tutoring programs in reading for elementary students at risk for reading difficulties? A meta-analysis of the intervention research. *Journal of Education Psychology* 92:605–19.

Gersten, R., Fuchs, L. S., Williams, J. P., and Baker, S. 2001. Teaching reading comprehension strategies to students with learning disabilities: A review of research. *Review of Educational Research*, 71:279–320.

Jenkins, J. J. 1979. Four points to remember: A tetrahedral model of memory experiments. In *Levels of Processing in Human Memory*, L. S. Cermak and F. I. M. Craik (Eds.), (pp. 429–46). Hillsdale, NJ: Lawrence Erlbaum.

Kame'enui, E. J., Simmons, D. C., and Coyne, M. D. 2000. Schools as host environments: Toward a school-wide reading improvement model. *Annals of Dyslexia*, 50:33–51.

Kirsch, I. S., Jungeblut, A., Jenkins, L., and Kolstad, A. 1993. *Adult Literacy in America: A First Look at the Results of the National Adult Literacy Survey*. Washington, DC: Department of Education.

Mastropieri, M. A., Scruggs, T. E., Bakken, J. P., and Whedon, C. 1996. Reading comprehension: A synthesis of research in learning disabilities. *Advances in Learning and Behavioral Disabilities*, 10B:201–27.

Mather, N., and Roberts, R. 1994. Learning disabilities: A field in danger of extinction. *Learning Disabilities Research and Practice*, 9:49–58.

McLeskey, J., Henry, D., and Axelrod, M. I. 1999. Inclusion of students with learning disabilities: An examination of data from reports to Congress. *Exceptional Children*, 66:55–66.

Moats, L. Summer 1995. The missing foundation in teacher education. *American Federation of Teachers*, 9:43–50.

Mosenthal, P. 1984. Reading comprehension research from a classroom perspective. In *Promoting Reading Comprehension*, J. Flood (Ed.), (pp. 16–29). Newark, DE: International Reading Association.

National Assessment of Educational Progress (NAEP). 1999. *1998 National Association of Educational Progress 1998 Reading Report Card.* Washington, DC: Department of Education, National Center for Educational Statistics.

Report of the National Reading Panel (NRP Report). 2000. Teaching children to read: Reports of the subgroups. Washington, DC: National Institute of Child Health and Human Development. Retrieved from: http://www.nichd.nih.gov/publications/nrp/report.htm

Paris, S. G., Wasik, B. A., and Turner, J. C. 1991. The development of strategic readers. In *Handbook of Reading Research*, Vol II. R. Barr, M. L. Kamil, P. B. Mosenthal, and P. D. Pearson (Eds.), (pp. 609–40). NY: Longman.

Pressley, M. 2000. Comprehension instruction in elementary school: A quarter-century of research progress. In *Reading for Meaning: Fostering Comprehension in the Middle Grades*, B. M. Taylor, M. F. Graves, and P. van den Broek (Eds.), (pp. 32–51). Newark, DE: International Reading Association.

Putnam, R. T., and Borko, H. 2000. What do new views of knowledge and thinking have to say about research on teacher learning? *Educational Researcher*, 29:4–15.

RAND Reading Study Group 2002. *Reading for Understanding: Toward a Research and Development Program in Reading Comprehension.* Retrieved January 4, 2002, from http://www.rand.org/multi/achievementforall/reading/readreport.html

Saint-Laurent, L., Dionne, J., Giasson, J., Royer, E., Simard, C., and Pierard, B. 1998. Academic achievement effects of an in-class service model on students with and without disabilities. *Exceptional Children*, 64:239–53.

Schumm, J. S., Moody, S. W., and Vaughn, S. 2000. Grouping for reading instruction: Does one size fit all? *Journal of Learning Disabilities*, 33:477–88.

Smith, M. C., Mikulecky, L., Kibby, M. W., Dreher, M. J., and Dole, J. A. 2000. What will be the demands of literacy in the workplace in the next millennium? *Reading Research Quarterly*, 35:378–83.

Snow, C. E., Burns, M. S., and Griffin, P. 1998. *Preventing Reading Difficulties in Young Children.* Report of the National Research Council. Washington, DC: National Academy.

Sparks, G. M. 1988. Teachers' attitudes toward change and subsequent improvements in classroom teaching. *Journal of Educational Psychology*, 80:111–17.

Swanson, H. L. 1999. Reading research for students with LD: A meta-analysis of intervention outcomes. *Journal of Learning Disabilities*, 32:504–32.

Talbott, E., Lloyd, J. W., and Tankersley, M. 1994. Effects of reading comprehension interventions for students with learning disabilities. *Learning Disability Quarterly*, 17:223–32.

Taylor, B. M., and Pearson, P. D. 2001. The CIERA school change project: Translating research on effective reading instruction and school reform into practice in high-poverty elementary schools. Retrieved from http://education.umn.edu/ci/taylor/taylor1.html

Thornberg, K. R., Hoffman, S., and Remeika, C. 1991. Youth at risk; Society at risk. *The Elementary School Journal*, 91:199–208.

Vaughn, S., Moody, S.W., and Schumm, J. S. 1998. Broken promises: Reading instruction in the resource room. *Exceptional Children*, 64:211–25.

Vaughn, S., Gersten, R., and Chard, D. 2000. The underlying message in LD intervention research: Findings from research syntheses. *Exceptional Children*, 67:99–114.

Venezky, R. L. 2000. The origins of the present-day chasm between adult literacy needs and school literacy instruction. *Scientific Studies of Reading*, 4:19–39.

Zigmond, N., and Baker, J. M. 1994. Is the mainstream a more appropriate educational setting for Randy? A case study of one student with learning disabilities. *Learning Disabilities Research and Practice*, 9:108–17.

Zigmond, N., Jenkins, J., Fuchs, L. S., Deno, S., Fuchs, D., Baker, J., Jenkins, L., and Couthino, M. 1995. Special education in restructured schools: Findings from three multi-year studies. *Phi Delta Kappan*, 76:531–40.

2
The Nature of Problems with Reading Comprehension

GETTING STARTED

✓ What factors contribute to difficulties with reading comprehension?
✓ Are there developmental changes in the relation of listening and reading comprehension?
✓ How do home and school experiences play a role in the nature and extent of students' problems with reading comprehension?
✓ What do the terms reading disability, learning disability, and dyslexia refer to?
✓ What are teachers' responsibilities for understanding the nature of comprehension problems among their students?

AN OVERVIEW OF COMPREHENSION AND COMPREHENSION PROBLEMS

What do we mean by the term, "reading comprehension"? Generally, it refers to an individual's understanding of a written text. However, sometimes the phrase is used as a general statement about a student's school achievement (e.g., "He has good reading comprehension"). When it is, we probably mean that the student is able to make sense of different texts, ones that are age-appropriate, under different circumstances in school-related activities, such as reading works of literature, reading textbooks for courses, reading and responding to questions on teachers' tests and standardized tests. Regardless, the concept of "comprehension" is similar. It is a process, rather than a particular product. The process is one through which the reader draws meaning from a text, based on his or her knowledge, the nature of the text and the author's message, the perceived purpose of reading, and the broader context in which the reading is carried out. Spiro (1980) described this process as one that involves constructing meaning; in his words:

Meaning does not reside in words, sentences, paragraphs, or even entire passages considered in isolation . . . What language provides is a skeleton, a blueprint for the creation of meaning. Such skeletal representations must then be enriched and embellished so that they conform with the understander's preexisting world views and the operative purposes of understanding at a given time. This process of knowledge-based, contextually influenced, and purposeful enrichment in comprehending language is what is referred to as "construction." . . . Constructed meaning is the interactive product of text and context of various kinds, including linguistic, prior knowledge, situational, attitudinal and task contexts, among others (pp. 245–246).

Note that Spiro is not restricting his explanation about comprehension to reading. In fact, it could be used for comprehension of oral language as well. The similarity of the process of comprehension of oral and written language may lead us to draw some inappropriate conclusions about the development of reading comprehension and the nature of problems that students have with reading comprehension. One might think that if the process is the same for oral and written language, students with comprehension problems will show similar difficulties on tasks of listening and reading comprehension, but that is not always the case. The developmental nature of reading comprehension and comprehension problems requires explanation.

Before children become readers of connected text, some of them have difficulties understanding spoken language. These children are very likely to have difficulties with reading comprehension that are similar to those they experience with oral language. (In fact, preschool children's language development is a good predictor of their reading comprehension years later.) We could regard these as children with general language comprehension problems.

Other children may have subtle problems with oral language comprehension that are not noticed by adults or picked up definitively by diagnostic tests. However, these mild problems may become more severe (and more evident to teachers) when the children are faced with comprehension of written, rather than oral language. This is because understanding by reading is more cognitively and linguistically taxing than understanding by listening.

Other children do not have problems with oral language at all, and in fact may excel in this area. They may have larger vocabularies than their peers. They may memorize the books read to them with ease. Yet, when they encounter reading, they have such difficulties learning the written language code that this becomes a barrier to their reading comprehension. If their problems learning to decode unfamiliar words and recognize common words persist, they are likely to experience other problems, ranging from fewer opportunities to learn from reading to negative attitudes toward reading and related activities (particularly writing).

The reading comprehension problems of these groups of children have different sources. In all three cases, we might assume that the children were raised in language-rich environments and that the language they are learning is their native language. Children who are learning English as a second language, children who come from culturally different backgrounds, and children who do not have adequate opportunities to learn language or are not exposed to literacy within their families have other challenges in learning to understand written texts. This fourth group is a complex one because of the diverse backgrounds and "risk" factors that the children bring with them to school.

Understanding different reasons for comprehension problems may help regular and special education teachers appreciate the challenges students face in becoming skilled readers. It may be apparent from the above discussion that the two major factors that play a role in reading comprehension are language comprehension and word decoding. In fact, these are the only two variables in the "simple model of reading" (Gough, Hoover, and Peterson 1996), which presents reading comprehension as the product of decoding and language comprehension. This model gives a helpful conceptual framework, but falls short of providing a complete explanation of additional factors that can play a role in the development of reading comprehension. In this chapter, we look further at the development of reading comprehension, including not only cognitive and linguistic factors that affect reading comprehension, but also aspects of metacognition, motivation, and other factors that play a role in students' reading achievement. We also discuss practical problems of identifying and addressing the needs of students with comprehension problems. It is important to understand the nature of comprehension problems so that this knowledge can be used to select instructional approaches that can foster the development of students' comprehension capabilities (Gersten et al. 2001).

READING AND LANGUAGE COMPREHENSION

Theoretical Models

Reading is a complex cognitive and linguistic activity. As a result, it should not be surprising that there is no single factor that accounts for the difficulties individuals have in becoming skilled readers. As Stanovich (1988) pointed out, although many studies have shown significant correlations between different reading-related processes (e.g., short-term memory, vocabulary), simple associations of this kind do not necessarily indicate a causal relation. In the search for causal factors, he suggested that the best candidate for an underlying cause of reading problems is "the phonological core deficit." That is, poor readers have difficulties grasping the sound structure of words. The ability to identify syllables (e.g., Say *napkin* without saying *nap*) or individual sounds in words (e.g., What is the first sound in *cat*?) and to manipulate sounds in words (e.g., Say *cat* without saying /k/) is called phonological awareness. Slow development of phonological awareness tends to result in difficulties learning the alphabetic code—the system by which the individual sounds of spoken words (phonemes) are represented by letters in written words. The ability to identify sounds in words and to know what letters represent those sounds is at the heart of the process of learning to decode written words—that is, to "sound out" words in written texts (Liberman, Shankweiler, and Liberman 1989).

Although lack of sensitivity to the sound structure in words certainly does hinder reading acquisition, we also know that this alone does not explain all reading disabilities and may not explain age-related changes in the characteristics of reading problems. As Scarborough (2001) pointed out, phonological awareness is itself influenced by vocabulary and grammatical knowledge. In addition, studies that have sought to boost the phonological awareness and decoding skills of children at risk for reading difficulties have not prevented reading problems down the road. For this reason, Scarborough suggested that the model of a single factor that leads to a series of increasingly serious reading-related problems (a "causal chain") is not a good theoretical model to explain reading disabilities.

If improving phonological processing does not remove the reading problem altogether, other sorts of cognitive and linguistic factors might play a role in the course of the development of reading capabilities. Following this line of reasoning, Scarborough (2001) proposed a model of reading disabilities in which the triggering event (e.g., phonological processing) leads to a variety of "symptoms" of reading difficulty (e.g., difficulties with decoding, lack of fluency of reading), and these difficulties may be compounded by other factors, such as the child's vocabulary knowledge or his or her interest in reading. This model holds potential for helping teachers and researchers think about the complexities of reading disabilities. It leads us away from the illusion that we can pinpoint a single cause for all disabilities, and it helps us understand why the particular characteristics of reading disabilities vary among individuals and change with age and experience.

One thing that is true, however, is that students who have difficulties with reading are likely to go on having such difficulties through their school years, even though the particular "symptoms" may change over time. According to Scarborough (2001):

> A daunting fact about reading (dis)abilities is that differences among school-children in their levels of reading achievement show strong stability over time, despite remedial efforts that are usually made to strengthen the skills of lower achievers. . . . Only about 5–10% of children who read satisfactorily in the primary grades ever stumble later, and 65–75% of children designated as reading disabled early on continue to read poorly throughout their school careers (and beyond) (p. 98).

The depressing figures that show the continuing problems of poor readers should be a call to action for all educators. To understand how to teach struggling readers effectively, it is helpful, if not necessary, to understand the complexities and developmental factors that contribute to reading disabilities. What are some of the factors that might contribute to reading problems, other than the phonological core deficit? Reading achievement is affected by the child's language development, particularly in the areas of expressive language, verbal ability, and linguistic awareness (e.g., grammatical awareness). Aspects of cognitive and metacognitive development may also play a role in an individual's acquisition of reading. Further, as noted earlier, both cognitive and linguistic aspects of development are likely to have a reciprocal relation with reading achievement. For instance, the extensiveness of children's vocabulary affects the ease with which they learn to read; however, reading also plays a major role in the development of children's vocabulary. Intrinsic and extrinsic factors are involved in these reciprocal causal relations. For example, we might imagine two children with similar difficulties learning the letters of the alphabet but who differed in their enthusiasm for activities designed to improve their emergent literacy. This might be because one grew up in a family that loved to read, whereas the other grew up in a family that owned few books and devoted little time to reading. The child who is eager to engage in reading activities is bound to make greater progress than the child who has no interest in reading (Baker and Wigfield 1999).

Unfortunately, there are many unanswered questions about the distinction between intrinsic and extrinsic factors—or the ways that they might influence one another. For example, Scarborough (1990) found that preschoolers who had a parent with dyslexia performed less well on language measures than preschoolers with parents who did not have reading problems. Further, the children of dyslexic parents subsequently showed difficulties learning to read. This pattern might be attributable to familiality, meaning that the children's language and reading abilities are affected by growing up with parents who have limitations (and limited interests) in these areas. The parents do not spend time reading, and the children tend to follow their lead. Alternatively, this pattern might suggest heritability, meaning that a tendency to have difficulties learning to read is genetically determined. Although genetic studies have shown that there is considerable heritability of phonological processing capabilities (which in turn affect decoding skill), very little is known about the heritability of factors like language that are directly relevant to reading comprehension (Olson and Gayan 2001). Because there is evidence that word reading and comprehension capabilities develop independently of one another, an important area for future research is the relation of intrinsic and extrinsic factors that affect comprehension.

Finally, teachers are well aware that the reading problems encountered by children change as they get older. This observation is supported by Scarborough's research (2001). In addition, she has shown that the development of reading-related capabilities is often not a steady progression, but one that is characterized by growth spurts and "quiet" periods in which there is little change. Because of the different developmental trajectories and the large number of language and cognitive factors that influence the development of reading skill, it is apparent that reading growth entails an extraordinarily complex set of interactions. We are left with the realization that we must carry out a thoughtful and complete assessment of students' reading-related capabilities and the contexts in which they are learning if we are to understand and provide appropriate assistance for their reading difficulties.

Development Changes in the Relation of Decoding and Comprehension

With the complexities of the process of learning to read in mind, we need to understand the major factors that influence the development of children's reading comprehension. Our first lesson is that the relation of reading and listening comprehension changes as children learn to read. In the first few years of learning to read, children with age-appropriate language development can understand much more challenging books through listening than they can read. As first graders, for example, they might listen to books like Seuss's *Horton Hatches the Egg* with comprehension and enjoyment. However, they do not have the necessary word reading skills to read such a book on their own. They can read Seuss's *Green Eggs and Ham* because the simple words in this story are in their reading vocabulary; however, this book, while it is enjoyed for its humor, presents few challenges to their language comprehension.

The relationship between listening and reading comprehension becomes stronger over the elementary years as children gain the word-reading skills they need to read books that match the level of their language comprehension. By about fifth grade, speed of word recognition is a stronger predictor of reading comprehension than accuracy. Language comprehension is also a significant predictor of reading comprehension (Curtis 1980). Thus, by about fifth grade, students' reading comprehension and listening comprehension performances are more closely related than they were when the students were younger (Sticht and James 1984). The developmental change described above is found among both good and poor readers. Aaron, Joshi, and Williams (1999) found that poor readers' word reading was the major component in reading comprehension in third grade, whereas word reading and listening comprehension were both significant factors in fifth and sixth grade. By sixth grade, rapid and automatic word recognition played a crucial role in comprehension.

From the very beginning, reading experience has an impact on the development of students' reading skill (Stanovich et al. 1996). Students who are successfully acquiring reading skill spend more time reading and read more difficult books than students for whom the acquisition process is very difficult. Because children who are already good comprehenders read more, they are likely to experience increases in vocabulary and knowledge bases that underlie future increases in comprehension efficiency. The less skilled readers read less and thus benefit less than their peers. Thus, the achievement gap between skilled and less skilled readers tends to widen not only on measures of text comprehension but also on other measures, such as vocabulary development (Stanovich et al. 1996). Skilled readers are also more likely to read with greater energy and interest than less skilled readers (McKenna, Kear, and Ellsworth 1995). As a result, they tend to be more highly motivated to monitor their own comprehension and take action when the text is not meaningful to them. Through these efforts, they are likely to pick up a greater array of strategies to support their reading comprehension (Paris, Wasik, and Turner 1991).

In short, students who have difficulties acquiring skill at word reading may start out with a specific problem, but after years of limited exposure to reading end up with a broader set of problems in the comprehension area, ranging from difficulties understanding complex grammatical structures to limitations in comprehension strategies. They may also dislike reading and may lack persistence when reading tasks become difficult. Interviewing fourth-grade poor readers, Juel (1988) found that they read little because they hated reading and because they had experienced failure with reading. Typically, they told her reading was boring, whereas good readers said that they liked reading because it gave them good ideas and they learned new things. Reading failure affects motivation for reading, which in turn affects how much children learn from and about reading (Baker and Wigfield 1999). The relation of basic word reading skill and motivation is one of the complex causal interactions that develop over time for children who struggle to learn to read.

Problems with Language Comprehension

Although some students with severe reading disabilities are found to be similar to peers with normally developing reading skill in listening or language comprehension (Stothard and Hulme 1996), other students with severe reading disabilities have not only phonological deficits and word reading problems but also language comprehension difficulties. For these students, the relative weakness in language comprehension is not simply the result of poor reading. Catts et al. (1999) reported a study of 183 second-graders identified as having significant difficulties with reading comprehension. Based on testing that had been carried out when the students were in kindergarten, the researchers determined that about 14% of them had phonological deficits alone, about 22% had oral language deficits alone, and 37% had deficits in both areas. Thus, 73% had deficits in some aspect of language. By way of comparison, for the good readers, about 86% had no language deficits; 5% had deficits in phonological processing alone, 6% had deficits in oral language alone, and 4% had problems in both aspects in kindergarten. These researchers found that many of the second graders identified as having word-reading problems showed problems in oral language in kindergarten.

Along similar lines, Aaron, Joshi, and Williams (1999) found evidence that not all reading disabilities are due to decoding problems. Not unlike the results of Catts et al. (1999), their results show that for older students with poor reading comprehension, some had decoding problems only, some had listening comprehension problems only, and a number had both types of problems. It seems reasonable to conclude, then, that low achievement in reading comprehension does not tell us *why* a given student is having difficulties with reading comprehension. As noted earlier, to reach an understanding of the underlying causes of an individual's reading comprehension problems, diagnosticians and teachers need to consider the student's pattern of developing language and reading capabilities. The student's listening and reading comprehension should be compared (with developmental norms in mind), and word decoding should be assessed, so that it can be determined whether problems with accuracy and facility with word reading are hindering the student's comprehension. We will return to the topic of distinguishing profiles of struggling readers in the chapter on assessment (Chapter 10).

A REVIEW OF FACTORS THAT INFLUENCE READING COMPREHENSION

While our primary focus is on reading comprehension, determination of the nature of reading difficulties requires an examination of factors that affect both word reading and reading comprehension. There are a number of cognitive and linguistic factors that are known to contribute to such problems.

Foremost among the factors that affect word reading skill are phonological processes. Phonological coding is defined as the representation of information about the sound structure of words in memory; it includes phonological awareness, word retrieval or naming, and verbal short term or working memory (Torgesen and Wagner 1998; Wagner et al. 1993). Stone and Brady (1995) found that less-skilled third-grade readers performed significantly less well than their age-mates and also than younger readers on tasks of verbal memory and speech production. Their analyses of the children's performance suggest that less skilled readers lack precise memory for the sounds in words (i.e., phonological representations) than the other children had. Intact phonological representations of words in spoken language appear to provide a basis for acquiring phonological awareness, which in turn is highly predictive of word reading achievement (Elbro, Borstrom, and Petersen 1998; Muter and Snowling 1998).

Ideally, children develop phonological awareness before and while they are learning to read. They show their awareness of sounds in words on such tasks as rhyming words (e.g., a word that rhymes with *bear* is *care*) or isolating sounds in words (e.g., What is the last sound in *pig*?). Such awareness is then associated with the process of reading and spelling written words (e.g., hearing three sounds in *pig* and identifying the letter that represents each one). Phonological awareness has been shown to have a reciprocal relation with reading development (Liberman, Shankweiler, and Liberman 1989; Perfetti et al. 1987). The greater the sensitivity to the sounds in words, the more successful beginning readers are likely to be at acquiring word-reading skill. However, the very process of learning to read fosters awareness of the sound structure of words.

Two other aspects of phonological processing are associated with reading skill: verbal working memory and rapid access to name codes in memory. Working memory is important to word reading because it is necessary to hold the sounds of words that are read in memory while they are processed for meaning. Students with limitations in working memory have trouble hanging on to and integrating all the words in sentences, particularly when the sentence is long and complex in structure and meaning. Working memory has an impact on both processing of words in sentences and on comprehension of the sentences (Daneman and Carpenter 1980).

Rapid, automatic naming of visual stimuli (often referred to as RAN) is considered by some to be a phonological process (e.g., Torgesen and Wagner 1998). Others have argued that the task of rapid naming has different processing requirements (Stone and Brady 1995). It may be related to the processing of the spelling of words (i.e., orthographic processing) (Bowers and Wolf 1993) and involve ease of retrieving the names of things (verbal labels) from memory. The ability to name objects, numbers, or letters rapidly (e.g., saying aloud the names of a list of letters like A D O S P) is a significant predictor of reading ability in many studies (Bowers 2001; Denckla and Cutting 1999). Slow naming characterizes some but not all cases of poor word reading. We will discuss problems with rapid naming further in the chapter on fluency (Chapter 3). Some poor readers have specific difficulties with phonological awareness; others, however, have deficits in both phonological awareness and naming. Students who have the most severe word-reading problems tend to be those with difficulties in both areas (Bowers and Wolf 1993).

A second factor that has been shown to predict performance on word reading measures is orthographic awareness, which refers to awareness of letter combinations or patterns and the specific spelling of words (Badian 2000; Berninger and Abbott 1994). Orthographic processing abilities have received much less attention than phonological processing abilities, but theories of reading acquisition generally indicate that the reader must link the understanding of the sound structure of a word with its spelling (Ehri 1992; Perfetti 1992). Furthermore, there are aspects of spelling that are not captured by analysis of the sounds in words. Some words have irregular elements or silent letters (e.g., *people, debt*); some words are homophones—they sound alike but have different spellings and meanings (e.g, *reign, rein,* and *rain*). Knowledge of the correct letter sequences of specific words (and associations with their phonology, morphology, grammatical roles, and meanings) is an important aspect of developing reading ability (Adams 1990; Berninger et al. 2001).

A third factor is oral language competence. Vocabulary, grammatical knowledge, and understanding of verbal concepts and relations all affect comprehension, but they also may affect acquisition of word-reading skill. In some studies designed to predict reading achievement from kindergarten or first grade, oral language plays a relatively minor role, but in other studies, language comprehension is found to be a significant predictor of word reading and comprehension (e.g., Catts et al. 1999). The strength of the relation may be affected by the particular measures of language that are used as predictors. In any case, after a few years in school, language comprehension variables become stronger predictors of reading comprehension (see Muter and Snowling 1998; Tunmer and Hoover 1992).

Related to (but distinct from) oral language are verbal ability and metalinguistic capabilities. Both combine aspects of language development with reasoning capabilities. Verbal ability refers to such traits as the ability to grasp verbal concepts and appreciate semantic relations. Metalinguistic capabilities (also called linguistic awareness) refer to the ability to reflect on and manipulate language, to treat it as an object of thought. Nagy and Anderson (1999) stated that reading is, by its very nature, a metalinguistic activity. As children learn to read and write, they acquire an explicit awareness of language forms and functions. The most important metalinguistic capability associated with early reading acquisition is phonological awareness (Tunmer, Herriman, and Nesdale 1989). As noted earlier, this is because awareness of the sound structure of words provides a foundation for acquiring the alphabetic code. However, other aspects of linguistic awareness have also been shown to contribute to reading achievement. These include grammatical awareness (Bowey 1986; Tunmer and Hoover 1992) and morphological awareness (Carlisle 1995; 2000). These two aspects of metalinguistic development may play a greater role in comprehension, once basic word reading skills have developed. They matter when aspects of linguistic form that affect meaning are critical to comprehension of texts.

HOME AND SCHOOL ENVIRONMENT: EXTRINSIC INFLUENCES ON THE DEVELOPMENT OF COMPREHENSION

Along with cognitive and linguistic processes, experience with books and exposure to a literate environment influence children's emergent literacy. When they read books with their parents and other caregivers, children develop an understanding of what books are like and how to handle them; they learn to expect certain elements in stories and to see relations between the pictures and the words (Clay 1985; Mason 1992). Listening to stories may foster development of the child's language comprehension and may help children develop "book language"—a way of talking (e.g., uncommon syntactic structures and language conventions) that is used in books but not in everyday conversation in their homes. Children who have read and talked about stories with members of their families also have begun to embrace a culture of literacy that prepares them for schooling.

Not surprisingly, the language of the home influences children's language development, which in turn plays a role in their ability to comprehend books. Quite simply, the amount of talk in the home influences children's language development. In one study, the number of words children learned between ages 1 and 3 reflected the amount and kind of talk in the home; further, the estimated vocabulary of three year olds was related to later achievement in reading (Hart and Risley 1995). Language practices in the home can affect the extent to which children think about words and word meanings and gain insights into ways to express ideas. (See Purcell-Gates 2000, for a more complete explanation of these relations). In one research project focused on the home-to-school links for at-risk children, the extensiveness of the vocabulary used in conversations and the support for literacy activities in the home were found to contribute to children's emergent literacy and ability to tell stories in kindergarten (Tabors, Snow, and Dickinson 2001).

In this same study, the characteristics of the teacher's discourse and curriculum also contributed to the prediction of children's emergent literacy. Although children arrive at school with basic language capabilities, communication in the classroom requires different vocabulary, grammar, language functions (pragmatics), and discourse genres (Wilkinson and Silliman 2000). Not knowing the standard ways of communicating in the classroom puts children at risk for learning little from their classroom experiences. The nature of talk in the classroom and the teachers' sensitivity to children's developing communicative competence are likely to affect their movement into literacy, their academic achievement, and their adjustment to school. Thus, talk in the classroom is as important as talk in the home. We can imagine, then, that students' innate language and cognitive capabilities are modulated by the home and school environment.

Undoubtedly, other home and school factors influence the development of reading-related capabilities. This brief review is not intended to be comprehensive, but it does suggest that the home and school contexts are important in shaping children's language and early literacy learning. Such factors as the amount the teacher talks with the students, the nature of classroom discourse, and the nature of the reading program may also contribute to children's developing reading capabilities, particularly as they interact with the children's linguistic and cognitive development.

COMPREHENSION PROCESSES AND SOURCES OF KNOWLEDGE

The above discussion has focused on factors that affect the development of both word reading and reading comprehension. An important question is whether there are some developing capabilities that specifically impact reading comprehension—that is, they do not affect oral language comprehension to the same degree. Perfetti, Marron, and Foltz (1996) identified six components that make up a fundamental list of potential sources of reading comprehension failure. Of these, four are considered to be processes, and two others are seen as sources of knowledge (as shown in table 2.1).

Of the four "processes," two we have discussed at some length already. As we have seen, decoding and word-naming speed provide access to information in written texts. At the same time, however, reading experience can affect decoding and word-naming speed. This is because children find it easier to read familiar than unfamiliar words. Furthermore, their understanding of texts helps them read words. They use information they garner from sentence contexts and analysis of word spellings and sounds to identify unfamiliar words (Tunmer and Chapman 1998). A good example of the value of context for word reading comes from a study by Adams and Huggins (1985). These researchers found that "irregular words" such as *stomach* were read more accurately when they were presented in a sentence (e.g., "The football hit him in the stomach") than in isolation. In several ways, then, language capabilities may affect lexical processes.

Working memory, as we noted earlier, includes the ability to hold information in memory while doing something with that information. Working memory may affect both word reading and comprehension, but it plays a larger role in reading than in language comprehension. This is because of the complexity of the process that must occur during reading: written strings of letters must be mapped onto words in long-term memory, and these must be held in working memory so that the meaning of the phrase or sentence can be constructed. When this process breaks down, comprehension is impeded. Studies have suggested that limitations in working memory may be implicated in reading problems (Swanson 1993; Yuill, Oakhill, and Parkin 1989).

Inference-making involves making connections and/or seeing elements of meaning that are not directly stated. The ability to make inferences is considered

Table 2.1   Sources of Comprehension Failure (adapted from Perfetti et al. 1996)

PROCESSES	KNOWLEDGE
Decoding; word naming speed	Word meanings
Working memory	Domain knowledge
Inference-making	
Comprehension monitoring	

by many to be a central problem for students who have specific comprehension problems (not word-reading problems) (Oakhill and Yuill 1996). The argument is that texts cannot be fully explicit, and in reading (more than in oral language) the reader must infer the intentions and meaning of the writer. In oral language, the listener has the benefit of prosody, vocal intonation, and non-linguistic context to help him or her interpret statements, but the reader does not have these benefits. We will pick up the topic of prosody again and discuss it at greater length in the chapter on fluency (Chapter 3).

The last of the processes, comprehension monitoring, refers to the reader's regulation and control of his or her own reading processes (Brown, Armbruster, and Baker 1986). Readers must ask themselves whether they understand the text while they are reading it or immediately afterward, and they must also have knowledge of fix-up strategies when comprehension failures are detected. Implicit awareness of fix-up strategies, to be effective, must be accompanied by procedures for selecting strategies that are helpful in resolving problems under different circumstances. For example, having detected a problem understanding a passage, one reader might decide to reread the passage, whereas another might look up an unfamiliar word from the passage in the dictionary. Students with reading problems are likely to be less tuned in to comprehension monitoring than their peers (Oakhill and Yuill 1996). Lack of self-monitoring while reading may be the result of a feeling of inadequacy, itself the result of repeated experiences with failure in their efforts to read for meaning. Because so many aspects of reading are problematic for poor readers, they do not feel "on top of the job," so to speak. In addition, struggling readers are likely to lack awareness of their own level of understanding (Baker and Anderson 1982). They also are not strategic readers (Paris, Wasik, and Turner 1991). They lack knowledge of ways to address problems with comprehension and make bad decisions about how to solve such problems in specific circumstances. We will discuss strategic reading at greater length in Chapter 4.

In examining the "knowledge" factors in Perfetti et al.'s scheme, we might be perplexed by the inclusion of "word meanings" under knowledge with no mention of other aspects of language comprehension. There is certainly solid research evidence to suggest that readers develop an understanding of word meanings through and for reading (Nagy, Herman, and Anderson 1985; Jenkins, Stein, and Wysocki 1984). However, grammatical knowledge also develops through reading—that is, some structural aspects of written sentences are learned through reading, not through oral uses of language. Grammatical awareness is related to achievement in reading comprehension (see Bowey 1986; Tunmer and Hoover 1992), and probably should be added to Perfetti et al.'s list. We include more discussion of the role of sentence comprehension and grammatical knowledge in Chapter 6.

Domain knowledge is the second of the sources of knowledge on this list of fundamental comprehension problems. Also referred to as background knowledge or prior knowledge, it has been found time and again to contribute significantly to comprehension of text passages (e.g., Anderson, Spiro, and Anderson 1978). It provides a framework for understanding ideas and recalling information in texts. Knowing something about the topic of a passage (e.g., tides) helps the reader integrate new information (e.g., the gravitational pull of the moon) into his or her knowledge base. However, sometimes prior knowledge can interfere with comprehension, and in some cases students may over-rely on prior knowledge, interpreting whatever they read in light of what they knew ahead of time instead of integrating prior knowledge with the information presented in a text. Finally, the issue is not just whether the reader has some appropriate domain knowledge, but whether he or she thinks to use it in the process of constructing meaning from text, and whether appropriate inferences are made to integrate prior knowledge and new knowledge from the text (Spiro 1980).

It seems likely that many kinds of "prior knowledge" play a role in reading comprehension. Prior knowledge can be used to refer not only to topical knowledge but also to knowledge of procedures and strategies used in reading (e.g., how and when to skim). For example, previous experience with a given post-reading task (such as free recall) may guide the readers' pace of reading, concentration, and use of particular strategies (e.g., look-backs). Procedural knowledge can be considered a component of metacognition (Brown, Armbruster, and Baker 1986), but like domain knowledge, it unquestionably plays a role in the act of reading. Perfetti et al. (1996) have this to say about knowledge:

> The importance of knowledge in comprehension, however, is not merely a matter of background or domain knowledge. Drawing an appropriate inference depends on having relevant knowledge activated when it is needed. Monitoring comprehension depends on having a sufficient base of knowledge so that an occasional "signal" of misapprehension is detected against a low noise background of adequate comprehension. Similarly, text inconsistency is a signal detection task, in which a mainly coherent representation of the text is a prerequisite (p. 159).

In short, sources of knowledge and component processes used in reading for meaning interact with one another, so that combinations of deficits might add measurably to the severity of comprehension problems. On the other hand, strengths in the knowledge areas might compensate, at least to some extent, for weaknesses in the component processes. Thus, for example, readers with memory difficulties might have a good store of word meanings and also be good at comprehension monitoring, and through use of these resources address at least some of the problems they encounter in constructing meaning from texts. It should not be assumed that all poor readers are equally deficient in all areas relevant to reading comprehension.

IDENTIFYING AND PROVIDING INSTRUCTION FOR STUDENTS WITH COMPREHENSION PROBLEMS: ISSUES FOR REGULAR AND SPECIAL EDUCATORS

Statistically, about a fifth of the students in most elementary classrooms (those in which students are not grouped by achievement) will show moderate to severe problems with reading comprehension. These problems have developed for a number of different reasons. Some students are simply experiencing "growing pains" as they struggle to handle increasingly complex reading tasks in school. Others have long-term difficulties with comprehension because of the kinds of underlying difficulties we have discussed in the previous sections. Of the students with long-term comprehension problems, some may do poorly on measures of comprehension because of word-reading difficulties, while others have specific comprehension problems, with or without word reading difficulties. Yet other students who struggle with comprehension may be in the process of learning English as their second language.

If these students are going to make progress in reading, they will need instruction that is appropriate for their learning needs. To make decisions about classroom instruction that addresses individual needs and still provides developmentally appropriate instruction in reading, the teacher should evaluate the needs of the weaker readers in the class. It is unlikely that all of these weaker readers will require or benefit from the same kind of help. For example, there may be no value to extending a program on phonics for those students whose word-reading skills are adequate—and this is likely to be the case for some students with reading disabilities and some students who are second language learners.

For students who are very significantly underachieving on standardized measures of reading comprehension, the teacher is well advised to turn to specialists in the school who can carry out a detailed assessment of the students' reading-related capabilities. A careful diagnostician can gather information about each of the areas we have discussed so far, making an effort to develop a full understanding of that students' strengths and weaknesses in reading-related areas. Test results tell only part of the story, however. It is important to gather information about their reading achievement in the classroom as well. Even knowing that a student has difficulties comprehending instructions as well as texts is just a starting point. Useful information about the developmental and educational history can be gathered from a student's parent and teachers, past and present. For example, it might help to know what efforts have already been made to address the students' reading problems. If the student is a second grader and received no special help in or out of the classroom in first grade, it might be appropriate to begin an in-class intervention with the help of specialists in reading. If, however, the student went through a Reading Recovery program in first grade and still has basic and severe difficulties reading connected texts, it would be appropriate to consider a referral for a special education evaluation.

Many students who are learning English while they go to school struggle with reading comprehension because their comprehension of spoken English is limited, relative to grade-level expectations. García (2000) reported that some researchers, who have compared the reading performance of bilingual students with their monolingual peers, found that the bilingual students' comprehension was affected by their status as second-language learners. They knew less about the topics, had difficulty with questions that required them to use appropriate background knowledge, did not know the meanings of many of the words, and so on. Although these problems may *seem* specific to students who are learning to read in a second language, they are not. Some monolingual students with reading comprehension difficulties experience the same problems as their bilingual peers. In general, it is not always possible to distinguish the profiles of students who appear to have biological causes for their learning problems from those whose reading problems appear to grow out of educational or environmental circumstances (Siegel 1992). As was discussed earlier, researchers generally agree about the most common reasons for reading comprehension difficulties, but there is no single characteristic or pattern of characteristics that lies behind all students' underachievement in reading comprehension (Cornoldi, De Beni, and Pazzaglia 1996).

A question teachers commonly ask is whether decisions about appropriate instruction in reading comprehension hinge upon the diagnosis of a reading disability. First, it is not appropriate to limit classroom assistance in reading comprehension to students diagnosed as having a reading or learning disability. All students with comprehension problems should be receiving help, whether it is in the regular education classroom or in a pull-out setting. Another point, however, is that intensive services outside the classroom should not always be considered a "last resort." Preventive tutoring for students at risk for reading problems may be called for. Short-term tutoring may help some students make up for lags in language and emergent literacy skills when they are beginning readers. However, a longer period of tutoring or more intensive work on reading may be needed for beginning readers who do not respond to such early intervention (Vellutino, Scanlon, and Lyon 2000).

Certainly, as we have noted already, when a student does not respond to individualized help within the classroom, it is appropriate to refer the student for assessment of a possible learning disability. The teacher plays a central role in helping school staff determine the appropriate educational services for a given student. Not only is the teacher most knowledgeable about the child's daily struggles and successes with reading, but also he or she has the opportunity to observe and record the child's response to in-class interventions. Response to such interventions is a rich source of diagnostic information (Fuchs and Fuchs 1998).

Terms for Reading Difficulties: Does it Matter What They're Called?

There is considerable confusion about the definitions and identifying criteria for diagnostic categories used with students with significant reading problems. Parents and teachers often ask whether *learning disability* and *reading disability* refer to different conditions. They also wonder how reading disability is different from *dyslexia*. Another common question concerns why some students with significantly poor reading comprehension achievement are not considered to have a disability.

The term *specific learning disability* was proposed by Samuel Kirk in the 1960s as a way to refer to students who have significant difficulties acquiring basic academic skills, despite having average or above average intellectual abilities.

Children identified as having a specific learning disability qualify for special education services in school. By law, students with learning disabilities have a right to a free and appropriate education. The definition given in PL 94-142, the Education for All Handicapped Children Act, is as follows:

> The term specific learning disability means a disorder in one or more of the basic psychological processes involved in understanding or using language, spoken or written, which may manifest itself in an imperfect ability to listen, think, speak, read, write, spell, or do mathematical calculations. The term includes such conditions as perceptual handicaps, brain injury, minimal brain dysfunction, dyslexia, and developmental aphasia. The term does not include children who have learning problems which are primarily the result of visual, hearing or motor handicaps, of mental retardation, of emotional disturbance, or of environmental, cultural, or economic disadvantage (USOE 1977, p. 65083).

It is important to note that reading is just one of a number of possible areas in which learning disabilities become evident in schools; others are listening, speaking, and mathematics. It is true, however, that most students (perhaps as many as 80%) who have learning disabilities have significant problems in reading (Lyon 1995). Thus, a student found to have a specific learning disability in the area of reading qualifies for special education services in his or her public school.

Numerous experts have criticized the definition of learning disabilities because the operational criteria do not specify the severity of the learning problems that make students eligible for special education services. The regulations simply require that there be either significant underachievement in reading relative to age or grade expectations or significant underachievement relative to one's learning potential (intellectual abilities). Other complaints about the definition focus on the vague reference to disorders in psychological processes and on the unrealistic premise that environment and intrinsic learning problems can be clearly distinguished, as is suggested by the last sentence of the definition.

The term *reading disability* is sometimes used to refer to one manifestation of a specific learning disability when underachievement is in the area of reading. However, it is also used more generally to refer to students with significant problems learning to read (that is, very low achievement on measures of reading), whether they fit the remaining criteria for specific learning disabilities or not. Over the last twenty years, there has been a heated debate over the requirement that a student's reading need be significantly below his or her learning ability (i.e., intellectual ability or IQ). Many researchers prefer the term reading disabilities, particularly as it refers to students whose significant underachievement in reading is caused by extreme difficulties acquiring word-reading skills, relative to age or grade-level peers. They argue that it is not necessary or even desirable to require that reading achievement be significantly weaker than the student's intellectual abilities. This is because of considerable evidence that the characteristics of reading disabilities are similar, regardless of students' intellectual ability

(Siegel 1992). Even though many researchers argue that IQ should not be used in the determination of a reading disability (see Fletcher et al. 1998), local and state educational agencies tend to comply with the regulations in federal law for identifying specific learning disabilities. Therefore, for the present, children found to have specific learning disabilities are those for whom there is a significant gap between their achievement and that of their peers or between their achievement and their intellectual capabilities.

The term *dyslexia* is in many respects comparable to the term reading disability. It is usually used to refer to students with severe difficulties with reading and spelling. *Developmental dyslexia* is used to specify problems with reading that have been evident from the early school years, when the student was first given instruction in reading. In contrast, *acquired dyslexia* (or *alexia*) is used to refer to severe difficulties with reading that begin in adulthood, following an insult to the brain, such as a stroke. In the same way that there have been numerous criticisms of the definition of "specific learning disabilities," many definitions of dyslexia have been found inadequate. A group of experts proposed a definition of dyslexia in 1995 that was intended to address some of the shortcomings of previous definitions; this definition is as follows (Lyon 1995):

> Dyslexia is one of several distinct learning disabilities. It is a specific language-based disorder of constitutional origin characterized by difficulties in single word decoding, usually reflecting insufficient phonological processing. These difficulties in single word decoding are often unexpected in relation to age and other cognitive and academic abilities; they are not the result of generalized developmental disability or sensory impairment. Dyslexia is manifest by variable difficulty with different forms of language, often including, in addition to problems with reading, a conspicuous problem with acquiring proficiency in writing and spelling (p. 9).

How do we distinguish the terms dyslexia and learning disabilities, when used to refer to severe difficulties learning to read? Again, learning disabilities is a more general term, as reading is just one of the manifestations of specific learning disabilities. At least in the above definition, it is suggested that dyslexia has a relatively specific cause (i.e., single word reading, reflecting difficulties with phonological processes), whereas causal factors are not specified in the federal definition of learning disabilities, except to say that these are "disorders in the understanding or use of language, spoken and written." Finally, there is a difference in common usage as well. The term *learning disability* is used in educational settings because it is tied to identification of the children who require special education services to address their reading problems, whereas the term *dyslexia* is likely to be used by those who do not work with state and federal regulations within school settings. These people include tutors in private practice, doctors, and researchers (among others).

Not all students with low achievement in reading comprehension qualify for labels such as learning disabilities or dyslexia, and this is as it should be. For example, it would be inappropriate to call a second-language learner with very low scores on a comprehension test learning disabled or dyslexic. Furthermore, in some schools that serve high numbers of students at risk for reading difficulties, many children in every classroom are not reading on grade level, as established by national norms. Here, too, it would be inappropriate to call these children learning disabled or reading disabled. Nonetheless, they need and deserve high quality instruction in reading that is appropriate to their needs, much as we would give to students found appropriately to have a learning disability.[1]

COMMONLY ASKED QUESTIONS

What kinds of questions might the regular or special educator ask the parents in order to understand developmental and family factors that might affect a students' reading achievement?

The classroom teacher and support services staff can benefit from information about the child's developmental and family background. Published topics and questions for family interviews are helpful for this purpose. An example of such an interview, along with thorough discussion of issues involved in interviewing, can be found in Sattler (1992). A thorough interview would include questions concerning health conditions, illnesses, or accidents that are pertinent to school learning (specifically in the area of reading). In addition, it is important to know if there have been any signs or medical diagnoses of unusual language or cognitive development. Because research has shown significant heritability for dyslexia, questions should also be asked regarding a history of reading difficulties and related problems (e.g., speech and language impairments) in the family. In addition, some understanding of cultural practices should be sought (e.g., do adults read to children?). Other questions might be added to an interview if the child is a second-language learner or comes from a culturally different background. For example, when did the child start learning the second language? Was the child taught to read in his or her native language? What languages are spoken in the home?

The information gained from an interview with a parent is likely to provide a better understanding of factors that cause or contribute to a child's reading difficulties. Typically, interview information is suggestive but not conclusive. In fact, as we have seen, a number of different intrinsic and extrinsic factors might collectively contribute to the child's difficulties learning to read. It is also possible that certain family factors might offset the negative psychological impact of a reading disability.

---

[1]It may be important to note that a meta-analysis has shown that students with learning disabilities experience more severe problems with reading than do poor readers who are not identified as learning disabled (Fuchs et al. 2000).

What is the relation of reading and writing disabilities?

Students who have word-reading problems are very likely to have spelling problems as well. Note that spelling is mentioned as an area of co-occurring difficulty in the working definition of dyslexia we discussed earlier. Similarly, students with reading comprehension problems are likely to have difficulties with written expression. This is because receptive language (reading and listening) serves as a foundation for expressive language (speaking and writing). Word-reading problems may respond more readily to instruction than spelling problems. In fact, adults who have overcome reading difficulties as children often continue to have spelling and writing problems as adults (Bruck 1993). Treiman (1995) reported that some studies find the spelling of dyslexics to be like that of younger, normally achieving children, whereas other studies find subtle differences, in that the dyslexics make more phonetically based spelling errors. Much more work is needed before we can tell whether spelling errors provide clear diagnostic markers of conditions such as dyslexia.

Teachers may want to consider teaching reading and writing together as "partners" in the communication process. It is also possible to use writing as an avenue to improve reading comprehension (Langer 1986). In some ways, experience with writing helps students learn to think about reading from a writer's perspective. They become more attuned to the ways writers order their ideas and argue their points, for example. Students with reading problems benefit from close links between instruction in reading and spelling and writing. Literacy programs designed to improve the reading skills of children with learning disabilities often include significant writing components (Englert and Mariage 1991).

How can teachers tell when to provide instruction in reading skills and when to provide accommodations or modifications?

It is important to provide instruction in reading skills for as long as it appears that a student can profit from such instruction. However, accommodations may be in order at various times during the school day, even when the children are receiving tutoring to improve their reading skills. For example, they might need help reading textbooks for science or social studies. They might benefit from listening to a work of literature while reading along in the book. They might need more time to complete reading or writing assignments. They might need to use a spell-checker or to be "forgiven" spelling errors in their compositions.

Accommodations are typically given to students with disabilities and students with such conditions as attention deficit disorder. However, teachers who believe in individualizing instruction in their classrooms are likely to provide normally achieving readers with accommodations on an as-needed basis, too. For example, a good reader who lacks the manual coordination to write clearly may be allowed to use special equipment (a pencil with a triangular grip or large-spaced lined paper). In short, an accommodation may be any way that a teacher helps a student with special needs learn and/or demonstrate his or her learning.

Schools tend not to offer remediation to older students with severe reading problems. After a number of years of basic tutoring in pull-out programs, students with learning disabilities are likely to regard remediation as boring and pointless (Guterman 1995). Right or wrong, it seems common at the high school level for regular education teachers to handle severe reading problems by providing accommodations and for special education teachers to provide subject-area tutoring instead of remediation. It is crucial, however, that schools and teachers do not prevent students from acquiring knowledge and skills by not providing accommodations. Students with reading comprehension disabilities have the same need as their peers to acquire knowledge in their content-area courses, and they may be able to do so only with appropriate accommodations and modifications in given courses. We will return to this topic in the chapter on reading in the content areas (Chapter 9).

In short, regular and special educators have the dual job of helping children learn to understand written texts and supporting their learning of information that is contained in such texts. Their collaboration is needed to determine appropriate methods of instruction and helpful or necessary adjustments to the students' learning tasks and materials. The students must have access to the same quality of learning as is available for students who do not have special needs in the area of reading.

REFERENCES

Aaron, P. G., Joshi, M., and Williams, K. A. 1999. Not all reading disabilities are alike. *Journal of Learning Disabilities*, 32:120–37.

Adams, M. J. 1990. *Beginning to Read: Thinking and Learning about Print.* Cambridge, MA: MIT Press.

Adams, M. J., and Huggins, A. 1985. The growth of children's sight vocabulary: A quick test with educational and theoretical implications. *Reading Research Quarterly*, 20:262–81.

Anderson, R. C., Spiro, R. J., and Anderson, M. C. 1978. Schemata as scaffolding for the representation of information in connected discourse. *American Educational Research Journal*, 15:433–40.

Badian, N. A. 2000. Do preschool orthographic skills contribute to prediction of reading? In *Prediction and Prevention of Reading Failure,* N. A. Badian (Ed.), (pp. 31–56). Baltimore: York Press.

Baker, L., and Anderson, R. I. 1982. Effects of inconsistent information on text processing: Evidence for comprehension monitoring. *Reading Research Quarterly,* 2:281–94.

Baker, L., and Wigfield, A. 1999. Dimensions of children's motivation for reading and their relations to reading activity and reading achievement. *Reading Research Quarterly,* 34:452–477.

Berninger, V. W., and Abbott, R. D. 1994. Multiple orthographic and phonological codes in literacy acquisition: An evolving research program. In *The Varieties of Orthographic Knowledge I: Theoretical and Developmental Issues,* V. W. Berninger (Ed.), (pp. 277–319). Dordrecht, The Netherlands: Kluwer Academic Publishers.

Berninger V. W., Abbott, R. D., Billingsley, F., and Nagy, W. 2001. Processes underlying timing and fluency: Efficiency, automaticity, coordination, and morphological awareness. In *Dyslexia, Fluency, and the Brain,* M. Wolf (Ed.), (pp. 383–414). Baltimore, MD: York Press.

Bowers, P. G. 2001. Exploration of the basis for rapid naming's relationship to reading. In *Dyslexia, Fluency, and the Brain,* M. Wolf (Ed.), (pp. 41–63). Baltimore, MD: York Press.

Bowers, P. G., and Wolf, M. 1993. Theoretical links among naming speed, precise timing mechanisms, and orthographic skill in dyslexia. *Reading and Writing: An Interdisciplinary Journal,* 5:69–85.

Bowey, J. A. 1986. Syntactic awareness in relation to reading skill and ongoing reading comprehension monitoring. *Journal of Experimental Child Psychology,* 41:282–99.

Brown, A. L., Armbruster, B. B., and Baker, L. 1986. The role of metacognition in reading and studying. In *Reading Comprehension: From Research to Practice,* J. Orsanu (Ed.), (pp. 49–75). Hillsdale, NJ: Lawrence Erlbaum.

Bruck, M. 1993. Component spelling skills of college students with childhood diagnoses of dyslexia. *Learning Disability Quarterly,* 16:171–84.

Carlisle, J. F. 1995. Morphological awareness and early reading achievement. In *Morphological Aspects of Language Processing,* L. B. Feldman (Ed.), (pp. 189–209). Hillsdale, NJ: Lawrence Erlbaum.

Carlisle, J. F. 2000. Awareness of the structure and meaning of morphologically complex words: Impact on reading. *Reading and Writing: An Interdisciplinary Journal,* 12:169–90.

Catts, H. W., Fey, M. E., Zhang, X., and Tomblin, J. B. 1999. Language basis of reading and reading disabilities: Evidence from a longitudinal investigation. *Scientific Studies of Reading,* 3:331–61.

Clay, M. 1985. Early detection of reading difficulties (3rd ed.). Portsmouth, NH: Heinemann Books.

Cornoldi, C., De Beni, R., and Pazzaglia, F. 1996. Profiles of reading comprehension difficulties: An analysis of single cases. In *Reading Comprehension Difficulties: Processes and Intervention,* C. Cornoldi and J. Oakhill (Eds.), (pp. 113–36). Mahwah, NJ: Lawrence Erlbaum.

Curtis, M. E. 1980. Development of components of reading skill. *Journal of Educational Psychology,* 72:656–69.

Daneman, M., and Carpenter, P. A. 1980. Individual differences in working memory and reading. *Journal of Verbal Learning and Verbal Behavior,* 19:450–66.

Denckla, M. B., and Cutting, L. E. 1999. History and significant of Rapid Automatized Naming. *Annals of Dyslexia*, 49:29–42.

Ehri, L. C. 1992. Reconceptualizing the development of sight word reading and its relationship to recoding. In *Reading Acquisition*, P. B. Gough, L. C. Ehri, and R. Treiman (Eds.), (pp.107–43). Hillsdale, NJ: Lawrence Erlbaum.

Elbro, C., Borstrom, I., and Petersen, D. 1998. Predicting dyslexia from kindergarten: The importance of distinctness of phonological representations of lexical items. *Reading Research Quarterly*, 33:39–60.

Englert, C. S., and Mariage, T. V. 1991. Making students partners in the comprehension process: Organizing the reading POSSE. *Learning Disability Quarterly*, 14:123–38.

Fletcher, J. M., Francis, D. J., Shaywitz, S. E., Lyon, G. R., Foorman, B. R., Stuebing, K. K., and Shaywitz, B. A. 1998. Intelligent testing and the discrepancy model for children with learning disabilities. *Learning Disabilities Research and Practice*, 13:186–203.

Fuchs, D., Fuchs, L. S., Mathes, P. G., and Lipsey, M. W. 2000. Reading differences between underachievers with and without learning disabilities: A meta-analysis. In *Research Syntheses in Special Education*, R. Gersten, E. Schiller, and S. Vaughn (Eds.), (pp. 81–104). Mahwah, NJ: Lawrence Erlbaum.

Fuchs, L. S., and Fuchs, D. 1998. Treatment validity: A unifying concept for reconceptualizing the identification of learning disabilities. *Learning Disabilities Research and Practice*, 13:204–19.

García, G. E. 2000. Bilingual children's reading. In *Handbook of Reading Research, Vol. III*, M. L. Kamil, P. B. Mosenthal, P. D. Pearson, and R. Barr (Eds.), (pp. 813–34). Mahwah, NJ: Lawrence Erlbaum.

Gersten, R., Fuchs, L. S., Williams, J. P., and Baker, S. 2001. Teaching reading comprehension strategies to students with learning disabilities: A review of research. *Review of Educational Research*, 71:279–320.

Gough, P. B., Hoover, W. A., and Peterson, C. L. 1996. Some observations on a simple view of reading. In *Reading Comprehension Difficulties: Processes and Intervention*, C. Cornoldi and J. Oakhill (Eds.), (pp. 1–13). Mahwah, NJ: Lawrence Erlbaum.

Guterman, B. R. 1995. The validity of categorical learning disabilities services: The consumers' view. *Exceptional Children*, 62:111–24.

Hart, B., and Risley, T. R. 1995. *Meaningful Differences in the Everyday Experience of Young American Children*. Baltimore: Paul H. Brookes Publishing Co.

Jenkins, J. R., Stein, M. L., and Wysocki, K. 1984. Learning vocabulary through reading. *American Educational Research Journal*, 21:767–87.

Juel, C. 1988. Learning to read and write: A longitudinal study of 54 children from first through fourth grades. *Journal of Educational Psychology*, 80:437–47.

Langer, J. A. 1986. *Children Reading and Writing: Structures and Strategies*. Norwood, NJ: Ablex.

Liberman, I. Y., Shankweiler, D., and Liberman, A. M. 1989. The alphabetic principle and learning to read. In *Phonology and Reading Disability*, D. Shankweiler and I. Y. Liberman (Eds.), (pp. 1–33). Ann Arbor, MI: University of Michigan Press.

Lyon, G. R. 1995. Toward a definition of dyslexia. *Annals of Dyslexia*, 45:3–27.

Mason, J. 1992. Reading stories to preliterate children. In *Reading Acquisition*, P. B. Gough, L. C. Ehri, and R. Treiman (Eds.), (pp.215–41). Hillsdale, NJ: Lawrence Erlbaum.

McKenna, M. C., Kear, D. J., and Ellsworth, R. A. 1995. Children's attitude toward reading: A national survey. *Reading Research Quarterly*, 30:934–956.

Muter, V., and Snowling, M. 1998. Concurrent and longitudinal predictors of reading: The role of metalinguistic and short-term memory skills. *Reading Research Quarterly,* 33:320–35.

Nagy, W. E., and Anderson, R. C. 1999. Metalinguistic awareness and literacy acquisition in different languages. In *Literacy: An International Handbook,* D. A. Wagner, R. L. Venezky, and B. V. Street (Eds.), (pp. 155–60). Oxford: Westview Press.

Nagy, W. E., Herman, P. A., and Anderson, R. 1985. Learning words from context. *Reading Research Quarterly,* 20:233–53.

Oakhill, J. and Yuill, N. 1996. Higher order factors in comprehension disability: Processes and remediation. In *Reading Comprehension Difficulties: Processes and Intervention,* C. Cornoldi and J. Oakhill (Eds.), (pp. 69–92). Mahwah, NJ: Lawrence Erlbaum.

Olson, R. K. and Gayan, J. 2001. Brains, genes and environment in reading development. In *Handbook of Early Literacy Research,* S. B. Neuman and D. K. Dickinson (Eds.), (pp. 81–94). New York: Guilford Press.

Paris, S. G., Wasik, B. A., and Turner, J. C. 1991. The development of strategic readers. In *Handbook of Reading Research, Vol II,* R. Barr, M. L. Kamil, P. B. Mosenthal, and P. D. Pearson (Eds.), (pp. 609–40). New York: Longman.

Perfetti, C. A. 1992. The representation problem in reading acquisition. In *Reading Acquisition,* P. B. Gough, L. C. Ehri, and R. Treiman (Eds.), (pp. 14–74). Hillsdale, NJ: Lawrence Erlbaum.

Perfetti, C. A., Beck, L., Bell, L., and Hughes, C. 1987. Phonemic knowledge and learning to read are reciprocal: A longitudinal study of first grade children. *Merrill Palmer Quarterly,* 33:283–19.

Perfetti, C. A., Marron, M. A., and Foltz, P. W. 1996. Sources of comprehension failure: Theoretical perspectives and case studies. In *Reading Comprehension Difficulties: Processes and Difficulties,* C. Cornoldi and J. Oakhill (Eds.), (pp.137–65) Mahwah, NJ: Lawrence Erlbaum.

Purcell-Gates, V. 2000. Family literacy. In *Handbook of Reading Research, Vol III,* M. L. Kamil, P. B. Mosenthal, P. D. Pearson, and R. Barr (Eds.), (pp. 853–70). Mahwah, NJ: Lawrence Erlbaum.

Sattler, J. M. 1992. *Assessment of children, 3rd edition.* San Diego: Jerome M. Sattler, Publisher.

Scarborough, H. S. 1990. Very early language deficits in dyslexic children. *Child Development,* 61:1728–734.

Scarborough, H. 2001. Connecting early language and literacy to later reading (dis)abilities: Evidence, theory, and practice. In *Handbook of Early Literacy Research,* S. B. Neuman and D. K. Dickinson (Eds.), (pp. 97–110). NY: Guilford Press.

Siegel, L. S. 1992. An evaluation of the discrepancy definition of dyslexia. *Journal of Learning Disabilities,* 25:618–29.

Spiro, R. J. 1980. Constructive processes in prose comprehension and recall. In *Theoretical Issues in Reading Comprehension,* R. J. Spiro, B. C. Bruce, and W. E. Brewer (Eds.), (pp. 245–78). Hillsdale, NJ: Lawrence Erlbaum.

Stanovich, K. E. 1988. The right and wrong places to look for the cognitive locus of reading disability. *Annals of Dyslexia,* 38:154–77.

Stanovich, K. E. West, R. F., Cunningham, A. E., Cipuelewski, J., and Siddiqui, S. 1996. The role of inadequate print exposure as a determinant of reading comprehension problems. In *Reading Comprehension Difficulties: Processes and Difficulties,* C. Cornoldi and J. Oakhill (Eds.), (pp.15–32). Mahwah, NJ: Lawrence Erlbaum.

Sticht, T. E., and James, J. H. 1984. Listening and reading. In *Handbook of Reading Research,* P. D. Pearson, R. Barr, M. L. Kamil, and P. B. Mosenthal (Eds.), (pp. 293–317). New York: Longman.

Stone, B., and Brady, S. 1995. Evidence for phonological processing deficits in less-skilled readers. *Annals of Dyslexia,* 45:51–78.

Stothard, S. E. and Hulme, C. 1996. A comparison of reading comprehension and decoding difficulties in children. In *Reading Comprehension Difficulties: Processes and Intervention,* C. Cornoldi and J. Oakhill (Eds.), (pp. 93–112). Mahwah, NJ: Lawrence Erlbaum.

Swanson, H. L. 1993. Working memory in learning disability subgroups. *Journal of Experimental Child Psychology,* 56:87–114.

Tabors, P. O., Snow, C. E, and Dickinson, D. K. 2001. Homes and schools together. In *Beginning Literacy with Language,* D. K. Dickinson and P. O. Tabors (Eds.), (pp. 313–34). Baltimore: Paul H. Brookes.

Torgesen, J. K., and Wagner, R. K. 1998. Alternative diagnostic approaches for specific developmental reading disabilities. *Learning Disabilities Research and Practice,* 13:220–32.

Treiman, R. 1995. Spelling in normal children and dyslexics. In *Foundations of Reading Acquisition and Dyslexia,* B. Blachman (Ed.), (pp. 191–218). Mahwah: Lawrence Erlbaum.

Tunmer, W. E., and Chapman, J. W. 1998. Language prediction skill. Phonological recoding ability, and beginning reading. In *Reading and Spelling: Development and Disorders,* C. Hulme and M. R. Joshi (Eds.), (pp. 33–67). Mahwah, NJ: Lawrence Erlbaum.

Tunmer, W. E., Herriman, M. L., and Nesdale, A. R. 1989. Metalinguistic abilities and beginning reading. *Reading Research Quarterly,* 23:134–58.

Tunmer, W. E., and Hoover, W. A. 1992. Cognitive and linguistic factors in learning to read. In *Reading Acquisition,* P. B. Gough, L. C. Ehri, and R. Treiman (Eds.), (pp. 175–214). Hillsdale, NJ: Lawrence Erlbaum.

United States Office of Education. (USOE). 1977. Definition and criteria for identifying students as learning disabled. *Federal Register,* 42 (250), p. 65083.

Vellutino, F., Scanlon, D. M., and Lyon, G. R. 2000. Differentiating between difficult-to-remediate and readily remediated poor readers: More evidence against the IQ-achievement discrepancy definition of reading disability. *Journal of Learning Disabilities,* 33:223–38.

Wagner, R. K., Torgesen, J. K., Laughon, P., Simmons, K. and Rashotte, C. 1993. The development of young readers' phonological processing abilities. *Journal of Educational Psychology,* 85:83–103.

Wilkinson, L. C., and Silliman, E. R. 2000. Classroom language and literacy learning. In *Handbook of Reading Research, Vol III,* M. L. Kamil, P. B. Mosenthal, P. D. Pearson, and R. Barr (Eds.), (pp. 337–60). Mahwah, NJ: Lawrence Erlbaum.

Yuill, N., Oakhill, J., and Parkin, A. 1989. Working memory, comprehension ability, and the resolution of text anomaly. *British Journal of Psychology,* 80:351–61.

3

Fluency and Its Relation to Reading Comprehension

GETTING STARTED

✓ How do automaticity of word reading and fluency of textual reading affect comprehension?
✓ What causes poor readers to have particular difficulties becoming fluent readers?
✓ How can classroom teachers help students become fluent readers?
✓ What are considered effective instructional methods to help struggling readers become fluent readers?

HOW DOES FLUENCY AFFECT COMPREHENSION?

Students need to read not only accurately, but also fluently in order to understand texts. When readers cannot read fluently, they may understand some of a passage or story, but comprehension is bound to be compromised. Why is this? One reason is the "no room to think" factor (Camp, Winbury, and Zinna 1981). If students are struggling with basic word recognition or decoding processes, they tend to devote such a large portion of their cognitive resources to this aspect of reading that there is little left over to devote to meaning. A second reason is the "forgetting" factor (Camp, Winbury, and Zinna 1981). If the reader is accurate in his or her word identification but still slow at this process, he or she is likely to have trouble maintaining information in memory long enough to make sense of it. Very slow reading is also likely to be accompanied by long pauses and regressions to earlier parts of the text, signs that the reader is attempting to integrate the meanings of words into a comprehensible text. By the end of a sentence, the reader may have lost information gleaned from the words at the beginning.

Accuracy and automaticity of word reading are characteristics we find in skilled readers at every age. To the adult skilled reader, word reading and indeed many aspects of reading appear to happen without conscious attention or deliberate action on the part of the reader (Laberge and Samuels 1974; Perfetti and Hogaboam 1975). Because skilled readers' word reading happens so effort-lessly, their subjective impression of reading is that they are processing words and sentences for meaning. However, fluent reading does not mean that the skilled reader is skipping over or not processing some words. Instead, it means that he or she recognizes most words in texts automatically—that is, immediately and without the need to use word-reading strategies consciously.

Automaticity and Fluency Are Not the Same

To understand the development of fluent reading, it helps to distinguish the terms automaticity and fluency. Ehri and Wilce (1983) have described the stages of acquir-ing word-reading skill that lead to automaticity. First, the reader needs to use strate-gies to recognize words (e.g., sounding out, making analogies to known words). With repeated exposures to words, connections among the sound, the spelling, and the meaning are established, and reading these words becomes less effortful. Such connections allow words to be identified in less than one second. This is why teach-ers tend to refer to words that readers recognize immediately as *sight words*. The term automaticity, like the term *sight word reading*, refers to the goal of rapid word recognition, whether these words are in passages or not. Teachers want their stu-dents to recognize words immediately and effortlessly. Fluency, on the other hand, refers to a smooth and relatively rapid reading of a text. For fluency to be achieved, most words in that text must be read with automaticity.

Of the two traits, fluency is the one that is more closely associated with good comprehension (Kuhn and Stahl 2000; Meyer and Felton 1999). This may be be-cause it refers to the reader's engagement with natural texts. Fluent reading is characterized by smooth reading of a passage, at a pace that reflects normal lan-guage delivery and with expression. There is a reciprocal relation between com-prehension and fluency. The better a reader's understanding of a passage, the more fluent his or her reading is likely to be. The more fluent the reader, the more likely it is that he or she will understand a passage.

How are improvements in fluency achieved for students with significant reading problems? An important starting point in answering this question is to repeat the point that improvements in accuracy may gradually lead to automatic-ity of word reading, which is a first step on the road to fluency. Some efforts have been made to determine whether students who need instruction to improve accuracy benefit from different sorts of instruction than those who are accurate, but not fluent, textual readers. Lovett, Ransby, and Barron (1988) identified groups of students for whom either speed or accuracy was the primary char-acteristic of their reading problem. These students received one of three treatments—decoding skills, oral and written language skills, or classroom sur-vival skills (the control condition). The accuracy-disabled students responded positively to the decoding skills treatment, as would be expected, while the rate-disabled students responded to both the decoding skills and oral and written lan-guage skills programs. The researchers suggested that the rate-disabled students benefited from practice on words, even though their word reading was not lack-ing in accuracy, as this practice fostered more fluent reading.

Automaticity of word reading may lead over time to fluency of passage reading, which in turn facilitates comprehension. Fluency makes it possible or at least likely that the reader will understand the text, although it does not guarantee that the reader *will* understand the text. An issue of some importance is whether the ability to infer words from context facilitates the accuracy, speed, and fluency of reading. Research has shown that skilled readers are so fast at recognizing words that hints from the passage about the identity of a word only sometimes aid word reading. On the other hand, less skilled readers are typically slow at reading words; as a result, there is time for clues from the passage context to influence the identification of unfamiliar words (Perfetti and Roth 1981). The less skilled reader may make more use of context than the skilled reader, but this does not always lead to accurate and fluent reading. Consider the following sentences: "The man was looking for the sponge he used to wash the car yesterday. First, he looked under the kitchen sink, and then he looked in the *garbage*." The skilled reader is likely to recognize the word *garbage* before the meaning of the sentence is processed. The less skilled reader who does not immediately recognize *garbage* might anticipate where car equipment is found and so might read the final word as *garage*. The reader's difficulty reading this word leads to dysfluent reading, as he or she pauses for a longer time than we would expect on the word *garage* and then, unsure that the sentence makes sense, rereads it, and eventually corrects the word-reading error.

Poor readers commonly have difficulties becoming fluent readers, even when they have acquired good word attack strategies and a fairly large store of sight words. For adult dyslexics, slow reading is a primary problem, even when they have the academic capabilities to go to college and graduate schools (Bruck 1990). Measures of word-reading speed are more powerful than measures of word-reading accuracy at distinguishing students with reading disabilities from peers matched for both chronological and reading age (Compton and Carlisle 1994). Nonetheless, problems with fluency are less commonly recognized and targeted for instruction than problems with word-reading accuracy. Most tests of word reading, including standardized tests and informal reading inventories, assess accuracy of word reading but do not assess fluency of passage reading.[2] If the tests used to evaluate students' progress in reading focus only on accuracy, teachers will be concerned about helping students become accurate word readers. They might assume that once students can decode most of the words in the books they read, they should be able to understand them. This assumption is flawed because it does not take into account the need for students to be fluent as well as accurate in their passage reading.

Reasons for Difficulties Attaining Automaticity and Fluency

The amount of practice in word reading students need to acquire automaticity varies a good deal for normally achieving and struggling readers (Ehri and Wilce

---

[2]At present, standardized and curriculum-based measures of speed of word and nonword reading are becoming popular. These are a good index of automaticity and provide an estimate of fluency.

1983; Manis 1985; Reitsma 1983). In general, however, less skilled readers need many more exposures to words before they recognize them immediately. Ehri and Wilce (1983) had normal readers and students with reading disabilities practice words and nonwords as many as 18 times. They found that the normally achieving readers, but not students with reading disabilities, read the familiar words as fast as they could name digits. In contrast, even with many exposures to the words, the students with reading disabilities had not developed a representation of the word in memory such that the verbal label could be retrieved immediately. These results suggest that students with reading disabilities have an underlying difficulty making connections between the sound and spelling of written words. It is important for teachers to appreciate that such students need much more practice reading words than their classmates before these words are securely stored in memory and can be retrieved instantaneously.

It appears that some students have particular trouble processing the sounds in words (a phonological deficit) while others have trouble processing the spellings (an orthographic deficit). Students who can not sound out regular nonsense words (e.g., *glurk*) may be thought of as having trouble working with phonological aspects of written words. Other students cannot recognize words that are not regular in their spelling (e.g., *people* or *island*), even when they have seen them many, many times. They may have particular difficulties storing an accurate orthographic image of a word's spelling in memory (Roberts and Mather 1997). Students who are very slow at learning to read and spell words are likely to have both problems.

As we discussed in Chapter 2, another reason for difficulties acquiring fluency stems from an underlying problem with "naming" speed, which refers to slow retrieval of the names of things from memory (Denkla and Rudel 1976; Denkla and Cutting 1999). Naming problems are evident not only when students are presented with letters and words but also when they are asked to name common objects, numbers, or colors rapidly. For example, students might be asked to name a series of color chips (e.g., red, blue, yellow) displayed in rows on a page as quickly as they can. Slow "namers" are significantly slower and less accurate than their peers at retrieving the correct word to identify the visually presented color chips (Wolf 1991). As Bowers (2001) has pointed out, such poor readers fail to abstract orthographic regularities after repeated exposure to written words and are severely limited in automaticity of word recognition. Through studies of neurological processing, Berninger and her colleagues have found that attention and "executive" processes (such as planning) play a role in the efficiency with which students carry out reading activities, and these (along with other mechanisms that affect timing) vary greatly among students who are not fluent readers (Berninger et al. 2001).

In one study, Bowers (1993) investigated the reading speed, before and after practice, for poor and average readers she followed from grade 2 through grade 4. She found that, when accuracy of word reading was controlled, speed of naming symbols (like numbers or colors) significantly explained the students' speed of reading, whether the passage was a new one or one that had been read at least four times. Finding verbal labels in one's head, therefore, is clearly one factor that stands in the way of achieving fluency for students who have significant problems learning to read. Similarly, Levy and her colleagues (see Levy 2001) provided fluency training for fourth graders who were fast or slow namers (based on performance on a measure of rapid automatized naming). The slow namers were in fact the slowest readers of passages. However, like the fast namers, they made significant gains on word naming when provided with practice. These researchers used passages that were relatively easy for the students to read, and they also used a time limit in the training so that the children would be motivated to try to read as fast as possible. Such measures may have influenced the students' growth in both fluency and comprehension.

In short, some students who have trouble with accuracy and automaticity of word reading are slow at retrieving verbal labels from memory, some have difficulties with phonological awareness and learning letter-sound relations, and some have trouble developing accurate mental representations of word spellings. When the naming or retrieval problem is accompanied by lack of awareness of the sound structure of words, researchers would say the student has a "double deficit" (Badian 1997; Bowers and Wolf 1993). Having both these problems has a greater impact on students' success in learning to read than either one alone. When students also have problems acquiring a sight vocabulary (i.e., words they have looked at hundreds of times are still not familiar to them), they are said to have a "triple deficit." These students typically have very severe problems acquiring accuracy, automaticity, and fluency of reading.

Another aspect of fluent reading that researchers have been concerned with is the student's ability to read with expression, which is apparent from the prosody and vocal intonation used by the student during oral reading. Prosody and intonation convey meaning. For example, in one oral language context, the question, "Where are you going?" might receive emphasis on the word "where" ("WHERE are you going?"), whereas in another the emphasis might be placed on the word "you" ("Where are YOU going?") The intent of the question is different with these two patterns of vocal emphasis. Some readers tend to read orally in a monotone. Because they put the same emphasis on every word, we might suspect that the words and sentences do not convey meaning to them. On the other hand, where we find a student reading with expression, we can expect that the student is reading for meaning.[3]

There are several different reasons for the links between prosody, non-fluent reading, and comprehension. One reason is that slow and inaccurate word reading may make it hard for the reader to read for meaning, a consequence being lack of expression in oral reading. Another reason is the reader's notion of the job of oral reading. He or she might think of oral reading as a process of calling out the words, without regard for natural stress patterns or comprehension. A third possibility is that some children have trouble appreciating the meaning of sentences, even when they can read the words. This may be because written sentences

---

[3]In some instances, students are excellent oral readers in the sense of reading passages accurately and with expression, but they lack comprehension. While a relatively rare condition, hyperlexia is evident when children experience a dissociation between ease of word reading and comprehension.

provide none of the prosodic clues that come with oral expression. These children find it hard to understand the meaning intended by the writer (Schreiber 1987). In several training studies, researchers have found that students' speech pauses become more natural as they become more fluent readers (Dowhower 1987; Herman 1985). In some studies, efforts have been made to provide prosodic "models" for the students. However, Young, Bowers, and MacKinnon (1996) found that repeated readings both with and without prosodic modeling led to improved fluency, and so they concluded that it was the repeated readings, not the prosodic modeling, that brought about significant improvement.

The Impact of Passage Context and Prior Knowledge on Fluency

Although it is clear that fluency may affect comprehension, there is relatively little written about the fact that poor comprehension can contribute to problems with fluency of reading. For most readers, context provides at least some facilitation for word recognition and (as noted earlier) may provide more support for poor readers than good readers. However, if a student does not understand the text passage, then context obviously cannot provide much support for the automaticity of word recognition or the fluency of reading. For example, Bruck (1990) found that adults with childhood diagnosis of dyslexia were quite slow at reading even common words in a text that was informative, but also quite humorous. According to her, one reason may be that these adults had relatively poor world knowledge and small vocabularies. Poorer understanding of the text might well have affected the degree to which these adults could use context to facilitate word recognition.

Levy (2001) has looked specifically at the role of context. Do readers gain more from repeated readings of connected texts or from repeated readings of words in lists? In a study that speaks to this issue, Levy and her colleagues (reported in Levy 2001) compared repeated encounters with words presented in lists and words presented in passages as they affected fourth-grade good and poor comprehenders' fluency and comprehension. The students in the "word list" practice condition played a computer game called "stop the clock" in which they read the words on lists as quickly as possible, these lists being made up of 108 target content words. The students in the passage practice condition encountered the same 108 words as they read different passages. Several weeks later, all of the students read two passages, and their accuracy, speed and comprehension were assessed. One passage contained the words both groups of students had practiced (albeit in different conditions) while the other did not contain any of the content words the students had practiced in either list or passage form. This passage assessed transfer of word reading automaticity from practiced to unpracticed words.

The results showed that both good and poor readers benefited from practice; even the poor readers read more fluently. On the transfer passage, both good and poor comprehenders read the passage more slowly than they had the passage with the trained words. Of particular interest was the fact that the transfer "benefit" was the same for those who had practiced the words on word lists and those who had practiced them in passages. The groups did not differ on comprehension, but this may be because the researchers had all the students read the passages several times before they tested their comprehension. The results suggest that practice on either word lists or passages that contain a number of the same words may result in improved fluency. Further evidence that practice with isolated words can affect comprehension comes from a study by Tan and Nicholson (1997) in which poor readers' word drill with flashcards led to improved comprehension.

It is important to keep in mind that the purpose of automaticity and fluency is to facilitate comprehension. The relation of different types of practice to improvement in comprehension is truly complex. We need to consider not only the severity of the naming problems of the students but also the types of words in lists and passages, the amount of practice students receive, and the way that comprehension is assessed. As a result, it is difficult to use research studies to compare practice on words lists and passages in terms of their benefits for comprehension. We need to keep in mind the virtually unanimous agreement that with sufficient repeated exposures to words (in lists or passages), students experience improved fluency in passage reading, which in turn is crucial for comprehension processes to work well.

A final note of caution is in order. Because fluency can be adversely affected by poor comprehension, we should not assume that we can make all students into more fluent readers simply by providing practice in word reading and repeated readings of passages. For some struggling readers, instruction in language comprehension, including both vocabulary and sentence comprehension, may also be needed to provide the foundation for fluent reading and comprehension.

APPROACHES TO INSTRUCTION

Drills on words in isolation may facilitate smooth and accurate reading of words in texts (Levy 2001; Mercer et al. 2000). Methods for improving word-reading speed involve repeated exposures to particular words or types of words that the students are learning to decode (that is, practice and review). These might involve word-reading drills, in which the student reads as many words as he or she can within a set time limit (e.g., 2 minutes). Such drills may involve old-fashioned flashcards, word lists, or computer programs that involve repeated practice sessions reading words quickly and accurately. Meyer and Felton (1999) reviewed a number of studies that focused on fluency among students who are poor readers. Their analysis showed that both rehearsal of words many times over (with a goal of improved accuracy and speed) and re-readings of passages were beneficial to the students.

Instructional methods designed to improve the fluency of reading natural texts are more clearly linked to comprehension than methods that involve practice on words in isolation. Different forms of practice with texts include independent reading (i.e., providing opportunities to read), practice reading with assistance of one kind or another, and repeated readings. Repeated reading can be assisted readings (re-reading texts with a skilled reader as a model and guide) and unassisted readings (re-reading texts independently) (e.g., Dowhower 1989; Kuhn and Stahl 2000; Meyer and Felton 1999). Each of these is discussed in turn.

Independent Reading Practice

A common recommendation for a method to help students become fluent readers is setting aside time for independent reading (Fielding, Wilson, and Anderson 1984). The general idea is that the best way to improve reading skills is to read as much as possible. In the same way that practice helps an athlete improve in agility and eye-hand coordination, characteristics that affect performance in sports like golf or tennis, practice in reading is thought to help the student recognize more and more words automatically, to develop good strategies for attacking unfamiliar words, and to monitor for comprehension—that is, to learn when and how to deploy other fix-up strategies when the text does not seem comprehensible. Belief in the value of extensive reading has lead to such educational practices as Sustained Silent Reading (a period of quiet, independent reading during the school day) and "book wars" (book-reading competitions which are thought to motivate students to spend time reading on their own). Such measures as these might contribute to students' reading proficiency.

Programs of independent reading are not often set up in such a way that the students read the same texts more than once. In fact, accomplishing a large amount of reading is often the goal. There is often no link to aspects of reading instruction (e.g., phonics or comprehension instruction). Finally, there is no assurance that students are reading books at a level that would be appropriate for developing fluency. Despite the limitations of independent reading as a component of a program on reading instruction, independent reading (and the amount of reading students do in that time) can contribute to improvement in reading, but clearly this is more likely the case for skilled than less skilled readers (e.g., Taylor, Frye, and Maruyama 1990).

For students with reading disabilities, practice alone may not provide sufficient support for the development of fluent reading. As poor readers, they have difficulties sustaining interest in reading. They are inefficient in processing information in texts, perhaps because they lack the ability to control and manage their own cognitive activities in a purposeful manner (Gersten et al. 2001). Motivation for self-improvement may be limited. Even when motivated, poor readers might not be wise about selecting books that they would benefit from reading. In a study of reading development in the elementary years, Juel (1988) informally assessed fourth graders' attitudes toward reading. She asked them, "Do you like to read?" A large number of the good readers responded affirmatively, whereas only a few of the poor readers did. Poor readers often said that they read little because they hated reading. One child said, "I'd rather clean the mold around the bathtub than read" (p. 442). For most poor readers, then, practice is most effective when it is linked to or accompanied by instruction.

Practice Reading with Assistance

Another form of practice involves providing support for reading through one of several means in situations where students are practicing by reading different texts. Means of support include shared book reading assisted by a student or adult, tape-recorded books that students can listen to as they watch the text, or computer software programs that provide texts and some guidance in word reading. These forms of support have been found to lead to improvements in accuracy and fluency of reading, including computers that provide support for word reading (e.g., Reitsma 1988).

Shany and Biemiller (1995) studied the effects of assisted reading practice over a four-month period on the rate and comprehension of at-risk third and fourth graders. They compared teacher-assisted practice (in which the student read aloud to the teacher, and the teacher supplied any word the child could not read) and tape-assisted practice (in which the child read the stories while simultaneously listening to the same text on tape). "Simultaneous" reading could be either oral or silent. The results showed significant gains in text reading rate and comprehension scores for the group with assisted practice, as compared to a control group. The students in the tape-assisted condition completed twice as much reading as those in the teacher-assisted condition. However, it may be important to note that the teacher was working with another student near-by and could monitor the tape-assisted child's work, as well as provide assistance if the child lost his or her place.

The results support the view that increased practice, carried out in the presence of the teacher, improves reading achievement. The amount of reading the students completed is also noteworthy, as most of the at-risk readers read through at least $2^{1}/_{2}$ "years" of basal readers in 64 days or 32 hours. The relationship between amount of reading and amount of progress is not clear, but the results provide evidence that in a relatively long-term study, the children showed improvement in reading comprehension. Still, the researchers pointed out that the progress a given student made in reading comprehension was not likely to exceed his or her listening comprehension. As noted earlier, fluency training by itself is not likely to turn students with developmental limitations in oral language comprehension into age-appropriate reading comprehenders.

Repeated Readings With and Without Assistance

Reading stories or passages more than one time is another way to improve fluency. The idea is that through repeated readings, students become faster and more accurate at recognizing both common function and content words (Samuels 1979). In fact, not only do repeated readings lead to improvements in fluency and comprehension of the passages that are reread, but also students gradually become more fluent when they read other (unpracticed) passages for the first time (Weinstein and Cooke 1992).

Kuhn and Stahl (2000) characterized repeated reading techniques as unassisted and assisted, depending on whether the reader receives guidance or not. In reviewing studies that have used repeated readings of these two types, these researchers found evidence that unassisted repeated readings sometimes led to improved accuracy, fluency, and comprehension, but assisted readings generally showed more positive results. Unassisted repeated readings might involve asking student to read a story and to read it again to themselves then or at a later time (e.g., at home). Two promising methods of assisted readings are the neurological impress method, which involves having the student shadow the adult's reading, and reading silently while listening to tape-recordings. For young and very slow readers, assisted repeated readings can involve "read alongs" (where the student has a live or audiotaped model of the passage) (Dowhower 1989). Poor readers have been found to benefit from listening to stories while they read along to themselves. Reading a passage silently as someone reads it aloud provides not only exposure to the pronunciation of the words but also experiences with natural phrasing and intonation. When the student's reading of a passage is about 60 words per minute, the teacher can shift from using *read-along* to *read-aloud* readings of the passage.

Two studies that compared assisted repeated reading (using listening while reading) and unassisted repeated readings found significant progress for both methods (Dowhower 1987; Rasinski 1990). Dowhower (1987) found that second graders in both types of instructional programs made significant gains in word accuracy and comprehension from the first to the last reading of a passage. Rasinski (1990) reported significant gains for third graders using repeated readings and listening-while-reading on word reading and reading speed. Comprehension was not ignored. Kuhn and Stahl (2000) pointed out that in these studies, students were required to tell about the passages they read. The particular methods of implementing repeated readings may make a difference in the amount of improvement the students experience.

Because fluency is such a pervasive problem among poor readers, a number of studies have been carried out to determine the extent to which poor readers benefit from training in fluency. One study that looked at the benefits of repeated readings for poor readers was carried out by Herman (1985). She had eight intermediate-grade students who were non-fluent readers practice five stories over a three-month period. She compared the rate and accuracy of the first and last readings of the initial story with the first and last readings of the final story. Comprehension was estimated by the quality of the word reading errors ("miscues"). After training, the students' rate and comprehension improved significantly. In addition, improvements were found not only on the repeated readings of particular passages but on different passages read thereafter. Although these results support the value of re-readings, they leave unanswered questions concerning how much practice is needed over a period of time in order to lead to long-term growth in reading comprehension.

In another study (O'Shea, Sindelar, and O'Shea 1987), fifth through eighth graders with LD were asked to read passages a number of times (1, 3, or 7 times), under two different conditions (i.e., given directions to read as quickly and accurately as possible, or given directions to remember the passage). The results showed more significant growth, both in terms of fluency and comprehension, between one and three readings, as compared to changes between three and seven readings. For this reason, the researchers recommended that instructional programs should not require more than three rereadings of a passage. Another finding of interest is that the students told to remember the story made gains in both fluency and comprehension, whereas the students told to read correctly and accurately made significant gains in fluency but not comprehension. These results suggest the importance of making comprehension a goal in fluency instruction programs for students with LD.

For severely disabled readers, repeated reading may be a very valuable step toward consolidation of reading skills. However, such training may not necessarily result in a shift from focus on word recognition skills to a focus on the meaning of the text. Roller (1994) reported a study of reading improvement during summer school for five 8- to 12-year old students who were severely reading disabled. The students worked with a tutor for 45 minutes a day; of this time 10 to 15 minutes were spent reading a new book and 10 to 15 minutes were spent rereading books they had already read. The instructional approach was meaning-based. An important question was the extent to which the student-teacher interactions would focus more on meaning than on accuracy of reading as the students progressed through their summer program. By the end of the program, the five students had read a total of 11 texts 38 times. The students' reading improved significantly in accuracy, and analysis of their interactions with their tutors indicated less emphasis on decoding. However, in only one of the five cases was a shift to primary concern for meaning evident. Roller suggested several reasons for this disappointing outcome. One is that, for some students, low accuracy continued to interfere with access to meaning. Another is that the students were reading relatively simple books. Although appropriate for their reading level (read at 90% accuracy), the stories lacked intrinsic interest and did not lend themselves to discussions of text interpretation. A third reason is that both the students and the teacher were aware that accuracy and fluency, not content, was an important goal of their reading sessions.

Using Repeated Readings in the Classroom

Kuhn and Stahl (2000) offered suggestions about how to use research-based principles to design programs of fluency instruction that can be used effectively in classrooms. They suggested using assisted reading as opposed to unassisted reading, as it takes advantage of the social interaction of classroom reading instruction. Although there are a number of different methods teachers can use, two that are thought to be particularly effective are echo reading and partner reading.

Echo reading involves having the teacher or a student read portions of the text; the class or reading partner echoes this reading word by word, phrase by phrase, or section by section. Partner reading can be carried out with readers of different ability (e.g., a good reader paired with a struggling reader), but this is not a requirement (Mathes, Simmons, and Davis 1992). (We discuss partner reading further in the chapter on elementary reading, Chapter 9). Peer-assisted reading strategies (PALS) can successfully include re-readings of passages. However, this method may be no more effective at improving reading fluency and comprehension than other methods. Vaughn and her colleagues (Vaughn et al. 2000) compared methods to improve fluency and comprehension used in third-grade classrooms: partner reading (designed to enhance fluency) and collaborative strategic reading (designed to enhance comprehension). They were interested in the effects of these two programs on students with identified reading disabilities and on students who were low-to-average readers. Over time, both average and low-achieving reading groups improved in fluency, and the results were similar for the two types of instructional programs. However, no significant gains in comprehension were found during the time period of the study.

For the benefit of both normally developing and struggling readers, repeated readings should be part of the routine reading activities, at least in second- and third-grade classrooms. One way to carry out repeated readings is to adjust the program of instruction in the basal reader to include re-readings. Hoffman (1987) designed such a program. The fluency component entailed several different activities and situations in which reading and re-readings occurred. First, the teacher read the passage from the basal to the students; he or she might then ask the students to echo-read the passage. Later, class time was allotted for practice reading, and the students also re-read the passage at home. The next day, the students read the same passage with a partner (both taking a turn reading it aloud). When Hoffman compared this fluency program with the instructional program suggested in the basal series, he found that the students who completed repeated readings made significant gains in fluency and comprehension. However, Hoffman raised the possibility that it was the increased amount of time these students' spent reading that contributed to their progress, not just the re-readings of the same passages. This suggestion serves as a reminder to us that repeated readings of passages may be one of a number of factors that contribute to improvements in students' fluency.

COMMONLY ASKED QUESTIONS

Should a student be an accurate reader before efforts are made to help him or her become a fluent reader?

Speed of passage reading should not be emphasized until some modicum of skill in basic word reading has been achieved. Pressing beginning readers to read more rapidly, for example, is likely to be counter-productive. Dowhower (1989) suggested that students should be able to read about 85% of the words in a passage accurately before repeated readings are initiated. However, repeated readings without an emphasis on speed can also contribute to students' sight word recognition. This may be because re-readings provide practice with words that appear over and over again in texts, such as prepositions, articles, and very common content words. The overlap of words in different passages may be one reason students make progress with repeated readings (Rashotte and Torgesen 1985).

Clearly, the nature of the texts we give to students will affect their progress toward becoming proficient readers. According to Hiebert and Martin (2001), "Particularly with children who are on the cusp of acquiring independent reading proficiency, characteristics of texts such as the presence of illustrations, the nature of the language, and the number of words can influence the kinds of experiences children and their teachers can have" (p. 361). These researchers have pointed out that both decodability and predictability of words in texts affect students' reading acquisition, but so also does the repetition of key words. All too often new "content" words appear only one or two times in a passage. As we noted earlier, it takes repeated exposures to a given word before students recognize it immediately.

In short, teachers who want their students to become fluent readers are well-advised to examine texts to determine whether content words appear in the passage more than once, whether most words are common and familiar, and whether a large percent of the words are decodable and/or predictable. If the texts used for repeated readings contain a high proportion of high frequency words, students should be able to receive the needed practice by repeated readings of different passages. Repeated exposures to high frequency words is beneficial even if the initial level of accuracy of the students' reading of the passage falls below 85% correct.

Do repeated readings lead to improvements in comprehension for students who struggle with reading?

Although repeated readings generally lead to improvements in fluency of reading, researchers have sometimes, but not always, found significant improvement in comprehension as well. Because improvement in comprehension is the ultimate purpose of such training, directions that focus students' attention on comprehension, as well as speed and accuracy, may be particularly important. Improved comprehension might be an explicit goal of rereading. When accuracy and speed are the only traits the students think the teacher cares about, they may "race the clock" and not worry about whether they have understood the passage at all. When students have a chance to solidify their understanding through rereading, performances on comprehension tasks may show improvement (Levy 2001; O'Shea, Sindelar, and O'Shea 1987).

Meyer and Felton (1999) found that fluency training helped students with various types of reading disability. In their experience, improvements in accuracy as well as fluency came with sufficient guided practice, and this practice included word lists or flash cards as well as passages. As for practice on isolated words, as we mentioned earlier, Tan and Nicholson (1997) found that when poor readers had lots of practice reading words presented in isolation, their comprehension improved.

Are repeated readings important at some grade levels but not others?

Most researchers have concerned themselves with fluency programs for students who have learned basic aspects of the code but for whom automaticity of word recognition and fluency of reading are still issues affecting their reading achievement. For normally developing readers, fluency of reading is a primary concern in the second and third grades. For struggling readers, issues of fluency are present for many years and may last into adulthood. Because fluency is so important for comprehension, problems with fluency need to be addressed throughout the years of formal schooling. For example, adolescents with reading disabilities who are reading content-area texts at a snail's pace need help with fluency. Dowhower (1989) has indicated that repeated readings can bring about improved fluency for mature students as well as for beginning readers.

For students with reading or learning disabilities, programs have been developed that have multiple components designed to improve automaticity of word reading and fluency of passage reading. Mercer and his colleagues (2000) studied one such program designed for middle-school students. This program was described as having various "fluency" components, although some are focused on automaticity, as we have defined this term. The "fluency-building" activities included work on rapid recognition of sound-symbol correspondences and word parts, recognition of high frequency words, and repeated readings of stories. The program used both a word list approach (i.e., speed drills that accompany the lessons on phonics programs and speed drills on common words) and a repeated passage reading approach. Mercer et al.'s study of this program showed that students with LD made significant gains over time, although it is not possible to tell whether all or just some of the fluency activities contributed to the students' progress.

Programs focused on automaticity of word recognition might be a particularly important component of a program designed to improve the reading achievement of older struggling readers (Mercer et al. 2000). Students may need to become not only accurate but also fast at reading words with specific orthographic patterns in order to make progress reading passages. Needless to say, opportunities to carry out repeated readings with natural texts are also crucial (Roller 1994). Even when students need to improve their word-reading skills, it is important for them to strive toward more fluent reading of texts.

What are the most important guidelines for teachers who would like to institute a program of repeated readings in their classrooms?

While many researchers have found benefits of training in fluency by using some form of repeated readings, some training programs appear to be more effective than others. One issue teachers need to consider is the difficulty of passages. Rashotte and Torgesen (1985) found that students made progress with repeated readings only when the passages were relatively "easy" for the students. Subsequent study of passage difficulty has supported these initial findings (Torgesen, Rashotte, and Alexander 2001). Reading passages are considered "easy" when students can read them with greater than 90% accuracy. This is roughly what is called the student's independent reading level. On the other hand, as noted earlier, Dowhower (1989) has suggested that 85% accuracy on a first reading would indicate that a passage is appropriate for repeated readings. Once a level of difficulty has been identified as appropriate for a given student, the teacher should make sure all passages are at that same level until the student shows significant improvement on subsequent readings. At this point, somewhat more challenging passages can be selected.

Teachers often wonder how many re-readings are needed for students to gain optimal benefits from re-exposure to a specific passage. This question comes with the recognition that too many re-readings may either turn off the students or lead to only trivial additional gains. In general, programs have been using three or four readings of a given passage as sufficient for the purpose of developing fluency over time (Meyer and Felton 1999). The hope is that with a long-term program of repeated readings, students will gradually need fewer re-readings to reach the point where they read at a normal rate for their age, with expression and with comprehension (O'Shea, Sindelar, and O'Shea 1987).

In some programs, students reread the same passage until they can read it accurately at a developmentally appropriate speed (e.g., 100 words per minute). It is not always easy to know how fast a given student ought to be reading (i.e., what speed to set as the "standard"). Obviously, both the difficulty of the passages and the students' word-reading skill affect expectations for improvement in reading speed. As a result, it seems more sensible to accept current evidence that the greatest improvements tend to come with the first few readings. Teachers have an easier time making sure that students have completed three rereadings than monitoring the speed with which students are actually reading particular passages.

Dowhower (1989) recommended that passages or stories used for practice be kept short, but Levy (2001) mentioned using longer passages than are typically used in studies in order to give students an opportunity to develop better understanding of the passage. Regardless of the length of passages, it is best if passages have some overlap of vocabulary (Rashotte and Torgesen 1985). Repeated exposures of words in different contexts may help strengthen students' memory for the words.

It is a good idea to have students keep track of their performance on first and final readings of a passage. Charts for both speed and accuracy can be kept. This method is not dissimilar from the oral reading measures (curriculum-based measures) for which the measurement of interest is the number of words read correctly in a minute (Shinn et al. 1992). Evaluation of a student's response to re-readings need not be done with every passage the student works on; instead, a record might be kept at regular intervals (e.g., once a month). Ideally, some measure of comprehension will be included in the evaluation process so that students are reminded that the goal of reading is not just speed but also understanding.

If a student is an extremely slow word reader, one recommendation is to use the read-along approach. However, when students are able to read the passage the first time at a rate of 60 words per minute or better, the teacher might want to shift to the independent repeated reading methods (unassisted methods) or to read-aloud methods.

In classroom settings, it may not be possible to maintain assisted readings, such as the read-along approach, on a daily basis. If this is the case, teachers might set up a "center" that provides equipment and procedures for students to work on their reading fluency. Equipment might include an array of books at appropriate levels, tapes and tape recorders, charts for students to keep a record of their performance, and so on. As noted earlier, it is important to help students attend to comprehension as well as accuracy and speed. For this reason, comprehension checks, which can come in the form of post-reading questions or a written recall, are an important aspect of effective programs in repeated readings.

REFERENCES

Badian, N. A. 1997. Dyslexia and the double deficit hypothesis. *Annals of Dyslexia*, 47:69–87.

Berninger, V. W., Abbott, R. D., Billingsley, F., and Nagy, W. 2001. Processes underlying timing and fluency of reading: Efficiency, automaticity, coordination, and morphological awareness. In *Dyslexia, Fluency, and the Brain*, M. Wolf (Ed.), (pp. 383–413). Baltimore, MD: York Press.

Bowers, P. G. 1993. Text reading and rereading: Determinants of fluency beyond word recognition. *Journal of Reading Behavior*, 25:133–53.

Bowers, P. G. 2001. Exploration of the basis for rapid naming's relationship to reading. In *Dyslexia, Fluency, and the Brain*, M. Wolf (Ed.), (pp. 41–63). Baltimore, MD: York Press.

Bowers, P. G., and Wolf, M. 1993. Theoretical links between naming speed, precise timing mechanisms, and orthographic skill in dyslexia. *Reading and Writing: An Interdisciplinary Journal*, 5:69–85.

Bruck, M. 1990. Word recognition skills of adults with childhood diagnoses of dyslexia. *Developmental Psychology*, 26:439–53.

Camp, L. W., Winbury, N. E., and Zinna, D. R. 1981. Strategies for initial reading instruction. *Bulletin of the Orton Society*, 31:175–88.

Compton, D. L., and Carlisle, J. F. 1994. Speed of word recognition as a distinguishing characteristic of reading disabilities. *Educational Psychological Review*, 6:115–40.

Denckla, M. B., and Cutting, L. E. 1999. History and significance of Rapid Automatized Naming. *Annals of Dyslexia*, 49:29–42.

Denckla, M. B., and Rudel, R. G. 1976. Rapid automatized naming: Dyslexia differentiated from other learning disabilities. *Neuropsychologia*, 14:471–79.

Dowhower, S. L. 1987. Effects of repeated reading on second-grade transitional readers' fluency and comprehension. *Reading Research Quarterly*, 22:389–406.

Dowhower, S. L. March 1989. Repeated reading: Research into practice. *The Reading Teacher*, 42:502–07.

Ehri, L. C., and Wilce, L. S. 1983. Development of word identification speed in skilled and less skilled beginning readers. *Journal of Educational Psychology*, 75:3–18.

Fielding, L. G., Wilson, P. T., and Anderson, R. C. 1984. A new focus on free reading: The role of trade books in reading instruction. In *The Contexts of School-Based Literacy*, T. E. Raphael and R. E. Reynolds (Eds.), (pp. 149–62). New York: Random House.

Gersten, R., Fuchs, L. S., Williams, J. P., and Baker, S. 2001. Teaching reading comprehension strategies to students with learning disabilities: A review of research. *Review of Educational Research*, 71:279–320.

Herman, P. A. 1985. The effect of repeated readings on reading rate, speech pauses, and word recognition accuracy. *Reading Research Quarterly*, 20:553–65.

Hiebert, E. H., and Martin, L. A. 2001. The texts of beginning reading instruction. In *Handbook of Early Literacy Research*, S. B. Neuman and D. K. Dickinson (Eds.), (pp. 361–76). New York: Guilford Press.

Hoffman, J. V. 1987. Rethinking the role of oral reading. *Elementary School Journal*, 87:367–73.

Juel, C. 1988. Learning to read and write: A longitudinal study of 54 children from first through fourth grades. *Journal of Educational Psychology*, 80:437–47.

Kuhn, M. R., and Stahl, S. A. 2000. *Fluency: A Review of Developmental and Remedial Practices*. University of Michigan, Center for the Improvement of Early Reading Achievement, Report #2-008.

LaBerge, D., and Samuels, J. 1974. Toward a theory of automatic information processing in reading. *Cognitive Psychology*, 6:293–323.

Levy, B. A. 2001. Moving the bottom: Improving reading fluency. In *Dyslexia, Fluency, and the Brain*, M. Wolf (Ed.), (pp. 357–79). Baltimore, MD: York Press.

Lovett, M. W., Ransby, M. J., and Barron, R. W. 1988. Treatment, subtype, and word type effects in dyslexic children's response to remediation. *Brain and Language*, 34:328–49.

Manis, F. R. 1985. Acquisition of word identification skills in normal and disabled readers. *Journal of Educational Psychology*, 77:78–90.

Mathes, P. G., Simmons, D. C., and Davis, B. I. 1992. Assisted reading techniques for developing reading fluency. *Reading Research and Intervention*, 31:70–7.

Mercer, C. D., Campbell, K. U., Miller, M. D., Mercer, K. D., and Lane, H. B. 2000. Effects of a reading fluency intervention on middle schoolers with specific learning disabilities. *Learning Disabilities Research and Practice*, 15:179–89.

Meyer, M. S., and Felton, R. H. 1999. Repeated reading to enhance fluency: Old approaches and new directions. *Annals of Dyslexia*, 49:283–306

O'Shea, L. J., Sindelar, P. T., and O'Shea, D. J. 1987. The effects of repeated readings and attentional cues on the reading fluency and comprehension of learning disabled readers. *Learning Disabilities Research*, 2:103–09.

Perfetti, C. A., and Hogaboam, T. W. 1975. The relationship between single word decoding and reading comprehension skill. *Journal of Educational Psychology*, 67:461–69.

Perfetti, C. A., and Roth, S. 1981. Some of the interactive processes in reading and their role in reading skill. In *Interactive Processes in Reading*, A. M. Lesgold and C. A. Perfetti (Eds.), (pp. 269–97). Hillsdale, NJ: Lawrence Erlbaum.

Rashotte, C. A., and Torgesen, J. K. 1985. Repeated reading and reading fluency in learning disabled children. *Reading Research Quarterly*, 20:180–88.

Rasinski, T. V. 1990. Effects of repeated reading and listening-while-reading on reading fluency. *Journal of Educational Research*, 83:147–50.

Reitsma, P. 1983. Printed word learning in beginning readers. *Journal of Experimental Child Psychology*, 36:321–39.

Reitsma, P. 1988. Reading practice for beginners: Effects of guided reading, reading-while-listening, and independent reading with computer-based speech feedback. *Reading Research Quarterly*, 23:219–35.

Roberts, R., and Mather, N. 1997. Orthographic dyslexia: The neglected subtype. *Learning Disabilities Research and Practice*, 12:236–50.

Roller, C. M. 1994. Teacher-student interaction during oral reading and rereading. *Journal of Reading Behavior*, 26:191–209.

Samuels, S. J. 1979. The method of repeated readings. *The Reading Teacher*, 32:403–08.

Schreiber, P. A. 1987. Prosody and structure in children's syntactic processing. In *Comprehending Oral and Written Language*, R. Horowitz and S. J. Samuels (Eds.), (pp. 243–70). New York: Academic Press.

Shany, M. T., and Biemiller, A. 1995. Assisted reading practice: Effects on performance for poor readers in grades 3 and 4. *Reading Research Quarterly*, 30:382–95.

Shinn, M. R., Good, R. H., Knutson, N., Tilly, W. D., and Collins, V. L. 1992. Curriculum-based measurement of oral reading fluency: A confirmatory analysis of its relation to reading. *School Psychology Review*, 21:459–79.

Tan, A., and Nicholson, T. 1997. Flashcards revisited: Training poor readers to read words faster improves their comprehension of text. *Journal of Educational Psychology*, 89:276–88.

Taylor, B. M., Frye, B. J., Maruyama, G. M. 1990. Time spent reading and reading growth. *American Educational Research Journal*, 27:351–62.

Torgesen, J. K., Rashotte, C. A., and Alexander, A. W. 2001. Principles of fluency instruction in reading: Relationships with established empirical outcomes. In *Dyslexia, Fluency, and the Brain*, M. Wolf (Ed.), (pp. 333–55). Baltimore, MD: York Press.

Vaughn, S., Chard, D. J., Pedrotty Bryant, D., Coleman, M., Tyler, B. J., Linan-Thompson, S., and Kouzekanani, K. 2000. Fluency and comprehension interventions for third-grade students. *Learning Disabilities Research and Practice*, 21:325–35.

Weinstein, G., and Cooke, N. L. 1992. The effects of two repeated readings interventions on generalization of fluency. *Learning Disability Quarterly*, 15:21–8.

Wolf, M. 1991. Naming speed and reading: The contribution of the cognitive neurosciences. *Reading Research Quarterly*, 26:123–41.

Young, A., Bowers, P., and MacKinnon, G. 1996. Effects of prosodic modeling and repeated reading on poor readers' fluency and comprehension. *Applied Psycholinguistics*, 17:59–84.

4

Comprehension Strategy Instruction

GETTING STARTED

✓ Why do poor readers often fail to use effective comprehension strategies?
✓ How can teachers address deficits in knowledge and use of strategies?
✓ What types of strategies should students learn?
✓ What are some factors to consider in designing a strategy instruction program?

THE ROLE OF STRATEGIES IN READING

Reading is a complex activity that requires the simultaneous application of a variety of cognitive processes. A skilled reader rapidly and accurately decodes the words, attaches meaning to words and sentences, connects text information to relevant background knowledge, maintains a mental representation of what he or she has already read, forms hypotheses about upcoming information, and makes decisions based on his or her purpose for reading—*all at the same time*. In this description, the reader is applying a number of strategies that facilitate the process of constructing meaning from text.

A strategy is often defined as an action, or a series of actions, undertaken to accomplish a particular goal (Dickson et al. 1998). More broadly conceptualized, strategy use includes one's *thoughts*, as well as actions, during the process of planning and carrying out a task and evaluating one's own performance. Although strategies can be consciously analyzed, we typically apply them so habitually and automatically that we may not be fully aware of our own strategy use unless we deliberately stop to think about our cognitive processes (Pressley, Goodchild et al. 1989). A person engaged in a complex activity may use many distinct, but related, strategies to accomplish his or her purposes. For example, a reader attempting to comprehend a text might begin by previewing the passage and activating prior knowledge about the topic. While reading, the person might make predictions, ask questions, construct representational images, and use the context to determine the meaning of an unfamiliar word. In response to difficulties, the reader might review, reread, or slow down.

Many poor readers have difficulty with strategy use. Children with learning disabilities (LD) have long been described as deficient in their spontaneous use of strategies (e.g., Torgesen 1977). Because of their failure to use strategies effectively and flexibly, children with LD and other low-achievers are often characterized as "inattentive," "passive," "maladaptive," and "disorganized" (Dickson et al. 1998). A number of explanations have been proposed for the limited strategy use often observed in these students. These include (a) deficiencies in metacognition, (b) a lack of proficiency in basic processes, and (c) an attitude of "learned helplessness."

Usually defined as "thinking about one's own thinking," metacognition has two primary components: knowledge and self-regulation. In order to use strategies effectively to aid reading comprehension, one must have knowledge of potentially useful strategies and understand when and why to apply them. One must be able to recognize the similarities between the current task and instances in which use of a given strategy was helpful in the past. Equally important are awareness of one's own capabilities and limitations, an appreciation of the demands of the task, and an understanding of the relationship between strategy use and comprehension. Self-regulation, the second component of metacognition involves monitoring and controlling one's actions *during* the reading process (Brown, Armbruster, and Baker 1986). Successful readers are aware of the state of their understanding as they read and take appropriate steps to correct comprehension failures. In response to such factors as changes in the difficulty of the text, limitations in prior knowledge about a given topic, and lapses in concentration or memory, good readers alter their strategies. They may reread portions of the text, slow down, pay closer attention to text structure, try to use context to determine the meaning of an unknown word, or stop and take a coffee break. Both aspects of metacognition—knowledge and self-regulation—are important predictors of good reading comprehension. Relative to skilled readers, poor readers tend to be less knowledgeable about strategies and their functions, less able to make judgments about the difficulty of a text, less aware of the requirements of different reading tasks, less sensitive to their own strengths and weaknesses, and less proficient at monitoring their comprehension and regulating strategy use accordingly (Brown, Armbruster, and Baker 1986; Dickson et al. 1998; Paris, Wasik, and Turner 1991).

Limited strategy use in children with LD has also been attributed to a lack of automaticity in basic processes, which creates a "bottleneck" (e.g., Perfetti and Hogaboam 1975) that prevents them from devoting attention to higher-level processes. For example, when decoding is a difficult and inefficient process, a child is forced to devote an enormous amount of attention and working memory capacity to word reading, and may not have sufficient cognitive resources to apply comprehension strategies. This difficulty is exacerbated by the fact that learning a strategy requires an initial investment of time and effort. At first, the conscious, deliberate application and monitoring of a strategy may consume most of a child's working memory capacity (Pressley, Symons et al. 1989). It is only through experience and practice that application of a strategy becomes efficient and automatic. Unless a child is able to apply a strategy quickly and easily, the time and effort involved may outweigh the benefits of using the strategy, at least from the child's point of view.

Finally, children who experience chronic academic difficulty may have acquired an attitude of "learned helplessness." Many students with LD and other low-achievers have a tendency to attribute academic outcomes to factors outside of their control. For instance, they may ascribe failure to a lack of ability and success to good luck. As a result, they may feel that nothing they do will make a difference, because they believe themselves to be at the mercy of external forces. Conversely, students who attribute academic outcomes to factors over which they have control, such as effort or strategy use, show greater persistence and are more likely to take an active role in the learning process (Licht 1993; Licht et al. 1985).

Years of school failure may put a child at risk for developing a passive, helpless attitude toward learning. Parents and teachers may also unintentionally foster the development of this attitude through their interactions with these children. There is evidence that adults tend to provide too much direct assistance to children with LD, give too much praise that is not related to performance, and offer too little encouragement to take strategic approaches to tasks (reviewed in Stone and Conca, 1993). There is also evidence of differences in the instruction provided for good versus poor readers. (See Palincsar et al. 1993, for a review.) For instance, Allington and McGill-Franzen (1989) found that teachers tended to ask different questions of good and poor readers. Good readers were more likely to be asked questions that stimulated inferential reasoning, whereas poor readers tended to be asked questions about factual information. Similarly, Collins (1982) found that good readers were more likely than poor readers to be encouraged to see reading as a problem-solving activity and to use strategies to work through difficulties. Poor readers, even in resource room settings, spend more time engaged in independent seatwork and less time interacting with the teacher or other students (e.g., Ysseldyke et al. 1989). Often little attention is given to comprehension instruction (e.g., Pressley et al. 1997; Moody et al. 2000; Vaughn, Moody, and Schumm 1998). In short, according to Palincsar et al. (1993), instruction for poor readers is often marked by "a general lack of attention to the knowledge, beliefs, and learning activities" (p. 250) that lead to the development of metacognitive abilities and effective strategy use.

From the abundance of research attention that has been devoted to strategy instruction during the past 20 years, there is mounting evidence that efforts to teach strategic reading do pay off. In fact, recent large-scale analyses of the learning disabilities research literature indicate that reading comprehension strategy training is one of the most effective instructional techniques for these students (e.g., Forness et al. 1997). Hence, there are very good reasons for teachers to evaluate critically and alter their instructional practices. However, given the complex set of intertwining factors that contribute to effective strategy use, it is essential that strategy instruction involve more than a brief presentation of the technique followed by a few practice exercises. There is evidence that instruction in reading comprehension strategies is most effective when it includes efforts to increase metacognition (Chan and Cole 1986; Graves 1986; Malone and Mastropieri 1992), ample opportunities for practice and generalization (Pressley, Goodchild et al. 1989), and attributional retraining (Borkowski, Weyhing, and Carr 1988; Schunk and Rice 1992).

Students are more likely to apply a strategy independently if they understand in what situations it is helpful and why. This involves learning to analyze the requirements of a task in order to make decisions about the strategies that will be most helpful in a given instance. If the task involves remembering and using information from the text for a specific purpose, the strategies one chooses to use would be different than those used in a reading situation in which there is no particular obligation to remember the details of what one has read. For example, tasks that require one to do something with information gained from reading—such as learn vocabulary terms related to the life cycle of the butterfly, write a report on butterflies, or identify a particular butterfly specimen—involve different sets of strategies from enjoying a fictional story about a butterfly. As was noted earlier, in order for a strategy to be truly useful, students must be able to apply it without undue effort. Initial attempts to use a strategy will likely involve time and effort, and students may well not see immediate benefits. Thus, it is important to provide them with sufficient practice to gain fluency and automaticity. If students are to learn to attribute improvement in reading comprehension to their own efforts to use strategies, they need to see tangible results. This can increase the likelihood that strategies will be maintained over time and generalized to other situations.

The remainder of this chapter includes (a) a discussion of four general types of strategies that have been shown to enhance reading comprehension, (b) a description of two recommended approaches to strategy instruction, and (c) some general guidelines for teachers.

TYPES OF READING STRATEGIES

Reading comprehension strategies may be grouped according to their function into four general categories: Preparatory, Organizational, Elaborative, and Executive. Preparatory or pre-reading strategies include such activities as accessing prior knowledge, determining one's purpose for reading, previewing text, and making predictions. Organizational strategies include identifying main ideas, summarizing, and mapping the text structure. Elaborative strategies involve integrating prior knowledge with textual information to form images, make inferences, and generate explanations that extend text information. Finally, executive strategies are those that involve recognizing and correcting comprehension "breakdowns" and making decisions about how to approach a task. This section includes a rationale for teaching each of these strategy types, a summary of supporting research, and several illustrative examples of each type.

Preparatory Strategies

A reader's knowledge base has a major influence on comprehension (e.g., Langer 1984). Readers who possess extensive networks of general knowledge and expertise in particular areas comprehend better and retain more information than those who are less knowledgeable. Moreover, as Pressley, Goodchild et al. (1989) observed, relevant prior knowledge may facilitate strategy use or even make the use of some strategies unnecessary. For example, a reader who already knows the meaning of a word does not need to use the context to determine its definition. However, many struggling readers have more limited vocabularies and less extensive funds of background knowledge than normal achievers. Another common problem is that students possess relevant knowledge but do not draw on it while reading (Brown, Armbruster, and Baker 1986; Cain and Oakhill 1999) Results from numerous studies indicate that poor readers are particularly likely to benefit from pre-reading strategies that involve activating prior knowledge, making predictions, previewing the text, and learning new vocabulary (e.g., Billingsley and Wildman 1988; Carr and Thompson 1996; Idol-Maestas 1985; Sachs 1983). Preparatory strategies are especially valuable when reading a text on an unfamiliar topic and may aid both poor readers and their normally achieving peers (Carr and Thompson 1996).

Two pre-reading strategies that have proven effective in both research studies and classroom practice are K-W-L (Ogle 1986) and TELLS Fact or Fiction (Idol-Maestas 1985). The K-W-L strategy consists of three basic steps:

K: Thinking about what I <u>K</u>now
W: Deciding what I <u>W</u>ant to find out
L: Remembering what I <u>L</u>earned

Before reading, children are taught to list and categorize what they already know about a topic and formulate questions about what they would like to learn from reading a passage on the topic. After reading, they summarize what they learned, check to see if their questions were answered, and decide what they still want to learn. A graphic organizer can be used for listing this information (See figure 4.1). TELLS Fact or Fiction is a multi-step procedure that includes studying the story title, examining the text for important words and difficult vocabulary, and deciding whether the passage is fact or fiction.

Another group of pre-reading strategies involves teaching students to make use of advance organizers or semantic maps constructed by the teacher (e.g., Sinatra, Stahl-Gemake, and Berg 1984). For more information on these techniques, see Chapter 7 on text structure and Chapter 9 on reading in the content areas.

Organizational Strategies

Identifying main ideas and summarizing text passages are skills that are particularly difficult for struggling readers. Often, main ideas are not directly stated and

K-W-L strategy sheet		
1. K—What we know	W—What we want to find out	L—What we learned and still need to learn

2. Categories of information we expect to use

A.   E.
B.   F.
C.   G.
D.

Figure 4.1   K-W-L: A teaching model that develops active reading of expository text. Figure from Ogle, Donna M. 1986, February. K-W-L: A teaching model that develops active reading of expository text. The Reading Teacher 39:564–70. Reprinted with the permission of Donna Ogle and the International Reading Association. All rights reserved.

must be inferred. Summarizing is a complex activity that involves paraphrasing and reorganizing information as well as distinguishing main ideas from supporting details. In a study of the summarizing abilities of good versus poor eighth grade readers, Winograd (1984) found that when asked to identify the most important information in a passage, poor readers often selected details that either were personally meaningful or could be easily visualized. In contrast, good readers were more likely to use text structure in identifying main ideas. Further, poor readers seemed unaware that a summary is a restatement of key ideas; in written summaries, they often failed to include the information they had previously identified as the most important.

The ability to identify key concepts is undoubtedly an essential component of good comprehension. In addition to enabling readers to "get the point," identifying and restating main ideas during reading is an effective means of checking comprehension. Training poor readers to reconstruct the gist after reading small segments of text may, in fact, "mimic certain monitoring strategies normally involved in reading" (Jenkins et al. 1987, p. 55).

In numerous studies, it has been shown that poor readers benefit greatly from learning strategies for identifying main ideas and summarizing text (e.g., Borkowski, Weyhing, and Carr 1988; Graves 1986; Jenkins et al. 1987; Malone and Mastropieri 1992; Weisberg and Balajthy 1990). In each of these studies, researchers trained children in upper elementary and middle school to use specific strategic procedures to identify important information. In most cases, the students were taught to use self-questioning techniques, asking themselves such questions as *Who or what is the passage about?* and *What is happening?* (e.g., Jenkins et al. 1987; Malone and Mastropieri 1992). Others included instruction in the function of details and how they differ from main ideas (e.g., Weisberg and Balajthy 1990). In some instances, the students were also asked to produce written restatements of important ideas (e.g., Jenkins et al. 1987; Weisberg and Balajthy 1990) or construct graphic organizers that represented the ideas in the passage (e.g., Weisberg and Balajthy 1990). Other researchers included instruction in identifying various kinds of text structures (i.e., compare-contrast, cause-effect.) as part of a strategy for identifying main ideas (e.g., Bakken 1995, cited in Mastropieri and Scruggs 1997; Smith and Friend 1986). (See Chapter 7 for a more detailed discussion of text structure).

Other researchers have developed and tested strategies for helping younger children identify key information in narrative text (e.g., Carnine and Kinder 1985; Idol 1987; Idol and Croll 1987; Nolte and Singer 1985). These strategies have typically involved training children to ask themselves questions about "story grammar" elements as they read: characters, setting, goals of the characters, actions taken, and outcome. Idol (1987) taught children to list this information on a "story map" (see figure 4.2) while reading. These techniques were shown to improve children's ability to answer comprehension questions and recall important story information.

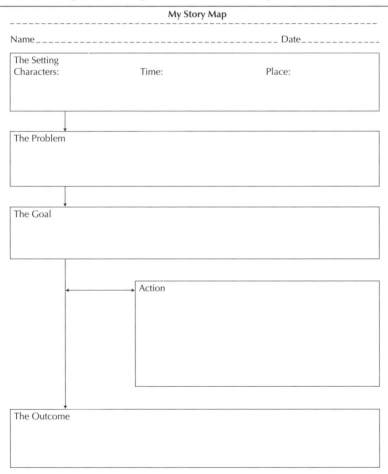

Figure 4.2   Components of the story map. From "Group story mapping: A comprehension strategy for both skilled and unskilled readers" by L. Idol, 1987, Journal of Learning Disabilities 20:196–205. Copyright (1987) by PRO-ED. Reprinted with permission

To summarize, identifying key ideas and reconstructing the gist of a passage while reading are important strategies that can improve significantly the comprehension of struggling readers, who tend to have difficulty distinguishing information that is central in the author's idea structure from colorful or personally relevant details. Strategic procedures for identifying main ideas and restating the gist are quite beneficial, particularly for upper elementary, middle school, and high school students who are confronting the challenges of reading expository text. Younger children may benefit from similar techniques that emphasize key elements of narrative text.

Elaborative Strategies

Like many of the pre-reading strategies, elaborative strategies involve the activation and use of background information. Elaborative strategies, which encourage children to integrate information in the text with their knowledge of the world, include various kinds of self-questioning procedures and the use of visual imagery. In contrast to organizational strategies, in which the emphasis is on identifying the author's main ideas, strategies in this category involve "reading between the lines" to elaborate upon and extend the author's ideas. The processes of asking and answering inference questions and representing information visually may leave students with deeper understanding and better memory for text content.

Self-questioning.   Traditional classroom dialogue typically involves three components: a question from the teacher, a student's response, and the teacher's evaluation of the student's answer (Gallego 1992). Teachers ask questions for a variety of reasons. Some of the most common are to assess comprehension, to highlight important information, and to stimulate higher-level thinking. Nolte and Singer (1985) pointed out that some teachers might also regard their questions as models for students to imitate. However, many students, including struggling readers, are unlikely to learn to ask themselves "teacher-like" questions from implicit modeling alone. Rather, they need explicit instruction and practice in the use of self-questioning. For this reason, many (if not most) comprehension strategies feature self-questioning techniques. As in the case of teacher questions, self-generated questions can serve many purposes. In addition to encouraging the activation of prior knowledge, aiding in the identification of main ideas, and serving as a tool for self-monitoring, self-questioning can prompt students to make inferences and generate explanations.

An example of a strategy that encourages inferential reasoning is "elaborative interrogation." Originally designed by Pressley and his colleagues (e.g., Pressley, El-Dinary, and Brown 1992), elaborative interrogation encourages students to attempt to infer unstated causal relationships by generating explanations for text information by asking "why" questions (e.g., *Why does it make sense that anteaters have long sharp claws? Why did Scrooge love money? Why was Tiny Tim happy even though he was crippled?*). Studies by Pressley and his colleagues, as well as by other researchers who trained students to use similar strategies (e.g., Chi et al. 1994; Trabasso and Magliano 1996), have demonstrated the effectiveness of this technique. In fact, students who reason through such logical explanations on their own typically learn and remember more than if the explanations are provided to them (e.g., Scruggs et al. 1993).

Research clearly suggests that elaborative interrogation is a powerful strategy for normally achieving and gifted children (e.g., Wood and Hewitt 1993; Wood et al. 1993) as well as adult readers (e.g., Woloshyn et al. 1990). However, the results of several studies indicate that it may be less beneficial for some struggling readers, especially those with low mental ability (e.g., Mastropieri and Scruggs 1997; Scruggs et al. 1993). These researchers concluded that an elaborative interrogation strategy might be very difficult for many poor readers to use independently because of the active reasoning, insight, and background knowledge required. However, with additional prompts (e.g., *What do anteaters eat? Where do ants live?*), the poor readers in these studies succeeded in generating explanations for such phenomena as an anteater's long, sharp claws. Other studies have yielded more encouraging results. For instance, Chi et al. (1994) found that both "skilled" and "less skilled" readers in the eighth and tenth grades benefited from a strategy that involved asking "why" questions.

To summarize, elaborative interrogation and similar self-questioning techniques have the potential to foster sophisticated inferential reasoning, enhance learning from text, and encourage students to view reading as a problem-solving activity. However, though these techniques are likely to benefit average and good readers, it may be unreasonable to expect poor readers, especially those with low cognitive ability, to apply them independently. Nonetheless, if additional support is provided to such students, in the form of guiding questions or other prompts, the process of reasoning their way to a solution may lead to deeper understanding and more lasting memory for text content.

Visual Imagery.   The use of visual imagery is one of the most celebrated reading comprehension strategies. It has a great deal of intuitive appeal, for many people claim to "see pictures" in their minds as they read. There is some evidence that the use of imagery increases engagement with a text and enriches the reading experience aesthetically (e.g., Cramer 1980; Irwin 1979; Long, Winograd, and Bridge 1989). The use of imagery also seems to enhance the memorability of information. Over the years, many studies have shown that memory for concrete, "imageable" material tends to be better than for more abstract material (e.g., Baddeley et al. 1975; Begg and Paivio 1969; Paivio 1986; Sadoski, Goetz, and Fritz 1993). Some researchers have further speculated that imagery is especially helpful for poor comprehenders with limited working memory. Imagery may allow such readers to retain some information in pictorial form, thereby reducing the demands on the verbal working memory system (e.g., Long, Winograd, and Bridge 1989; Oakhill and Patel 1991).

Studies in which children are taught to pause during reading and form pictures in their minds have generally yielded positive results (e.g., Clark et al. 1984; Gambrell and Bales 1986; Gambrell and Jawitz 1993; Oakhill and Patel 1991; Rose, Cundick, and Higbee 1983). However, in a large-scale analysis of the research literature, Mastropieri and Scruggs (1997) noted that although the outcomes of imagery training studies are positive overall, the effects are not as great as for a number of other comprehension interventions. There are a number of reasons this might be so.

Weisberg (1988) agreed that imagery might increase children's awareness of the content of passages and improve comprehension of literal, concrete material, such as descriptions of characters and settings in stories. However, she argued, imagery may not be particularly useful for representing logical relationships among events and ideas. Although concrete information that can easily be visualized does tend to be memorable (e.g., Sadoski, Goetz, and Fritz 1993), this phenomenon may actually cause problems for poor comprehenders. As Winograd's (1984) study illustrated, poor readers tend to view imageable or interesting details as the most important information in a passage. They may not understand the relationship between this supporting material and the broader concepts it illustrates. There is also evidence that only certain kinds of images are associated with good comprehension. In a recent study, McCallum and Moore (1999) found that children whose images accurately reflected text content had better comprehension of important concepts than those whose images were tangentially related to the text or were inaccurate representations of the information. In other words, children who did not understand what they read in the first place were unable to form the kinds of images that support comprehension and memory of text content. These results raise questions about whether "quality" imagery is a cause or an effect of good comprehension.

In conclusion, teaching children to form images as they read may be beneficial. Imagery strategies can usually be taught relatively quickly and easily (Billingsley and Ferro-Almeida 1993), and imagery may encourage active engagement with the text and improve memory, especially for concrete material. However, we recommend that teachers not limit instruction in reading comprehension to imagery training. Effective use of imagery requires sufficient proficiency in basic language processing. In fact, Clark et al. (1984) suggested that a prerequisite for imagery instruction might be at least a fourth-grade reading level. After all, it is impossible for a child to form accurate representational images if a text contains an excessive number of words the child does not understand or cannot decode. Thus, imagery training is no substitute for vocabulary or language instruction. We also recommend that imagery instruction be combined with strategies for identifying main ideas or representing the relationships among ideas, perhaps through graphic organizers.

Executive Strategies

As noted earlier, students with LD and other poor readers may lack metacognitive knowledge about strategy use and skill in monitoring their understanding as they read. Recall that metacognition has both knowledge and self-regulatory components. In order to apply strategies effectively, students not only need knowledge of strategic procedures, but must also understand how features of the text, requirements of the task, and characteristics of the reader affect the kinds of strategic activities that are required. Students also need to learn to regulate strategic processes as they read. We are classifying as executive strategies (a) techniques for evaluating the text, the task, and reader characteristics to plan strategic activities and (b) techniques for monitoring and regulating strategy use.

It is not sufficient to teach students to apply strategic procedures blindly (Brown, Armbruster, and Baker 1986); rather they need to understand when the strategy is likely to be useful and why. Once they have been exposed to a variety of strategies, students can be taught to ask themselves a series of questions before reading about the text (e.g., *Is it fact or fiction? Is it easy or difficult?*), the task (e.g., *What is my purpose for reading? Do I need to remember what I read? Do I need to focus on the main points or the details?*), and their own characteristics (e.g., *Will I be able to remember what I read? Do I know much about this topic? How interested am I in this topic?*). Answers to these questions can be used to decide which strategies would be most useful in a given situation.

Several researchers have designed and tested strategies for accomplishing specific reading-related tasks. An example is the Question-Answer Relationships (QARs) technique (Raphael 1986). Children are taught to categorize questions in terms of whether the answer can be found in the text ("In the Book" questions) or whether the reader must rely on his or her own knowledge ("In My Head" questions). (See figure 4.3).

In the Book QARs	In My Head QARs
Right There The answer is in the text, usually easy to find. The words used to make up the questions and words used to answer the question are **Right There** in the same sentence.	**Author and You** The answer is *not* in the story. You need to think about what you already know, what the author tells you in the text, and how it fits together.

Think and Search (Putting It Together)
The answer is in the story, but you need to put together different story parts to find it. Words for the question and words for the answer are not found in the same sentence. They come from different parts of the text.

On My Own
The answer is not in the story. You can even answer the question without reading the story. You need to use your own experience.

Figure 4.3   Illustrations to explan QARs to students. Figure from Raphael, T. E. 1986, February. Teaching question answer relationships, revisited. The Reading Teacher 39 (6):516–22. Reprinted with permission of Taffy Raphael and the International Reading Association. All rights reserved.

This technique may make children more aware of the relationship between textual information and prior knowledge and enable them to make appropriate decisions about which strategies to use as they seek answers to questions (e.g., skimming through the text to find an answer versus drawing on background information). This technique has proven to be especially beneficial for low-achieving students and those with LD in the elementary grades (Raphael 1984; Simmonds 1992).

An important finding in many strategy training studies has been that students are both more successful at using strategies and more likely to transfer strategy use to new situations when the strategic procedure includes self-monitoring steps (e.g., Graves 1986; Jenkins et al. 1987; Malone and Mastropieri 1992; Wong and Jones 1982). Many self-questioning strategies require students to reread or look back at the text if they cannot answer the questions. Graves (1986), for example, asked the children to stop during reading and ask themselves, *Do I understand what the whole story is about?* If they could not answer this question, they were to reread the passage. Vaughn and Klingner (1999) taught children to distinguish portions of a passage that they understood well ("clicks") from spots where comprehension broke down for some reason ("clunks"). Such techniques can help poor readers become more aware of how to recognize and repair break-downs in comprehension.

In short, the metacognitive aspect of strategic behavior should be a central theme in strategy instruction. In the following section, we describe several possible methods for teaching strategies, all of which include metacognitive elements.

APPROACHES TO STRATEGY INSTRUCTION

The goals of strategy training are independent application by the student, maintenance of the strategy over time, and generalization to related tasks. Most practitioners agree that quality strategy instruction for poor readers needs to include a carefully structured process for gradually releasing responsibility for application and self-regulation to the student, for as Pressley, Goodchild et al. (1989) noted, maintenance and transfer rarely follow from "simple instruction about how to execute a strategic procedure" (p. 315). Figure 4.4 from Duke and Pearson (2002) illustrates a model of instruction in which the teacher initially assumes primary responsibility for task completion.

During a process of guided practice, teacher and student assume joint responsibility. Finally, the teacher relinquishes all responsibility to the students. To facilitate this process, task difficulty needs to be carefully controlled, and students need to be given ample opportunities to practice a strategy and apply it in a variety of authentic contexts.

Though the goals of strategy instruction are not contested, researchers and practitioners disagree about the best means of accomplishing them. A variety of methods have been advocated for teaching strategies and related metacognitive skills. These vary in the degree to which the teacher controls and directs instruction, in the degree to which the strategies are broken down into small, sequential

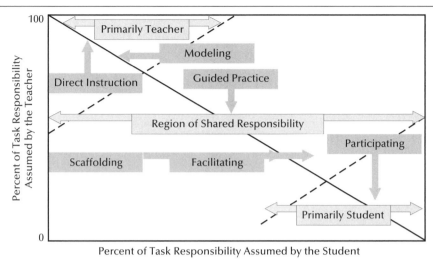

Figure 4.4   Gradual Release of Responsibility: As one moves down the diagonal from upper left to lower right, students assume more, and teachers less, responsibility for task completion. There are three regions of responsibility: primarily teacher in the upper left corner, primarily student in the lower right, and shared responsibility in the center. From Duke, N., and Pearson, P. D., 2002. Effective Practices for developing reading comprehension. In *What Research Has to Say About Reading Instruction*, 3rd ed., A Forstrup and J. Samuels (Eds.). Newark, DE: International Reading Association. Reprinted with permission of P. D. Pearson.

steps, and in the context in which they are taught. At one end of the continuum are instructional methods in which the teacher maintains tight control over the instructional process, provides extremely explicit directions and explanations, and teaches strategies in step-by-step fashion, making sure students have mastered one step before moving on to the next. At the other end of the continuum are methods guided by a "constructivist" paradigm. A learning environment is created that allows students to construct knowledge and develop self-regulation capabilities with a lesser degree of explicit instruction while temporary assistance or "scaffolding" is provided by a teacher.

In the next section, we will describe in detail several methods of strategy instruction that have solid research support: the Strategies Intervention Model, Direct Explanation, Reciprocal Teaching, and Transactional Strategies Instruction. The Strategies Intervention Model, developed by researchers at the University of Kansas (Deshler and Lenz 1989) and Direct Explanation (Duffy and Roehler 1987; Duffy et al. 1986; Duffy et al. 1987) involve explicit, teacher-directed instruction. In contrast, in Reciprocal Teaching (Palincsar and Brown 1986; 1988), rooted in constructivist philosophy, strategies are introduced and practiced in small, collaborative groups in which the teacher is a participant and a guide. Transactional Strategies Instruction (Pressley and Wharton-McDonald 1997) is an adaptation of Reciprocal Teaching and Direct Explanation that incorporates elements of both. Though these various approaches to strategy instruction are quite different, if implemented systematically, all have the potential to foster independent use, maintenance, and generalization.

The Strategies Intervention Model

The Strategies Intervention Model was developed by Deshler, Schumaker, and their colleagues at the Institute for Research on Learning Disabilities at the University of Kansas (see Ellis et al. 1991; Lenz, Ellis, and Scanlon 1996). This group has designed a very systematic approach to strategy instruction that incorporates elements of direct instruction and cognitive behavior modification. The emphasis is on teaching a core group of strategies that promote academic and social success. Not surprisingly, many of the strategies developed by this group of researchers involve reading comprehension. These include paraphrasing, self-questioning, visual imagery, and error monitoring. Each of the strategies is designated by an acronym, each letter of which represents a step in the strategic procedure. For example, the paraphrasing strategy is known is RAP:

1. **R**ead a paragraph.
2. **A**sk yourself, "What were the main ideas and details of this paragraph?"
3. **P**ut the main idea and details in your own words.

Students are given explicit rules for carrying out each step, and the acronym serves as a mnemonic device to trigger recollection of these rules.

The instructional procedure involves two stages: acquisition of the strategy and generalization of the strategy. At each stage, the student is asked to make a commitment to learning and using the strategy. Instruction begins with an explanation of the rationale for the strategy and situations in which it would be useful. Then the teacher models the strategy, using a think-aloud process. Students rehearse the steps of the strategy until they have memorized them. They are given teacher-directed practice and feedback as they learn to use the strategy. Initially, they apply the strategy to simple materials, then gradually progress to grade-level text. When students have demonstrated that they can use the strategy effectively, the process of generalization begins. The teacher provides many examples of the strategy and frequently reminds students of when the strategy can be used. They are given carefully structured guided practice in applying the strategies to actual school assignments and are encouraged to prompt themselves to use the strategies with self-talk. Throughout the procedure, there is a great deal of teacher explanation and feedback. Student progress is monitored along the way, and supplementary instruction and feedback are provided. This approach has generally proven to be effective in enhancing the academic performance of students with LD and other low achievers (see Ellis, Lenz, and Sabornie 1987a, 1987b). The University of Kansas program is often advocated as a tool for providing adolescents with the academic and social skills needed for success in school and life; however, the basic approach to strategy instruction has broader applications and has been successfully used with younger students.

Direct Explanation

The Direct Explanation approach (Duffy and Roehler 1987; Duffy et al. 1986; Duffy et al. 1987) involves introducing and teaching a single strategy at a time to mastery before others are introduced. Students are given explicit, detailed information about the purpose of the strategy, steps in the strategic procedure, ways to implement the strategy, and the conditions under which it might be useful. Instruction is accompanied by plenty of concrete examples, modeling, and practice. The teacher provides very carefully crafted explanations, demonstrations, and modeling. Active involvement on the part of the students is encouraged, but the teacher remains in control of the instructional process. With the Direct Explanation approach, emphasis is placed on the *thought processes* involved in using the strategy. Duffy and Roehler (1987) provide the following illustration of the modeling process in teaching the strategy of using context clues and background knowledge to determine the meaning of a word:

> I want to show you what I do when I come to a word I don't know the meaning of. I'll talk out loud to show you how I figure it out. [Teacher reads] 'The cocoa steamed fragrantly.' [Teacher says] Hmmm, I've heard that word 'fragrantly' before, but I don't really know what it means here. I know one of the words right before it though, 'steamed.' I watched a pot of boiling water once and there was steam coming from it. The water was hot, this must have something to do with the cocoa being hot. Okay, the pan of hot cocoa is steaming on the stove. That means steam is coming up and out, but that still doesn't explain what 'fragrantly' means. Let me think about the hot cocoa on the stove and try to use what I know about cocoa as a clue. Hot cocoa bubbles, steams, and smells! Hot cocoa smells good! [Teacher rereads] 'The cocoa steamed fragrantly.' That means it smelled good! (Duffy and Roehler 1987, p. 517).

There are five steps in the Direct Explanation approach to strategy instruction:

1. The teacher explains the focus of the lesson, naming the strategy, explaining the steps in the strategy, and discussing when and why it is useful.
2. The teacher models the use of the strategy, with emphasis on the reasoning process involved in applying it to solve a comprehension problem.
3. The teacher provides guided practice. If students have difficulty, the teacher provides further modeling and demonstration of the reasoning process.
4. The students practice the strategy independently.
5. The students are given opportunities to apply the strategy in other contexts.

Another strategy is introduced only when students demonstrate that they have mastered the first strategy. Eventually children are given practice integrating all of the strategies they have learned and making decisions about which strategy is most useful in a given situation. This procedure has been shown to improve significantly the comprehension and metacognitive awareness of low achievers in the third through fifth grades.

Reciprocal Teaching

In contrast to the more teacher-directed approaches described above, with Reciprocal Teaching (Palincsar and Brown 1986; 1988), students and teacher are mutually involved in the instructional process. Reciprocal teaching is based on Vygotsky's (1978) social constructivist theory of learning, which suggests that children gradually gain the ability to regulate their own behavior and cognitive processes by internalizing the overt explanatory language of adults. Hence, there is an emphasis on the role of the social interaction in the learning process. In reciprocal teaching, strategy instruction occurs as the teacher and a small group of students engage in a dialogue during the reading process, with the goal of joint construction of meaning from a text. Kucan and Beck (1997) suggested that "what distinguished Palincsar and Brown's work was not the particular strategies that were taught but rather the process through which the students would learn, or the mechanism for students' internalization of the strategies" (p. 281). In another departure from other approaches to strategy instruction, several complementary strategies are introduced simultaneously. Instruction is generally less explicit than in the direct explanation approach, with more left for the student to infer. However, the instructor tries to make the covert processes employed by good readers obvious to the students through modeling and explanations. As students gain the ability to apply the strategies, the teacher gradually reduces the frequency and explicitness of prompts and supports.

The reciprocal teaching process includes daily sessions of about 30 minutes each that proceed until students have mastered a set of reading comprehension strategies: *summarizing* (identifying and paraphrasing main ideas), *questioning* (formulating and answering questions about the content), *clarifying* (recognizing and correcting "breakdowns" in comprehension), and *predicting* (forming hypotheses about upcoming events or information). The strategies are introduced, modeled, and practiced *briefly* in isolation during the first few sessions. The goal during this phase of instruction is exposure to the strategies, not complete mastery. In the next phase, students are then asked to apply all four strategies in "guided interactive practice." During this process, the teacher works with a small group of students (four to seven). The students and teacher take turns assuming the role of "teacher" or discussion leader. After reading a segment of the text silently, the discussion leader summarizes the content, asks questions "that a teacher might reasonably ask" (Brown and Palincsar 1987, p. 87), discusses and clarifies difficulties (if any), and makes a prediction about upcoming content. The discussion leader then invites other students to generate additional questions, make predictions, and ask for clarification. Another student assumes responsibility for leading the discussion of the next segment of text, and the process is repeated. The strategies are applied *when appropriate* in the context of actual reading. For instance, if there is nothing in the text segment that the students did not understand, there is no need to use the clarification procedure. The sessions usually have a ritualized structure at first, but as students become more comfortable with the procedure and more adept at applying the strategies, interactions among the group members become more natural. The only constraint is the requirement that all four strategic activities are used in the course of the discussion (Palincsar et al. 1993).

Early in the process, the teacher may need to model most or even all components of the strategies. As students become more proficient in using the strategies, the teacher supplies prompts, modeling, and explanations only as needed. For example, if the student discussion leader cannot formulate a question, the teacher might suggest a means of starting the question (e.g., *Where was . . .*). If this does not help, the teacher could model a question (e.g., *I might ask the question "Where was the treasure buried?"*) or suggest that the student supply a fact rather than ask a question. The teacher also provides corrective feedback (e.g., *I think you forgot an important idea.*) and praise. In time, as students become more proficient at applying the strategies, the teacher provides less support. To build metacognitive awareness, each session begins with a review of the strategies, the importance of using them, and reasons that using a strategy leads to better comprehension. It is suggested that each session end with having the students read a passage independently and answer comprehension questions. This allows the teacher to assess progress and provides feedback to the students on their performance. Students should be encouraged to attribute their improvement to use of the strategies.

Reciprocal teaching was initially designed for use with middle school students who had reasonably good decoding but poor comprehension. The students included in many of the original studies were seventh graders who, in spite of low achievement, had not been officially classified as having LD (Brown and Palincsar 1987). The procedure was implemented primarily with expository text. In both carefully controlled laboratory studies and application in school settings, students made improvement both in reading comprehension and in metacognitive awareness. Further, strategy use was maintained over time (Brown and Palincsar 1987). In later studies, Palincsar and Brown experimented with adapting the procedure for use with younger children. They have reported success in using reciprocal teaching with children in kindergarten through second grade (Brown and Palincsar 1987; Olson and Platt 2000). The primary procedural difference is that the text was read aloud to the children. For a more detailed discussion of reciprocal teaching and examples of dialogue, see Brown and Palincsar (1987), Palincsar and Brown (1986; 1988), or Olson and Platt (2000).

There are a number of other strategy instruction methods that are based on the principles used in Reciprocal Teaching. These include POSSE (Englert and Mariage 1991) and Collaborative Strategic Reading (Vaughn and Klingner 1999). Like reciprocal teaching, these techniques involve teaching a set of related strategies in a small-group context in which students take turns leading discussions. However, they differ somewhat in their particulars. For instance, with POSSE, greater emphasis is placed on predicting and mapping the author's organizational structure, and Collaborative Strategic Reading includes a more explicit procedure for monitoring comprehension and correcting problems.

Transactional Strategies Instruction

As noted earlier, both Reciprocal Teaching and the more teacher-directed approaches are supported by research. Either method of strategy instruction can be effective if sufficient time is devoted to the instructional process, and if students are given plenty of practice opportunities with increasing emphasis on independent application. Teachers may, in fact, wish to consider including components of both approaches. Recent research (Swanson 1999) indicates that comprehension instruction for students with LD is most effective when explicit instruction is combined with an interactive, small-group approach such as Reciprocal Teaching. Moreover, in a review of the research on Reciprocal Teaching, Rosenshine and Meister (1994) concluded that the technique is more likely to be effective if teachers spend time teaching the strategies directly before starting the interactive phase of the training. These findings suggest that it may be overwhelming for many poor readers to try to apply four strategies simultaneously before they have been mastered individually in isolation. Such students may need very explicit instruction and guided practice in, for example, formulating questions about text before they can integrate this skill independently with other strategic activities. Such direct and on-going teacher coaching is one of the goals of a more flexible, educator-devised approach that Pressley and his colleagues (e.g., Pressley and Wharton-McDonald 1997) call Transactional Strategies Instruction. Teachers select a small repertoire of strategies such as prediction, question generation, identifying and resolving "breakdowns" in comprehension, mental imagery, summarization, relating prior knowledge to text content, and so on. Some of the characteristics of the approach are (a) long-term instruction, often carried out throughout the school year rather than merely over the course of a few weeks, (b) teacher modeling and direct explanation of the strategies, throughout the school day and in a variety of different contexts, with explicit explanation of where and when the students could use a given strategy, and (c) student modeling and discussion of the strategies, with strategy use serving as a vehicle for dialogue in small-group reading activities. This approach gives teachers some flexibility in terms of which strategies are taught and how discussion in reading groups is structured. As noted earlier, it also allows for more extensive teacher support, provided on an as-needed basis. The effectiveness of this approach has recently been demonstrated in a number of studies (reviewed in Pressley and Wharton-McDonald 1997).

Like Reciprocal Teaching and related approaches, Transactional Strategy Instruction features "thinking aloud" (Kucan and Beck 1997) and provides a forum for students to learn not only what other readers do but *how* they do it. In addition to the teacher modeling, students have the opportunity to witness their peers engaging in the reading and thinking process. Moreover, students receive extensive practice in integrating multiple strategies during the reading process and in making decisions about which strategies to apply and when. Finally, interaction in small group settings may help students gain the academic and social skills they need to participate meaningfully in "Book Clubs" and other cooperative learning activities (see Chapters 8 and 9). However, as we discuss in the following section, there are many factors involved in making decisions about how to approach strategy instruction. What is effective in a given situation may not work well in another.

COMMONLY ASKED QUESTIONS

There is clearly a dizzying array of choices for the teacher who wants to include strategy instruction in a reading comprehension program. Which strategies to teach, how to teach them, and how to get students to use them are common concerns. Making these decisions requires consideration of the factors introduced in Chapter 1: characteristics of the learners (e.g., age, decoding ability, working memory capacity, prior knowledge), the nature of texts and tasks, the setting, and the instructional preferences of the teacher. In this section, we offer some general guidelines and suggestions for maximizing the effectiveness of strategy instruction.

Which strategies should a teacher teach?

Most experts agree that it is better to select a few strategies and teach them thoroughly and systematically than to give students superficial exposure to many. But which strategies? One way of answering this question is to consider the four general classes of strategies described earlier: preparatory, organizational, elaborative, and metacognitive. These correspond to four basic strategic activities that are important in effective reading: activating background information before reading, abstracting important ideas, integrating textual information with prior knowledge, and monitoring comprehension. Choosing one or more strategy from each category to teach is a reasonable approach. In fact, the four component strategies included in reciprocal teaching (predicting, summarizing, questioning, and clarifying) correspond to the four categories. However, in deciding which particular strategies to emphasize, one should consider the age and ability level of the students, what type of text they are reading, and how they are expected to use information gained from reading.

Learner Characteristics.   Teachers should be aware that most strategy training studies have involved students in the upper elementary and middle school grades. Certain strategies may be effective only for students who have attained a reasonable degree of proficiency in decoding. A beginning reader who is putting a great deal of energy into word reading probably will not be able to apply a complex strategic procedure at the same time. However, some strategies are appropriate for younger children. Both Pressley (1976) and Borduin, Borduin, and Manley (1994) successfully taught a simple imagery strategy to second graders, and some self-questioning techniques, such as KWL, can be used with younger children. It is also possible to adapt some of the procedures for use with young children or less skilled decoders. For instance, recall that

Brown and Palincsar (1987) were able to use the reciprocal teaching procedure with young children if the text was read aloud to them.

Unfortunately, there has been very little research on application, maintenance, and generalization of strategies in children of different ages. However, some established findings from the developmental literature have implications for strategy instruction. It has been shown that metacognitive abilities increase with age and experience. For this reason, younger children will probably need more explicit instruction than older children both in strategy use and in metacognitive awareness (Harris and Pressley 1991). It is also likely that younger children will need more time and practice than older children to master a strategy. Working memory also increases with age (e.g., Case 1985), so older children will likely be able to apply more complex strategic procedures than younger children.

As we discussed in Chapter 2, working memory capacity is often related to reading comprehension. Poor readers, particularly those with lower mental ability, often have serious weaknesses in working memory that limit the extent to which they can manage to read and simultaneously implement a complex strategic procedure, even with a great deal of practice (Pressley, Goodchild et al. 1987). In this case, use of the strategy is unlikely to have a significant impact on comprehension, and there is a good chance that the student will decide it is not worth the effort. Unfortunately, we lack data on the approximate working memory capacity needed to execute various strategies. However, we offer a few suggestions when working with students with working memory limitations. (1) Choose a simple procedure with fewer steps to memorize and/or provide student with a list of steps as a reminder. (2) Break a complex procedure into component skills, teach them separately, and then work on integrating. For instance, if using a Reciprocal Teaching approach, provide extensive instruction in the strategies separately before asking the student to combine them. (3) Experiment with imagery and visual organizers. Some researchers (e.g., Long, Winograd, and Bridge 1989; Oakhill and Patel 1991) have speculated that using visual imagery may help reduce demands on verbal working memory. Visual organizers might also be useful in that they provide students with a written record of key ideas from the text. Students might be taught to review the visual organizer created from one portion of a text before reading the next portion. Unfortunately, efforts to remediate deficits in working memory have not been promising (Swanson 2000). Thus, it is important that these students learn to compensate for weaknesses in working memory through strategic activities.

Some strategies—most notably elaborative strategies—are highly dependent on background knowledge. An individual with a limited knowledge base may not be able to use them very effectively. For example, if a student attempting to use elaborative interrogation does not have the necessary knowledge base to supply a logical answer to a "why" question, the strategy will probably not be of much help. Other elaborative strategies may be more appropriate for students without an extensive knowledge base. For instance, Willoughby, Wood, and Khan (1994) found that for students with limited background knowledge in a given area, imagery was more effective than elaborative interrogation. In addition to having less well developed knowledge bases, several studies have demonstrated that poor readers may be overly dependent on background knowledge (e.g., Lipson 1982; Maria and MacGinitie 1982), distorting new information to conform to their expectations or failing to recognize instances in which their prior knowledge differs from information in the text. Such readers may have difficulty making accurate inferences, correcting misconceptions, or learning anything new through reading. Along with activating prior knowledge, strategies that encourage attention to the idea structure in a text or that involve comparing prior knowledge and beliefs with information in the text might be helpful. For example, the final step in KWL requires students to summarize what they learned. At this point they might be asked to consider whether anything in the text surprised them or contradicted what they thought they knew about the topic.

The Nature of the Text. The kinds of strategies needed vary according to the type of text a student is reading. Some strategies are general enough that they can be applied across text types, others are designed primarily for readers of specific types of texts. Some are relevant only to narrative texts while others are more useful to readers of expository texts. Even general strategies often need to be applied differently when reading different types of text. For instance, making predictions is an important strategy to employ regardless of what type of text one is reading. However, the nature of one's predictions will differ with text type. In the case of narrative text, predictions typically involve future events. In contrast, with an expository text such as a textbook passage, predictions generally involve speculation about upcoming information. In the case of an opinion essay, hypotheses about the author's viewpoint and how he or she might develop the argument are more relevant.

As we mentioned earlier, a very important metacognitive skill is the ability to match strategies with text and task demands. Ideally—in time—students will be exposed to a variety of strategies that serve different purposes and learn to use them in appropriate situations. However, when making decisions about how to *begin* strategy instruction, we recommend considering what type of text the student is most likely to be reading. Young children who are primarily reading simple fictional stories would benefit from strategies that involve understanding "story grammar" (see Chapter 8). Similarly, for older students in literature classes, strategies for identifying themes, sources of conflict, etc. would be beneficial (see Chapter 9). However, in content classes at the middle and secondary levels, students typically read far more expository text than narrative. Many struggling readers, even those who comprehend stories relatively well, struggle with the demands of reading and learning from textbooks and other informational text (e.g., Armbruster, Anderson, and Meyer 1991). Thus, for students who are learning to read expository text, it is beneficial to emphasize organizational strategies that draw their attention to the author's idea structure, such as those that feature graphic organizers or semantic maps.

The Nature of the Task.   An important consideration is what students will be expected to do with information from texts? Will they use the text to answer questions? Write a book report? Share what they learned with their classmates? Use the information to solve a problem or design an experiment? How important is it for them to remember what they read? Do they need to remember only the main points, or are details important too? Different tasks clearly dictate the use of different strategies. Teachers should select and teach strategies that will help students meet task expectations. In most content area classes, especially at the middle and secondary levels, students are expected not only to read for understanding but also to remember and use text information. Using graphic organizers, producing written summaries, and making notations in the margins of a text are examples of strategic activities that may not only improve comprehension but also strengthen memory for what was read. Additionally, they provide the student with a written record of key text information that can be the basis of a book report or an oral presentation. Such notes can also be used for review and study. A common classroom assignment is to answer study questions after reading. The QAR strategy described earlier can help students learn to provide appropriate answers to different types of questions. By explicitly explaining the connection between the use of a given strategy and the requirements of a given task, teachers can help students learn to evaluate a task independently and select an appropriate strategy or set of strategies.

How should teachers go about teaching strategies?

Earlier in this chapter, we presented several research-supported methods of strategy instruction. All are time intensive and require a serious commitment on the part of the teacher. However, which method is preferable may depend largely on the setting and how a teacher chooses to organize instruction in his or her classroom.

The Nature of the Setting.   The setting in which instruction is delivered often imposes constraints on how strategies can be taught. In a resource room, it tends to be somewhat easier for a teacher to tailor instruction to the needs of individual students. Though one-to-one instruction is a rare luxury in today's schools, even in the resource room (Moody et al. 2000), it is usually possible in resource settings to work intensively with small groups of students who have common academic needs. In such a situation, Reciprocal Teaching and related approaches are likely to work well. However, the Reciprocal Teaching procedure requires that a teacher be available to give undivided attention to a small group of students for a relatively long period of time (about a half hour), at least in the initial stages of instruction. Unless the other students in the class are able to work independently or in groups with minimal teacher involvement, Reciprocal Teaching may not be feasible in a general classroom setting with a sole teacher. However, it is becoming increasingly popular for special education teachers to provide services to student within the classroom rather than in resource settings. In such a co-teaching situation, working with a small group of students may be more practical. (See Chapter 9 for further recommendations on teaching strategies in small, collaborative groups in the general classroom.)

Direct Explanation and the Strategies Intervention Model more readily allow for full-class instruction followed by practice activities in which the teacher circulates among the students. However, before taking such an approach, it is important to consider the needs of *all* the students in a heterogeneous classroom. A finding in some strategy-training studies is that the strategies benefit poor readers but not good readers (e.g., Chan and Cole 1986; Dole, Brown, and Trathen 1996; Oakhill and Patel 1991). Often, as Oakhill and Patel (1991) noted, good readers devise strategies on their own that are just as effective as the ones being taught. Forcing good readers to use cumbersome strategic procedures may, in fact, do more harm than good. Not only may the strategy not help them, but they may also lose interest and motivation. Dole, Brown, and Trathen (1996) reported the case of a high-achieving student who resisted using a strategy (which involved filling out a story map) and whose performance actually declined over the course of the treatment. It is thus important to determine if a student really *needs* to learn a particular strategy before teaching it. Nonetheless, there are a few strategies that have consistently proven to be beneficial for readers of differing ability levels. One of these is elaborative interrogation, which is helpful for normally achieving and even gifted students (though it may be less helpful for some poor readers). By assigning students to different groups, it may be possible to differentiate instruction so that students are taught the strategies that best match their needs. In addition to varying the particular strategies that are taught, teachers can vary the explicitness with which a strategy is taught and the amount of practice provided. Poor readers can be provided with very explicit, systematic instruction while high achieving students might be challenged to develop and share their own strategies with one another.

Instructional Preferences.   Some teachers are more comfortable with a direct, step-by-step approach to strategy instruction in which the procedure for fostering independent application is clear-cut. When this is the case, Direct Explanation or the Strategies Intervention Model might be a better instructional choice than Reciprocal Teaching. Some teachers are skilled at supplying just enough support at the right times and at gradually relinquishing control over the discussions to the students. Others find it difficult to "let go" and be a participant in the discussion rather than the leader. However, some research indicates that the effectiveness of reciprocal teaching and related techniques depends on a teacher's willingness to do just that (Englert and Mariage 1991).

Some teachers routinely use small-group instruction in their classes. In these cases, the students are probably used to working cooperatively, and strategy instruction in small groups would not involve a dramatic shift in the existing classroom organization. Other teachers prefer the more traditional approach of providing most instruction to the full group and having students work independently on practice activities. Although small-group instruction probably offers more flexibility in terms of tailoring strategy instruction to individual needs, strategy training can be done on a class-wide basis. In situations in which all or most of the students need work on reading comprehension, such as in lower-track content classes at the secondary level, this approach might be preferable.

In short, if a teacher carefully considers the possibilities and limitations of his or her academic setting and preferred instructional style, it is more likely that strategy instruction will be offered systematically and on a long-term basis. If, on the other hand, an instructional method is not compatible either with the setting or a teacher's style, the teacher may soon discard strategy instruction as a failed experiment.

How do teachers get students to use strategies?

A common concern of teachers is that students do not continue to use strategies after the instructional period or transfer strategic procedures to new situations (e.g., reading a textbook for a different class). As Pressley, Goodchild et al. (1989) pointed out, strategy instruction should not be regarded as a "quick fix." Rather, it may take a long time, a great deal of practice, and frequent reminders or "refresher courses" for a strategy to become habitual and automatic. In addition to providing ample opportunities for practice during the instructional process, there are a number of things teachers can do to help ensure that students continue to use the strategies they are taught (see also Harris and Pressley, 1991; Pressley, Goodchild et al. 1989).

1. Throughout the day and across the curriculum, remind students of instances in which a strategy could be applied. Make it clear through modeling and suggestions that strategies are not just for "reading group." Provide explicit examples of generalization. For instance, if a student has learned to use visual imagery when reading stories, illustrate how the same strategy can help the student understand a math word problem.

2. Enlist the support of other teachers. As Harris and Pressley (1991) noted, "Several teachers consistently modeling and prompting appropriate use of a strategy across different tasks and settings can make a meaningful difference in generalization" (p. 398). If the strategies were taught in the resource room, it is valuable to show children explicitly how they transfer to tasks in the general classroom. For instance, if a student learned to apply K-W-L in the resource room, his or her social studies teacher could point out that this technique is also useful when reading the textbook. Students might also be encouraged to consider how a strategy should be modified when applied to a different kind of text, a different task, or in a different context. For instance, when using imagery to visualize the scenario in a math word problem, it is more important to construct an accurate image than when visualizing the setting of a story.

3. Encourage students to adapt strategies to make them more personally useful. This might include omitting steps as a student gains skill in using a strategy. For instance, when a student consistently demonstrates proficiency in identifying an author's organizational framework, mapping the structure on a graphic organizer may be a time-consuming step that is no longer necessary or helpful.

4. In a similar vein, students might be encouraged to conduct their own tests of a strategy's effectiveness. For instance, they might try reading two sections of a textbook chapter, paraphrasing the main idea of each paragraph in one instance and

not in the other. They could then compare their accuracy on the study questions at the ends of the sections. Frequent informal assessments of comprehension can make students more aware of their increasing progress, especially if the results are graphed. This can help them learn to attribute improvement to strategy use realistically, which in turn can increase motivation to use strategies.

REFERENCES

Allington, R. L., and McGill-Franzen, A. 1989. School response to reading failure: Instruction for Chapter 1 and special education students in Grades two, four, and eight. *Elementary School Journal*, 89:529–42.

Armbruster, B. B., Anderson, T. H., and Meyer, J. L. 1991. Improving content-area reading using instructional graphics. *Reading Research Quarterly*, 26:393–416.

Baddeley, A. D., Grant, S., Wight, E., and Thomson, N. 1975. Imagery and visual working memory. In *Attention and Performance*, V, P. M. A. Rabbitt and S. Dornic (Eds.), (pp. 205–17). New York: Academic Press.

Begg, I., and Paivio, A. 1969. Concreteness and imagery in sentence memory. *Journal of Verbal Learning and Verbal Behavior*, 8:821–27.

Billingsley, B. S., and Ferro-Almeida, S. C. 1993. Strategies to facilitate reading comprehension in students with learning disabilites. *Reading and Writing Quarterly*, 9:263–78.

Billingsley, B. S., and Wildman, T. M. 1988. The effects of prereading activities on the comprehension monitoring activities of learning disabled adolescents. *Learning Disabilities Research*, 4:36–44.

Borduin, B. J., Borduin, C. M., and Manley, C. M. 1994. The use of imagery training to improve reading comprehension of second graders. *Journal of Genetic Psychology*, 155:115–18.

Borkowski, J. G., Weyhing, R. S., and Carr, M. 1988. Effects of attributional retraining on strategy-based reading comprehension in learning-disabled students. *Journal of Educational Psychology*, 80:46–53.

Brown, A. L., Armbruster, B. B., and Baker, L. 1986. The role of metacognition in reading and studying. In *Reading Comprehension: From Research to Practice*, J. Orasanu (Ed.), (pp. 49–75). Hillsdale, NJ: Lawrence Erlbaum.

Brown, A. L., and Palincsar, A. S. 1987. Reciprocal teaching of comprehension strategies: A natural history of one program for enhancing learning. In *Intelligence and Exceptionality: New Directions for Theory, Assessment, and Instructional Practice*, J. D. Day and J. G. Borkowski (Eds.), (pp. 81–132). Norwood, NJ: Ablex.

Cain, K., and Oakhill, J. V. 1999. Inference making ability and its relation to comprehension failure in young children. *Reading and Writing*, 11:489–503.

Carnine, D, and Kinder, B. D. 1985. Teaching low performing students to apply generative and schema strategies to narrative and expository material. *Remedial and Special Education*, 6:20–30.

Carr, S. C., and Thompson, B. 1996. The effects of prior knowledge and schema activation strategies on the inferential comprehension of children with and without learning disabilities. *Learning Disability Quarterly*, 19:48–61.

Case, R. 1985. *Intellectual development*. Orlando, FL: Academic Press.

Chan, L. K. S., and Cole, P. G. 1986. The effects of comprehension monitoring training on the reading competence of learning disabled and regular class students. *Remedial and Special Education*, 7:33–40.

Chi, M. T. H., de Leeuw, N., Chiu, M., and La Vancher, C. 1994. Eliciting self-explanations improves understanding. *Cognitive Science*, 18:439–77.

Clark, F. L., Deshler, D. D., Schumaker, J. B., Alley, G. R., and Warner, M. M. 1984. Visual imagery and self-questioning: Strategies to improve comprehension of written material. *Journal of Learning Disabilities*, 17:145–49.

Collins, J. 1982. Discourse style, classroom interaction and differential treatment. *Journal of Reading Behavior*, 14:429–37.

Cramer, E. H. 1980. Mental imagery, reading attitude and comprehension. *Reading Improvement*, 17:135–39.

Deshler, D. D., and Lenz, B. K. 1989. The strategies instructional approach. *International Journal of Disability, Development and Education*, 36:203–24.

Dickson, S. V., Collins, V. L., Simmons, D. C., and Kame'enui, E. J. 1998. Metacognitive strategies: Research bases. In *What Reading Research Tells Us About Children with Diverse Learning Needs*, D. C. Simmons, and E. J. Kame'enui (Eds.), (pp. 295–360). Mahwah, NJ: Erlbaum.

Dole, J. A., Brown, K. J., and Trathen, W. 1996. The effects of strategy instruction on the comprehension performance of at-risk students. *Reading Research Quarterly*, 31:62–84.

Duffy, G. G., and Roehler, L. R. 1987. Teaching skills as strategies. *The Reading Teacher*, 40:514–21.

Duffy, G. G., Roehler, L. R., Meloth, M. S., Vavrus, I. G., Book, C., Putnam, J., and Wesselman, R. 1986. The relationship between explicit verbal explanations during reading skill instruction and student awareness and achievement: A study of reading teacher effects. *Reading Research Quarterly*, 21:327–52.

Duffy, G. G., Roehler, L. R., Sivan, E., Rackliffe, G., Book, C., Meloth, M. S., Vavrus, I. G., Wesselman, R., Putnam, J., and Bassiri, D. 1987. Effects of explaining the reasoning associated with using reading strategies. *Reading Research Quarterly*, 22:347–68.

Duke, N., and Pearson, P. D. 2002. Effective practices for developing reading comprehension. In *What Research Has to Say About Reading Instruction*, 3rd ed., A. Farstrup and J. Samuels (Eds.). Newark, DE: International Reading Association.

Ellis, E. S., Lenz, B. K., and Sabornie, E. J. 1987a. Generalization and adaptation of learning strategies to natural environments: Part 1, Critical agents. *Remedial and Special Education*, 8:6–20.

Ellis, E. S., Lenz, B. K., and Sabornie, E. J. 1987b. Generalization and adaptation of learning strategies to natural environments: Part 2, Research into practice. *Remedial and Special Education*, 8:21–3.

Ellis, E. S., Deshler, D. D., Lenz, B. K., Schumaker, J. B., and Clark, F. L. 1991. An instructional model for teaching learning strategies. *Focus on Exceptional Children*, 23:1–24.

Englert, C. S., and Mariage, T. V. 1991. Making students partners in the comprehension process: Organizing the reading "POSSE." *Learning Disability Quarterly*, 14:123–38.

Forness, S. R., Kavale, K. A., Blum, I. M., and Lloyd, J. W. 1997. Mega-analysis of meta-analyses. *Teaching Exceptional Children*, 29:4–9.

Gallego, M. A. 1992. Collaborative instruction for reading comprehension: The role of discourse and discussion. In *Promoting Academic Competence and Literacy in School*, M. Pressley, K. R. Harris, and J. T. Guthrie (Eds.), (pp. 223–42). New York: Academic Press, Inc.

Gambrell, L. B., and Bales, R. J. 1986. Mental imagery and the comprehension monitoring performance of fourth- and fifth-grade poor readers. *Reading Research Quarterly*, 21:454–64.

Gambrell, L. B., and Jawitz, P. B. 1993. Mental imagery, text illustrations, and children's story comprehension and recall. *Reading Research Quarterly*, 28:265–73.

Graves, A. W. 1986. Effects of direct instruction and metacomprehension training on finding main ideas. *Learning Disabilities Research*, 1:90–100.

Harris, K. R., and Pressley, M. 1991. The nature of cognitive strategy instruction: Interactive strategy construction. *Exceptional Children*, 57:392–404.

Idol, L. 1987. Group story mapping: A comprehension strategy for both skilled and unskilled readers. *Journal of Learning Disabilities*, 20:196–205.

Idol, L., and Croll, V. J. 1987. Story-mapping training as a means of improving reading comprehension. *Learning Disability Quarterly*, 10:214–29.

Idol-Maestas, L. 1985. Getting ready to read: Guided probing for poor comprehenders. *Learning Disability Quarterly*, 8:214–29.

Irwin, J. W. 1979. College readers' mental imagery, reading ability, and attitude toward reading. *Reading Improvement*, 16:124–29.

Jenkins, J. R., Heliotis, J. D., Stein, M. L., and Haynes, M. C. 1987. Improving reading comprehension by using paragraph restatements. *Exceptional Children*, 54:54–9.

Kucan, L., and Beck, L. L. 1997. Thinking aloud and reading comprehension research: Inquiry, instruction, and social interaction. *Review of Educational Research*, 67:271–99.

Langer, J. A. 1984. Examining background knowledge and text comprehension. *Reading Research Quarterly*, 19:468–81.

Lenz, B. K., Ellis, E. S., and Scanlon, D. 1996. *Teaching Learning Strategies to Adolescents and Adults with Learning Disabilities*. Austin, TX: PRO-ED.

Licht, B. G. 1993. Achievement-related beliefs in children with learning disabilities: Impact on motivation and strategic learning. In *Strategy Assessment and Instruction for Students with Learning Disabilities*, L. J. Meltzer (Ed.), (pp. 195-220). Austin, TX: PRO-ED.

Licht, B. G., Kistner, J. A., Ozkaragoz, T., Shapiro, S., and Clausen, L. 1985. Causal attributions of learning disabled children: Individual differences and their implications for persistence. *Journal of Educational Psychology*, 77:208–16.

Lipson, M. Y. 1982. Learning new information from text: The role of prior knowledge and reading ability. *Journal of Reading Behavior*, 14:243–61.

Long, S. A., Winograd, P. N., and Bridge, C. A. 1989. The effects of reader and text characteristics on imagery reported during and after reading. *Reading Research Quarterly*, 24:353–72.

Malone, L. D., and Mastropieri, M. A. 1992. Reading comprehension instruction: Summarization and self-monitoring training for students with learning disabilities. *Exceptional Children*, 58:270–79.

Maria, K., and MacGinitie, W. 1982. Reading comprehension disabilities: Knowledge structures and non-accommodating text processing strategies. *Annals of Dyslexia*, 32:33–59.

Mastropieri, M. A., and Scruggs, T. E. 1997. Best practices in promoting reading comprehension in students with learning disabilities. *Remedial and Special Education*, 18:197–213.

McCallum, R. D., and Moore, S. 1999. Not all imagery is created equal: The role of imagery in the comprehension of main ideas in exposition. *Journal of Reading Psychology*, 20:21–60.

Moody, S. W., Vaughn, S., Hughes, M. T., and Fischer, M. 2000. Reading instruction in the resource room: Set up for failure. *Exceptional Children*, 66:305–16.

Nolte, R. Y., and Singer, H. 1985. Active comprehension: Teaching a process of reading comprehension and its effects on reading achievement. *The Reading Teacher*, 38:24–31.

Oakhill, J., and Patel, S. 1991. Can imagery training help children who have comprehension problems? *Journal of Research in Reading*, 14:106–15.

Ogle, D. M. 1986. K-W-L: A teaching model that develops active reading of expository text. *The Reading Teacher*, 39:564–70.

Olson, J. L., and Platt, J. M. 2000. *Teaching Children and Adolescents with Special Needs* 3rd ed. Upper Saddle River, NJ: Merrill.

Palincsar, A. S., and Brown, A. L. 1986. Interactive teaching to promote independent learning from text. *The Reading Teacher*, 39:771–77.

Palincsar, A. S., and Brown, A. L. 1988. Teaching and practicing thinking skills to promote comprehension in the context of group problem-solving. *Remedial and Special Education*, 9:53–9.

Palincsar, A. S., Winn, J., David, Y., Snyder, B., and Stevens, D. 1993. Approaches to strategic reading instruction reflecting different assumptions regarding teaching and learning. In *Strategy Assessment and Instruction for Students with Learning Disabilities: From Theory to Practice*, L. J. Meltzer (Ed.), (pp. 247–70). Austin, TX: PRO-ED.

Paivio, A. 1986. *Mental Representations: A Dual Coding Approach.* New York: Oxford University Press.

Paris, S. G., Wasik, B. A., and Turner, J. C. 1991. The development of strategic readings. In *Handbook of Reading Research*, Vol II, eds. R. Barr, M. L. Kamil, P. B. Mosenthal, and P. D. Pearson (pp. 609–40). New York: Longman.

Perfetti, C. A., and Hogaboam, T. W. 1975. The relationship between single word decoding and reading comprehension skill. *Journal of Educational Psychology*, 67:461–69.

Pressley, M., Goodchild, F., Fleet, J., Zajchowski, R., and Evans, E. D. 1989. The challenges of classroom strategy instruction. *The Elementary School Journal*, 89:301–42.

Pressley, M., Symons, S., Snyder, B. L., and Cariglia-Bull, T. 1989. Strategy instruction research comes of age. *Learning Disability Quarterly*, 12:16–30.

Pressley, M., and Wharton-McDonald, R. 1997. Skilled comprehension and its development through instruction. *School Psychology Review*, 26:448–66.

Pressley, M., Wharton-McDonald, R., Hampston, J. M., and Echevarria, D. 1997. A survey of the instructional practices of grade five teachers nominated as effective in promoting literacy. *Scientific Studies of Reading*, 1:145–60.

Pressley, M., El-Dinary, P. B., and Brown, R. 1992. Skilled and not-so-skilled reading: Good information processing and not-so-good information processing. In *Promoting Academic Competence and Literacy in School*, M. Pressley, K. R. Harris, and J. T. Guthrie (Eds.), (pp. 91–127). New York: Academic Press, Inc.

Raphael, T. E. 1984. Teaching learners about sources of information for answering comprehension questions. *Journal of Reading*, 27:303–11.

Raphael, T. E. 1986. Teaching question-answer relationships revisited. *The Reading Teacher*, 39:516–23.

Rose, M. C., Cundick, B. P., and Higbee, K. L. 1983. Verbal rehearsal and visual imagery: Mnemonic aids for learning disabled children. *Journal of Learning Disabilities*, 16:352–54.

Rosenshine, B., and Meister, C. 1994. Reciprocal teaching: A review of the research. *Review of Educational Research*, 64:479–530.

Sachs, A. 1983. The effects of three prereading activities on learning disabled students' reading comprehension. *Learning Disability Quarterly*, 6:248–51.

Sadoski, M., Goetz, E. T, and Fritz, J. B. 1993. Impact of concreteness on comprehensibility, interest, and memory for text: Implications for dual coding theory and text design. *Journal of Educational Psychology*, 85:291–304.

Schunk, D. H., and Rice, J. M. 1992. Influence of reading-comprehension strategy information on children's achievement outcomes. *Learning Disability Quarterly*, 15:51–64.

Scruggs, T. E., Mastropieri, M. A., Sullivan, G. S., and Hesser, L. S. 1993. Improving reasoning and recall: The differential effects of elaborative interrogation and mnemonic elaboration. *Learning Disability Quarterly*, 16:233–40.

Simmonds, E. P. M. 1992. The effects of teacher training and implementation of two methods for improving the comprehension skills of students with learning disabilities. *Learning Disabilities Research and Practice*, 7:194–98.

Sinatra, R. C., Stahl-Gemake, J., and Berg, D. N. 1984. Improving reading comprehension of disabled readers through semantic mapping. *The Reading Teacher*, 37:22–9.

Smith, P. L., and Friend, M. 1986. Training LD adolescents in a strategy for using text structures to aid recall of instructional prose. *Learning Disabilities Research*, 2:38–44.

Stone, C. A., and Conca, L. 1993. The origin of strategy deficits in children with learning disabilities: A social constructivist perspective. In *Strategy Assessment and Instruction for Students with Learning Disabilities: From Theory to Practice*, L J. Meltzer (Ed.), (pp. 23–59). Austin, TX: PRO-ED.

Swanson, H. L. 2000. Are working memory deficits in readers with learning disabilities hard to change? *Journal of Learning Disabilities*, 33:551–66.

Swanson, H. L. 1999. Reading research for students with LD: A meta-analysis of intervention outcomes. *Journal of Learning Disabilities*, 32:504–32.

Torgesen, J. K. 1977. The role of nonspecific factors in the task performance of learning disabled children: A theoretical assessment. *Journal of Learning Disabilities*, 10:27–34.

Trabasso, T., and Magliano, J. P. 1996. How do children understand what they read and what can we do to help them? In *The First R: Every Child's Right to Read*, M. Graves, P. van den Broek, and B. Taylor (Eds.), (pp. 158–81). New York: Columbia University Teachers College Press.

Vaughn, S. and Klingner, J. K. 1999. Teaching reading comprehension through collaborative strategic reading. *Intervention in School and Clinic*, 34:284–92.

Vaughn, S., Moody, S., and Schumm, J. S. 1998. Broken promises: Reading instruction in the resource room. *Exceptional Children*, 64:211–25.

Vygotsky, L. S. 1978. *Mind in Society: The Development of Higher Psychological Processes*. Cambridge, MA: Harvard University Press.

Weisberg, R. 1988. 1980s: A change in focus of reading comprehension research: A review of reading/learning disabilities research based on an interactive model of reading. *Learning Disabilities Quarterly*, 11:149–59.

Weisberg, R., and Balajthy, E. 1990. Development of disabled readers' metacomprehension ability through summarization training using expository text: Results of three studies. *Reading, Writing, and Learning Disabilities*, 6:117–36.

Willoughby, T., Wood, E., and Khan, M. 1994. Isolating variables that impact on or detract from the effectiveness of elaborative interrogation. *Journal of Educational Psychology*, 86:279–89.

Winograd, P. 1984. Strategic differences in summarizing texts. *Reading Research Quarterly*, 19:404–25.

Woloshyn, V. E., Willoughby, T., Wood, E., and Pressley, M. 1990. Elaborative interrogation facilitates adult learning of factual paragraphs. *Journal of Educational Psychology*, 82:513–24.

Wood, E., and Hewitt, K. L. 1993. Assessing the impact of elaborative strategy instruction relative to spontaneous strategy use in high achievers. *Exceptionality*, 4:65–79.

Wood, E., Miller, G., Symons, S., Canough, T., and Yedlicka, J. 1993. Effects of elaborative interrogation on young learners' recall of facts. *The Elementary School Journal*, 94:245–54.

Wong, B. Y. L., and Jones, W. 1982. Increasing metacomprehension in learning disabled and normally-achieving students through self-questioning training. *Learning Disability Quarterly*, 5:228–40.

Ysseldyke, J. E., Thurlow, M. L., O'Sullivan, R., and Christensen, S. L. 1989. Teaching structures and tasks in reading instruction for students with mild handicaps. *Learning Disabilities Research*, 4, 78–86.

5

Vocabulary and
Reading Comprehension

GETTING STARTED

✓ How are vocabulary and reading comprehension related?
✓ How do reading difficulties affect vocabulary development?
✓ What is the difference between incidental and intentional word learning?
✓ What methods of instruction are most effective in helping struggling readers develop their word knowledge?

VOCABULARY AND COMPREHENSION OF TEXTS: A RECIPROCAL RELATION

How Are Vocabulary Knowledge and Reading Comprehension Related?

It should not be surprising that the depth and breadth of a reader's vocabulary affects his or her reading comprehension. After all, words are meaning-bearing units, and they serve as the foundation for communicating ideas and information. Comprehension of sentences involves processing of successive words and integrating their meanings to construct idea units (Just and Carpenter 1987). Understanding individual words in a passage does not necessarily mean that a reader will fully understand ideas conveyed by those words; however, not understanding a large number of words (especially those central to the ideas of the passage) will certainly make understanding the passage exceedingly difficult.

Because knowing words related to the topic of a text is likely to contribute to comprehension of that text, it is not surprising that a person's vocabulary and reading comprehension capabilities are apt to be significantly related. This is true at all grade levels and in different languages and countries around the world (e.g., Anderson and Freebody 1983). How might we explain this general relation of understanding words and understanding passages? One reason for the relation of vocabulary and reading comprehension is that both depend on an individual's language-learning abilities. Some people are simply better at learning language than others, and innate verbal ability affects both understanding words and understanding ideas conveyed in sentences and discourse. Some students with disabilities in language learning are likely to lag behind their peers in the development of their word knowledge as well as aspects of comprehension. This developmental lag affects their reading comprehension as well as their oral language comprehension.

A second factor that accounts for the relation of vocabulary and comprehension is the mutual dependence on the extensiveness of an individual's world experiences. World knowledge can be acquired first-hand (e.g., one's experiences) or second-hand (e.g., by reading). Sometimes referred to as background knowledge or prior knowledge, world knowledge provides both words and a framework with which to understand ideas and information presented through these words. Thus, a student who has experienced or read about sailing and navigation at sea is likely to know such maritime words as *anchor*, *yacht*, and *buoy*. Knowledge about boating and the words used to express this knowledge go hand-in-hand.

Word knowledge and world knowledge develop together and together influence comprehension. Even in the preschool years, the kind and amount of language in the home, the kinds of experiences the child has, and the opportunities he or she has to learn words vicariously from various sources (e.g., story book reading, dinner table talk) may influence vocabulary development, which in turn influences comprehension performance in later years (e.g., Dickinson and Tabors 2001; Hart and Risley 1995). The richness of experiences in school is also a significant influence: teachers and parents can foster the acquisition of knowledge by providing opportunities for diverse learning experiences in the classroom and in the surrounding community, including reading books to children (Dickinson, Cote, and Smith 1993).

One factor that affects the relation of vocabulary and reading comprehension is the development of the child's basic reading skills, as these provide access to ideas and information in the text. As Mezynski (1983) has suggested, poor decoding or word reading skill hinders students' learning of new words, as well as acquisition of ideas and information from written texts. Lack of adequate word-reading skills may also mean that a child with a good vocabulary cannot use this word knowledge to understand text passages that he or she is given to read. Thus, a good oral vocabulary must be accompanied by good word-reading skills for there to be a positive relation between vocabulary and comprehension. Lack of automaticity of word recognition and/or dysfluent reading, which were discussed in Chapter 3, are also bound to stand in the way of accessing words and ideas in written texts.

Vocabulary, background knowledge, and reading comprehension are likely to vary widely in any given elementary classroom, but the reasons for strengths or weaknesses in these areas may be different for different children. For example, children from low-income homes are likely to have fewer extensive experiences in the world around them, and the amount and kind of talk in the home may limit their early vocabulary development (Hart and Risley 1995; Snow, Burns, and Griffin 1998). For children in such circumstances, there is a continuing developmental lag in vocabulary knowledge, even after the children have been in school for a number of years. This lag is one reason for relatively poor performance on measures of reading comprehension (White, Graves, and Slater 1990). A second example is children with language disabilities. Their vocabulary may be different from that of their peers on school entry not because of inadequate experiences in the home but because of relative weaknesses in language-learning abilities. For them, access to ideas and information in texts is impeded because depth and breadth of vocabulary is limited and because language comprehension is compromised in other respects (Kamhi and Catts 1986). In addition, many poor readers experience weaknesses in syntactic and semantic foundations of comprehension of words and passages (e.g., McKeown 1985).

The Effects of Reading Difficulties on Vocabulary Acquisition

When students struggle with reading, the teacher cannot make any assumptions about the relation of their reading difficulties and their vocabulary development. It is imperative that information be gathered about the students' capabilities and development in all of the areas discussed thus far: the extensiveness of the student's vocabulary, background knowledge, language comprehension, and reading skills. This information can be used to develop a profile of each poor reader's strengths and weaknesses with regard to vocabulary learning (Carlisle 1993).

Most students with significant reading difficulties have particular problems acquiring word reading skills and becoming fluent readers. Of these students, some have difficulties with oral language acquisition and others do not. The students with "pure" reading disabilities are likely to learn vocabulary effectively through listening, but not through reading. Because of their problems with accuracy and fluency of word reading, they are likely to read books that are below grade level and are therefore not likely to contain new words or new meanings for familiar words. Thus, the opportunities to learn words by reading are very limited. In addition, they often dislike reading and lack the motivation to read as much as their peers do (Juel 1988). When they do read, they may also engage less actively in constructing meaning from the text (Paris, Wasik, and Turner 1991).

The relation of vocabulary and reading achievement is one of reciprocal causation (Stanovich 1986). That is, the children with better word knowledge usually learn to read more easily than their peers, and once they acquire basic reading skills, the reading that they do fosters further development of their vocabulary. In contrast, poor readers may not have significant problems with vocabulary learning when they enter school, but their reading problems lead to slower vocabulary development over time.

As noted earlier, students with relatively low verbal ability or with language-learning disabilities make slower progress than their peers for reasons that are not simply due to their reading difficulties. The breadth and depth of their word knowledge is affected by difficulties with semantic and conceptual aspects of word learning. Students with limited word knowledge, relative to their peers, also have less precise knowledge about words (Curtis 1987; McKeown 1985). For example, Curtis (1987) found that students who have earned low scores on vocabulary tests tend to define words in terms of the contexts in which they have heard them used. They lack a more general understanding of the word. In contrast, students who earned high scores on vocabulary tests were able to give more abstract definitions, showing that they understood the central features of the word's meaning. By way of an example, she reported that college students generally picked the correct meaning of *surveillance* from a set of options on a multiple-choice test. However, if they were asked to define the word, high vocabulary students gave a synonym (e.g., "watch"), whereas low vocabulary students described the context in which the word was used (e.g., "surveillance is what the police do in crime situations").

Simmons and Kame'enui (1990) found that students with learning disabilities (LD) followed this pattern. They gave 10- and 12-year-old students with LD and normally developing peers a task that involved defining words. The students with LD were less able to define words than were their normally achieving peers. Thereafter, the students were given an identification task for any definition item where their response was inaccurate or incomplete. The students with LD often showed recognition of the meanings of words they could not define. Simmons and Kame'enui did not sort their students into groups with specific reading disabilities or broader language-learning disabilities. Still, such a practice might help a teacher determine whether a particular student who is weak in reading skills is likely to learn vocabulary with relative ease from oral contexts or whether he or she will need language instruction to develop the semantic and conceptual foundations of word learning.

One study that did focus on verbal ability as a way to estimate the potential for vocabulary learning was carried out by Fawcett and Nicolson (1991). These researchers separated adolescents with dyslexia into two groups (high and low verbal ability) and then provided a summer program in vocabulary instruction. This program was carried out at home, involving interactive lessons with their parents; word learning, therefore, was through oral language usage, not reading. The results showed that the students with stronger verbal ability made much greater progress than did the students with weaker verbal ability. These results should be a reminder to teachers that not all students with reading disabilities have deficits in word learning. However, students with good verbal ability but significant problems with reading accuracy and fluency are likely to acquire vocabulary much more readily from oral language contexts, such as discussions in content area courses, than from reading.

Incidental Word Learning

During the school years (kindergarten through 12th grade), on average students learn about 3,000 words each year. This means that students with better language-learning abilities and more experience with language may be learning 5,000 words a year, whereas students with language learning problems may learn as few as 1,000 words a year (Beck and McKeown 1991). Where do the students learn all these words? Relatively few of these words are learned through direct instruction of vocabulary in school (Beck and McKeown 1991; Nagy and

Herman 1987). It is estimated that no more than about 300 words are learned through vocabulary lessons in a given year. For example, if a teacher required students to learn 20 words a week for 30 weeks, the students would have worked on 600 words. Of these 600, perhaps half will be retained in memory some time after the weekly vocabulary quiz. Obviously, 300 words is a very small portion of the number of words students learn in a year. Most of the words they learn are encountered in their daily lives; the learning process is called incidental word learning.

Learning words by listening and speaking is an incremental process. Students may learn a little about a word from inferring its meaning in a particular context, but it may take numerous other encounters with that same word to develop a full understanding of what it means and how it is used. For example, in a discussion of resources from the sea in one fourth-grade class, the teacher told the students that seaweed was used to feed to livestock. Most of the children did not know the word *livestock*, but they could tell that it referred to something alive. They might guess that it referred to domesticated animals (pets or farm animals), because it is in these contexts that people feed animals.

When will the students acquire a more complete understanding of this word? Right away, if someone asks the teacher to explain the word. If this does not happen, further learning will not occur until the word is encountered again, and who knows when that might be for these fourth graders. Given the incremental nature of word learning, we appreciate an important point about word learning: "knowing" a word is not like knowing the dictionary definition. Knowing a word may fall anywhere along a continuum of depth of knowledge. At one end is a simple association (e.g., knowing that insulation has something to do with houses). Toward the middle may be knowledge of a specific meaning (e.g., knowing that insulation keeps heat in a house in winter). At the other end of the range is understanding various meanings of a word, understanding fine-grained distinctions concerning how a word is used, and/or understanding figurative uses (e.g., knowing that insulate can mean setting oneself apart from others or from a situation).

Context matters in incidental word learning. The richness of the oral discourse in the classroom affects the opportunities to learn new words. The teacher's use of words and interest in talking about words may affect the depth of their understanding. This is true for reading as well. The extensiveness of reading experience and the presence of some (but not too many) unfamiliar words in reading materials affects students' word learning while reading. Some researchers have argued that most of the incidental word learning that students do after about the fourth grade is through reading (Fielding, Wilson, and Anderson 1984; Nagy and Herman 1987). There is evidence, however, that students make significant improvements in word knowledge through units of instruction in content-area courses such as science (Carlisle, Fleming, and Gudbrandsen 2000).

Studies of word learning through reading have shown that even with just one reading of a passage, students are likely to have inferred the meanings of some words, with varying levels of precision, from one or more encounters with them. Several factors influence incidental word learning through reading. One of these is the number of times a word is repeated in the passage (Jenkins, Stein, and Wysocki 1984). The second is the nature of "clues" to the word's meaning that are present in the surrounding text (Nagy, Herman, and Anderson 1985). For example, in the following sentence, there are clues to the meaning of *hatchet* to provide the basis for a reasonable guess that this is a tool for cutting wood: "Father wanted to trim some dead branches from the tree in front of our house, so he sent me to the garage to find the hatchet." A third factor is the degree of unfamiliarity of the word itself and the other words in the passage. Schatz and Baldwin (1986) found that unusual or uncommon words in naturally occurring texts may not be learned through incidental exposure to them. A fourth factor is the word-reasoning abilities of the student, as we have discussed. Some students are more adept at identifying helpful clues to the meaning of an unknown word than others. In short, the more a person knows about words, the more he or she is likely to learn about unfamiliar words during reading.

Poor readers have been found to learn fewer words from reading than good readers (Jenkins, Stein, and Wysocki 1984). As noted earlier, struggling readers tend to read easier books and fewer books than their peers, and they care less about reading, so that the incentive to learn from reading is relatively low. In fact, for both good and poor readers, the level of difficulty of the text is an issue. If students read books that are moderately challenging, they have a better opportunity to learn new words than if they read books that are easy for them (Carver 1994). On the other hand, if the text contains too many unfamiliar words and concepts, word learning will be very difficult. This is in part because useful clues to a word's meaning will be hard to come by. The same principle pertains to learning from oral contexts. Students ordinarily learn some words through listening to their teachers and classmates and taking part in interactive discussions that involve using words they are becoming more familiar with. However, students whose previous knowledge of a given topic is limited, relative to that expected by the teacher, are likely to be overwhelmed by the many unfamiliar words that are used to discuss the topic. For students who are struggling readers or whose vocabulary development lags behind their peers, incidental word learning is a slow and challenging process in both oral and written language contexts (see Carlisle, Fleming, and Gudbrandsen 2000).

APPROACHES TO INSTRUCTION

Thus far, the discussion of word learning has emphasized the importance of incidental word learning as it relates to vocabulary growth and achievement in reading comprehension. In schools, however, word learning is not left to chance. For this reason, we need to concern ourselves with intentional as well as incidental word learning. Because of its importance for comprehension, experts in reading recommend some form of vocabulary instruction. Furthermore, it is generally recognized that learning vocabulary is a crucial part of content-area learning in science and other domains. However, even though there are many studies of methods of vocabulary instruction that have yielded significant improvements (NRP Report 2000), teachers are understandably uncertain about the best way or ways to go about fostering vocabulary development among their students, with a particular eye toward optimal long-term benefits. For the short term, teachers can ask students to learn words that are important to the topic under study. For the long term, teachers want to instill curiosity about words and good word-learning habits in their students—habits that include being attentive to unfamiliar words and trying to understand familiar words used in new ways in different contexts, whether these are academic and non-academic. As McKeown and Beck have noted, "because instruction cannot cover all words that students need to know, and because some people are much less efficient word learners than others, it is important to encourage independent word learning" (1988, p. 44).

What do students need to learn? Graves (2000) has pointed out that students need a variety of skills to support their word learning. These include methods of learning words while reading, such as context analysis, which refers to using clues from a passage to infer the meaning of unfamiliar words, and structural analysis, which refers to using word parts to infer the meanings of words. We will say more about these strategies shortly. In addition, students need to learn how to use the dictionary and thesaurus. As surprising as it may seem, these resources often do not yield helpful information to students because of the complexity of the wording of definitions (Scott and Nagy 1997). Dictionary entries tend to be most useful to people who already have a good sense of the meaning of the word they are looking up! Finally, students need to realize that there are different ways to learn words and to deal with unknown words they encounter during reading. Teachers can help them become aware of the benefits of putting effort into this aspect of their school work.

How can teachers help students with these general aspects of word learning? Teachers would do well to provide explanations of word-learning strategies, procedures for using these strategies, and opportunities to practice using them. They should also consider teaching a variety of word-learning strategies that are appropriate in their content area. In addition, as Graves (2000) pointed out, much can be achieved if the teacher models the attitudes and skills he or she hopes students will learn—for example, expressing curiosity about words, turning to the dictionary to check the meanings of words, and introducing word games.

What particular methods do researchers recommend, particularly for students with reading difficulties? We present different methods grouped in the following way: (a) reading or listening to books, (b) intentional learning of contextual-analysis strategies, (c) discussion of words drawn from reading materials, (d) associative memory techniques, (e) structural analysis (learning to use word part clues), and (f) computer-based programs.

Reading and Listening to Books

There are several studies that have shown that young students learn words by listening to books read aloud. Kindergarten children have been found to learn words from stories that their teachers read to them three times (Eller, Pappas, and Brown 1988). Stahl, Richek, and Vandevier (1991) also documented growth in word knowledge when sixth graders listened to stories their teachers read to them.

A number of experts in reading (e.g., Fielding, Wilson, and Anderson 1984; Nagy, Herman, and Anderson 1985) have argued that the best way to learn words is to read. In keeping with the earlier discussion of incidental word learning, the more reading students do, the more they have opportunities to learn words or to increase their understanding of words they know at some level. In discussing the benefits of free reading, Fielding, Wilson, and Anderson (1984) acknowledged that oral language experience is the main source of new words learned by young children. "However, there is reason to believe that beginning in about the third grade, reading becomes a more important source of vocabulary growth than oral language for most people" (p. 152). In part, this is because school textbooks that are intended to increase students' knowledge also contain numerous unfamiliar words, words that students must learn in order to acquire that content knowledge. With independent reading in mind, these researchers also argued for the life-long benefits of pleasure reading.

As we discussed in the chapter on fluency (Chapter 3), teachers have taken this advice to heart and introduced programs like SSR (Sustained Silent Reading) or DEAR (Drop Everything And Read). There are also "book wars" in many schools, which provide an incentive for students to read lots of books. These are motivating methods to get children reading, and there is evidence that the amount of reading children do is related to their growth in their vocabulary and comprehension capabilities (Anderson, Wilson, and Fielding 1988; Greaney 1980).

Nonetheless, if free reading is considered by schools to be a way that teachers can foster vocabulary growth, two potential problems need to be addressed. One is that not all the books students choose to read on their own are difficult enough to introduce them to new words (Carver 1994). On the other hand, students with poor reading skills may select reading materials that are too difficult for them in an effort to keep up with their peers. An important rule of thumb for guiding students toward books at an appropriate level of difficulty is that there should be no more than 5 words in 100 that are hard for a given student to read. The second problem is that the students who particularly need to develop their vocabulary are those with reading and language-learning problems, and these are the students who do not and will not read much on their own. As a result, although independent reading is very valuable, it should not be the only method teachers use to foster development of vocabulary.

Inferring Meanings From Context

Because incidental word learning is the way most words are learned, efforts have been made to find ways to teach students how to infer the meanings of words from context. Kuhn and Stahl (1998) reviewed fourteen studies designed to teach students to infer meanings from context. Typically, in these studies students have been taught a step-wise process to use and types of context clues to look for. Then they are given practice using the process and identifying context clues that are available. The steps in the process vary in different studies (Buikema and Graves 1993; Herman and Dole 1988; Jenkins, Matlock, and Slocum 1989; White, Sowell, and Yanagihara 1989), but they often include the following:

- ✓ Write the unknown word
- ✓ Look for passage clues
- ✓ Write the passage clues below the word
- ✓ Think about what the word might mean, based on the clues
- ✓ Try this meaning in the passage to see if it makes sense
- ✓ If it does, move on to see if there are helpful clues later in the passage. If it does not make sense, revise your guess about the meaning of the word.

The types of context clues that should be taught are a matter of debate. Sternberg, Powell, and Kaye (1983) have recommended teaching a number of different types of clues (e.g., temporal, spatial). However, Carnine, Kame'enui, and Coyle (1984) found that students with learning disabilities could take advantage of only a few of these, the most useful one being synonyms. One limitation of this study (as is true of others as well) is that the period devoted to teaching context clues and helping students use them was very short. Other researchers have suggested that many students need extensive discussion and guided practice if they are going to learn to use context clues effectively on their own (Patberg, Graves, and Stibbe 1984).

Students must use their semantic and conceptual knowledge to infer meanings of words from context (whether oral or written language is involved). Not surprisingly, therefore, younger students and students with limited language or cognitive capabilities will have difficulty learning new words by this method. This includes students with language-learning disabilities. The presence of limitations in cognitive or linguistic development does not necessarily mean that teachers should avoid instruction in using context clues to learn new words. In fact, such instruction may help students compensate for their native difficulties with incidental word learning. Nonetheless, the plan for instruction should be carefully thought out. The amount of guided practice that is provided, as well as the number and types of clues the students are given to work with, should be adjusted so that the student benefits from the use of inferential methods.

Discussion of Vocabulary Drawn From Reading Materials

Although only a small number of words are learned through direct instruction in the classroom, there are benefits to learning words that are used to discuss a specific topic. One advantage is accessing and sharing prior knowledge about a topic, and in doing so linking the topical words to the students' awareness of appropriate knowledge about the topic. For example, preteaching vocabulary from stories they were about to read was found to enhance fifth graders' comprehension of stories (Wixson 1986). Although no one method has been singled out as the best method (Beck and McKeown 1991), researchers have studied effective programs of vocabulary instruction to determine how they differ from less effective programs. Stahl and Fairbanks (1986) found that effective methods involved both definitional and contextual sources of information. Thus, effective learning took place when students studied definitions for words but also studied words in natural sentences or passages so that they could see how the words were used.

McKeown and Beck (1988) and Mezynski (1983) identified three characteristics of vocabulary instructional programs that had a significant impact on reading comprehension. These are (a) breadth of training, (b) repeated exposures to words, and (c) active processing of information about the meanings of words. In McKeown and Beck's studies, breadth of instruction was termed "rich" instruction, as it entailed using a variety of activities. These might include relating meanings of words in their uses in particular contexts or comparing words with similar meanings. Students were encouraged to extend the use of words outside the classroom. Working on words over time (including at home) was particularly important for lower-achieving students who tended to have difficulty learning words on their own.

McKeown and Beck recommended guidelines for selecting words from reading materials, such as literature or textbooks. They suggested previewing texts in order to select words that are central to the ideas of the readings and also "interesting and generally useful." Words of "general high utility" might be words like *unique* and *gregarious*, as opposed to words like *divertimento* or *nebula*. The teacher also needs to decide whether the words might be introduced in a "narrow" or a "rich" way. This is done by taking into account what else needs to be done to prepare the students for the unit, and what other instructional activities are planned. It is important to realize that not all words require a "rich" knowledge for purposes of a given unit. If the Greek myth focused on Arachne and her weaving ability, words like *loom* and *spindle* might be taught in a narrow way, on the assumption that middle-school students would not need a deep knowledge of weaving to understand the myth or to understand other Greek myths they would be reading. In short, decisions about the instructional program must take into account a variety of factors associated with the goals and materials of the curriculum.

The method recommended by these researchers has been found to be effective for low-achieving students. One important aspect is the introduction of words for discussion before the passage is read by the group. Another is the follow-up activities that provide an opportunity for students to built lasting memories of the meanings of words as they are used in a particular context. For example, McKeown and Beck mentioned challenging students to find uses of taught words outside of class. They also suggested activities like "stump the class," where children bring to class words they think no one will know. The children then teach these words to their classmates (with some teacher assistance). Such activities stimulate students' interest in words and word knowledge. They also may enrich the verbal environment for children at home as well as at school.

In content area courses, students may learn vocabulary effectively by participating in interactive discussions that focus on the important terms used in a given unit of study. Although these are discussed in Chapter 9, we give a brief overview of interactive discussion as a word-learning strategy here. Bos and Anders (1990) compared three interactive strategies (e.g., semantic mapping, semantic feature analysis, and semantic/syntactic feature analysis) with definition instruction as methods for junior high students with LD to learn vocabulary that was found in a chapter about fossils in their science textbook. The definition instruction involved directly teaching the meanings of terms and carrying out such follow-up activities as oral recitation and memorization. The interactive strategies involved discussion in which the teacher and students activated prior knowledge and predicted relations among the terms. For semantic mapping, the group constructed a hierarchical relationship map, whereas for semantic feature analysis the teacher and students predicted relations among concepts using a relationship matrix. An example of a matrix for semantic feature analysis, developed by Nagy (1988), is given in figure 5.1. Notice that it provides a way to distinguish similar terms, based on their semantic features. For instance, a shed and a shack are both crude structures; however, a shed is used for storage, whereas a shack is inhabited by people.

The results of this study showed that interactive discussions and activities produced better vocabulary learning and higher scores on comprehension measures for students with LD than did learning definitions. The researchers suggested that interactive learning strategies focused students' attention on the passage context and on the relations among concepts and words in the unit of study. Similarly, sharing ideas and activating prior knowledge are benefits of these methods. Methods such as rich, elaborated vocabulary instruction can facilitate reading comprehension for students with LD.

Discussion of unfamiliar words has been found to be an effective way of learning vocabulary. Researchers have found that when teachers presented unfamiliar words in context and asked students to offer possible meanings, the ensuing

	for people	for animals	for storage	big/fancy	small	crude/rough	permanent	portable
house	+	−	~	○	○	○	+	−
shack	+	−	−	−	+	+	?	−
shed	−	−	+	−	+	+	?	−
barn	−	+	○	−	−	○	+	−
tent	+	−	~	−	○	○	−	+
mansion	+	−	~	+	−	−	+	−
. . .								

Figure 5.1   Matrix for a semantic feature analysis. The marks in the cells are arrived at through class discussion. From Nagy, W. E. 1988. Teaching vocabulary to improve reading comprehension (p. 15). Newark, DE: International Reading Association. Reprinted with permission of William E. Nagy and the International Reading Association. All rights reserved.

discussion led to significant improvement of their understanding of the words (Jenkins, Matlock, and Slocum 1989). Discussion of vocabulary can be carried out in literature discussion groups. In a study carried out by Fisher, Blachowicz, and Smith (1991), fourth-grade students in mixed ability reading groups worked cooperatively in groups of four. Each group member had a role with specific responsibilities for each day; these roles were discussion director, vocabulary researcher, literary luminary, and secretary-checker. The four roles rotated each day. The vocabulary researcher selected five or six words from the chapter of the book they were reading to teach the group members. Along with identifying appropriate meanings for the words, the vocabulary researcher led a discussion about the words and asked students to derive meanings from context. The vocabulary researcher would confirm their predictions or give a better meaning. The fourth graders' performance on a vocabulary test showed that they had made noticeable gains in their understanding of the words they discussed in their groups. A method such as this one may help students take an interest in words and understand the value of studying unfamiliar words in texts they read. Although mixed-ability groups were formed in this study, it is not clear whether struggling readers or students with LD actually benefited from group discussion of words.

Another discussion method was explored in a study by Stahl and Kapinus (1991). Fifth graders were given difficult words that were in the passage they were about to read. The teacher provided a short definition of each word. Students were then asked to think of "possible sentences" containing the words that might be in the passage they were about to read. These were written on the blackboard. When students finished contributing possible sentences, they read the chapter or passage. The class then discussed the possible sentences, determining whether they were true or not. "Untrue" sentences were modified. In this study, the technique of Possible Sentences was compared to semantic mapping; in comparison to pretest performance, the Possible Sentences group showed stronger learning of target vocabulary than the semantic mapping group. The technique appeared to help students access prior knowledge and share knowledge and experiences with each other. Furthermore, it might foster students' ability to consider the meanings of words as they are used in different contexts. This method holds promise for students who struggle with reading and language-learning, but further study is needed.

Associative Memory Methods

Another method recommended for use with students with reading or LD in content-area courses is the mnemonic method, and most commonly among this family of methods, the key word method. The mnemonic method provides specific assistance in the recall of information; it is thought to be appropriate for students with LD because they are likely to have difficulties committing information to memory (Scruggs and Mastropieri 1990). The keyword method has been used in different content areas and with various types of words, such as scientific root words or learning the accomplishments of important people, where the students have to learn to associate a word with its meaning or a word with another word.

Vocabulary learning via the keyword method links an acoustic cue to a pictorial representation associated with the meaning. The association need not make a lot of sense; in fact, the novelty of the link may be a central feature of its memorability. The keyword is a word that is acoustically similar to the target word. For example, in one study 6th, 7th and 8th graders with LD, training in mnemonic learning involved word parts and dinosaur names (Veit, Scruggs, and Mastropieri, 1986). The researchers compared the mnemonic condition and a comparison condition. An example of the mnemonic condition involves learning the word part *ornith* (as in the word ornithology, which is the study of birds). To learn the word part *ornith*, the student was given a picture of a bird with an oar over its shoulder. The bird stands for *ornith*, and the oar is the associated keyword. When the student is asked to define *ornith*, he or she presumably would recall the oar over the bird's shoulder and in this way retrieve the first sound of the word and its associated meaning. For the comparison condition, the student was given a picture of a bird only (that is, without the keyword) and presumably would learn bird as a definition for *ornith* by association.

The keyword method has been linked to better recall and better comprehension for students with LD in a large number of studies, most typically in comparison to a control condition that employed direct instruction (Scruggs and Mastropieri 1990; Veit, Scruggs, and Mastropieri 1986). Furthermore, students with LD trained in the keyword method to learn English vocabulary showed better transfer of the learning strategy to another type of word (Italian words) than students trained to use directed rehearsal (McLoone et al. 1986). Other mnemonic methods are also thought to be effective for students with learning or reading disabilities. One of these is the "peg word" method, which involves the use of rhyming words to facilitate the recall of numbered or ordered information (e.g., the first ten amendments to the Constitution).

Some critics have expressed the concern that students using mnemonic methods may learn, but not truly understand the information. On the contrary, Mastropieri, Scruggs and Fulk (1990) have suggested that mnemonic instruction may facilitate, rather than inhibit, comprehension. A different concern surfaced in a study by Pfeiffer (1999), who found that the keyword method, as compared to pairing words with meanings linked to associated background information, works well if the students are given the word and asked to come up with the definition, but not if the students are given the definition and asked to recall the word. This may be because the definition does not trigger recall of the acoustically similar keyword. Understandably, there are also concerns about the time-consuming process of developing the materials for use with mnemonic methods The teachers need to select the words to be learned, invent the keywords, and so on. Although the mnemonic method has been used with middle-school and junior-high students in content-area courses, it is likely to be less effective with younger students.

Using Word Part Clues

Along with analysis of the passage context to infer word meanings, students can be taught to infer meanings from analysis of meaning-bearing parts of words.

These include prefixes, base or root words, and suffixes. Learning to analyze word parts may be very important as students move into the middle school years. Nagy et al. (1989) have estimated that about 60% of the unfamiliar words middle school students encounter in the books they read are morphologically complex words with relatively transparent structure and meaning, such as *replacement* or *undamaged*. Awareness of the structure of complex words is likely to pay off in terms of both vocabulary development and reading comprehension (e.g., White, Power, and White 1989).

Some studies have shown that deriving word meanings from morphological analysis is only partially successful in getting the student close to knowing the full meaning of a word (Wysocki and Jenkins 1987). Students (particularly those who are younger or less able readers) may focus particularly on the base word, neglecting analysis of the syntactic and semantic aspects of some suffixes. For example, students may indicate that they understand the word *talkativeness*, but their sense of knowing this word may derive entirely from their familiarity with the word *talk*. Their neglect of the two suffixes that follow the base word becomes apparent when they are asked to use the word in a sentence and produce such sentences as "My cousin was talkativeness, and she spent all her time on the telephone."

Nagy and Herman (1987) have emphasized the value of combining analysis of word structure and context to determine the meanings of unfamiliar words during reading. A student who devotes some attention to analyzing the words' parts in relation to the whole might be able to come to an understanding of the possible meaning of the word. Then, examination of context clues can often provide a way to check the estimated meaning of the word. For example, consider the sentence: "With *readjustment* of its legs, the stool was once again at the right height." Analysis of the parts of *readjustment* would yield the probable meaning of "state of changing again," and clues in the sentence (e.g., "once again") provide some confirmation that the outcome of the structural analysis process was helpful in understanding the word.

Henry (1988, 1999) has studied a program of instruction that includes a focus on structural analysis and word etymology. This first part of this program involved teaching words of Anglo-Saxon origin, because the base word is usually a free-standing word form that students may recognize (e.g., *helpless* or *unavoidable*). Next, Latinate prefixes, suffixes, and root words are taught; root words are usually not free-standing (e.g., *duc* means to lead and is found in such words as *induce* and *reduce*). Finally, students learn Greek roots and compounds (e.g., *microphone*). Henry's research has indicated that students with and without learning disabilities make significant improvements in word learning, as well as in word reading and spelling skill.

Computer Programs

Computer programs have been developed primarily as a way to increase instructional time without placing greater demands on the time teachers need to spend working on vocabulary (Johnson, Gersten, and Carnine 1987). Other advantages of computer-aided instruction include the opportunity to individualize the content, to self-pace the lesson, to provide immediate feedback for the students, and to give a wealth of opportunities for repetition and practice. Proponents of computer-aided instruction have also argued that computers are motivating for students with LD.

"Drill and practice" software programs appear to be the most widely used methods of computer-based vocabulary learning. In adopting such methods, teachers should consider the characteristics of effective vocabulary programs discussed above in relation to the computer-aided instruction. For example, through selection menus, the teacher can control the particular words to be learned (and the number in a given set). In addition, the amount and type of practice may need to be monitored even though students work on their own. Providing "extra reviews," for instance, has been found to lead to quicker recall and better transfer to passage comprehension (Johnson, Gersten, and Carnine 1987). Software programs for vocabulary development have often been used with high school students. The ability to work independently over a period of time on abstract tasks may be an important prerequisite for selecting students who would benefit from computer-aided instruction in vocabulary.

A recent development is using synthesized speech to present the words for learning to students with LD. In one case study report, sixth-grade students with LD made greater gains in vocabulary when synthesized or digitized speech was a component of the software program than when it was not (Hebert and Murdoch 1994). The speech component may have been effective because students could hear the words they were learning and thereby develop an understanding of the relationship of the pronunciation and the spelling. In addition, hearing the words may have made them aware that they had some previous knowledge of them. That is, the words were in their oral "recognition" vocabulary, even if they were not recognized in print.

Some research projects with students with reading problems have focused on presentation of passages for reading on the computer screen (Reinking and Rickman 1990). In one such study, sixth graders read passages either in print form (with a dictionary or glossary they could use) or on a computer (with either mandatory or optional assistance with the meanings of unfamiliar words). The students who read the passages on the computer with mandatory assistance scored significantly higher on a vocabulary test that measured knowledge of target words. Whether this method would assist students with reading disabilities is not known. However, the authors suggested that their results support further exploration of the use of computer-mediated texts to develop reading comprehension capabilities.

COMMONLY ASKED QUESTIONS

How do teachers go about selecting a method or methods of vocabulary instruction?

Teachers are advised to pick methods of vocabulary development that are appropriate for the students' abilities and needs, as well as the goals of instruction and the difficulty of the materials. In addition, methods for learning vocabulary should be selected on the basis of their suitability to task and content-area requirements. When teaching diverse groups of students in content areas, for example, a fifth-grade social studies teacher might use pre-reading vocabulary study with the text but also the keyword method to learn specific terms. On the other hand, a fifth-grade reading and language arts teacher might use group selection and discussion of key words when students are in the literature discussion groups and follow up with dictionary skills in language arts. There is further discussion of appropriate instructional methods to ensure comprehension of content-area textbooks in Chapter 9. In a resource room or clinical setting, a teacher has more opportunity to design a program of vocabulary instruction to suit the needs of a given student. Such a setting may be particularly beneficial for students who need to develop conceptual and semantic foundations for word learning (Oetting, Rice, and Swank 1995).

Use of a variety of methods to teach vocabulary is supported by research, and as we pointed out earlier, no one method is ideal for every situation in which students might be expected to expand their vocabulary. Stahl and Fairbanks (1986) recommend a combination of direct instruction, discussion, and elaboration activities. Direct instruction appears to be particularly important for students who are poor at reading and/or language learning. By direct instruction, we mean being explicit with students: telling them what they will be learning and why, telling them how to learn the material, modeling the learning process, and providing practice and explanation for problems that crop up over time. In addition, as we pointed out earlier, we need to make sure poor readers have the access strategies they need to learn words and ideas from texts (Mezynski 1983). Regular and special education teachers should work together to make sure that poor readers continue to develop the decoding strategies they need to identify unfamiliar words in texts. If the students cannot read the words, it is unlikely that they will learn or remember their meanings.

How can teachers use independent reading to foster vocabulary development?

If independent reading is included as a natural way to foster vocabulary development, teachers should keep several points in mind. First, the books students read should be interesting to them and moderately challenging for them. These conditions ensure opportunities for students to increase the depth and breadth of their word knowledge. Second, poor readers may need support in order to benefit from independent reading. They are likely to benefit from reading books aloud with a peer or an adult, repeated readings, and other techniques that improve fluency and may also foster word learning. Discussion of literature (or content-area passages) may also foster vocabulary development, particularly if students are encouraged to talk about the words in the text (see Fisher, Blachowicz, and Smith 1991).

Independent reading can best be regarded as one of a number of different methods teachers use to foster the development of students' vocabulary. Although it should not be the sole method used, it is crucial that students get as much reading experience as possible. To some extent, all of us learn to read by reading—and this particularly pertains to vocabulary development during reading (Cunningham and Stanovich 1991).

How do teachers coordinate vocabulary development across the curriculum?

It is important for teachers to consider vocabulary development across the curriculum. In this way, it is possible to plan to meet different instructional goals in different settings. For example, if the language arts teacher is intending to work on dictionary skills, other content-area teachers can have the student make use of these skills for purposes of reinforcement and improving their word learning in different domains. Teachers might use team meetings of grade-level curriculum committees to coordinate the goals and methods of vocabulary instruction within a school.

Teachers who work with middle-school students with language-learning disabilities might need to determine whether the students are "overloaded" in terms of the number of words they are expected to learn for their different content area courses each week. Requiring students to learn too many words, particularly if they are unrelated to one another, may be counter-productive, as it may overload their capacities for comprehension and recall.

What tips do researchers give teachers?

Numerous researchers have offered suggestions concerning characteristics of effective instruction in vocabulary (Johnson and Pearson 1984; McKeown and Beck 1988; Nagy 1988; Stahl 1986). These pertain to all students, including those with reading and language-learning problems (Carlisle 1993). To summarize these, effective instruction

✓ Provides exposure to different meanings of words
✓ Provides illustrations of word usage in natural contexts
✓ Builds conceptual and semantic foundations for word knowledge
✓ Builds understanding of links among members of word families
✓ Assists efforts to derive meanings from context
✓ Provides ways to remember word meanings
✓ Integrates new information with prior knowledge
✓ Facilitates opportunities for meaningful use

REFERENCES

Anderson, R. C., and Freebody, P. 1983. Vocabulary knowledge. In *Theoretical Models and Processes of Reading*, 3rd ed, H. Singer and R. B. Ruddell (Eds.), (pp. 343–71). Newark, DE: International Reading Association.

Anderson, R. C., Wilson, P. T., and Fielding, L. G. 1988. Growth in reading and how children spend their time outside of school. *Reading Research Quarterly*, 23:285–303.

Beck, I. L., and McKeown, M. G. 1991. Conditions of vocabulary acquisition. In *Handbook of Reading Research*, Vol 2. R. Barr, M. L. Kamil, P. B. Mosenthal, and P. D. Pearson (Eds.), (pp. 789–814). New York: Longman.

Bos, C. S., and Anders, P. L. 1990. Effects of interactive vocabulary instruction on the vocabulary learning and reading comprehension of junior-high learning disabled students. *Learning Disability Quarterly*, 13:31–42.

Buikema, J. L., and Graves, M. L. 1993. Teaching students to use context clues to infer word meanings. *Journal of Reading*, 36:450–57.

Carlisle, J. F. 1993. Selecting approaches to vocabulary instruction for the reading disabled. *Learning Disabilities Research and Practice*, 8:97–105.

Carlisle, J. F., Fleming, J. E., and Gudbrandsen, B. 2000. Incidental word learning in science classes. *Contemporary Educational Psychology*, 25:184–211.

Carnine, D., Kame'enui, E. J., and Coyle, G. 1984. Utilization of contextual information determining the meaning of unfamiliar words. *Reading Research Quarterly*, 19:188–204.

Carver, R. 1994. Percentage of unknown vocabulary words in text as a function of the relative difficulty of the texts: Implications for instruction. *Journal of Reading Behavior*, 26:413–38.

Cunningham, A. E., and Stanovich, K. E. 1991. Tracking the unique effects of print exposure in children: Associations with vocabulary, general knowledge, and spelling. *Journal of Educational Psychology*, 83:264–74.

Curtis, M. E. 1987. Vocabulary testing and instruction. In *The Nature of Vocabulary Acquisition*, M. G. McKeown and M. E. Curtis (Eds.), (pp. 37–51). Hillsdale, NJ: Lawrence Erlbaum.

Dickinson, D. K., Cote, L., and Smith, M. W. 1993. Learning vocabulary in preschool: Social and discourse contexts affecting vocabulary growth. In *The Development of Literacy Through Social Interaction*, C. Daiute (Ed.), (pp. 67–78). San Francisco: Josey-Bass Publishers.

Dickinson, D. K., and Tabors, P. O. 2001. *Beginning Literacy with Language: Young Children Learning at Home and School*. Baltimore: Brookes Publishing Company.

Eller, R. G., Pappas, C. C., and Brown, E. 1988. The lexical development of kindergartners: Learning from written context. *Journal of Reading Behavior*, 20:5–24.

Fawcett, A. J., and Nicolson, R. I. 1991. Vocabulary training for children with dyslexia. *Journal of Learning Disabilities*, 24:379–83.

Fielding, L. G., Wilson, P. T., and Anderson, R. C. 1984. A new focus on free reading: The role of trade books in reading instruction. In *The Contexts of School-Based Literacy*, T. E. Raphael and R. E. Reynolds (Eds.), (pp. 149–62). New York: Random House.

Fisher, P. J. K., Blachowicz, C. L. Z., and Smith, J. C. 1991. Vocabulary learning in literature discussion groups. In *Learner Factors/Teacher Factors: Issues in Literacy Research and Instruction*, J. Zutell, S. McCormick, L. L. A. Caton, and P. O'Keefe (Eds.), (pp. 201–09). Chicago: National Reading Conference.

Graves, M. F. 2000. A vocabulary program to complement and bolster a middle-grade comprehension program. In *Reading for Meaning: Fostering Comprehension in the Middle Grades*, B. M. Taylor, M. F. Graves, and P. van den Broek (Eds.), (pp. 116–35). Newark, DE: International Reading Association.

Greaney, V. 1980. Factors related to amount and type of leisure time reading. *Reading Research Quarterly*, 15:337–57.

Hart, B., and Risley, T. R. 1995. *Meaningful differences in the everyday experiences of young American children*. Baltimore: Paul H. Brookes.

Hebert, B. M., and Murdoch, J. 1994. Comparing three computer-aided instruction output modes to teach vocabulary to students with learning disabilities. *Learning Disabilities Research and Practice*, 9:136–41.

Henry, M. K. 1988. Beyond phonics: Integrated decoding and spelling instruction based on word origin and structure. *Annals of Dyslexia*, 38:258–75.

Henry, M. K. 1999. A short history of the English language. In *Multisensory Teaching of Basic Language Skills*, J. R. Birsh (Ed.), (pp. 119–39). Baltimore: Paul H. Brookes.

Herman, P. A., and Dole, J. A. 1988. Theory and practice in vocabulary learning and instruction. *Elementary School Journal*, 89:43–54.

Jenkins, J. R., Matlock, B., and Slocum, T. A. 1989. Two approaches to vocabulary instruction: The teaching of individual word meanings and practice deriving word meaning from context. *Reading Research Quarterly*, 24:215–35.

Jenkins, J. R., Stein, M. L., and Wysocki, K. 1984. Learning vocabulary through reading. *American Educational Research Journal*, 21:767–87.

Johnson, D., and Pearson, P. D. 1984. *Learning Vocabulary through Reading*, 2nd ed. New York: Holt, Rinehart and Winston.

Johnson, G., Gersten, R., and Carnine, D. 1987. Effects of instructional design variables on vocabulary acquisition of LD students: A study of computer-assisted instruction. *Journal of Learning Disabilities*, 20:206–13.

Juel, C. 1988. Learning to read and write: A longitudinal study of 54 children from first though fourth grades. *Journal of Educational Psychology*, 80:437–47.

Just, M. A., and Carpenter, P. A. 1987. *The Psychology of Reading and Language Comprehension*. Boston: Allyn and Bacon.

Kamhi, A. G., and Catts, H. W. 1986. Toward an understanding of developmental language and reading disorders. *Journal of Speech and Hearing Disorders*, 51:337–47.

Kuhn, M. R., and Stahl, S. A. 1998. Teaching children to learn word meanings from context: A synthesis and some questions. *Journal of Literacy Research*, 30:119–38.

Mastropieri, M. A., Scruggs, T. E., and Fulk, B. M. 1990. Teaching abstract vocabulary with the keyword methods: Effects on recall and comprehension. *Journal of Learning Disabilities*, 23:92–6, 107.

McKeown, M. G. 1985. The acquisition of word meaning from context by children of high and low ability. *Reading Research Quarterly*, 20:482–96.

McKeown, M. G., and Beck, I. L. 1988. Learning vocabulary: Different ways for different goals. *Remedial and Special Education*, 9:42–52.

McLoone, B. B., Scruggs, T. E., and Mastropieri, M. A. 1986. Memory strategy instruction and training with learning disabled adolescents. *Learning Disabilities Research and Practice*, 2:45–53.

Mezynski, K. 1983. Issues concerning the acquisition of knowledge: Effects of vocabulary training on reading comprehension. *Review of Educational Research*, 53:253–79.

Nagy, W. E. 1988. *Teaching Vocabulary to Improve Reading Comprehension*. Newark, DE: International Reading Association.

Nagy, W., and Anderson, R. C. 1984. The number of words in printed school English. *Reading Research Quarterly*, 19:304–30.

Nagy, W. E., and Anderson, R., Schommer, M., Scott, J. A., and Stallman, A. C. 1989. Morphological families and word recognition. *Reading Research Quarterly*, 24, 262–82.

Nagy, W. E., and Herman, P. A. 1987. Breadth and depth of vocabulary knowledge: Implications for acquisition and instruction. In *The Nature of Vocabulary Acquisition*, M. G. McKeown and M. E. Curtis (Ed.), (pp. 19–45). Hillsdale, NJ: Lawrence Erlbaum.

Nagy, W. E., Herman, P. A., and Anderson, R. 1985. Learning words from context. *Reading Research Quarterly*, 20:233–53.

National Reading Panel (NRP) Report. 2000. Retrieved from: http://www.nichd.nih.gov/publications/nrp/report.htm

Oetting, J. B., Rice, M. L., and Swank, L. K. 1995. Quick incidental learning (QUIL) of words by school-age children with and without SLI. *Journal of Speech and Hearing Research*, 38:434–45.

Paris, S. G., Wasik, B. A., and Turner, J. C. 1991. The development of strategic readers. In *Handbook of Reading Research*, Vol II. R. Barr, M. L. Kamil, P. B. Mosenthal, and P. D. Pearson, (Eds.), (pp. 609–40). New York: Longman.

Patberg, J. P., Graves, M. F., and Stibbe, M. A. 1984. Effects of active teaching and practice in facilitating students' use of context clues. In *Changing Perspectives on Research in Reading/Language Processing and Instruction*, J. A. Niles and L. A. Harris (Eds.), (pp. 146–51). Rochester, NY: National Reading Conference.

Pfeiffer, J. 1999. *Long-term retention of novel information learned via the keyword mnemonic method*. Unpublished dissertation. Evanston, IL: Northwestern University.

Reinking, D., and Rickman, S. S. 1990. The effects of computer-mediated texts on the vocabulary learning and comprehension of intermediate-grade readers. *Journal of Reading Behavior*, 22:395–411.

Schatz, E. K., and Baldwin, R. S. 1986. Context clues are unreliable predictors of word meanings. *Reading Research Quarterly*, 21:439–53.

Scott, J. A., and Nagy, W. E. 1997. Understanding the definitions of unfamiliar verbs. *Reading Research Quarterly*, 32:184–200.

Scruggs, T. E., and Mastropieri, M. A. 1990. Mnemonic instruction for students with learning disabilities: What it is and what it does. *Learning Disability Quarterly*, 13:271–80.

Simmons, D. C., and Kame'enui, E. J. 1990. The effect of task alternatives on vocabulary knowledge: A comparison of students with and without learning disabilities. *Journal of Learning Disabilities*, 23:291–97, 316.

Snow, C. E., Burns, S., and Griffin, P. 1998. *Preventing reading difficulties in young children.* Washington, DC: National Academy Press.

Stahl, S. A. 1986. Three principles of effective vocabulary instruction. *Journal of Reading*, 29:662–68.

Stahl, S. A., and Fairbanks, M. M. 1986. The effects of vocabulary instruction: A model-based meta-analysis. *Review of Educational Research*, 56:72–110.

Stahl, S. A., and Kapinus, B. A. 1991. Possible sentences: Predicting word meanings to teach content-area vocabulary. *The Reading Teacher*, 45:36–43.

Stahl, S. A., Richek, M. A., and Vandevier, R. J. 1991. Learning meaning vocabulary through listening: A sixth-grade replication. *National Reading Conference Yearbook*, 40:185–92.

Stanovich, K. E. 1986. Matthew effects in reading: some consequences of individual differences in the acquisition of literacy. *Reading Research Quarterly*, 21:360–406.

Sternberg, R. J., Powell, J. S., and Kaye, D. B. 1983. Teaching vocabulary-building skills: A contextual approach. In *Classroom Computers and Cognitive Science*, A. C. Wilkinson (Ed.), (pp. 121–43). New York: Academic Press.

Veit, D. T., Scruggs, T. E., and Mastropieri, M. A. 1986. Extended mnemonic instruction with learning disabled students. *Journal of Educational Psychology*, 78:300–08.

White, T. G., Graves, M. F., and Slater, W. H. 1990. Growth of reading vocabulary in diverse elementary schools: Decoding and word meaning. *Journal of Educational Psychology*, 82:281–290.

White, T. G., Power, M. A., and White, S. 1989. Morphological analysis: Implications for teaching and understanding vocabulary growth. *Reading Research Quarterly*, 24:283–04.

White, T. G., Sowell, J., and Yanagihara, A. January 1989. Teaching elementary students to use word-part clues. *The Reading Teacher*, 302–08.

Wixson, K. K. 1986. Vocabulary instruction and children's comprehension of basal stories. *Reading Research Quarterly*, 21:317–29.

Wysocki, K., and Jenkins, J. 1987. Deriving word meanings through morphological generalization. *Reading Research Quarterly*, 22:66–81.

6

Sentence Comprehension Instruction

GETTING STARTED

✓ How does the ability to reflect on and manipulate syntax aid a reader?
✓ What are some explanations for the difficulty poor readers often experience in comprehending sentences?
✓ What kinds of sentences tend to be most problematic?
✓ How can teachers address sentence-level difficulties

INTRODUCTION

Effective comprehension of sentences is essential in forming an accurate and co-herent understanding of a text as a whole. As a reader proceeds through a text, he or she constructs meaning on a gradual basis. Information from each succes-sive sentence is taken in and related to previous information. At any given mo-ment, a competent reader may be expected to have only a partially complete understanding of a passage. Such a reader might have many unanswered ques-tions and may even have drawn some erroneous conclusions on the basis of in-complete information. As the reader continues through the text, however, he or she will likely update his or her understanding by adding new information, re-solving ambiguities, and correcting misperceptions to arrive at ever more com-plete and accurate comprehension of the text (Oakhill, Garnham, and Vonk 1989; Radvansky and Zacks 1997).

Obviously, there are many factors involved in a skilled reader's construction of meaning. Among these are accurate and fluent word reading, vocabulary knowledge, access to relevant background information, awareness of text and paragraph structure, effective comprehension monitoring, and application of strategies. Each of these topics is discussed elsewhere in this book. This chapter will be devoted to another important component of comprehension—the ability to understand individual sentences and to link the ideas in a given sentence to ideas in the sentences that come before and after it. The chapter is divided into three main sections: (1) a discussion of the difficulties poor readers often exhibit with sentence comprehension; (2) a description of specific types of sentences and cohesive elements that are likely to pose difficulties for less skilled readers; and (3) recommended approaches for addressing sentence-level difficulties.

THE RELATIONSHIP BETWEEN GRAMMATICAL AWARENESS AND READING

A common element of all natural languages is grammar, or syntax. Derived from the Greek word for "arrangement," syntax has been defined as "the way in which words are arranged to show relationships of meaning within (and sometimes between) sentences" (Crystal 1987, p. 94). The syntactic system of a language includes non-arbitrary rules for combining words and morphemes into phrases and clauses and for organizing these structures into sentences. There are constraints on which elements of a sentence can be moved and where they may be relocated. For instance, in English a statement can be transformed into a question by reversing the positions of the subject and verb: *John is happy* can be converted to *Is John happy?* but not to *John happy is.*

Linguist Noam Chomsky (1965), who developed one of the most influential theoretical frameworks of syntax, argued that human beings are biologically predisposed to acquire language, that we are born with the ability to learn the syntactical rules that bind elements of language together, just as we are born with the capacity to walk. Indeed, within an astonishingly brief time and with little or no explicit instruction, children throughout the world manage to master the complex and highly abstract syntactic systems of their native languages. Very young children learn to classify words by grammatical function (i.e., nouns, verbs, adjectives, etc.) and discover the principles governing the ordering of words (e.g., adjectives come before nouns), the creation of plurals, and the formation of past-tense verbs. Throughout their preschool years, they learn to combine words into sentences of increasing variety and complexity until, by the age of five, their language is remarkably adult-like in its basic form. Moreover, well before children begin combining words in their spoken language, there is evidence that they comprehend the effect of syntax on meaning. For instance, 17-month olds understand the difference between *Big Bird tickled Cookie Monster* and *Cookie Monster tickled Big Bird* (Golinkoff and Hirsh-Pasek 1987, cited in Tager-Flusberg 1993). Children may also use syntax as a clue to the meanings of words as they acquire new vocabulary (e.g., Gleitman 1990).

It should be noted that young children's knowledge of syntax is largely implicit. That is to say, they are not young linguists or grammarians who can explain the principles of subject-verb agreement or label the parts of speech. Nonetheless, as children grow older, they develop a greater capacity to think consciously about the language they hear and use, acquiring such metalinguistic abilities as phonological and syntactic awareness. Tunmer, Nesdale, and Wright (1987) have defined syntactic awareness as "the child's ability to reflect upon and to manipulate aspects of the internal grammatical structure of sentences" (p. 25). Children demonstrate this ability when they perform such tasks as determining whether or not a sentence is grammatically acceptable (e.g., *Bill has two puppy*); correcting grammatical errors in sentences; supplying appropriate words in cloze activities (e.g., *Michael was born a long time* ____); and rearranging scrambled sentences (e.g., *Rides Sally bike her*). In numerous studies over the years, researchers have found a strong association between performance on tasks such as these and reading ability (Bentin, Deutsch, and Liberman 1990; Bowey 1986a; Fowler 1988; Pratt, Tunmer, and Bowey 1984; Siegel and Ryan 1988; Tunmer, Nesdale, and Wright 1987; Vogel 1975; Weaver 1979). Children who perform well on measures of grammatical awareness tend to be good readers. Moreover, groups of good readers typically outperform groups of poor readers on such tasks.

These findings lead to the question of how grammatical awareness aids readers. One possibility is that readers with greater sensitivity to syntax are better able to monitor the accuracy of their reading. In fact, Bowey (1986b) found children with stronger syntactic skills were more likely to correct oral reading errors that resulted in grammatically or semantically unacceptable sentences. Similarly, Tyler and Nagy (1990) found that in comprehending difficult sentences, skilled readers at the high school level were more likely than poor readers to make use of syntactic information in suffixes, which indicates the part of speech of a word. For example, *indecisive* is an adjective while *indecision* is a noun. As Tunmer (1989) noted, "A strategy that syntactically aware children are able to use is to check that the meanings they assign to the words of spoken or written discourse conform to the surrounding grammatical context" (p. 105). Grammatical awareness may also improve both comprehension and memory for what was read by enabling children to cluster individual words into meaningful syntactic units such as phrases (Tunmer and Bowey 1984, cited in Bowey 1994).

Although in most studies grammatical awareness has been more strongly associated with comprehension than with decoding, a number of researchers have found significant correlations between syntactic ability and decoding (e.g., Bowey 1986b; Willows and Ryan 1986). Grammatical awareness may facilitate the development of decoding and word recognition skills by enabling children to use the constraints imposed by syntax to identify unknown words. In several studies, children with stronger syntactic and semantic skills proved to be better at using context to identify words that they had been unable to decode in isolation (e.g., Nation and Snowling 1998; Rego and Bryant 1993). As Rego and Bryant (1993) observed, children "are more likely to make the right guess if they know that the next word could be an adjective or a noun but not a verb" (p. 236).

In spite of the strong association between grammatical manipulation tasks and reading ability, we are not sure why poor readers have difficulty with these tasks. A number of explanations have been put forth. One proposed explanation is that syntactic awareness is but one aspect of a more general delay or deficit in language. In a review of the literature on the topic, Bowey (1994) argued that the tasks that researchers have used to assess grammatical awareness might also be measuring other aspects of language ability. If this is so, it may be that a deficit in "grammatical awareness" is often part of a global language problem. There is ample evidence that children who display language impairments or delays in the preschool years are at risk for later reading problems (Bishop and Adams 1990;

Catts et al. 1999; Dement and Gombert 1996; Rescorla 2000; Scarborough 1990, 1991; Siegel and Ryan 1988). In fact, results from a number of studies indicate that early deficits in language are predictive of reading difficulties well into the adolescent years (Butler 1988; Goulandris, Snowling, and Walker 2000; Rescorla 2000). The preschoolers who have the greatest chance of developing reading problems seem to be those who have problems *understanding* spoken language (Morice and Slaghuis 1985; Nation and Snowling 1998). However, even children whose difficulties are limited to expressive language may be at risk. In a recent study, Rescorla (2000) found that young adolescents who had good language comprehension as toddlers but who were late talkers performed significantly less well than those with normal language development on measures of vocabulary, grammar, and reading.

Secondly, some researchers claim that it is limitations in working memory that cause what appear to be deficits in syntactic skills. Fowler (1988) argued that many of the tasks used to assess grammatical awareness (e.g., sentence correction, cloze activities) place high demands on working memory in that they require "the child to hold the entire sentence in memory, derive some meaning from it, and typically perform some more complex function" (p. 75). Hence, some of these tasks may be measuring working memory rather than syntactic awareness per se. A number of researchers have found that poor readers did not exhibit deficits in their understanding of syntax itself when the memory demands of the tasks were reduced (Fowler 1988; Smith et al. 1989). In fact, results of some studies have indicated that syntactic awareness may not predict reading ability after the effects of working memory have been statistically controlled (e.g., Gottardo, Stanovich, and Siegel 1996).

Finally, some of the linguistic deficits observed in poor readers may be a *consequence* of their reading disabilities rather than the *effect* of preexisting language problems. Since good readers tend to read more than poor readers, they are exposed to more sophisticated language and concepts. This allows them to expand their vocabularies, increase their understanding of complex syntax, build a fund of background knowledge, and learn to read strategically. They are then able to bring an abundance of knowledge and skills to their future reading that poor readers do not have because of their more limited experience with the printed word (Stanovich 1986). Indeed, the results of several longitudinal studies indicate that, over time, poor readers may experience a decline in verbal intelligence (Bishop and Butterworth 1980) and in language and vocabulary (Share and Silva 1987). Thus, poor readers may have limited syntactic knowledge because they have done relatively little reading. As Tunmer (1989) noted, the language in text is less embedded in context than oral language generally is. Meaning cannot be conveyed or clarified through gestures, facial expressions, or prosody. Sentences tend to be longer and more complex with many ideas integrated into a single sentence. Clauses and sentences are linked together with conjunctive devices that a child may rarely, if ever, encounter in everyday conversational language (*moreover, although, consequently,* etc.). Poor readers who do little independent reading or who are able to read only very simple texts may receive little exposure to the language in grade-level reading material. As a result, they may lag behind their peers in their ability to comprehend the more complex syntax of written discourse and in the development of metalinguistic abilities such as grammatical awareness.

What conclusions can we draw about the nature of problems with sentence comprehension from these somewhat contradictory research results? It is probably safe to say that all three explanations have merit. Children with a history of language deficits or delays, those with weaknesses in working memory, and those who have had little exposure to the vocabulary and syntax in grade-level texts are likely to have difficulty comprehending sentences. In the following section, we examine some specific types of sentences that may be particularly problematic for poor readers.

POTENTIAL DIFFICULTIES IN SENTENCE COMPREHENSION

Throughout childhood and adolescence, normally achieving students gain the ability to understand and use increasingly complex syntactical patterns (Nippold 1998). Poor readers may lag behind their peers, continuing to experience difficulties with challenging syntax well after it has been mastered by most of their agemates. According to Maria (1990), the types of sentences that are most difficult for school age children "tend to be those that are exceptions in some way to the common order of information presentation (in English) and are more likely to be found in written English than in oral English" (p. 135). Educators should be aware of specific sentence structures and devices for connecting sentences that may cause difficulties for struggling readers. This information can help teachers identify potentially problematic portions of text and plan remedial activities. In this section of the chapter, we have included examples of some of the syntactical patterns and cohesive elements that research and experience suggest are among the most difficult for poor comprehenders.

Simple Sentences

A simple sentence consists of a single independent clause. Because they are typically shorter than compound and complex sentences and contain fewer ideas, simple sentences are usually comprehended with relative ease. However, short sentences are not necessarily easier to process than longer ones. Simple sentences with the following elements may be challenging for poor comprehenders.

Passive Constructions.   Passive sentences violate the more common Subject-Verb-Object order (e.g., *The bird ate the worms*). In a passive construction, the person or thing that is acted upon appears earlier in the sentence than the person or thing performing the action, and a simple action verb is replaced by a verb phrase (e.g., *The worms were eaten by the bird.*). Young children and those with language impairments tend to rely on their knowledge of the world when interpreting passive sentences. Hence, they may have no difficulty with a sentence about a familiar situation such as *The worms were eaten by the bird.* However, a sentence describing a less plausible scenario (e.g., *The bird was eaten by the worms.*) might be misinterpreted, as might a sentence in which either party could potentially perform the action (e.g., *The truck was hit by the car.*).

Word Order.   Sometimes the position of a word can alter the meaning of a sentence. For instance, *John caught only three fish* is very different from *Only John caught three fish.* Similarly, *We painted the house red* means something altogether different from *We painted the red house.*

Double Negation.   Two negative words (e.g., *not, never*) or prefixes (e.g., *un-, mis-, dis*) in a sentence cancel one another out, producing a positive statement. For example, *John's plan is not unreasonable* means that John's plan might work, and *Sally would never not do her homework* means that Sally can be counted on to do her homework. Students who overlook one of the negatives or who have difficulty with the logic can easily misinterpret such sentences (McNeil 1987). Interpretation can be further complicated by the fact that the meaning of a sentence with double negation is often more subtle than a simple positive statement. Consider the following:

Speaker 1: *Are you happy?*
Speaker 2: *I am not unhappy.*

The second speaker's response to the question suggests a neutral feeling rather than happiness.

The Effect of Little Words.   Students with reading difficulties often omit, insert, or substitute small words such as articles. In many cases, this does not have a dramatic adverse effect on comprehension; however, sometimes it does. Consider the case of *few* and *little* as opposed to *a few* and *a little.*

The captain's diary offered *few* clues about the location of the treasure.
The captain's diary told us *little* about the location of the treasure.

A student who is not familiar with these syntactical patterns is likely to insert "a" into these sentences, producing a more familiar structure. Such a student would probably conclude, erroneously, that the diary would help the treasure seekers.

Verb Phrases.   The use of less common verb tenses and addition of auxiliary (helping) verbs might result in confusion for some poor readers (e.g., *We should have done our homework. She had been working hard all day.*).

Compound and Complex Sentences

A *compound* sentence consists of a two or more independent clauses linked with a coordinating conjunction (e.g., *and, but, so*). A *complex* sentence contains one independent clause and at least one dependent clause linked by a subordinating conjunction (e.g., *because*, *although*.) According to Nippold (1998), sentences that contain an independent clause plus a verbal such as an infinitive or participial phrase are also classified as complex. A *compound-complex* sentence contains at least two independent clauses and one or more dependent clauses.

Compound and complex sentences may pose difficulty for poor comprehenders for a variety of reasons. First, as noted earlier, these sentences are often (though not always) longer than simple sentences. Longer sentences tend to have greater "concept density." In other words, many ideas are packed into a single sentence via dependent clauses, embedded clauses or phrases, and plural subjects or predicates. Processing such sentences places a burden on our limited-capacity working memory system. Readers with weaknesses in working memory or those who lack fluency (see Chapter 3) may have difficulty retaining incoming information long enough to grasp the connections among all the ideas in a lengthy, concept-dense sentence.

According to the "kernel distance theory" of Fry, Weber, and DePierro (1978), the more words that intervene between the subject and predicate, the more difficult a sentence will be to process. See table 6.1 for examples of embedded clauses and phrases that interrupt the main clause. Sentences with embedded clauses have received intense scrutiny by researchers because they can be notoriously difficult to process, even by some adult readers. As would be expected, struggling readers tend to have difficulty in comprehending such sentences (Mann, Shankweiler, and Smith 1984; MacGinitie, Katz, and Maria 1980, cited in Maria 1990). MacGinitie, Katz, and Maria for instance, presented 4th and 5th graders with sentences in which a relative clause was embedded between the subject and the verb (e.g., *The witch who yelled at the children grabbed the box.*). When asked who grabbed the box, many of their research participants replied, "the children."

Table 6.1   Examples of Introductory or Embedded Phrases and Clauses

Appositive	• My neighbor, *a corporate attorney*, purchased a yacht. • *A corporate attorney*, my neighbor purchased a yacht.
Elaborated subject	• Breeds *such as collies, cocker spaniels, and golden retrievers* were represented at the dog show.
Prepositional phrase	• The horse *with the brown coat and the black mane* is in the lead.
Relative clause	• Many birds *that live in the tropical rain forest* are extremely colorful.
Infinitive phrase	• The first diver *to compete in the event* made many mistakes.
Participial phrase	• *Tied to the post with a frayed rope,* the dog was barking furiously.
Adjectives or Participles	• *Tired, frustrated, disheveled, and ready to cry,* Matilda finally gave up on getting the car out of the ditch by herself.

Embedded or introductory phrases and clauses are examples of syntactic constructions that are encountered infrequently in conversational language. These elements may be unfamiliar to children who have relatively little experience with sophisticated, "literate" language. (See table 6.1 for examples.)

Grasping the meaning of complex and compound sentences hinges on comprehension of the conjunctions that link clauses. The conjunctions are used to express a variety of relationships including temporal (e.g., *before, since, as*); causal (e.g., *so, because*); adversative (e.g., *but, although, while*); and conditional (e.g., *if, unless*). It has been documented in numerous studies that comprehension and use of these connecting expressions improve gradually throughout childhood and adolescence (see Nippold 1998 for a review). For instance, McClure and Steffensen (1985) asked students in Grades 3, 6, and 9 to complete sentences with the coordinating conjunctions *and* and *but*, and the subordinating conjunctions *because* and *even though* (e.g., *He bought a TV because* _____.). By the sixth grade, most of the children had mastered the use of *and, but* and *because*, but performance on *even though* continued to improve through the ninth grade. McClure and Steffensen also found that at every grade level, performance on their sentence completion task was significantly correlated with vocabulary and reading ability. Readers who overlook or do not understand a conjunction may miss the author's point or interpret the ideas as unrelated. As McClure and Steffensen (1985) noted, such readers may comprehend individual clauses but fail to understand the sentence as a whole.

Conjunctions involving temporal (e.g., *before, after, when*) and causal (e.g., *because, so*) relationships are usually mastered earlier than those involving adversative (e.g., *although, even though*) and conditional relationships (e.g., *if, unless*). However, young children may have difficulty with temporal and causal sentences if the order of the clauses differs from the order events would have in the real world (McNeil 1987). For instance, *After I did my homework, I had a snack* might be understood better than *I had a snack after I did my homework*. This is particularly true in instances when the events could logically occur in either order. Some children may also be confused by the fact that some conjunctions can denote two different relationships (Maria 1990). For instance, *while* can express a temporal relationship (*I read the newspaper while I ate breakfast.*) or an adversative relationship (*My sister likes chocolate chip cookies while I prefer brownies.*)

A final type of sentence that has received a great deal of research attention is the "garden path" sentence. The initial part of a garden path sentence suggests an interpretation that turns out to be incorrect; the reader is thus forced to backtrack and either reread the sentence or rely on memory to reinterpret it. A common type of garden path sentence results when the word *that* has been omitted:

Jane knew the answer to the math problem was incorrect.
The cotton clothing is made from grows in the South.

Although such sentences are relatively rare in natural text, they do occur from time to time, giving good readers pause and creating difficulty for struggling readers.

Cohesive Ties Between Sentences

Language, spoken or written, is more than a collection of unrelated sentences. Rather, speakers and writers use a variety of techniques to establish links between as well as within sentences. Halliday and Hasan (1976) were the first to describe and systematically classify the means by which texts are bound together, or made cohesive.[4] Their book, *Cohesion in English*, is still considered the authoritative text on the subject. See table 6.2 for a summary of their taxonomy of cohesive ties. The first four categories of cohesive ties (Reference, Substitution, Ellipsis, and Lexical Cohesion) involve situations in which the cohesive tie replaces the word or phrase to which it refers. For example, a pronoun may be used instead of a noun, a synonym or superordinate term instead of a related word. These cohesive ties streamline language by eliminating unnecessary repetitions and serve as "glue" to bind sentences together. The fifth category, conjunction, we have already discussed in the context of compound and complex sentences.

Table 6.2   Cohesive Ties

REFERENCE: A word that cannot be understood in its own right. It must make reference to something else for its interpretation. Examples:
- Truckers transport all kinds of products from one part of the country to another. *They* spend many hours on the road.
- This is my favorite restaurant. I come *here* often for lunch.

SUBSTITUTION: A word that is used in place of another word, phrase, or clause. Examples:
- My friend will have the sirloin steak. I'll have *the same*.
- Everyone seems to think he is guilty. If *so*, he should offer to resign.

ELLIPSIS: Words are left out. Examples:
- I enjoyed seeing the paintings at the art gallery. Most [*of the paintings*] were done by local artists.
- Did Bob eat the rest of the pie? He must have [*eaten the pie*].

LEXICAL COHESION: The same term, a synonym, superordinate term, or a closely related word is used to make connections across sentences. Examples:
- As Tom stood on the street corner, he saw a man come running out of the bank. *The man* flew down the street and jumped into the passenger seat of a black car.
- Yesterday I picked a bushel of corn, two baskets of beans, and a large bag of squash. I don't know what I'm going to do with all these *vegetables*.

CONJUNCTION: Links are made between two ideas so that the understanding of the second idea is related to the understanding of the first idea. Examples:
- I tried for three hours to solve the puzzle. *However*, I finally gave up and looked at the answer.
- We need to arrive at the concert early. *Otherwise*, it will be impossible to get good seats.

---

[4]Cohesion should not be confused with the related concept of coherence. Coherence is a broader term that includes text structure, organization, and internal consistency as well as cohesion between sentences. While cohesion is a property of text itself, coherence is, in part, achieved through the reader's efforts to construct meaning (Moe and Irwin 1986).

All types of cohesive ties may be found *within* sentences as well as between. Cohesive ties within sentences are generally easier for readers to understand (Barnitz 1986; Geva and Ryan 1985), primarily because the cohesive tie is in close proximity to its referent. A sentence (or several sentences) may come between a cohesive tie and the word, phrase, or clause to which it refers. In these cases, a reader must be able to hold an idea in one sentence in memory long enough to connect it with the cohesive tie in another sentence. Research suggests that working memory limitation is a likely cause of difficulty in integrating information across sentences (Barnitz 1986; Oakhill 1994). Dysfluent readers and those who lack familiarity with cohesive techniques also may have difficulty making links between sentences.

Personal pronouns are by far the most common type of cohesive tie, making up over 70% of all the cohesive elements in basal readers (Baumann 1987). Pronouns tend to be easier for children to understand than other types of cohesive ties (Barnitz 1986). Poor comprehenders, however, may have difficulty even with seemingly very straightforward, unambiguous cohesive devices. For instance, Yuill and Oakhill (1988) compared the ability of good and poor comprehenders to determine the referents of cohesive ties occurring in stories. Initially, the children were asked to decide what the cohesive ties "stood for" or "pointed back to." If they were unable to respond, they were asked a more direct question. For instance, in the case of a text segment such as *Bill went fishing. He carried his rod to the bus stop*, the children would be asked, "Who carried his rod to the bus stop?" There were dramatic differences between the good and poor comprehenders. The poor comprehenders made many errors, even when they were asked direct questions about who did what. Older poor readers may also experience difficulty with cohesion; Fayne (1981) reported similar results in a study involving 10th and 11th grade students.

Halladay and Hason's (1976) last category of cohesive ties is conjunctions. In addition to the conjunctions that occur within sentences (see above discussion of compound and complex sentences), conjunctive adverbs (e.g., *therefore, however, consequently, nevertheless, rather, furthermore, moreover, conversely*) are frequently used to link sentences and, sometimes, larger units of text. Nippold, Schwarz, and Undlin (1992) explored the comprehension and use of adverbial conjuncts in students between the ages of 12 and 23. Comprehension increased from 79% at age 12 to 94% by age 23. Although the more difficult conjunctive adverbs (e.g., *conversely, moreover*) are rare in books written for children (Nippold, Schwarz, and Undlin 1992), they occur frequently in expository text at the high school and college levels. Hence, mastery of these terms may have to do with the amount of exposure a student receives to high-level academic writing, and they may be a source of difficulty for struggling readers at the secondary level.

Inferences

Not all relationships among ideas are explicitly stated. Sometimes it is up to the reader to infer the connections between ideas and use prior knowledge to fill in gaps. Inferences are required when a cohesive tie is either omitted altogether or is somewhat ambiguous. Consider the following example (adapted from Cain and Oakhill 1999):

> *Debbie wrapped her bathing suit in her towel. She put the bundle in her backpack.*

The reader must infer that "bundle" refers to the towel-encased bathing suit. In another example, the cohesive tie has been eliminated altogether:

> *A flash of lightning was followed by a deafening thunderclap. The lights suddenly went out.*

The causal relationship between the thunderstorm and the power outage is not explicitly stated and must be inferred. In the absence of a connective such as *as a result,* understanding the cause of the power failure may be dependent on background knowledge or prior experience with power outages during thunderstorms. In other situations, the problem is not an ambiguous or absent cohesive tie, but the fact that readers must integrate details in the text with background knowledge to make a judgment about what is happening in a sentence. For instance, in a sentence such as *They set off for home, pedaling as fast as they could* (from Cain and Oakhill 1999), the reader must draw on knowledge about conveyances that can be pedaled to conclude that the characters are riding bicycles.

Difficulty in making inferences can be an important reason for comprehension failure. Geva and Ryan (1985), for instance, found that skilled readers in the fifth and seventh grades were better than average or poor readers at inferring relations between sentences when explicit cohesive ties were absent. Moreover, unlike the good readers, who comprehended passages equally well whether or not they had explicit cohesive ties, the comprehension of average and poor readers was adversely affected by omission of conjunctions.[5]

Cain and Oakhill (1999) found that poor comprehenders were as accurate as good readers at answering questions about information that was explicitly stated. However, they were less successful than good comprehenders on questions that required inferences (e.g., *Where did Debbie put her towel? How did the children travel home?*). Even though the poor comprehenders possessed the necessary background knowledge to make the inferences (e.g., they mentioned bicycles when asked what sorts of things could be pedaled), they did not make use of this knowledge. Cain and Oakhill concluded that poor readers often approach reading with different goals than do good readers. They may be more focused on accuracy of word reading than on comprehension. Moreover, they may be "poor at knowing when and how to relate knowledge to the text in order to supply missing details" (p. 501).

---

[5]In an effort to produce textbooks that are appropriate for children in a given grade, authors typically use readability formulas to calculate grade level. In many formulas, readability is based in part on sentence length. In an effort to shorten sentences, authors may omit conjuctions, producing two simple sentences rather than a complex or compound sentence. According to the readability formulas, this should make the text more comprehensible. However, according to Maria (1990), this practice may be a mistake. A string of short sentences is not always easier to understand than a single complex or compound sentence, for if conjunctions are omitted, relationships among the ideas have to be inferred.

Sometimes sentences require an analysis of the context in order to be accurately interpreted. For instance, a sentence such as *It's cold in here* can be either a simple statement of fact or an implied request to turn up the heat. A comment such as *That's nice* can be a truthful statement, a white lie, or sarcasm, depending on the situation. Demorest et al. (1984) found several developmental trends in children's abilities to interpret false remarks accurately. Children ages 6, 9, and 13 and college-age adults were asked to decide on the basis of contextual information whether a character in a story was being sincere, purposively deceptive, or sarcastic. Six-year olds tended to take most remarks as sincere, relying solely on what the speaker said as evidence of belief and purpose. By nine and 13, children were better able to use the facts of the situation and the speaker's behavior to distinguish sincere from false and sarcastic remarks. Poor readers may have difficulty "reading between the lines" in such circumstances. Pearl et al. (1991), for instance, found that 7th and 8th grade students with learning disabilities (LD) were less likely than nondisabled students to recognize the deceptive statements of story characters.

METHODS OF INSTRUCTION

In spite of an abundance of research on the relationship between grammatical awareness and reading comprehension, research on effective techniques for enhancing sentence-level comprehension is sparse, especially for students with reading disabilities. Researchers who have explored the relationship between grammatical awareness and reading (e.g., Siegel and Ryan 1984) have often advocated that syntactic skills be targeted in remedial programs for poor readers. However, there have been very few studies investigating the effects of efforts to heighten children's understanding of syntax. An important question is whether or not improvements in grammatical awareness lead to more general improvements in reading comprehension. Based on what we know so far, the answer seems to be "yes." Some techniques have proven to be beneficial, though not in every study and not for every struggling reader.

In a recent study, Layton, Robinson, and Lawson (1998) provided lessons in syntactic awareness to a group of fourth graders with a range of reading abilities. Their training emphasized understanding of the "jobs words do" in sentences. Compared to a control group, these students proved to be better at articulating that there are rules of syntax, explaining what some of the rules are, and reflecting on their own performance on tasks requiring syntactic knowledge. However, children who received the training performed no better than those who did not on measures of oral reading and reading comprehension. Though disappointing, these results suggest that, while there may be some benefit in making children aware of the functions of grammatical elements, such training may not transfer to reading, at least not for children in the early elementary grades. More promising are techniques that involve active manipulation of sentence components.

Weaver (1979) and White, Pascarella, and Pflaum (1981) taught children a strategy for constructing sentences from scrambled words. The participants in the White et al. study were 30 students with LD in the upper elementary grades who were reading, on average, at about a second grade level. Working in groups of 3 or 4, the children were taught to locate the verb first, then to ask themselves a series of questions (*Who? To whom? What? Where? When? Why? How?*) to arrange the rest of the words. Afterwards, they asked themselves if the sentence made sense. In a series of lessons, the children proceeded from constructing simple sentences to complex sentences with multiple clauses. Compared to a control group (who had completed traditional sentence-skill exercises from a basal reading series), the children in the experimental group made significant gains in reading comprehension. However, it is important to note that the children who benefited the most were those whose initial reading achievement was higher. The poorest readers in the group (those reading at around a first grade level) did not make significant improvement. The authors speculated that for these children, the effort required for reading words interfered with their focusing on meaning.

In a more recent study, Gillon and Dodd (1995) identified a group of 10- to 12-year-old children with average or above intelligence who had a history of speech/language disorders, who were reading well below grade level, and who were making only very gradual improvement in reading. They implemented a six-month-long intervention program for these students that involved instruction in both phonological processing (practice with segmenting, manipulating, and blending sounds) and syntactical skills. The syntactic training included a number of activities that, like the scrambled-word exercise described above, involved manipulation of sentence components. For instance, the children expanded simple sentences to construct complex and compound sentences, arranged scrambled words and phrases to make sentences, combined short sentences to create longer ones, and learned to use conjunctions. In this case, the results were quite dramatic. On average, the children's grade equivalency scores on a standardized reading test increased 1.5 years for decoding and 2 years for reading comprehension over the course of the six-month instructional period. The gains in decoding were due primarily to the phonological training, although both phonological and syntactic instruction contributed to gains in comprehension. However, like White, Pascarella, and Pflaum (1981), Gillon and Dodd found that the students with the most severe reading disabilities did not benefit from the syntactic instruction. For these students, only the phonological training had a significant impact on their reading comprehension.

The results of these studies have a number of implications for the classroom. First, tasks like those described above that require students actively to manipulate sentences may increase awareness of syntax, which, in turn, may improve comprehension. Merely learning to identify syntactical elements and explain their function is probably not enough; rather, students need to explore the internal structure of sentences by creating, combining, and expanding them. Sentence combining, in particular, has received a fair amount of research support as a tool for enhancing the comprehension of poor readers (e.g., Neville and Sears 1985; Straw and Schreiner 1982) as well as improving writing skills (e.g., Smith and Combs 1980; Straw and Schreiner 1982). Secondly, it is important to keep in mind that these activities may not be of benefit to all poor readers. In the case of students with very limited decoding skills, Gillon's and Dodd's (1995) findings would suggest that time might be better spent on word-reading instruction. However, it is not known what the long-term effects of instruction might be for such students. It is possible that once their decoding skills have improved sufficiently, they will be able to make use of previously acquired grammatical knowledge. Moreover, syntactic instruction might have a positive effect on listening comprehension (Straw and Schreiner 1982). Nonetheless, it is probably not reasonable for teachers to expect immediate reading-related benefits for students with very limited decoding skills.

As we have seen, many struggling readers have difficulty in using the clues provided by conjunctions and other cohesive ties to make connections between the clauses in complex and compound sentences and between separate sentences. The following are some ideas for helping students understand conjunctions and other cohesive ties. Unfortunately, at this point, most have not been tested on children with reading or learning disabilities in controlled research studies. However, in the clinical experience of a number of reading experts (e.g., Maria 1990; McNeil 1987), they have proven to be helpful for poor readers.

Understanding compound and complex sentences often depends on grasping the relationships among ideas. Some students benefit from explicit instruction in the meaning of conjunctive elements. There are so many conjunctions that it may be difficult for teachers to know where to begin. Pulver (1986) suggests selecting the conjunctions that are causing problems for students and that are needed to understand grade-level text. Before beginning instruction, teachers might want to analyze the language of the literature students are reading, identify frequently occurring conjunctions, and assess students' understanding of these terms. Maria (1990) and Pulver (1986) offer several ideas for assessment activities. For instance, students may be asked to complete sentences that contain a variety of conjunctions:

> *I wanted to play with my friend, but* _____.
> *I took my dog for a walk even though* _____.
> *I ran all the way home because* _____.

Another possibility is to create cloze activities in which student are asked to fill in the blank with an appropriate conjunction. Teachers may wish to use sentences from actual textbooks to create these assessment activities.

> *Movies often show octopuses attacking divers,* _____ *they really swim away if a person comes close to them* (from Maria 1990).

It is usually most effective to teach conjunctions in related groups, such as a set of conjunctions expressing adversative (e.g., *but, even though, however*) or causal relationship (e.g., *so, because, as a result*). Teachers might wish to integrate instruction on conjunctions with content area concepts (see Chapter 9). For instance, as Pulver (1986) notes, causal relationships are particularly important in the study of history, and sentences with causal conjunctions occur frequently in social studies text. Maria (1990) points out that authors often use adversative conjunctions to contradict common misperceptions, as the octopus sentence above illustrates. Mastering these conjunctions can help children learn new information from expository text that contradicts what they believe to be true.

The following are some possible practice activities:

- Rewording sentences using different but related conjunctions (e.g., *but* vs. *even though*).
- Combining sentences using specific conjunctions.
- Having students discuss how changing the conjunction alters the meaning of a sentence (McNeil 1987): *She cooks* (and, while, where, if, because, so, but) *he does the dishes.*
- Altering the text to draw students' attention to conjunctions. Geva and Ryan (1985) found that for fifth and seventh grade readers of all ability levels, comprehension was enhanced when they read versions of text in which conjunctions were underlined and capitalized. When students' attention was drawn to connecting words, they seemed more likely to attempt to integrate ideas within or between sentences. A related idea is to train students to locate and underline conjunctions as they read.
- Filling in the blank (either within or between sentences) with an appropriate conjunction. This activity may be useful in helping students understand text in which connectives have been omitted and relationships must be inferred. Pulver (1986) suggests the following strategy for identifying and comprehending implicit relationships:
  1. Look at where the sentences come together; think about how the sentences are related to one another.
  2. Think about what you already know about the topic.
  3. Try to insert a conjunction between the two sentences that contain related ideas. Does the new sentence make sense?

Many students, even skilled readers, have never consciously thought about authors' use of cohesive devices (McNeil 1987). As a means of drawing students' attention to cohesion, McNeil suggests having them identify all the words that "stand for" other words, phrases, or clause in a short, familiar passage. After locating the cohesive ties, students can be asked to determine the antecedent of each and to classify the cohesive ties in terms of the kind of element they replace: noun, verb, phrase or clause, related word. This activity can be followed by a discussion of how and why writers use cohesive ties. For good readers, an activity such as this may be all that is necessary to encourage greater attention to the connections between sentences. However, struggling readers will likely need more explicit instruction. The following are some recommendations for students who have difficulty understanding cohesion. As Maria (1990) notes, these activities may not only improve comprehension but also help students write more cohesively.

- Have students match the cohesive tie with its antecedent. There are several ways to do this. Students may draw arrows from the cohesive ties to the words they replace (Baumann and Stevenson 1986), write the antecedent above the cohesive tie, or write the same number over words that are linked (McNeil 1987). Some students may benefit from applying one of these techniques as they read.

- Have children read a passage and answer questions that require comprehension of cohesive ties.

> *Mary scored two goals in the soccer game last night. Her teammate, Susan, did too.*

> Whose teammate is Susan?
> What did Susan do?

- Delete pronouns from a passage and have students fill in the blanks.
- Give students a passage in which names and other sentence components have been unnecessarily repeated. Ask them to substitute cohesive ties for the repetitious information.
- At times, the antecedent of a pronoun may be somewhat ambiguous. Some children may need to be taught how to use "clues" such as number and gender to figure out what pronouns stand for.

> *Joe and Laura went to the beach. He played in the water while she looked for shells. Afterwards, they had a picnic lunch.*

In other instances, children may need to draw on background knowledge and reasoning skills to determine the most probable antecedent of a pronoun. In the following example, *it* more likely refers to the mall than to the bank since John was able to conduct his business at the bank.

> *John went to the mall after he deposited some money in his account at the bank. It was closed.*

McNeil (1987) suggests having students generate a list of strategies they can apply when they are unsure what a pronoun stands for. If they are still not sure after using clues in the sentence, they should be encouraged to read on, for the next sentence may hold a further clue (Clark 1986):

> *John went to the mall after he deposited some money in his account at the bank. It was closed. So he was unable to buy his sister a birthday present.*

On the other hand, the next sentence sometimes requires a revision of one's original hypothesis:

> *John went to the mall after he deposited some money in his account at the bank. It was closed. However, he used the ATM.*

The activities described here may help many poor readers become more aware of the function of cohesion and better able to relate one sentence to another. For some additional ideas, see Baumann and Stevenson (1986).

COMMONLY ASKED QUESTIONS

What are some ways to integrate work on sentence comprehension into contextual reading?

The activities described above may be useful in helping students acquire better "sentence sense." However, there are a number of problems with relying exclusively on decontextualized exercises for sentence level instruction. First, children become bored with worksheet or workbook activities that they perceive as uninteresting and repetitious "busywork." Secondly, students with learning problems often have great difficulty transferring what they have learned in one context to other situations (see Chapter 4 for a more extensive discussion of this problem). Unless students receive explicit instruction on how to apply what they have learned in isolated exercises to "real" reading, they may fail to do so, thus defeating the purpose of the exercises. Finally, creating sentence exercises "from scratch" that are tailored to the needs of particular students probably requires time and a level of individualization that is not feasible for most classroom teachers. (Teachers in resource settings might be in a better position to address the needs of students who have difficulty with specific aspects of sentence comprehension.)

Decontextualized activities certainly have their place. They are a good way to introduce a concept or provide additional practice with specific skills. However, we recommend that teachers also address sentence level comprehension in the context of authentic literature. An excellent way to do this is to integrate sentence-level instruction into the Reciprocal Teaching process. Reciprocal Teaching, which is described in detail in Chapter 4, is one of several techniques for teaching strategic reading. Its highlights include extensive teacher modeling, collaboration between teacher and students, and gradual movement toward independent application of reading strategies. Reciprocal Teaching involves four key strategies (Questioning, Clarifying, Predicting, and Summarizing) that can be applied to sentence-level comprehension difficulties.

We recommend that teachers read through the text in advance to identify potentially challenging sentences and portions of text (e.g., place where a text-connecting inference is required). In the course of Reciprocal Teaching or a related approach, the teacher can model questions to ask that will help clarify the meaning of these sentences (e.g., *Who is doing the action? What are they doing? Where are they? What happened first? Why did this happen?*). Harris and Sipay (1990) recommend responding to incorrect answers with *How do you know?* or *Why do you think so?* to encourage children to use the text to justify their answers and, in the process, possibly rectify misunderstandings. The teacher can also use the Clarifying step to point out difficult sentences and encourage students to discuss their meaning. Maria (1990) recommends asking students to restate difficult sentences in their own words to ensure that they understand. Students should also be encouraged to use both their background knowledge and the overall context when trying to comprehend challenging sentences.

Unlike the carefully controlled texts used in practice exercises, authentic texts are often complex and "messy." They may not be particularly well organized or cohesive. Relationships between sentences are not always made clear, and the referents of cohesive ties are sometimes ambiguous. Sometimes this is intentional on the part of the writer. Often authors will introduce a topic in a way that is designed to create confusion or pique curiosity, then proceed to clarify and develop their ideas. At other times, the reader's confusion may stem from a poorly written text. Many struggling readers tend to assume that all breakdowns in comprehension are their own fault, so they may not be aware of instances when a text is genuinely hard to understand (Clark 1986). Clark recommends teaching students to identify confusing parts of the text and apply problem-solving strategies. He created the following hierarchy of problem-solving options, ranging from the least disruptive of the reading process to the most disruptive and effortful.

1. Ignore the problem and read on. This may be a good option if the problem is very minor or not crucial to the overall meaning.
2. Suspend judgment and read on in hopes that the author will later clarify the problem.
3. Form a tentative hypothesis and read on to see if it is confirmed later on.
4. Reread current or prior text. This is the best course of action when ambiguities or contradictions are not resolved via other strategies.
5. Ask for help.

Clark (1986) recommends that the teacher model this problem-solving process during the course of Reciprocal Teaching. When something in the text is genuinely difficult to understand, the teacher can model his or her confusion and explain to the students why the text is unclear. In this way, the teacher can illustrate the fact that even good readers are occasionally stumped. Gradually, more responsibility should be placed on the students for spotting ambiguities or inconsistencies and applying the problem-solving strategies.

How can teachers expose children who do very little reading to complex language?

As we discussed earlier, less well-developed syntactic skills may be a cause of reading difficulties as well as an effect of limited exposure to complex language. There are a number of things that teachers and parents can do to compensate for a lack of reading, both formally and informally. First, teachers and parents can make a conscious effort to model complex syntax in their conversations with children and to ask questions of children that encourage them to elaborate upon and extend their ideas (Dickinson and Tabors 2001; Sawyer and Butler 1991). Fey et al. (1993) taught a group of parents of preschool children with delays in syntactical development how to provide language instruction in the context of daily activities. The parents were encouraged to elaborate on their children's language and create opportunities for them to use specific syntactical constructions. For instance, if the child responded to a question about a picture with "Eating cookie," the parent could add, "Yes, the boy is eating a cookie" and encourage a similar response from the child. This approach proved to be beneficial for the children in the study. Teachers of older children can model the syntax that is used in grade-level reading material and give students opportunities to imitate it.

Like many researchers, Alverman (1983) found that relative to their age mates, children with reading disabilities were less successful at comprehending a variety of complex sentence structures. However, she also found a significant correlation between the syntactic complexity of the books the children had either read themselves *or* listened to and their language development. These results support the advice that has long been given to parents and teachers of children with reading disabilities: Read to them. Exposing children to books that are linguistically more complex than they are capable of reading on their own may enhance their ability to comprehend more complex syntactic structures, which, in turn, may aid their reading. As Sawyer and Butler (1991, p. 69) note, "For some, perhaps, reading achievement can be even more effectively served through the ears (listening comprehension) than through the eyes (word attack)." Books on tape, instructional videotapes, and CD ROMs may be equally effective in exposing children to sophisticated syntax and vocabulary.

A reasonable question involves the optimal level of material for reading aloud. Obviously, one should not select material with syntax or vocabulary so far beyond the child's level of language comprehension that he or she becomes overwhelmed or bored. However, while syntactical abilities arguably play a critical role in comprehension, it is important to keep in mind that a variety of factors affect a person's ability to construct meaning. In this chapter, we have focused almost exclusively on the text itself and the limitations poor readers may have in dissecting its grammar. However, other reader-related factors, such as background knowledge, interest level, strategy use, and motivation also affect comprehension. If a student has the requisite topic-related knowledge and is interested and motivated, difficult syntax, in and of itself, may not be a serious impediment to comprehension. A case in point is the immensely popular Harry Potter series. The author, J. K. Rowling, was turned down by a number of publishers when she approached them with the first book in the series (Bouquet 2000). Among their concerns was that her sentence structure was too complex for children. Rowling refused to compromise and eventually found a publisher willing to take a chance on her book. As a result, millions of children have not only learned to enjoy reading but have also gained a greater appreciation for (and quite possibly greater metacognitive awareness of) language itself.

REFERENCES

Alverman, D. 1983. Reading achievement and linguistic stages: A comparison of disabled readers and Chomsky's 6-to-10-year-olds. *Journal of Research Developments in Education*, 16:26–31.

Barnitz, J. G. 1986. The anaphora jigsaw puzzle in psycholinguistic and reading research. In *Understanding and Teaching Cohesion Comprehension*, J. W. Irwin (Ed.), (pp. 45–55). Newark, DE: International Reading Association.

Baumann, J. F. 1987. Anaphora in basal reader selections: How often do they occur? *Journal of Reading Behavior*, 19:141–58.

Baumann, J. F., and Stevenson, J. A. 1986. Teaching students to comprehend anaphoric relations. In *Understanding and Teaching Cohesion Comprehension*, J. W. Irwin (Ed.), (pp. 95–123). Newark, DE: International Reading Association.

Bentin, S., Deutsch, A., and Liberman, I. Y. 1990. Syntactic competence and reading ability in children. *Journal of Experimental Child Psychology*, 48:147–72.

Bishop, D. V. M., and Adams, C. 1990. A prospective study of the relationship between specific language impairment, phonological disorders, and reading retardation. *Journal of Child Psychology and Psychiatry*, 31:1027–50.

Bishop, D. V. M., and Butterworth, G. E. 1980. Verbal-performance discrepancies: Relationship to birth risks and specific reading retardation. *Cortex*, 16:375–90.

Bouquet, T. December 2000. The wizard behind Harry Potter. *Reader's Digest*, 94–101.

Bowey, J. A. 1986a. Syntactic awareness and verbal performance from preschool to fifth grade. *Journal of Applied Psycholinguistics*, 15:285–308.

Bowey, J. A. 1986b. Syntactic awareness in relation to reading skill and ongoing reading comprehension monitoring. *Journal of Experimental Child Psychology*, 41:282–99.

Bowey, J. A. 1994. Grammatical awareness and learning to read: A critique. In *Literacy Acquisition and Social Context*, E. M. H. Assink (Ed.), (pp. 122–49). London: Harvester Wheatsheaf/Prentice Hall.

Butler, K. G. 1988. Preschool language processing performance and later reading achievement. In *Preschool Prevention of Reading Failure*, R. L. Masland and M. W. Masland (Eds.), (pp. 19–51). Parkton, MD: York Press.

Cain, K., and Oakhill, J. V. 1999. Inference making ability and its relation to comprehension failure in young children. *Reading and Writing*, 11:489–503.

Catts, H. W., Fey, M. E., Zhang, X., and Tomblin, B. 1999. Language basis of reading and reading disabilities: Evidence from a longitudinal investigation. *Scientific Studies of Reading*, 3:331–61.

Clark, C. H. 1986. Instructional strategies to promote comprehension of normal and non-cohesive text. In *Understanding and Teaching Cohesion Comprehension*, J. W. Irwin (Ed.), (pp. 125–136). Newark, DE: International Reading Association.

Chomsky, N. 1965. *Aspects of the Theory of Syntax*. Cambridge, MA: MIT Press.

Crystal, D. 1987. *The Cambridge Encyclopedia of Language*. Cambridge, England: Cambridge University Press.

Demont, E., and Gombert, J. E. 1996. Phonological awareness as a predictor of recoding skills and syntactic awareness as a predictor of comprehension skills. *British Journal of Educational Psychology*, 66:315–32.

Demorest, A., Meyer, C., Phelps, E., Gardner, H., and Winner, E. 1984. Words speak louder than actions: Understanding deliberately false remarks. *Child Development*, 55:1527–34.

Dickinson, D. K., and Tabors, P. O. 2001. *Beginning Literacy with Language: Young Children Learning at Home and School*. Baltimore, MD: Paul H. Brookes Publishing.

Fayne, H. R. 1981. A comparison of learning disabled adolescents with normal learners on an anaphoric pronomial reference task. *Journal of Learning Disabilities*, 14:597–99.

Fey, M. E., Cleave, P. L., Long, S. H., and Hughes, D. L. 1993. Two approaches to the facilitation of grammar in children with language impairment: An experimental evaluation. *Journal of Speech and Hearing Research*, 36:141–57.

Fowler, A. E. 1988. Grammaticality judgments and reading skill in grade 2. *Annals of Dyslexia*, 38:73–94.

Fry, E., Weber, J., and DePierro, J. 1978. A partial validation of the kernel distance theory for readability. In *Reading: Disciplined Inquiry in Process and Practice*, P. D. Pearson and J. Hansen (Eds.), (pp. 121–24). Clemson, SC: National Reading Conference.

Geva, E., and Ryan, E. B. 1985. Use of conjunctions in expository texts by skilled and less skilled readers. *Journal of Reading Behavior*, 17:331–46.

Gillon, G., and Dodd, B. 1995. The effects of training phonological, semantic, and syntactic processing skills in spoken language on reading ability. *Language, Speech, and Hearing Services in Schools*, 26:58–68.

Gleitman, L. R. 1990. The structural sources of word meaning. *Language Acquisition*, 1:3–55.

Gottardo, A., Stanovich, K., and Siegel, L. 1996. The relationships between phonological sensitivity, syntactic processing, and verbal working memory in the reading performance of third-grade children. *Journal of Experimental Child Psychology*, 63:563–82.

Goulandris, N. K., Snowling, M. J., and Walker, I. 2000. Is dyslexia a form of specific language impairment? A comparison of dyslexic and language impaired children as adolescents. *Annals of Dyslexia*, 50:103–20.

Halliday, M. A. K., and Hasan, R. 1976. *Cohesion in English*. London: Longman.

Harris, A. J., and Sipay, E. R. 1990. *How to Increase Reading Ability: A Guide to Developmental and Remedial Methods*, 9th ed. White Plains, NY: Longman.

Layton, A., Robinson, J., and Lawson, M. 1998. The relationship between syntactic awareness and reading performance. *Journal of Research in Reading*, 21:5–23.

Mann, V. A., Shankweiler, D., and Smith, S. T. 1983. The association between comprehension of spoken sentences and early reading ability: The role of phonetic representation. *Child Language*, 11:627–43.

Maria, K. 1990. *Reading Comprehension Instruction: Issues and Strategies.* Parkton, MD: York Press.

McClure, E., and Steffensen, M. 1985. A study of the use of conjunctions across grades and ethnic groups. *Research in the Teaching of English*, 19:217–36.

McNeil, J. D. 1987. *Reading Comprehension: New Directions for Classroom Practice.* Glenview, IL: Scott Foresman.

Moe, A. J., and Irwin, J. W. 1986. Cohesion, coherence, and comprehension. In *Understanding and Teaching Cohesion Comprehension*, J. W. Irwin (Ed.), (pp. 3–8). Newark, DE: International Reading Association.

Morice, R., and Slaghuis, W. 1985. Language performance and reading ability at 8 years of age. *Applied Psycholinguistics*, 6:141–60.

Nation, K., and Snowling, M. 1998. Individual differences in contextual facilitation: Evidence from dyslexia and poor reading comprehension. *Child Development*, 69:996–1011.

Neville, D. D., and Sears, E. F. 1985. The effect of sentence combining and kernel-identification training on the syntactic component of reading comprehension. *Research in the Teaching of English*, 19:37–61.

Nippold, M. A. 1998. *Later Language Development: The School-age and Adolescent Years.* Austin, TX: PRO-ED.

Nippold, M. A., Schwarz, I. E., and Undlin, R. A. 1992. Use and understanding of adverbial conjuncts. *Journal of Speech and Hearing Research*, 35:108–18.

Oakhill, J. 1994. Individual differences in children's text comprehension. In *Handbook of Psycholinguistics*, M. A. Gernsbacher (Ed.), (pp. 821–48). New York: Academic Press.

Oakhill, J., Garnham, A., and Vonk, W. 1989. The on-line construction of discourse models. *Language and Cognitive Processes*, 4:263–86.

Pearl, R., Bryan, T., Fallon, P., and Herzog, A. 1991. Learning disabled students' detection of deception. *Learning Disabilities Research and Practice*, 6:12–16.

Pratt, C., Tunmer, W. E., and Bowey, J. A. 1984. Children's capacity to correct grammatical violations in sentences. *Journal of Child Language*, 11:129–41.

Pulver, C. J. 1986. Teaching students to understand explicit and implicit connectives. In *Understanding and Teaching Cohesion Comprehension*, J. W. Irwin (Ed.) (pp. 69–82). Newark, DE: International Reading Association.

Radvansky, G. A., and Zacks, R. T. 1997. The retrieval of situation-specific information. In *Cognitive Models of Memory*, M. A. Conway (Ed.), (pp. 173–213). Cambridge, MA: MIT Press.

Rego, L. L. B., and Bryant, P. E. 1993. The connection between phonological, syntactic, and semantic skills and children's reading and spelling. *European Journal of Psychology of Education*, 8:235–46.

Rescorla, L. 2000. Do late-talking toddlers turn out to have reading difficulties a decade later? *Annals of Dyslexia*, 50:87–102.

Sawyer, D. J., and Butler, K. 1991. Early language intervention: A deterrent to reading disability. *Annals of Dyslexia*, 41:55–79.

Scarborough, H. S. 1990. Very early language deficits in dyslexic children. *Child Development*, 61:1728–43.

Scarborough, H. S. 1991. Early syntactic development of dyslexic children. *Annals of Dyslexia*, 41:207–20.

Siegel, L. S., and Ryan, E. B. 1984. Reading disability as a language disorder. *Remedial and Special Education*, 5:28–33.

Siegel, L. S., and Ryan, E. B. 1988. Development of grammatical-sensitivity, phonological, and short-term memory skills in normally achieving and learning disabled children. *Developmental Psychology*, 24:28–37.

Share, D. L., and Silva, P. A. 1987. Language deficits and specific reading retardation: Cause or effect. *British Journal of Disorders of Communication*, 22:219–26.

Smith, S. T., Macaruso, P., Shankweiler, D., and Crain, S. 1989. Syntactic comprehension in young poor readers. *Applied Psycholinguistics*, 10:429–54.

Smith, W. L., and Combs, W. E. 1980. The effects of overt and covert cues on written syntax. *Research in the Teaching of English*, 14:19–38.

Stanovich, K. 1986. Matthew effects in reading: Some consequences of individual differences in the acquisition of literacy. *Reading Research Quarterly*, 20:360–406.

Straw, S. B., and Schreiner, R. 1982. The effects of sentence manipulation on subsequent measures of reading and listening. *Reading Research Quarterly*, 17:339–52.

Tager-Flusberg, H. 1993. Putting words together: Morphology and syntax in the preschool years. In *The Development of Language*, 3rd ed. J. B. Gleason (Ed.), New York: Maxmillian.

Tunmer, W. E. 1989. The role of language-related factors in reading disability. In *Phonology and Reading Disability: Solving the Puzzle*, D. Shankweiler and I. Y. Liberman (Eds.), (pp. 91–131). Ann Arbor: University of Michigan Press.

Tunmer, W. E., Nesdale, A. R., and Wright, A. D. 1987. Syntactic awareness and reading acquisition. *British Journal of Developmental Psychology*, 5:25–34.

Tyler, A., and Nagy, W. 1990. Use of derivational morphology during reading. *Cognition*, 36:17–34.

Vogel, S. 1975. *Syntactic Abilities in Normal and Dyslexic Children*. Baltimore: University Park Press.

Weaver, P. 1979. Improving reading comprehension: Effects of sentence organization instruction. *Reading Research Quarterly*, 15:127–46.

White, C. V., Pascarella, E. T., and Pflaum, S. W. 1981. Effects of training in sentence construction on the comprehension of learning disabled children. *Journal of Educational Psychology*, 73:697–704.

Willows, D., and Ryan, E. 1986. The development of grammatical sensitivity and its relationship to early reading achievement. *Reading Research Quarterly*, 21:253–66.

Yuill, N. M., and Oakhill, J. V. 1988. Understanding of anaphoric relations in skilled and less skilled comprehenders. *British Journal of Psychology*, 79:173–86.

7

Texts and Discourse Comprehension

GETTING STARTED

✓ How and why does comprehension vary with different text genres and media forms?
✓ What is meant by "text structure"? And how does the structure of a text affect comprehension and recall?
✓ Why do poor readers have difficulties becoming aware of discourse characteristics and text structures?
✓ What methods are effective in teaching poor readers sensitivity to discourse factors and text structures?

VARIATION IN TEXTS AND DISCOURSE

Texts are integrated expressions of an author's feelings, thoughts, and ideas. Texts can be oral as well as written, but because our focus is on reading, we are concerned primarily with the nature of written texts and the challenges of understanding and learning from them. These texts are permanent, static artifacts (Alexander and Jetton 2000). In the form of books, they sit on shelves in libraries, schools, and homes waiting to be read. When they are read, the individual reader completes the communication process, but he or she also takes away personal reactions, ideas, and information from the text. Though the text itself does not change, what is taken away by a reader depends on that reader. Comprehension of texts is a dynamic process.

A person's understanding of a particular written text is a matter of not just the characteristics of the text itself but also the knowledge and reading skill of the reader. Certainly, the nature of the discourse in the text and the content do matter a great deal. Even an experienced adult reader will struggle to make sense of a technical report, particularly in an unfamiliar content area. The reader may lack the vocabulary and background knowledge to follow the explanations. Children who are learning to read have additional challenges. They may have trouble reading the words or understanding the conventions of communication associated with a given genre—for example, a play or a poem. We need to be aware,

139

too, that students in today's schools encounter a variety of types of texts. There are different genres, such as poems, plays, stories, novels, essays and textbooks. There are also different forms of media, such as hypermedia and interactive media.

Understanding the relation of texts and reading comprehension is made even more complex when we take into consideration the varied characteristics of written discourse. Consider expository texts (also known as informational texts). Expository texts vary in rhetorical structure. For example, the purpose might be to explain causes (e.g., why leaves on deciduous trees turn color in the fall), or it might be to tell events in the order in which they occurred (e.g., what happened when Daniel Boone crossed the Appalachian mountains). Texts also vary in terms of the order of presentation of ideas and information and the explicitness with which the organization is presented to the reader. Sometimes the main point of the article is stated at the beginning, whereas at other times the writer leaves it to the reader to figure out what the main point is. The relations among ideas may vary as well.

Two other text-based factors affect comprehension. These are the complexity of the language and discourse patterns. The familiarity of the vocabulary and sentence structures makes a difference. We discussed these and related aspects of linguistic complexity in Chapters 5 and 6. In addition to these factors, the ways that words and sentences are related to one another affect the coherence of the discourse. By coherence, we mean the ease with which the reader can understand the ideas and information in a text, as they are related to one another and contribute to the reader's construction of a mental representation of the meaning of the text.

Along with the structure of the text, we need to consider the content, or the knowledge base that the text draws on or refers to. Comprehension may be challenging if the information is abstract, replete with unfamiliar concepts, and so on. The clarity of the presentation of information (e.g., Are ideas elaborated? Are examples given?) may also affect comprehensibility. Further, the mapping between the particular information in a text and the reader's knowledge structures may or may not be straightforward.

Thus far, we have identified four aspects of the texts that are likely to influence comprehension—genre, text structure, linguistic complexity, and content. We have indicated, too, that characteristics of the reader affect comprehension of different texts. Readers vary in their background knowledge of the content of the text, their experience with the genre, and their ability to handle the language of the text. In addition, researchers have found that there are developmental changes in students' understanding of the types of logical relations writers use to explain ideas (e.g., Horowitz 1987). For instance, children grasp temporal relations before they understand causal relations. In fact, young children are apt to confuse temporal and causal relations. They might think that when two events occur one right after the other, the first one caused the second. For example, the arrival of the train at the station caused the whistle to blow. There are also differences between normally achieving and low achieving readers in the appreciation of texts and discourse structures. We will discuss these at greater length later in this chapter.

In schools, the context in which particular texts are read also affects the ease with which students understand them and can learn from them. The teacher sets the goals, assigns tasks, and establishes the nature of the learning activities in the classroom (the situation organizer). The choice of interactive tasks and the learning activities (such as shared reading and discussion) might make it easier for students to learn from a difficult text than if they were to read the material on their own and try to master new concepts with no support. Because this is the case, it is important to consider how teachers can provide appropriate support for students who might have difficulties reading content-area texts—a topic we return to in Chapter 9.

The teachers' goals and uses of texts can affect students' long-term retention, not just their ability to complete assignments on a day-to-day basis. If the ideas and information are abstract and seemingly outside the realm of "useful" knowledge for young students, little may stay with them for future use. For example, eighth graders in a physical science course might retain little if they simply read and study a chapter on the separation of substances, including distillation and filtering, in order to take a test. However, if the teacher helps them put the ideas to use, they might end up with an enduring sense of the value of the new knowledge. The teacher might give them the assignment of finding out why bottled water is such a popular commodity today. What is wrong with tap water or well water? What are the pros and cons of drinking distilled water?

This chapter deals with the nature of written texts and the ways reader and context variables interact with texts to affect comprehension and learning. We focus on genres of written texts, text and discourse structures, and content. Because the difficulty of understanding given texts is in large part determined by the reader's abilities, interests, and knowledge, as well as the context in which the text is read, we include discussion of the interactions of these factors.

GENRE AND TEXT STRUCTURE

It takes experience to appreciate different written-language genres. For example, exposure to poetry (oral or written) provides a foundation for understanding conventions of writing poetry and of communicating with others through this genre. The most prevalent genres for school-age students involve forms of narration and exposition, including stories, novels, newspaper articles, essays, textbooks, and the like. Increasingly, students are also exposed to different forms of electronic media, including interactive computer programs and the web.

Traditional texts and electronic texts have different characteristics, according to Alexander and Jetton (2000). One distinguishing dimension is whether they are linear or nonlinear in nature. Traditional forms of written discourse are linear, as is indicated by the fact that any actions the reader takes to understand the text depend on his or her own initiative. In contrast, electronic texts are nonlinear. They are "connected discourse accompanied by a database management system that guides or prompts readers to reaccess or extend the main text through associative computer-based links to other informational screens" (p. 290). Because of these links, computer technologies provide ready access to a variety of types of information from different sources on a given topic, and they facilitate learning from multiple texts as well. For example, having read a book about witchcraft in early New England settlements (a linear text), a student may then go the library and check out *The Crucible*, a play on the same topic. Another student with access to the Internet can search for information on the topic of witchcraft. He or she might be able to read legal papers on the witchcraft trials or religious tracts on Puritan beliefs and might find out about various works of literature inspired by the persecution of witches. As Alexander and Jetton (2000) have pointed out, computer technologies have changed how we teach and learn from texts, but we still do not know whether technological advances have led to better knowledge acquisition. Still, educators cannot simply "sit back and wait to see what happens. Today's students are already learning with and from these technologies" (p. 288).

The three types of text that are most relevant to learning in school are narrative, expository, and a mixture of the two. In the early elementary years, children read mostly narratives. Their exposure to informational texts is quite limited, and in fact, relatively few informational texts are available at the elementary reading levels, should teachers want to use them (Duke 2000). At about fourth grade, students encounter expository or informational texts in their content-area courses (e.g., social studies). Textbooks contain primarily expository texts, but they may also include mixed texts. Mixed texts have characteristics of both narration and exposition. For example, in a chemistry textbook, personal accounts, such as Marie Curie's discovery of radioactivity, may be used as an introduction to an explanation of the nature of radioactive elements.

The transition from reading mostly narrative to mostly informational texts is not an easy one for many students in the late elementary years. Many find it difficult to understand texts that contain unfamiliar discourse structures, vocabulary, and concepts, and this is often what informational texts are like (Englert and Hiebert 1984; Flood, Lapp, and Farnan 1986). There has been considerable criticism of the text structure and discourse characteristics of textbooks in recent years. Textbooks for content areas such as science and social studies are too often written in such a way that the ideas and information are hard to grasp (Beck and McKeown 1989). As a result, many students, not just those who are underachieving readers, have trouble learning from textbooks. The problems of comprehending and learning from textbooks are compounded by the lack of instruction in how to learn from such sources of information. (See Chapter 9 for further discussion of this topic.)

FORMING A MENTAL REPRESENTATION OF A TEXT

A reader who enjoys reading certain types of texts, such as books about nature, acquires not only vocabulary that refers to the natural world, but also an appreciation for ways of knowing within that discipline. In reading words, sentences, and paragraphs, the reader links ideas and information within the text itself and also between the text and the reader's knowledge of that particular topic. Thus, text-driven and knowledge-driven processes are interwoven (Goldman and Rakestraw 2000) and are the basis for formation of a coherent mental representation of the text. This mental representation contains ideas and information as they are related to one another, linked where possible to prior knowledge. In the reader's mind, the text is not just a collection of random bits of information but is instead organized in a way that aids both understanding and retrieval of information (van den Broek 1990). Making links between ideas within the text and between content of the text and prior knowledge requires inferential processes. To build on an example given by van Oostendorp and Goldman (1999), a reader of an article about urban development might find references to New York City and also to the Big Apple. Some readers will realize that the second term refers to the first; this they knew before they read the article. Other readers would have to infer from the context that the Big Apple was another name for New York City. Inferences are required at all levels of text processing and are a crucial determinant of the quality and nature of the mental representation a given reader constructs as he or she reads a particular text.

Text Structure and Idea Relations

A reader uses a particular arrangement of ideas and information (the structure of the text) as a kind of framework into which individual events or pieces of information are fit. Without awareness of the structure of a written text, a reader's understanding may be fragmented and poorly organized, and recall of the text is jeopardized. Experience reading different types of texts builds awareness of text structures. Once a reader gains such awareness, he or she can develop expectations about the text structure, sometimes without reading more than a sentence or two of the text. For example, the title of a selection in a fifth-grade basal reader is "Incredible Journeys," and the first sentence states "You probably know that birds fly south for the winter, but did you know that butterflies do, too?" The reader is likely to expect a description of the seasonal migrations made by butterflies. Using this expectation, the reader can readily follow the writer's train of thought.

Through her studies of expository texts, Meyer (1984) identified five top-level rhetorical structures. These are collection or list, description, cause, comparison, and problem-solution. (Other researchers have presented similar schemes for the major types of rhetorical structures.) Familiarity with expository texts is bound to help students become accustomed to the ways writers organize their thinking about and connect ideas. In addition, the development of children's cognitive abilities provides a foundation for understanding and distinguishing different types of idea relations (Horowitz 1987). In general, students have a harder time acquiring and using awareness of expository than narrative text structures. There are several reasons for this. One is that narratives tend to be characterized by temporal relations, and readers can focus on the particular job of inferring the relation of causal factors in the narrative chain of events. Information texts, on the other hand, can have any of the five rhetorical structures listed above. A second reason is that children are exposed to narratives from the time they are very young. The time ordering that characterizes narratives becomes familiar as they listen to their parents and siblings tell about their experiences and about events in the community. In contrast, they have less exposure to "informational" texts in the elementary years (Duke 2000).

The relations among ideas within a passage also need to be understood in terms of their relative importance. We tend to use the term "main ideas" to refer to the central points (whether stated or implied) in expository text and "main events" in narrative text. Attention to the major points is a powerful way to support comprehension and memory of text. In fact, results of studies have shown that readers who are good at identifying main ideas are also likely to recall the details or less important ideas as well (e.g., Meyer 1984). Main ideas serve as a kind of framework in which details and subsidiary ideas are held in place.

Closely related to these aspects of text organization is understanding of the logical relations of ideas and information at the local (as opposed to global) level. Connections among ideas and the resulting organization of the passage information are thought to capture fundamental patterns of human thought. Ideas and their relations to one another may be represented explicitly. Explicit statements of main ideas or of the organization of a text are most helpful to readers when they come early in the text (Day and Zajakowski 1991). When an explicit statement of a main idea starts a paragraph, we call this statement a topic sentence. In the following topic sentence, "The farmers' use of the land affected the quality of the water in the river in two ways," note that we are given not only the topic (how the farmer's land use affected water quality) but also a signal about how the idea will be developed (explanation of the "two ways").

Signals of this sort exist within the body of paragraphs, not just at the beginning. Signals are verbal cues that alert the reader to the organization and idea relations in the text that follows. The particular signals are likely to indicate the relation of ideas within a paragraph or passage. If a paragraph provides a list of ideas or reasons, the signals might be "one," "another," "yet another." If the paragraph gives events in time order, the signals might be "first," "then," "finally." If the paragraph involves comparison, the signals might be "similarly," "on the other hand," "however."

Meyer (1984) used the term *signaling* to refer to various linguistic devices that a writer might use to help the reader follow the structure of a text. Because signaling helps the reader understand the organization of ideas, it affects both comprehension and recall. In both narrative and informational texts, other devices are used to help the reader follow the writer's train of thought. These include repetitions of key words and phrases and the use of pronoun references (i.e., cohesive devices, as discussed in Chapter 6). In addition, the writer conveys the organization of ideas through rhetorical devices such as explicit statements of the purpose or graphic devices such as indentation of paragraphs or bullets to list points.

Not all texts contain clear devices to direct the reader's attention to idea relations. When signals are not used, the reader must determine the relation of ideas from the content. As noted earlier, the need to infer relations may affect the reader's appreciation of the coherence of the text, which in turn may affect the nature of the mental representation that is constructed during reading. Inexperienced or struggling readers may have particular difficulties understanding texts that rely on their ability to infer idea relations. Needless to say, these different characteristics of texts (i.e., explicit statements of main ideas, use of signaling, the nature of idea relations) interact with one another. Notice that example (a) below provides an implicit statement of a causal relation, and no signaling is used. Because of these traits, the cause-effect relations might be hard for young readers to appreciate. In contrast, in example (b), young readers are likely to understand the temporal relations that are marked by signaling (i.e., *at the same time, then*).

(a) The toddler raced around the corner and ran directly into the little table by the door. The table toppled over and the lamp crashed to the floor, breaking into many pieces.
(b) The hummingbird drank the nectar from the flower, at the same time collecting pollen on her neck. Then, at the next flower some of this pollen rubbed off on the petals and was left behind.

As these examples show, the discourse structure varies in terms of how much help is given the reader. We have seen that comprehension of texts is affected by the nature of the rhetorical or logical relations among ideas, the explicitness of statements of the main ideas, and the use of devices to signal structure and relations. These can interact with one another, too, making the text that much harder or easier for the reader to understand and remember.

Background Knowledge Usually, But Not Always, Facilitates Comprehension

One final consideration is the content of the text as it is related to the reader's knowledge in that domain. The reader's familiarity with the content area may affect the ease with which he or she can develop a coherent mental representation of the text. If the reader has some appropriate knowledge of the topic about which he or she is reading, the comprehension process becomes one in which old information and ideas are adapted to include new information and ideas. As a result, the reader who has background information to start with retains more of the details and general points in a passage than the reader with little or no background knowledge (Stahl et al. 1991). In contrast, a reader with no prior knowledge of a topic must start from scratch, building an understanding of unfamiliar concepts, words, and ideas.

Of course, background knowledge is not an all-or-none proposition. Nonetheless, readers with "high" knowledge are better able to identify and recall central ideas and to integrate information than readers with "low" knowledge. For elementary students reading history texts, McKeown and Beck (1990) found that students' recall was characterized by simple associations; their answers to questions showed that they did not perceive connections among ideas, and they sometimes misunderstood events and relations of events. One reason may be that the students' lacked familiarity with the topics covered in the history text.

Sometimes the reader's previous experience or knowledge interferes with his or her comprehension of the text. Researchers have shown that when prior knowledge conflicts with passage information, readers tend to rely on their prior knowledge (Alvermann, Smith, and Readance 1985). When this happens, the reader is likely to interpret passage information in the light of his or her prior knowledge and to distort the meaning of the text. This problem may be particularly pronounced in the case of poor readers who have difficulty in the first place taking information from the text. Perhaps because of difficulties with linguistic processing, poor comprehenders might stick with what they knew before reading rather than including information from the text in their up-dated knowledge base (Maria and MacGinitie 1982).

Roller (1990) has argued that text structure and prior knowledge can work together to support understanding and recall of the text. Text structure may support comprehension and recall best when the passage is moderately familiar. In this situation, the reader can use text structure to infer relations among concepts. However, when the reader knows a lot about the topic, the text structure is not so helpful. When the content is very familiar, a clearly delineated text structure may not be necessary for understanding how ideas about that topic are related to one another. On the other hand, if the passage content is entirely unfamiliar, the organization of the text might not provide adequate compensation for the reader.

Voss and Bisanz (1985) found that in reading baseball passages, both "low knowledge" and "high knowledge" readers made use the passage structure to construct relations among ideas. However, the high knowledge readers were more successful at seeing idea relations, presumably because of their familiarity with the game of baseball. A later study showed interactions between three factors: knowledge, text structure, and reading comprehension skill (Voss and Slifies 1996). It appears that poor readers depend more on explicitly marked text structure than good readers do as a support for their understanding of texts, whether the topics are familiar and unfamiliar (Goldman and Rakestraw 2000). They are less able to infer structural relations on their own.

Comprehension of Narrative and Informational Texts by Poor Readers

With experience, most students gradually develop awareness of the rhetorical structures used in written texts, but it is important that teachers facilitate the development of this awareness, because it plays an important role in comprehension and learning. Below fifth grade, students have difficulty seeing the relative importance of different ideas in informational texts. Similarly, students with reading and learning disabilities (LD) tend to be delayed in their comprehension of the different text structures of informational texts (Weisberg and Balajthy 1989). Both micro-textual clues to meaning (e.g., relational words within sentences) and macro-textual clues to meaning (e.g., signal words like *then, first, finally*) present challenges because of limitations in the development of their language comprehension capabilities. Poor readers can be overwhelmed by the process of integrating ideas presented by the language of the texts. This happens (at least in part) because they cannot organize the information in their heads; they cannot sort out the important from the less important information. If poor readers are unable to demonstrate awareness of the overarching themes or ideas, they are also likely to have difficulty relating details and subsidiary ideas to these main themes.

Awareness of story grammar, which refers to the basic elements of stories, is typically picked up by children as they listen to and then read stories in their preschool years, but children who are struggling readers are slower at developing an awareness of story grammar. This is evident from the stories they tell and from their comprehension of stories they read (Montague, Maddux, and Dereshiwsky 1990), as they are less likely to attend to the main characters, the setting, the problem that gets the story events underway, and the like. Another way to think about story structure is by conceiving of the events as forming a causal chain; on this chain are events that are directly linked to one another. For example, in the story of Goldilocks and the Three Bears, Goldilocks was hungry so she ate the bear's porridge, and she was tired so she climbed into Baby Bear's bed to sleep. These events are on the causal chain. If the story included discussion of less central events, such as what Mother Bear did to make the porridge, those events would be off the causal chain, and because they are not crucial links in the chain of events, they would be less likely to be remembered by the reader. The causal chain, which links one event to the next, may not be grasped by young children and students with reading disabilities. Montague, Maddux and Dereshiwsky (1990) gave students of three age groups (4–5, 7–8, and 10–11 years), with and without LD, two tasks that required processing of story grammar: retelling stories and writing stories. They found that the students with LD performed less well than their peers in terms of amount and type of information in their stories. In this study, students with LD, compared to their peers, demonstrated a less well-developed understanding of story grammar. However, even if they recalled fewer story statements than their peers, students with LD still recalled more statements on the causal chain than off the causal chain (Wolman 1991; Wolman, van den Broek, and Lorch 1997). Two factors that affect long-term recall of story information are the students' reading ability and the complexity of the causal structure of the story.

In the same way that awareness of story grammar affects comprehension and recall of narratives, awareness of expository structures affects understanding and recall of information from expository passages. Researchers have found an impact of awareness of text structure on comprehension by comparing students' recall of well-ordered passages and passages with randomly ordered sentences. In one study (Taylor and Samuels 1983), fifth and sixth graders who were aware of text structure recalled more from the well-ordered than the scrambled passages. In contrast, the children who were less aware performed similarly on scrambled and normal passage.

The results of other studies have also indicated that young students and struggling readers are not adept at using text structure as an aid to memory retrieval (Richgels et al. 1987). Englert and Thomas (1987) studied the awareness and use of text structure by younger (third and fourth grades) and older students with LD (sixth and seventh grades), as well as normally achieving students. Students read and selected sentences to add to a text; the correct choices were those that fit the structure of the passage. The students were also asked to write two sentences to add to some passages. Again, the question was whether they would write sentences that suited the structure of the passage. The passages were all expository, including description, enumeration, sequence, and comparison/contrast. The results showed that the students with LD were less sensitive to the text structures than their peers and that lack of awareness contributed to their difficulties reading and writing passages. They were less able to appreciate idea relations and to predict the kind of information that would be likely to come next.

In this study difficulty detecting and using text structures as an aid to comprehension was not the result of word reading problems. What other reasons have been given? There are a number of possible explanations. One is that poor readers have difficulties with language learning; this includes learning both micro-structural and macro-structural properties of language. The micro-structural level leads to the kinds of difficulties processing sentences that were discussed in Chapter 6. Macro-structural properties include the logical relations implied by signaling terms, as discussed earlier in this chapter. Evidence of difficulties processing linguistic structure can be found in students' retelling of information passages that they have read (Carlisle 1999). Poor readers' recall protocols are less well organized and less substantive than those of their peers. A second reason may be their inexperience analyzing written texts. They spend less time engaging with written texts and may be reluctant to analyze passages for meaning. A third reason is that the students with reading problems are less adept than their peers at implicit learning of appropriate strategies for remembering and organizing information (Englert and Thomas 1987). Kletzien (1991) studied the strategies that good and poor readers reported using on a cloze procedure reading task. One finding was that the students used organizational strategies more on passages of medium difficulty than on those of high or low difficulty. Furthermore, the total number of strategies poor readers used declined as the passages became more difficult. Her results suggest that reading ability and passage difficulty affect students' use of strategies to perform reading tasks.

For poor readers, acquiring an awareness of text structure may be particularly important. Such awareness leads to an appreciation of organizational factors and experience using the structure of the text as a way to remember information. Deliberate use of a strategy of analyzing the structure of texts may also lead to more active processing and greater effort to understand and remember what is read. Awareness of text structure is not a panacea for all of the problems associated with understanding and learning from different genres and texts, but it is likely to enhance the coherence of the reader's mental representation of texts.

APPROACHES TO INSTRUCTION

Among researchers, there is general consensus that text structure can be taught to students and that awareness of text structure can improve reading comprehension. There are important implications of these research results, not only for instruction of students who are poor readers but also for educators responsible for selecting textbooks and trade books for students to read. Goldman and Rakestraw (2000) suggested that students can be taught to identify and follow text structures as they read; this requires teaching them to identify particular types of structures (e.g., comparison, cause). Students can also be taught to create graphic aids that represent text structures. For most students, acquiring a solid grasp of story grammar is easier than becoming adept at recognizing expository structures. One reason for this is that there are different ways to relate ideas and organize information in informational passages (Gersten et al. 2001).

One approach that has received considerable attention is teaching students story grammar. Such instruction involves helping students learn to recognize the basic components of stories. These include (but are not limited to) characters, setting, the problem (or initiating event), and the solution. Sometimes questions are used to focus attention on these components (e.g., What is the setting? Who are the characters?). Often, a story map is used, and with this aid, students create a graphic display of basic story elements (Idol and Croll 1987). Story grammar instruction has been shown to improve story comprehension of both good and poor readers from first grade through high school. In fact, in one study (Hayward and Schneider 2000), preschoolers with language impairments improved in their recall of story information and their story production after they had received seven weeks of instruction in story grammar components.

In general, story grammar instruction helps poor readers improve both their recall of story elements and their comprehension of stories, although there is not always an improvement in overall reading comprehension. Idol and Croll (1987) demonstrated that a story map was effective in improving the story comprehension of students who were poor readers in first grade. Direct instruction of an advanced story map procedure has also been shown to increase story grammar knowledge of students with LD in the sixth and eighth grades (Gardill and Jitendra 1999). On retell measures, students included more story elements; they also showed improvement in their basal passage comprehension. However, improvement in reading stories in basals or anthologies has not been found in all such research studies. For example, story grammar instruction helped high school students with LD to recall important elements in stories but did not affect their performance on detail-oriented questions that followed stories in a high school anthology (Gurney et al. 1990). Differences in results may stem from the variation in the severity of reading problems among the study participants and from the nature of the instructional programs.

Specific information about the use of graphic organizers for story grammar training can be found in case studies of five intermediate-level students with comprehension problems carried out by Idol and Croll (1987). The students were taught to use a template called a story map, which is shown in Chapter 4 (figure 4.2). In the training phase, they read a story with the teacher and were aided in locating the information to complete the map.

After the map had been completed, the students retold the story and answered comprehension questions. When a student reached stability at the

criterion level of 80% correct on the comprehension measure, the story map procedure was stopped. The results showed that all five students made progress on
various post-reading measures (e.g., answering implicit and explicit questions,
story retelling), and four of the five maintained their improved performance after
the intervention was over. Because students tended to provide more information
about story components in their retellings, the researchers inferred that the use of
the story map affected their awareness of story components, which, in turn, affected their story comprehension.

Instruction in story grammar has been compared to some other methods of
improving comprehension of narratives. In one study (Short and Ryan 1984),
fourth graders were instructed in a strategy for finding story grammar elements
in stories; a second group received both the strategy instruction and attribution
training, whereas a third group received only attribution training. The attribution training procedures emphasized students' learning of the relation between
effort and reading outcomes. Five self-statements were used to help the children
take a more active stance in their reading. The story grammar strategy focused
on the children's learning of five questions; these were: (a) Who is the main
character? (b) Where and when did the story take place? (c) What did the main
character do? (d) How did the story end? (e) How did the main character feel?
Training in the use of these questions took place over three sessions. During the
sessions, students in the strategy conditions were prompted to vocalize the
"wh" questions, to note question cues in the margin (e.g., MC standing for main
character), and to underline the story information answering the question. This
strategy training (with and without attribution training) led to better performance on post-treatment measures than the attribution training alone. One reason for progress seemed to be a greater attention to self-monitoring of
comprehension.

In a similar manner, instruction in the structure of expository passages has
been shown to benefit poor readers. Here, too, graphic organizers have been
found to be beneficial to students, even if they are not always more effective than
other methods (Griffin and Tulbert 1995). For example, Simmons, Griffin, and
Kame'enui (1988) compared teachers' pre-reading use of graphic organizers,
post-reading use of graphic organizers, and traditional instructional activities
suggested by the sixth-grade science book (e.g., activating prior knowledge,
questioning and discussion). Their poor readers in these three conditions did
equally well on the short-term probes and on a post-test following treatment.
However, the pre-reading graphic organizer group did better than the others on
a delayed posttest.

Graphic organizers that show different relations between ideas have been
used to improve both the reading and writing of expository texts (Flood, Lapp,
and Farnan 1986; Griffin and Tulbert 1995). Figure 7.1 from Flood, Lapp, and
Farnan (1986) shows a plan for reading and writing exposition paragraphs.
Notice that it provides the structure for the student, on the assumption that after
repeated uses, the student will internalize the relations of ideas captured by the
graphic organizer. In this example, the student is learning to articulate a main
idea and to present ideas or details to support it.

Step 1. Teacher helps student select topic and list background knowledge
    Topic: _____
    Facts I already knew about the topic   1. _____
                                        2. _____
                                        3. _____
                                        4. _____
                                        5. _____

Step 2. Student turns to other sources of information
    Facts I have learned about the topic

	Source	Fact
	1. (reference material, e.g., encyclopedia) _____	1. _____
	2. (reference material) _____	2. _____
	3. (teacher) _____	3. _____
	4. (other informed adult or child) _____	4. _____
	5. (miscellaneous) _____	5. _____

Step 3. Student plots the paragraph
    Theme or main idea _____
        Supporting details   1. _____
                                  2. _____
                                  3. _____
                                  4. _____
                                  5. _____

Step 4. Student writes the expository paragraph
    My final paragraph

_____
_____
_____
_____
_____

Note: To help children focus on the task, the teacher will want to start by putting the blank form for each step on a separate piece of paper and handing them out to be used one step at a time.

Figure 7.1   Steps in learning to write an expository paragraph. From Flood, James, Lapp, Diane, and Farnan, Nancy. 1986, February. A reading-writing procedure that teachers expository paragraph structure. The Reading Teacher 39 (6):556–62. Reprinted with permission of James Flood and the International Reading Association. All rights reserved.

In one study (Sinatra, Stahl-Gemake, and Berg 1984), a semantic map was given to poor readers in grades 2 through 8 as a pre-reading activity; it was applied to both narrative and expository passages. The semantic map presented concepts or events in a visual graphic way, showing relations among ideas. For both narration and exposition, the students with LD performed significantly better on the comprehension questions after studying the semantic map in a pre-reading phase. The use of a semantic map, which portrayed relations of ideas in the passage, was compared to the "verbal readiness" approach, which involved a directed reading lesson in which the teacher wrote new vocabulary words on the chalkboard and discussed new content with the students before reading. Most of the students with LD showed improvement with each of these conditions.

According to the researchers, the teachers found the semantic map useful as a pre-reading activity because it demonstrated visually the relation of main and subordinate ideas.

Instruction in summarization is not a pre-reading method but rather involves teaching the student to extract the main ideas from the text (see chapter 4). Typically, students are asked to read a short passage and to reduce the information to the bare facts. Then this central information is written down. The summary provides a framework for recall of information in the text. Students become better at recalling not only main ideas but also details that are not in the summary. Weisberg and Balaithy (1989) found that summarization training improved poor readers' awareness of their own comprehension problems and processes.

Another form of instruction that may help struggling readers attend to the organization of texts involves teaching students to find main ideas (Graves 1986). The expectation is that if students recall the most important ideas, they are likely to retain supportive details as well (Meyer 1984). Stevens (1988) tested methods for teaching remedial reading students in grades 6 through 11 strategies for identifying the main idea and metacognitive strategies for checking their main idea hypotheses. The effectiveness of this training was compared to that of three other conditions: training in classification skills, training in a combination of the strategies and classification skills, and a control group that received only practice exercises. All of the training was carried out on microcomputers with a program that provided instruction in the main idea identification strategy and then a self-checking strategy. After training, students practiced the strategy in a multiple-choice format. The remedial students made more improvement in comprehension when they were given strategy training than when they simply practiced finding main ideas in passages. However, improvement was not evident when they were given passages with new content. Thus, while comprehension strategies focused on self-monitoring may have improved the poor readers' ability to identify main ideas, lots of guided practice, independent application, and discussion of the strategies may be needed to assure that students have fully adopted them and have taken to using them on their own. As noted in Chapter 4, it is important that students be aware of the usefulness of strategies to increase their comprehension and recall of passages.

TECHNOLOGY AND TEXT STRUCTURE

We noted in the beginning of this chapter that there are differences in the ways readers interact with traditional printed texts (i.e., linear texts) and electronic texts (i.e., non-linear texts). Computers have introduced many different systems though which non-linear texts are available for students who are learning to read or using reading to learn in different domains. Unfortunately, there are still very few studies that provide solid information about the benefits of computers, hypermedia, and multimedia for the development of reading comprehension. Kamil, Intrator, and Kim (2001) reported that between 1986 and 1996, only 2% to 5% of all of the research articles on reading and writing focused on the role of technology.

Still, non-linear texts hold the promise of providing various kinds of assistance and support for poor readers (Kamil, Intrator, and Kim 2001). Such texts are characterized by options presented to the reader to work with or supplement work on a given text or reading activity. These options are not available to the reader of written texts, who in some ways must be more self-sufficient. For example, traditional printed materials do not include options for ancillary learning activities and cannot provide feedback about the accuracy of one's comprehension. Textbooks often have pre-reading and follow-up activities and may provide ways for the reader to assess his or her comprehension, but these lack the array and flexibility of options available with computer programs.

Meyer and Rose (1998) have described various options available for reading and learning in a computer environment that are thought to be helpful for students with special needs. Three categories of options and examples of each are presented in figure 7.2. Some options have to do with the way reading materials are presented; other options pertain to ways to support students' use of the program; still other options are geared toward fostering interest and providing challenges for readers.

As is evident from this table, the computer environment offers the individual reader some decisions that might affect comprehension and learning or might simply make reading easier or more comfortable. Unfortunately, there are few studies to evaluate the effectiveness of different aspects of reading within a computer environment. Still, because of growing use, it is important to consider ways that computer programs might support comprehension. Some provide help for basic reading skills, such as providing the pronunciation or meaning of an unfamiliar word. Specifically, there might be an option to highlight a word and request from a menu the pronunciation of that word. The use of talking books has been the focus of some studies (Reitsma 1988), and the results are promising. In some, comprehension increases with access to digitized speech support (see

Options for presentation of reading material:
- Variable text, background, and highlight color
- Read aloud in synthetic or digital speech
- Phonemes words, phrases, sentences read aloud on request

Options for expression or support of students' motor and strategic systems:
- Ways to respond to the text (e.g., text, recorded speech, images)
- Supports for spelling and typing words (e.g., voice recognition systems)
- Opportunities to explore the text and images by manipulating them
- Supports such as leading questions, suggested strategies, and templates

Options for supporting interests and needs for challenge:
- Opportunity to choose materials and tailor activities to one's needs, preferences, and skill levels
- Opportunities to read and write in real-life contexts
- Tools and resources to create original work
- Timely and appropriate feedback

Figure 7.2   Computers as flexible learning environments

Kamil, Intrator, and Kim 2001). Other programs provide support for students' knowledge base other than in the area of vocabulary. For example, there might be an option to click on an icon that provides a video clip giving background information. "Dynamically combining text and narratives with illustrations and sound, multimedia applications, such as CD-ROMs, the Internet, and hypertext, are offering new modalities for using and acquiring literacy" (Kamil, Intrator, and Kim 2001, p. 774). Furthermore, there is some suggestion that students with poor background knowledge benefit from multimedia learning. A third way in which computer programs support reading is by providing feedback and recommendations for correcting errors. Some programs are also designed to support the development of reading strategies, usually by modeling them for the reader. This might include, for instance, the use of a graphic organizer to record ideas and facts from the text.

Meyer and Rose (1998) have provided explanations of components of software programs designed to aid struggling readers, but they also have indicated that such programs suffer from a number of limitations. For example, the interaction components lack the kinds of flexibility that are truly needed to support the learning of students with different profiles of reading skill. These researchers have also pointed out that there are few studies to guide us in evaluating the effectiveness of computer technologies in assisting students with special needs. This may be because it is seemingly impossible to account for the many factors that affect reading in computer environments. The effectiveness of reading instruction in computer environments may depend on the teacher's philosophy and knowledge, the availability of software programs and computers themselves, the tasks and classroom contexts for learning, and the characteristics of the students.

We need to keep in mind two different views of computers as they are used as tools for reading. One view is that students learn from the computer. The computer is the learning environment. In this case, computers provide only general advantages, such as immediate feedback. Research on computer-based instruction "compares favorably with conventional instruction in terms of learning outcomes" (Labbo and Reinking 1999, p. 484). A second view is that students learn *with* a computer. In this case, the technology and software enable the student's learning. "The computer plays an active role in fundamentally shaping orientations to learning, content and tasks" (Labbo and Reinking 1999, p. 483). Many students are using computer-based technologies to assist their learning in and out of school. The ready access to information offered through the Internet has made the notion of gathering information from different sources a much broader and richer experience. It is arguably a faster and more feasible process than going to the library to learn about a topic.

The pace and kinds of change taking place today are sobering—so much so that it is hard to know quite what to expect reading and learning from written texts to be like in another generation. Various experts agree that changes in computer technologies are causing us to reconsider our definition of literacy and our approaches to teaching it (Meyer and Rose 1998). Furthermore, traditional literacy alone will not be an appropriate end goal in the near future. To quote Leu

(1997), "changes in the strategic knowledge required to navigate traditional text environments have been glacial; changes in the strategic knowledge required to navigate Internet environments are meteoric" (p. 65). We are going to need to reconceptualize our view of reading and processes of learning to read as we become more invested in the use of computer technologies in classrooms.

COMMONLY ASKED QUESTIONS

How can teachers tell whether students are having specific difficulties with comprehension that are attributable to lack of awareness of text structures?

Having read this chapter, teachers might think that their students are likely to have problems with text comprehension that stem from lack of awareness and appropriate use of text structure to aid comprehension and recall. They might wonder how to find out whether this is, in fact, the case. Free recall is the task that most researchers use to determine whether the reader has attended to the text structure, and this is probably the most informative method for teachers. Teachers can benefit from asking students to read a short passage and then retell the passage as best they can. If the teacher tape-records this retelling and then transcribes it, he or she can examine the extent to which the student recalls main ideas and also the extent to which the recall protocol accurately portrays the organization and substance of the passage that was read. This is a difficult task for all students, whether they are struggling readers or not, so it is a good idea to give the student more than one opportunity to retell a passage that was read. With a bit of experience, most students get used to reading the passage with the retelling task in mind—that is, they concentrate a bit more than they might otherwise, and they may even think ahead about how they will organize the retelling.

In retelling a passage they have read, many poor readers have a tendency to spill out all of the ideas and details that come to mind, without regard for order or relative importance. If their recall protocols are scored on the basis of the main points in the passage, poor readers are very likely to do less well than more skilled readers (Carlisle 1999). Teachers can also score the students' recall of key content words (Fuchs, Fuchs, and Maxwell 1988). Here, too, the less able readers are likely to show less recall for the important terms that were used in the passage.

Because other factors also affect comprehension and learning from text, it is important that the teacher consider other reasons for poor recall of main ideas or lack of awareness of the organization of the text. Two such factors are the students' background knowledge and their language capabilities (e.g., vocabulary). As noted earlier, students with little prior knowledge of a given topic are likely to have difficulties identifying main ideas and integrating information (McKeown and Beck 1990). Recall protocols might suggest that they have retained unassimilated bits of information from the passage.

How do teachers select methods for teaching students awareness of text structures?

Because texts are so varied, no one method for improving students' awareness of text structures will work well for all genres and types of text structures. As is recommended in Chapter 4, teachers should make sure their students learn to use a variety of strategies. Students also need to know when and why each strategy or study method might be helpful. Along with teaching different strategies, the teacher should give the students lots of opportunities for guided practice, as well as opportunities to select strategies and use them on their own. Students' views of effective ways to analyze the structure of passages may be shared in a group discussion. Such discussion may also be a way to encourage students to personalize their study skills and learning strategies.

Because students have different learning styles and modality preferences, it is a good idea to offer options. For example, one strategy to use during or after reading is to make an outline of the key information in the text. Some students find traditional outlining helpful because it forces them to consider the relative importance of the ideas. A very different strategy to use during or after reading is making a concept map. This involves placing the main idea in a center circle and then placing words and phrases in circles linked to the main idea or to other subsidiary ideas. In a model developed by Lapp, Flood, and Hoffman (2000), the relation is written along the line that attaches one key word or phrase to another. Some students find this system preferable because it is not linear but still makes them think about relations of the information and ideas to the topic.

Teachers should make sure that the strategies suit the reading demands the students are encountering at school. It is not appropriate to teach awareness of story grammar to high school students if they are not reading stories on a regular basis. Along similar lines, some strategies may be too difficult for young students, given their level of cognitive development and ability to regulate and monitor their own reading and study skills. This may be true for summarization, for instance. Pressley and his colleagues (1989) have suggested that students below fifth grade do not benefit from training in summarization. On the other hand, young students (both normally achieving and struggling readers) appear to benefit from the use of graphic organizers that make text structures apparent.

In some cases, it is recommended that students be taught to recognize particular types of informational texts, including, lists, comparison, cause, and so on. Such instruction is often carried out with clear exemplars of each kind of relation. For example, the following might serve to illustrate a paragraph with an implicit causal structure:

> Bob bought an ivy plant at the store and took it home. Two days later, the leaves were wilted, and the plant looked generally bedraggled. Bob thought it might be getting too much sunlight, so he moved it to a shadier spot. The next day, the plant looked worse. Then it occurred to him that the plant might need water. Half an hour after he gave it a pitcher full of water, the plant looked as perky and green as it had the day he bought it.

One difficulty with this type of instruction is that natural texts often do not have just one type of text structure. Even within a given paragraph, the top-level relation may be comparison, but the body of the paragraph may be riddled with lists or examples. Because of the complexity of natural texts, students may need extended time for practice using their knowledge of informational text structures in guided lessons with discussion about the importance of ideas, their relations, and the structure or organization of the text.

On what basis should teachers select texts for beginning readers?

In recent years, we have seen many changes in the texts that are available for teaching beginning reading. Some types of reading materials have a long history. For example, decodable texts are descendents of the linguistic readers of several decades ago. Linguistic readers provide many instances of words with similar rime patterns in a given passage. Because texts had lots of rhyming words, they gave the students practice in recognizing specific decodable elements within words (e.g., "Stan can fan the man"), but they were criticized because they were not meaningful or interesting.

Teachers became interested in more "authentic" literature in the 1980s, and in fact children's literature was more engaging for the children (and the teachers, too). However, struggling readers had a hard time with the number of different words —and the complexity of these words. One solution was the development (or selection) of predictable texts. These rely heavily on repeated phrases and words, so that the total number of "new" words students read is limited. The burden on the beginning reader of trying to read many new words in a short text is minimized by repeating words, phrases, and sentences. Predictable texts tend to use common words (high frequency words) to aid children in their acquisition of a sight vocabulary. However, some of these words may have complex letter-sound relations, and these pose challenges for young readers (Hiebert and Martin 2001).

Teachers can find published anthologies of both types today—those that feature decodable texts and those that tend more toward predictable texts, although in the last five years, most basal series have tried to include a large proportion of decodable words. Teachers can also make use of "little books" that have been written for different levels of reading skill. These may be published as supplementary materials, or they may be sold as an alternative to anthologies. The "leveling" of the little books, which places them in a sequence of gradually increasing difficulty, may help students receive practice reading books successfully (Hoffman et al. 2000). Gradual increases in difficulty of the texts help students maintain their sense of being able to read and understand the different books they are given.

In terms of comprehension, beginning readers generally do not challenge the comprehension capabilities of children. Nonetheless, from reading books even at the primer level, they will learn something about genre or discourse types (e.g. poetry, stories) and about text structures (e.g., story grammar). Recently published basal readers are likely to be made up of a variety of types of discourse, including not only narratives but also informational texts. Most of these are authentic pieces of writing. Still, regardless of the type of text used with beginning readers, teachers should have other instructional activities for the purpose of developing comprehension capabilities on a regular basis. Such activities include listening to books read aloud (with discussion of them afterward), word study (focused on meaning), telling stories, explaining personal experiences to classmates (as in sharing time), explaining observed phenomena in the classroom (e.g., the hatching of an egg), and the like. The more "talk" (i.e., extended discourse) there is in a classroom, the greater the likelihood that the students will be able to read complex texts with understanding from the late elementary years on.

REFERENCES

Alexander, P. A., and Jetton, T. L. 2000. Learning from text: A multidimensional and developmental perspective. In *Handbook of Reading Research*, vol III, M. L. Kamil, P. B. Mosenthal, P. D. Pearson, and R. Barr (Eds.), (pp. 285–310). Mahwah, NJ: Lawrence Erlbaum.

Alvermann, D. E., Smith, L. C., and Readance, J. E. 1985. Prior knowledge activation and the comprehension of compatible and incompatible text. *Reading Research Quarterly*, 20:420–36.

Beck, I. L., and McKeown, M. G. 1989. Expository text for young readers: The issue of coherence. In *Knowing Learning and Instruction: Essays in Honor of Robert Glaser*, L. B. Resnick (Ed.), (pp. 47–66). Hillsdale, NJ: Lawrence Erlbaum.

Carlisle, J. F. 1999. Free recall as a test of reading comprehension for students with learning disabilities. *Learning Disability Quarterly*, 22:11–22.

Day, J. D., and Zajakowski, A. 1991. Comparisons of learning ease and transfer propensity in poor and average readers. *Journal of Learning Disabilities*, 24:421–26, 433.

Duke, N. K. 2000. 3.6 minutes per day: The scarcity of informational texts in first grade. *Reading Research Quarterly*, 35:202–24.

Englert, C. S., and Hiebert, E. H. 1984. Children's developing awareness of text structures in expository materials. *Journal of Educational Psychology*, 76:65–74.

Englert, C. S., and Thomas, C. C. 1987. Sensitivity to text structure in reading and writing: A comparison between learning disabled and non-learning disabled students. *Learning Disabilities Quarterly*, 10:93–105.

Flood, J., Lapp, D., and Farnan, N. 1986. A reading-writing procedure that teaches expository paragraph structure. *The Reading Teacher*, 556–62.

Fuchs, L. S., Fuchs, D., and Maxwell, L. 1988. The validity of informal reading comprehension measures. *Remedial and Special Education*, 9:20–8.

Gardill, M. C., and Jitendra, A. K. 1999. Advanced story map instruction: Effects on the reading comprehension of students with learning disabilities. *Journal of Special Education*, 33:2–17, 28.

Gersten, R., Fuchs, L. S., Williams, J. P., and Baker, S. 2001. Teaching reading comprehension strategies to students with learning disabilities: A review of research. *Review of Educational Research*, 71:279–320.

Goldman, S. R., and Rakestraw, J. A. 2000. Structural aspects of constructing meaning from text. In *Handbook of Reading Research*, vol III, M. L. Kamil, P. B. Mosenthal, P. D. Pearson, and R. Barr (Eds.), (pp. 311–35). Mahwah, NJ: Lawrence Erlbaum.

Graves, A. W. 1986. Effects of direct instruction and metacomprehension training on finding main ideas. *Learning Disabilities Research*, 1:90–100.

Griffin, C. C., and Tulbert, B. L. 1995. The effect of graphic organizers on students' comprehension and recall of expository text: A review of the research and implications for practice. *Reading and Writing Quarterly*, 11:73–89.

Gurney, D., Gersten, R., Dimino, J., and Carnine, D. 1990. Story grammar: Effective literature instruction for high school students with learning disabilities. *Journal of Learning Disabilities*, 23:335–42, 348.

Hayward, D., and Schneider, P. 2000. Effectiveness of teaching story grammar to preschool children with language impairments: An exploratory study. *Child Language, Teaching, and Therapy*, 16:255–84.

Hiebert, E. H., and Martin, L. A. 2001. The texts of beginning reading instruction. In *Handbook of Early Literacy Research*, S. B. Neuman and D. K. Dickinson (Eds.), (pp. 361–76). New York: The Guilford Press.

Hoffman, J. V., Roser, N. L., Salas, R., Patterson, E., and Pennington, J. 2000. Text leveling and little book in first-grade reading. University of Michigan: *Center for the Improvement of Early Reading Achievement, Technical Report #1-010.*

Horowitz, R. 1987. Rhetorical structure in discourse processing. In *Comprehending Oral and Written Language*, R. Horowitz and S. J. Samuels (Eds.), (pp. 117–60). New York: Academic Press.

Idol, L., and Croll, V. J. 1987. Story-mapping training as a means of improving reading comprehension. *Learning Disability Quarterly*, 10:214–29.

Kamil, M. L., Intrator, S. M., and Kim, H. S. 2001. The effects of other technologies on literacy and literacy learning. In *Handbook of Reading Research*, Vol. III, M. L. Kamil, P. B. Mosenthal, P. D. Pearson, and R. Barr (Eds.), (pp. 771–88). Mahwah, NJ: Lawrence Erlbaum.

Kletzien, S. B. 1991. Strategy use by good and poor comprehenders reading expository text of differing levels. *Reading Research Quarterly*, 26:67–86.

Labbo, L. D., and Reinking, D. 1999. Theory and research into practice: Negotiating the multiple realities of technology in literacy research and instruction. *Reading Research Quarterly*, 34:478–92.

Lapp, D., Flood, J. and Hoffman, R. P. 2000. Using concept mapping as an effective strategy in content area instruction. In *Content Area Reading and Learning: Instructional Strategies*, 2nd edition, D. Lapp, J. Flood, and N. Farnan (Eds). (pp. 291–305.) Boston: Allyn and Bacon.

Leu, D.J. 1997. Caity's question: Literacy as deixis on the Internet. *The Reading Teacher*, 51:62–7.

Maria, K., and MacGinitie, W. H. 1982. Reading comprehension disabilities: Knowledge structures and non-accommodating text processing strategies. *Annals of Dyslexia*, 32:33–59.

McKeown, M. G., and Beck, I. L. 1990. The assessment and characterization of young learners' knowledge of a topic in history. *American Educational Research Journal*, 27:688–726.

Meyer, B. J. F. 1984. Organizational aspects of text: Effects on reading comprehension and applications for the classroom. In *Promoting Reading Comprehension*, J. Flood (Ed.), (pp. 113–38) Newark, DE: International Reading Association.

Meyer, A., and Rose, D. H. 1998. *Learning to Read in the Computer Age*, Vol 3: From reading research to practice. Cambridge, MA: Brookline Books.

Montague, M., Maddux, C. D., and Dereshiwsky, M. I. 1990. Story grammar and comprehension and production of narrative prose by students with learning disabilities. *Journal of Learning Disabilities*, 23:190–97.

Pressley, M., Johnson, C. J., McGoldrick, J. A., and Kurita, J. A. 1989. Strategies that improve children's memory and comprehension of text. *Elementary School Journal*, 90:3–32.

Reitsma, P. 1988. Reading practice for beginners: Effects of guided reading, reading-while-listening, and independent reading with computer-based speech feedback. *Reading Research Quarterly*, 23:219–35.

Richgels, D. J., McGee, L. M., Lomax, R. G., and Sheard, C. 1987. Awareness of four text structures: Effects on recall of expository text. *Reading Research Quarterly*, 22:177–96.

Roller, C. 1990. The interaction between knowledge and structure variables in the processing of expository prose. *Reading Research Quarterly*, 25:79–89.

Short, E. J., and Ryan, E. B. 1984. Metacognitive differences between skilled and less skilled readers: Remediating deficits through story grammar and attribution training. *Journal of Educational Psychology*, 76:225–35.

Simmons, D. C., Griffin, C. C., and Kame'enui, E. J. 1988. Effects of teacher-constructed pre- and post-graphic organizer instruction on sixth-grade science students' comprehension and recall. *Journal of Educational Research*, 82:15–21.

Sinatra, R. C., Stahl-Gemake, J., and Berg, D. N. October 1984. Improving reading comprehension of disabled readers through semantic mapping. *The Reading Teacher*, 22–9.

Stahl, S. A., Hare, V. C., Sinatra, R., and Gregory, J. F. 1991. Defining the role of prior knowledge and vocabulary in reading comprehension: The retiring of number 41. *Journal of Reading Behavior*, 23:487–508.

Stevens, R. J. 1988. Effects of strategy training on the identification of the main idea of expository passages. *Journal of Educational Psychology*, 80:21–6.

Taylor, B. M., and Samuels, J. 1983. Children's use of text structure in the recall of expository material. *American Educational Research Journal*, 20:517–28.

van den Broek, P. W. 1990. Causal inference and the comprehension of narrative texts. In *The Psychology of Learning and Motivation: Inferences and Text Comprehension,* Vol 25, A. C. Graesser and G. H. Brower (Eds.), (pp. 175–94). San Diego: Academic Press.

van Oostendorp, H., and Goldman, S. R. 1999. *The Construction of Mental Representations during Reading.* Mahwah, NJ: Lawrence Erlbaum.

Voss, J. F., and Bisanz, G. L. 1985. Knowledge and the processing of narrative and expository texts. In *Understanding Expository Texts: A Theoretical and Practical Handbook for Analyzing Explanatory Text*, B. K. Britton and J. B. Black (Eds.), (pp. 173–98). Hillsdale, NJ: Lawrence Erlbaum.

Voss, J. F., and Silfies, L. W. 1996. Learning from history text: The interaction of knowledge and comprehension skill with text structure. *Cognition and Instruction*, 14:45–68.

Weisberg, R., and Balajthy, E. 1989. Transfer effect of instructing poor readers to recognize expository text structure. In *Cognitive and Social Perspectives for Literacy Research and Instruction: 38th yearbook of the NRC*, S. McCormick and J. Zutell (Eds.), (pp. 279–85). Chicago: National Reading Conference.

Wolman, C. 1991. Sensitivity to causal cohesion in stories by children with mild mental retardation, children with learning disabilities, and children without disabilities. *The Journal of Special Education*, 25:135–54.

Wolman, C., van den Broek, P., and Lorch, R. F. 1997. Effects of causal structure on immediate and delayed story recall by children with mild mental retardation, children with learning disabilities, and children without disabilities. *The Journal of Special Education*, 30:439–55.

8

Teaching Comprehension at the Elementary Level

GETTING STARTED

✓ What is the relation of acquisition of word-reading skill among beginning readers and performance in reading comprehension several years later?
✓ What is the relation of language development and reading comprehension?
✓ What instructional methods and/or established reading programs are designed to improve the comprehension of struggling readers in the elementary years?
✓ What kinds of instructional formats are effective for reading comprehension instruction and practice for struggling readers?

FIRST STEPS IN BECOMING A READER

In the primary grades, the biggest challenge children face is learning the code; they need to understand how their oral language is written down. Without this understanding, they cannot read. They need to learn strategies for recognizing unfamiliar words, and they need to learn to recognize familiar words rapidly and accurately. Practice reading texts, whatever their source (e.g., basal readers, leveled books), helps them become fluent readers. Although we expect children will become adept at word reading through the elementary years, we also expect them to gather experience with the structure and content of different types of written texts and with the process of interpreting texts. Ideally, they also learn to enjoy reading—to see reading as a source of interesting ideas and information, to be entertained by stories or poems, and to see themselves as readers. Certainly, the more children read, the better readers they are likely to become.

With the current interest in helping all children learn to read in the early elementary years, one might expect methods of elementary reading instruction to reflect recent research on effective practices. However, from the perspective of the teachers, teaching children to read is not substantially different today from the way it was thirty or forty years ago. Baumann et al. (2000) carried out a modified replication of a study of reading instruction in 1963 involving a survey to which elementary teachers responded. These researchers found a number of similarities in teachers' responses then and now: teachers said they worked with heterogeneous classes, spent a significant amount of time on reading and literacy instruction, provided instruction in phonics, and administered standardized reading tests (as required). Furthermore, on both surveys, teachers stated that meeting the needs of struggling readers was their biggest challenge. The researchers also found two important differences. One is that today's teachers said that they use a "balanced" approach to literacy instruction, whereas in the 1963 survey teachers were more likely to use a skills-based approach. Basal readers that use a balanced approach include more instruction in phonics than was true in the past, but they also include a heavy emphasis on authentic children's literature and a full array of literacy activities (e.g., writing, linking literacy to other content areas). Thus, the term *balanced* means combining a code-emphasis and a meaning-emphasis. A second difference is that today's teachers are offered more opportunities for professional development.

In terms of research on effective instruction in reading comprehension, over the last decade, we have seen a greater interest in comprehension, and research studies have shown that comprehension strategies can be taught effectively as early as second grade (Brown et al. 1996). Still, in a recent review, Pressley (2000) remarked that even though the research community supports teaching comprehension, such instruction is not common in elementary schools. Particularly in first and second grades, much more emphasis is placed on teaching children to be independent readers (i.e., making sure they can read connected text accurately and fluently) than on teaching comprehension. However, by the late elementary years (grades 4 and 5), basic reading skills are generally in place, and teachers are likely to put more emphasis on children's understanding of texts and their ability to acquire information from them.

The emphasis on helping children acquire word-reading skills in first and second grades is not misplaced. The better word readers in these grades are the ones who are more successful at comprehension several years later (e.g., Juel 1988). The summary of the National Reading Panel Report (2000, p. 9) is as follows:

> First graders who were taught phonics systematically were better able to decode and spell, and they showed significant improvement in their ability to comprehend text. Older children receiving phonics instruction were better able to decode and spell words and to read text orally, but their comprehension of text was not significantly improved.

Phonemic awareness and letter-name knowledge may be the best predictors of reading achievement in kindergarten, but by first grade, students' ability to decode familiar and unfamiliar words is a strong predictor of later reading achievement. Although it is clear that phonics is one component of a good program in early literacy, not all programs that include phonics are equally effective, particularly at supporting the developing reading skills of the weakest readers.

For example, Brown and Felton (1990) found that children identified as at-risk for reading disability at the end of their kindergarten year benefited more in terms of improvement in reading-related areas from structured, systematic phonics than phonics taught in the context of reading texts. Struggling readers need something other than the occasional phonics lesson in balanced literacy basals.

There is no shortage of programs that might fill this need, and it is difficult for teachers to determine which of the many supplemental reading programs available in schools today will truly help their children learn to read, especially those who are risk for reading failure. Hiebert and Taylor (2000) analyzed different interventions that were given to first graders and to second graders in order to determine whether children who received specially designed programs made more progress in reading than peers who received the regular reading instruction in their classrooms. They studied programs that differed on various dimensions (e.g., pull-out versus in-class), and they also had an opportunity to examine the characteristics of programs that seemed to lead to significant growth among the children who were struggling with reading. The results showed that, in general, for both grade levels, the children who received the special programs made significantly greater progress than their "status quo" peers. One important conclusion drawn by these researchers is that about 75% of the children in the bottom quartile can be brought up to the average range, if they are taught in groups of two or three, and about a third of the children in the bottom quartile can make this kind of progress, if taught in groups of six or seven students. In short, with well-designed interventions, a large portion of the children who are failing to learn to read in first and second grades can be taught to read.

Even in the well-designed classroom interventions explored by Hiebert and Taylor, a small number of children still have severe problems learning to read by the end of second grade. For these children, there is likely to be a prolonged period of concentration on the "basics": phonological awareness, phonics, and practice with texts at an appropriate reading level (Clark and Uhry 1995). Children who are severely challenged in their attempts to learn to read may receive some or all of their reading instruction in a setting apart from the regular classroom. Such instruction may supplement skills taught in the classroom or provide more extensive instruction in areas of particular need (e.g., explicit phonics). However, even if the child receives all of his or her reading instruction in a pull-out setting, there is no guarantee that the program will be truly individualized or that the instructional materials will differ from those used in the regular education setting (Vaughn, Moody, and Schumm 1998). The nature of the instructional program is a major concern here, not just the fact that the child is taught in a pull-out setting.

The decision to supplement or replace the reading instruction of the regular education class may depend on the severity of the child's reading difficulties and other learning problems as well as criteria for eligibility for special education services in the school district or state. However, many teachers are hesitant to refer children struggling with the initial stages of learning for special programs because of the belief that they should be given time to catch on to reading. In contrast to this position, experts are now arguing that it is far better to provide help early on, with the hope of preventing reading problems from developing, than to wait for such problems to develop (Snow, Burns, and Griffin 1998; Vellutino, Scanlon, and Lyon 2000). Some researchers are working with school personnel to develop models of instruction in regular classes that meet the needs of students who are struggling to learn to read (e.g., Jackson et al. 1999). This might be accomplished by having adequately trained personnel in first-and second-grade classes and including in the instructional program the elements that are most needed by students who are having trouble breaking the code (e.g., phonological awareness, phonics). Although such programs might provide the kind of instruction most beginning readers can benefit from, they still might not meet the needs of the weakest readers.

There is another issue we need to keep in mind as we examine the relation of early reading instruction and reading comprehension. Some educators and researchers seem to assume that when students' word-reading problems have been successfully remediated, so that words are read accurately and smoothly, they will be at the level of their normally achieving peers in comprehension as well. That is, they believe struggling readers do not need any more help with comprehension than their normally achieving peers need. To quote Clark and Uhry (1995), "while children with dyslexia may have difficulty with comprehension (and not all do), this difficulty is not the primary problem. These children should respond to the same sort of reading comprehension instruction that is appropriate for all children" (p. 104). For both regular and special educators, the emphasis in kindergarten and the early elementary years is on preventing reading problems by intensive work on phonological awareness and phonics (Torgesen, Wagner, and Rashotte 1997; Scanlon and Vellutino 1997). These views may give a misleading idea about the relation of decoding and comprehension, and they may lead to a general neglect of comprehension instruction in the elementary years, including oral as well as written language comprehension.

Before children are able to read connected text, comprehension can be developed by a joint focus on oral language and literacy. Although many early elementary literacy programs have goals for development of oral language, the amount of time and programmatic effort devoted to these goals may be minimal. For example, teachers may help children learn new words only when questions about the meanings or uses of words are encountered in books that the teacher reads aloud to the children. As part of a study of support for literacy development in homes and schools, Dickinson, Tabors, and their colleagues (2001) interviewed preschool teachers and observed their classroom reading and language practices. The results show marked differences in the teachers' estimates of time spent on oral language activities and time actually devoted to these activities. A similar pattern might be found in elementary classes as well.

THE LANGUAGE-LITERACY CONNECTION

Teachers should be aware of the value of linking classroom practices that foster language and literacy development in the elementary years. Tabors, Snow, and Dickinson (2001) reported that the receptive vocabulary of kindergartners in their home-school study was significantly related to the students' receptive vocabulary and reading comprehension in both grades 4 and 7. This means that, in general, the kindergartners with relatively limited vocabulary continued to have limited vocabulary and tended to be less skilled at reading comprehension in fourth and seventh grades. Although many students will have no unusual difficulties with comprehension once they are equipped with basic word reading skills, others struggle with aspects of language comprehension even before reading instruction begins. Students in different "risk" categories, such as those in inner city schools and those whose native language is not English, stand to benefit a great deal from high quality, systematic programs focused on oral and written language comprehension.

Catts and his colleagues (1999) have argued that attention to comprehension of oral and written language is valuable for all children even in the early elementary years, but is particularly crucial for those with early signs of reading problems. These researchers found that a large portion of struggling readers have problems with language learning that hinder the development of their reading comprehension. Furthermore, studies show that, even among groups of children without known disabilities, there are large individual differences in vocabulary and language comprehension before they begin school (Hart and Risley 1995; Dickinson and Tabors 2001). It is important for parents and teachers to realize that preschool children's vocabulary and language comprehension are related to their reading comprehension years later, for better or for worse (Tabors, Snow, and Dickinson 2001; Scarborough 2001).

Tabors, Snow, and Dickinson's (2001) research showed that home and school factors might affect the relationship between kindergarten language and later literacy. Such factors might include the type of reading program, the amount of reading a child does, and the experiences the child has with his or her family. Thus, home and school environments have the potential of compensating for each other. A supportive, language-rich home environment can counteract partially the influence of an unstimulating school program. The reverse is true, too: a supportive learning environment in school can counteract, to some extent, the influence of a home that is unstimulating in terms of language and literacy. Thus, excellent schools (in Tabors, Snow, and Dickinson's case, preschools) have the potential of making up for below average support for language and literacy in the home.

The above conclusions suggest all the more reason schools should provide children with instructional support for developing language comprehension skills, particularly as they may be applied to literacy activities. With our nationwide concern for making sure that all children can read by the end of third grade, elementary reading programs should include components focused on not only word reading, but also vocabulary and comprehension skills. Children should not be left to their own devices when it comes to figuring out how to understand and learn from written texts. How can teachers support children's developing comprehension capabilities *before* they can read and *while* they are learning to read? In answering this question, our particular emphasis is on the nature of the relation of language and literacy acquisition as they mutually reinforce each other.

In theory, becoming literate leads to development of an individual's oral language capabilities. However, it is also true that children's oral language development affects their literacy acquisition. We discussed this sort of reciprocal relation in Chapter 2. For our present purposes, we are interested in one part of this relation: what kinds of changes in oral language come with children's introduction to literacy? First, experience with written language heightens children's linguistic awareness (Watson 2001). Take phonological awareness as an example. As they come to understand the alphabetic writing system and master letter-sound correspondences and the spelling of words, children develop an awareness of the sound structure of words, particularly phonemic awareness, which refers to appreciation of the individual sounds that make up words (e.g., /b/-/a/-/g/- in *bag*). Similarly, grammatical awareness is fostered by learning to read. In fact, skilled readers are more sensitive to the grammaticality of sentences than less skilled readers (Bowey 1994). Through exposure to written language, children also develop a better sense of words and the ways they are represented in writing. For instance, young children use sound spelling before they master conventional spelling; they might write "Once upon a time" as "wunzupon atime." Despite evidence that literacy fosters linguistic awareness, Watson (2001) pointed out that we cannot claim that exposure to written language is the direct cause. This is because studies have shown that some aspects of linguistic awareness develop among people who are not literate. Therefore, it may be best to think of literacy as fostering a broader array of metalinguistic understandings than is fostered by exposure to oral language alone.

Another way that literacy affects language development is through exposure to decontextualized language. Decontextualized language is language used to refer to events and ideas that are not shared at that moment between communication partners. Written discourse tends to be less personal and more abstract than oral discourse. In reading and writing, there is a greater distance between the two engaged in communication than there is in listening and speaking. Because there is no face-to-face communication and because the discourse is often not directed to a specific audience, the reader has to make more inferences about the probable meaning. As they become readers, children must learn a different means of communicating and different strategies for figuring out the meanings of texts than they use in oral communication. It is not that oral language is simpler or easier to understand, but rather that the ways of taking meaning from oral and written texts are quite different (Halliday 1987).

As we noted in Chapter 2, the language children are exposed to at home and in school influences the development of their language comprehension (which in turn influences their comprehension of written texts). In the home, children's experiences differ in terms of the nature of discussion at the dinner table and the extent to which they are encouraged to take part in conversations (Dickinson and Tabor 2001; Hart and Risley 1995). The closer the family's language practices are to those used in school and school books, the more likely the children will move smoothly into literacy.

It is not just the home environment that shapes children's language but also the oral language practices in schools. Many uses of language in school are unlike those used in most home settings. For example, family members are not likely to ask one another to answer questions that they already know the answer to. In the first years of schooling, children are immersed in an environment with unfamiliar discourse practices, and their ability to learn how to engage in these practices will influence their success in school. One example of a school discourse practice is defining words. As Watson (2001) pointed out, at home children are seldom asked to give explicit definitions of words, whereas such a request is common at school. An example she gave involves the child's identification of an object in a show-and-tell kindergarten classroom as "an enchanted egg." The teacher then asked the child what enchanted means. The child responded, "It means there's something inside it" (p. 50). Even if teachers do not specifically ask for definitions, they nonetheless are likely to seize occasions to ask children to explain things—what happened to the egg, where they got it, why they brought the egg to show to others. According to Watson (2001), "the discourse is organized around signification and interpretation rather than enactment or experience" (p. 50). Whereas discourse that focuses on personal experiences is common as an everyday use of language outside of school, the more analytic and reflective language practices in classrooms draw on and build the capabilities children will need to be effective in constructing meaning from written texts.

Talk in school also differs from talk at home in the choice of topics and the implicit rules for participating in efforts to understand and share ideas (Wilkinson and Silliman 2000). Unlike talk at home, talk at school often focuses on events, ideas, and information topics that are not present for the children to examine and refer to (i.e., what a penguin looks like and where it lives). Such talk also involves following different speakers' turns and learning to make a bid for a turn in order to contribute to the discussion. Some children learn faster than others how to follow the thread of a discussion and contribute to the process of constructing an understanding of ideas and events. Children who are successful at learning how to participate in school discussions are in a position to learn from each other and share ideas. Comprehension becomes a dialogic process. Children who are more adept at school talk are also the children who are more able to read from multiple sources on a topic and negotiate "meanings" contributed by peers who have different perspectives on the topic.

Clearly, children face many challenges as they learn how to meet the communicative demands of the classroom, and this is where the teacher plays a crucial role. For example, in the early elementary years, children like to be called on and will say whatever is on their minds, even if what they have to contribute is only remotely related to the topic. The teacher plays a particularly important role in helping the group see how a given child's ideas and experiences contribute to the discussion. By the late elementary years, most children can be expected to be capable of referential communication; that is, they can use language to help each other follow the connections between ideas and pieces of information (Lloyd 1990). They are aware that as speakers they need to communicate coherently, and as listeners they need to monitor the speaker's statements for meaning and to request clarification when it is needed. Classrooms in which group discussion is valued are places where children learn to contribute their views and knowledge and shape them through discussion with others (Lloyd 1990). Not all classrooms provide this sort of support for the development of children's oral language comprehension and expression.

What is the teacher's role in this process? The teacher facilitates discussion by providing direction, organization, and a support system of sorts. The teacher's role is particularly important in the elementary years because children's ability to negotiate understandings with others is still in its formative stages. It has become common to use the metaphor of scaffolding (Bruner 1983) to describe the way teachers provide support for children's learning, removing the support when it is no longer needed. Adults can facilitate the process by serving a number of different roles. These include redirecting children's attention to what is relevant, interpreting a child's statement for the group, or alerting a child (or the group) about a communication failure (Lloyd 1990). Teachers can also set the pace of the discussion, model turn-taking, and help children who are predominantly on-lookers contribute something of importance to the group discussion.

In discussing referential communication, we emphasize the importance of children learning how to participate in group discussions directed toward negotiating understanding of events, ideas, and information. In whatever form they take (e.g., small groups, cooperative learning), instructional conversations provide a mechanism for the individual to learn strategies for understanding written texts. As noted above, some children are more likely to move smoothly into ways of learning by talking than others. Unfortunately, "the small-group processes that promote positive effects for learning are not well understood" (Wilkinson and Silliman 2000, p. 351). Nonetheless, the children who have difficulties learning how to take a constructive role in discussions appear to also have difficulties comprehending written texts (Wallach and Butler 1994). For this reason, teachers are encouraged to integrate language with literacy learning across the curriculum and grade levels.

Fostering Linguistic Awareness and Metacognition

Along with providing opportunities to learn from and through discussion, teachers can support children's language development by finding ways to foster their linguistic awareness. Linguistic awareness refers to children's sensitivity to the forms and functions of language. "Awareness" of language is demonstrated when children treat language as an object of thought. They might reflect on the forms or meanings of words. They might show an awareness of changes in meaning that occur when the order of words in a sentence is changed (e.g., "The man painted the white fence" as compared to "The man painted the fence white"). They might show that they can manipulate words or sentences to meet specific demands (e.g., changing a passive to active voice as in "The dog was chased by the boy" to "The boy chased the dog").

Metalinguistic functioning is different from normal uses of oral language in that attention is not simply on content but rather on form, or more particularly the relation of form and meaning. In everyday conversation, listeners focus on the meaning intended by the speaker, generally ignoring grammatical errors and incompletely expressed ideas. In contrast, readers need to focus on the relation of form and meaning, and this involves functioning at a metalinguistic level. According to Nagy and Anderson (1999), reading is ultimately a metalinguistic activity. Aspects of linguistic awareness that are related to literacy acquisition include phonological awareness, syntactic awareness, and morphological awareness (Bowey 1994; Tunmer, Herriman, and Nesdale 1988). Bowey (1994) has argued that grammatical awareness contributes to children's ability to assemble words into meaningful syntactic groups as they are read. Doing so is particularly important for understanding written language because written language provides little by way of information about prosodic and situational cues—ways that grammatical structures are determined in oral language. For instance, in the sentence, "John stole the car," we do not know whether to be surprised that it was John who stole the car or whether it is only what John stole (the car) that is striking. In oral language, more emphasis would be placed on "John" to convey the first of these meanings and on "car" to convey the second meaning. Grammatical awareness may also help children notice reading errors when the sentence, as read, does not make sense—and thus provides an opportunity to correct the reading of the sentence. In this way, grammatical awareness is important for comprehension monitoring.

Aspects of phonological, morphological and grammatical awareness distinguish students who are good and poor readers in the elementary years (see Bowey 1994; Rubin 1988; Tunmer, Herriman, and Nesdale 1988). While there is much we still do not understand about instruction to improve students' metalinguistic development, efforts to improve metalinguistic functioning may be an important way to support students' acquisition of literacy (Menyuk 1999). Teachers can provide numerous informal opportunities to think about language. They can encourage children to be curious about language by modeling their own interest in words, word meanings, and so on (e.g., What is a *fork* in the road?). Informal activities can be tied to classroom routines (e.g., having children line up to go to lunch on the basis of the number of syllables in their first name). Teachers can use nursery rhymes and songs to heighten children's awareness of the sounds structure of words and of prosody. They can share jokes that depend of the sounds and meanings of words for their humor, and they can teach word games, such as Pig Latin.

Reading and Discussing Books with Children

Reading books to children is an activity teachers commonly include in preschool and kindergarten classrooms. Most first-grade teachers read to their children, and teachers of older students would be well advised to read books aloud to their students as well. Teachers who share their love of reading may help children develop a love for literature and an eagerness to become readers themselves. For preschool and kindergarten children, some important benefits of listening to books and discussing them have been outlined by Mason (1992). First, children develop their listening comprehension. This might include developing an understanding of common text structures, such as stories. They also learn new words or new meanings for familiar words from listening to books read aloud (Elley 1989). Second, children learn book language. They learn ways that language is used in books, including conventions such as "once upon a time" and unusual syntactic structures, as in "'Not I,' said the cow." Third, children learn about the forms and functions of written language. They learn (albeit implicitly) to distinguish narratives from information texts and fairy tales from real-life narratives. Finally, by looking at books that are read to them, they have opportunities to learn the conventions of writing. They may even learn to recognize common words.

Children can develop comprehension capabilities through listening to stories and through participation in guided discussion of stories and information texts. However, researchers have found that not all home and school book reading experiences have equal value for children's language and literacy development (e.g., Beck and McKeown 2001; Scarborough, Dobrich, and Hager 1994). It is the nature of the discussion that accompanies and follows the reading of the book that most influences children's developing understanding of written texts (Dickinson and Tabors 2001; Morrow 1990). Adults can assist children in their efforts to learn from texts by encouraging responses and by providing information to make it possible for them to use personal experiences to understand events. Adults help children learn the process of jointly constructing meaning from texts.

Shared experiences talking about books is one way for children to gain experience with decontextualized language (Beck and McKeown 2001). Talking about stories and information books may help children become accustomed to discourse that focuses on events and ideas that are not in the here-and-now. Children come to realize that because the writer and reader cannot communicate face to face, readers must work to make sense of parts of the texts that are confusing. Researchers agree that it is the *quality* of talk about written texts that fosters children's literacy (Beck and McKeown 2001; Dickinson and Smith 1994; Mason 1992). Talking about books may enhance development of language as it is used in school classrooms and in books. Dickinson and Smith (1994) found that one particular style of book reading (performance-oriented style) that involved considerable discussion before and after the reading of the book, supported vocabulary growth more than two other styles of book reading (co-constructive and didactic-interactional) that involved less rich exchanges about the books. Thus, shared book reading in the elementary years is most likely to be beneficial when children participate in the construction of meaning and in sharing their ideas about events, characters' motives and the like. Whitehurst and Lonigan (2001) have referred to such discussions as dialogic reading. It is up to the parent or teacher to facilitate discussion through asking questions that probe and extend children's thinking and link their past experiences with their understanding of the information in books. Dialogic reading becomes a kind of conversation with children that grows out of the reading of a book together.

Various programs of book reading have been investigated in research studies with the goal of understanding effective ways to engage children in book-reading experiences. One example is a program called Text Talk, developed by Beck and McKeown (2001). At the heart of the program is a series of questions that the teacher poses during reading of a book. These prompt the children to think about and connect ideas and events in the book. The teachers are encouraged to avoid constrained questions—that is, questions that lend themselves to one-word answers, such as "when they started scrubbing, what came off?" (The answer is "dirt"). Instead, they should ask open-ended questions that require students to describe or explain text ideas, such as "why" questions: "Why did they call Harry a strange dog?" The teachers are encouraged to follow up initial questions in productive ways when the children struggle to answer them. In this way, they provide support for the children's ability to connect and explain ideas and events. In Text Talk teachers also ask the children to explain meanings of key words. The children repeat the words and discuss their meanings in the text; the teacher rereads the text to show how the word is used in the story. This component provides an added impetus to children's language development.

Two other features of this program are noteworthy. One feature is the selection of challenging books. Beck and McKeown found that the books should be both challenging and interesting to the children so that they are motivated to put effort into the process of understanding and talking about the text. On the other hand, care is taken not to choose books that are outside the realm of the children's understanding. Based on their studies of Text Talk methods, the researchers recommended selecting books with an event structure (i.e., narratives), rather than a series of situations (e.g., books with facts about animals), in order to make it possible for children to develop understanding of extended texts. A second feature concerns the pictures. In Text Talk, the children hear and discuss the story before they are shown the pictures. In this way, they must depend on the linguistic content for interpretation, not on the pictures.

Other researchers have recommended that book reading include information texts as well as narrative texts (Duke 2000; Duke and Kays 1998; Pappas 1993). In general, discourse that provides information to another person is familiar to children. In their homes, they are likely to listen to explanations about how things work (e.g., how to turn on a flashlight; how to load film in a camera). Discussion with parents and older siblings may center on explanations of events (e.g., why bees sting people) or explanations of processes (e.g., how to warm food in a microwave oven). Shared reading of information texts provides a foundation for understanding written discourse structures and genres other than stories. Children also enjoy learning about the world around them from books.

Methods for Fostering the Development of Comprehension

Thus far, we have seen that activities designed to foster language development and to support comprehension (oral and written) are likely to benefit all children, whether they are at risk for comprehension difficulties or not. The main reason is that a child's proficiency in reading *depends* on his or her oral language development. Reading is a complex language activity. Language is the content as well as the means of learning. The types of instruction and learning activities used with elementary children provide both a context and an opportunity for children to develop their language and literacy knowledge. However, because reading comprehension is so dependent on orchestrating higher-level thinking skills, early elementary students have trouble learning some comprehension strategies, in particular those that are place heavy demands on reasoning and awareness of one's own mental processes (Pressley et al. 1989).

The development of comprehension capabilities may not always be effectively brought about by direct instruction alone. In a review of constructivist approaches to teaching reading, Stanovich (1994) concluded:

> Research has indicated that explicit instruction and teacher-directed strategy training are more efficacious when the focus is developing decoding skill. This is essentially true for at-risk children, children with LD, and children with special needs. In contrast, successful interventions directed at comprehension processes are more likely to have the characteristics of dialectical constructivism—where self-discovery and holistic principles will be more apparent (p. 270).

There are many questions still about how to approach the process of providing effective instruction in comprehension in the early elementary years, particularly in cases where children have limited language and/or cognitive development. Quite often teachers in the elementary years combine direct explanations of strategies with follow-up practice and guidance in appropriate use of strategies so that the students become accustomed to using them on their own. The combination of explicit instruction with guided learning through group discussion may be the best general model for elementary school teachers who have students with learning disabilities in their classes (Swanson 1999). An added benefit of group discussions is that they can be used to share thoughts about how effective students find different procedures or activities to be. Discussion of strategies is thought to heighten students' metacognitive awareness. Such discussion may involve teaching children to think about their own thinking. One probable result is that they will become "thinking readers." Thoughtful planning of ways to make students aware of their own reading habits and practices may be particularly important for struggling readers (Paris and Oka 1986).

APPROACHES TO INSTRUCTION

Teaching Comprehension Strategies

Regular and special educators may choose among a variety of strategies and procedures for ensuring that texts are understood. In their survey of instructional practices used by special educators who were nominated as effective literacy teachers, Rankin-Erickson and Pressley (2000) found that three comprehension methods were reported as being used by all of the second-grade teachers they interviewed. These were finding the main idea, predicting upcoming events, and activating prior knowledge. Almost all of the special educators also taught awareness of text elements (e.g., sequences of events), pre-taught passage vocabulary, and held pre-reading discussions.

Pressley and his colleagues (1989) reviewed methods of teaching reading comprehension that have been found to be effective through intervention studies. In this review, they first examined strategies that take "a few steps" for the student to execute and are relatively easy to teach. Three of these are summarization, imagery, and story-grammar. (All of these methods were discussed in Chapter 4.) For students in fifth grade or below, summarization may not be a promising approach, as there are indications that young students find it hard to distinguish the important and less important information. Imagery might be helpful for some readers and some texts, but it is hard to develop "mental pictures" when texts contain abstract ideas and intricate relations between ideas and information. In general, the more complex the language and the text structures, the more difficulty students are likely to have applying this technique. Nonetheless, creating mental images has been shown to be an effective method with students with specific comprehension problems (Oakhill and Patel 1991). Teaching story grammar has also been found to benefit struggling readers. This method was discussed both in Chapter 4 (on comprehension processes) and Chapter 7 (on text and discourse structures). Numerous studies have found that awareness of story grammar can help poor readers at the elementary level improve their comprehension and recall of narratives (e.g., Idol and Croll 1987; Montague, Maddux, and Dereshiwsky 1990).

One other simple-to-teach and easy-to-learn strategy described by Pressley et al. (1989) is question-generation. Question generation is often used with older students, but in Reciprocal Teaching, where four types of questions are used consistently, question-generation has been quite effective in fostering comprehension of early elementary students, including those who are poor readers (Palincsar 1991). Furthermore, Reciprocal Teaching has been effective in improving first graders' listening comprehension when the teacher has read texts aloud for the group and stopped at points in the text to answer questions. Before beginning the Reciprocal Teaching sessions, the children were introduced to the four question types (i.e., strategies). Thereafter, the teacher-led instruction took place every day for 20 minutes a day for 20 days. The passages, drawn from basal readers, were expository. On the post-testing, which involved listening to a passage and answering ten questions about it, the children who were included in the reciprocal teaching group out-performed another group of children who did not receive this same instruction.

Although question-generation can benefit poor readers and children at risk for reading comprehension problems, question-answering strategies may be more successful when taught to older students with reading problems. These require that students learn about the different types of questions teachers and textbooks ask, and knowing these, figure out how to answer the questions. Pressley et al. (1989) concluded that distinctions among the types of questions were difficult for children in the elementary years. Minimally, this method requires extensive training, so that it can not be considered an "easy-to-teach" method for poor readers in the elementary years.

In the category of comprehension methods that are harder to teach and take longer to learn, Pressley et al. (1989) focused primarily on ways to teach students to activate prior knowledge and to use that knowledge to support understanding and learning from text. While in general there is consensus that activating prior knowledge is valuable for the purpose of understanding a text, studies have shown that prior knowledge can interfere with memory of passage information when the two were not compatible. For example, Pressley et al. (1989) cited a study carried out by Lipson with fourth, fifth, and sixth graders who were enrolled in schools with particular cultural or religious affiliations. The passages they read were not always congruent with the children's religious and cultural knowledge, and on these passages the students tended to distort the information from the passages in their recalls. Because it is likely that conflicts between prior knowledge and text information will occur, students should be taught to watch out for the possibility of such conflicts. When a conflict occurs, they might make an effort to recall the information that is in the text or try to identify the basis for the conflict. Both detecting and resolving such conflicts are difficult for elementary students with reading problems. Analytic processes, such as these, require considerable instruction and support from the teacher.

Systems like K-W-L (Ogle 1986) are quite helpful for bringing prior knowledge to mind. Here the teacher helps the students activate prior knowledge, prepares them for thinking about the content of the text, and provides a way to review what is learned. A system such as this one is an appropriate way to activate and incorporate prior knowledge during reading at the elementary level, even if it does not always prevent over-reliance on prior knowledge. The importance of activating prior knowledge and the particulars of Ogle's K-W-L method are discussed at some length in Chapter 4.

Elementary students can benefit from this and other methods designed to help them understand and learn from texts. Reflecting on reader ability differences, Pressley and his colleagues (1989) concluded that "poor readers benefit more than good readers from story-grammar training, instructions as to how to answer questions about text, and prior knowledge activation. Thus, it makes sense to emphasize these skills as part of remedial reading" (p. 24). While the above discussion appears to emphasize individual strategies that might be taught to elementary readers, the current wisdom is to teach combinations of strategies. For example, Pressley and his colleagues developed a strategy package with many components; called Transactional Strategy Instruction, it has been found to be beneficial for students with reading difficulties and for children in the early elementary years (Brown et al. 1996; Pressley et al. 1992). (See Chapter 4 for further discussion of this method.)

Reading Groups: Talking About Texts

As in listening and talking about books read aloud, children make gains in developing critical reading capabilities by talking with others about books or passages in books they are reading. They become used to reflecting on thematic complexities, developing an explanation for the motives of characters, and learning about the world. Comprehension is not a single outcome; in fact, it may be conceptualized as a process of developing and evolving understandings of texts. The "others" involved in this learning process include not only parents and teachers, but also peers. It is not surprising, then, that there are a number of models for providing a social context in which students can learn how to understand written texts. Some include the teacher as a guide and facilitator of the discussion; others do not. It is not possible to consider all of these models here, so we have chosen to review the underlying principles of three systems that use literature discussion as a means of learning how to understand written texts. These include Questioning the Author (Beck et al. 1997), Collaborative Reasoning (Anderson et al. 2001; Chinn, Anderson, and Waggoner 2001), and Book Clubs (Raphael and McMahon 1994).

Literature discussion groups grew out of the "whole language" philosophy in the 1980s. These required teachers to create small-group formats within regular classes and to learn how to talk about books with students in these groups without "dictating" how the students were to understand the books. Guidelines are available for teachers who choose to participate in the small group discussion in this way (e.g., McGee, Courtney, and Lomax 1994). The teachers may need to model ways to talk about books so that the children in the group learn how to contribute meaningfully to the discussion. However, teachers need to adopt ways of guiding without directing. This may involve a difficult adjustment when the rest of the school day has the teacher in his or her role as director of the students' learning.

A helpful explanation of the ways teachers can facilitate students' discussion of literature can be found in Beck et al. (1997). In their model, teachers help the students with their discussion by the queries they introduce (as will be discussed shortly). However, teachers also need to learn to use other discussion moves. Six of these moves are listed below.

- Marking: Teachers respond to students' comments to draw attention to a particular idea.
- Turning back: Teachers make students responsible for thinking through a problem; in addition this term refers to directing the students' attention to the text as a way to clarify their thinking.
- Revoicing: Teachers interpret unclear statements made by students by rephrasing the ideas.
- Modeling: Teachers show students how to talk about or explain ideas and in this way provide a model for them to learn from.
- Annotating: Teachers provide information to fill in gaps.
- Recapping: Teachers pull together and summarize major ideas students have constructed up to that point in the discussion.

One way to use groups for reading discussion is Book Clubs (Raphael, Florio-Ruane, and George 2001; Raphael and McMahon 1994). Here the small groups are made up of student members, while the teacher serves as a guide, wandering from group to group to monitor and assist in the deliberations as needed. In the Book Club programs, the small group discussion is just one part of the literacy program. For instance, there are times when the whole class meets together to hear reports from the individual groups or to be given information by the teacher about literary devices that the students might not be able to figure out on their own. Goatley, Brock, and Raphael (1995) carried out a study to determine whether fifth-grade students who were at risk for or identified as having reading difficulties would benefit from participation in Book Clubs. This paper reported on one group that included three students who qualified for special services; one had participated in Chapter 1, one had received reading instruction through special education, and one received ESL services for second-language learning. The researchers examined the participation of these students in the group discussion, knowing that it was quite possible that students who had trouble reading would not be actively engaged. It was a noticeable challenge for these students to move from teacher-directed context for learning to one that was student-directed. Still, the researchers found evidence of significant growth in the students' comprehension strategy use and in their ability to support each other's meaning construction. Teachers' and students' satisfaction with the Book Club experiences for struggling readers make it clear that student-guided discussions of books, as in Book Clubs, offer numerous advantages for poor readers.

Another approach is called Questioning the Author (Beck et al. 1997). Like Text Talk, it involves groups of students engaged by the teacher in discussion of literature, searching together for the meaning that the author intends to communicate. The teacher, who guides the discussion, asks "initiating queries" after segments of the text are read, often to help the group summarize the text up to that point. Three types of initiating queries are as follows: "What is the author trying to say here? What is the author's message? What is the author talking about?" (Beck et al. 1997, p. 45). Then, after reading the entire selection, the teacher provides "follow-up queries" to encourage the students to elaborate on their thoughts about the text passage and to clarify their thinking about what they read. Examples of follow-up queries are as follows: "What does the author mean here? Does the author explain this clearly?" (p. 45). There are also special queries that are recommended for use with narrative texts. Planning lessons is compared to a rehearsal for a stage production, because the teacher functions as both director and actor, but must also select the text and make decisions about the segments of text that will be the topic of discussion. Finally, it is very important for the teacher to learn how to facilitate the students' discussion. As in other types of teacher-led discussions of reading, the teacher needs to become familiar with— indeed, comfortable with—different discussion moves that he or she might make.

A model quite different from this one is Collaborative Reasoning (Anderson et al. 2001; Chinn, Anderson, and Waggoner 2001). This system is based on the assumption that different approaches to discussion have different instructional "frames" (Chinn, Anderson, and Waggoner 2001). These frames reflect implicit decisions about four issues; these are as follows: (1) What is the literacy stance toward the book or story? (2) Who has interpretive authority? (3) Who controls the speaking? and, (4) Who controls the topic of discussion? Unlike recitations (teacher-directed discussions), in Collaborative Reasoning the teacher and students share control over the topic, and the students have interpretive authority.

In terms of control over turns, the students are free to speak when they wish, but the teacher retains control through the questions she asks to scaffold the discussion. Collaborative Reasoning is less dependent on teacher control than Questioning the Author but more dependent on teacher control than Book Clubs. Along with differences in instructional frames, the interpretive stance of Collaborative Reasoning is different from that of the other models: it is primarily critical and analytic. Students are asked to address issues and provide arguments or reasons to support their thinking. Developing skill at reasoning depends on the students' appreciation of the process of presenting arguments and counter-arguments, understanding of the process of building a case based on evidence, and appreciation of the need to see others' perspectives.

Anderson and his colleagues investigated the feasibility of implementing Collaborative Reasoning in fourth-grade classrooms. The children were from socio-economically diverse rural schools. They were organized into groups based on their reading levels. The discussions took place after students had read a given book. A central question was chosen for purposes of fostering discussion, specifically the ability to formulate and exchange critical arguments. For instance, the story "Making Room for Joe" concerned a family that has an uncle with Down syndrome who had to find a new place to live. The question for this story was: "Has the family made the right decision to have Uncle Joe live with them?" (Chinn, Anderson, and Waggoner 2001, p. 383). In the discussion, students were expected to provide arguments for or against their decision, weigh the value of evidence offered by other students in support of their positions, and decide whether to maintain or change their original stances. The results of two studies suggest that the students learn methods of argumentation that are not just based on mimicry of other students. The teachers and students were successful at implementing Collaborative Reasoning, and students who participated in the groups showed greater engagement and more use of higher cognitive level processes than students in "recitation" settings (Chinn, Anderson, and Waggoner 2001).

One value of Collaborative Reasoning is its potential for improving students' metacognition. Because the structure of arguments is abstract, forms of argumentation learned in one situation may be subject to transfer or generalization to other situations. Children appear to gain awareness of ways to talk about literature; they learn argument strategies when they see that a particular strategy is a useful tool in a discussion, useful for persuading others. Anderson et al. (2001) have shown that the use of particular argument strategies is subject to the "snow-ball effect," meaning that once used in a group successfully, a given strategy is likely to be used by other members of the group with increased frequency in subsequent story discussion sessions. Such strategies include ways to gain the floor for a classmate (i.e., "What do you think, Sam?"), positioning in relation to a classmate's argument (i.e., "I agree (or disagree) with Leslie because . . ."), learning how to hedge when uncertain (e.g., "The accident could have happened . . ."), and presenting story evidence to support an argument (e.g., "In the story, it said —"). As appealing as this method for running literature discussion is, there is a need for studies that include students with reading comprehension difficulties.

As is the case with other arrangements for literature discussion, students with reading problems could carry out the reading in a variety of ways (e.g., having the story read aloud to them). Still, we do not know how well students with reading problems would fare in the process of learning forms of argumentation from their peers.

Supplemental Instruction: Pull-out Programs

Reading Recovery.   Reading Recovery was designed to prevent the onset of serious reading problems by intervening early. This pull-out program was developed by Marie Clay in New Zealand for first-grade children struggling with reading. In the US, first graders are usually considered candidates when they are achieving in the lowest 20% on reading tests. The program offers intensive, one-to-one instruction in 30-minute lessons daily for 30 to 60 lessons. The approach involves observing and analyzing the reading behaviors the child has learned and, on the basis of this information, determining how to help the child improve in reading. The teachers, who are specifically trained to teach this program, follow a prescribed lesson plan. Each lesson includes re-reading previously read books, writing and reading sentences, and reading a new book. The focus is on word and sentence level skills; there are no program components specifically focused on reading comprehension. Although the lesson plan is fixed, the teacher selects books and ways of working with the child that fit the child's needs. Once the child reaches a level of reading that is about average for his or her classmates, the one-to-one instruction is terminated. While Reading Recovery has been found to improve many students' reading, the program may not be suitable for students with severe reading difficulties. Children who make little progress are discontinued (that is to say, dropped from the program)(Shanahan and Barr 1995). Another problem is that the gains children make during their period of instruction may not be lasting. Studies have shown that children who had Reading Recovery instruction did not consistently perform better than children in other reading programs on a variety of reading measures six months to a year later (Center et al. 1995; Shanahan and Barr 1995).

Tutoring in Reading.   Many supplementary reading programs in the elementary years involve one-to-one or small group tutoring in basic reading skills, particularly phonological awareness, phonics, and oral reading of appropriate texts. Various programs have been explored in recent years, with the purpose of exploring methods that might be effective in addressing basic reading deficits (e.g., Foorman, Francis, and Fletcher 1998). Comprehension is not usually a major component in such programs. The goal is to help children develop text-reading skills so that the students are poised to acquire skill in comprehension.

When provided early in the school years, tutoring in reading may prevent serious reading problems from developing and aid in the identification of students who are likely to incur severe problems learning to read (Hiebert and Taylor 2000). Vellutino and his associates (2000; Scanlon and Vellutino 1997) have carried out several studies in which they have identified the students at-risk for reading failure in kindergarten or the beginning of first grade and then studied the effectiveness of a tutoring program in reading. Children were tutored every day for 30 minutes for approximately fifteen weeks. Tutoring was tailored to meet the needs of the individual child, but fifteen minutes of each session was devoted to reading connected text in order to foster strategies for word identification. Other instructional activities included phonological awareness activities, phonics, and development of a sight vocabulary. These researchers found that a sizable proportion of the children at-risk for reading difficulties had caught up to their normally achieving peers after half a year of remediation. A small percent continued to perform below the 30th percentile on tests of basic reading skills. Daily tutoring of the type used in this study turned out to be an effective way to distinguish the children who needed a boost at the beginning from those who had significant and recalcitrant problems learning to read. Like Marie Clay, who developed Reading Recovery, these researchers argued that some children do not come to school with experiences with literacy and language that enable them to learn to read, while others have more lasting difficulties and need more extensive individual tutoring in reading. These are the children who are likely to have innnate reading disabilities.

Tutoring programs for older elementary students are more likely to include a comprehension component. Olson and his colleagues (Olson et al. 1997; Wise and Olson 1995) studied a supplemental program that involved reading stories on a computer that provided speech support for targeted words. The ROSS program provided assistance in word reading by segmenting words at the onset-rime and syllable levels; the student pressed a particular key on the keyboard to hear the sounds of different segments or to hear the whole word. In one study, second through sixth graders with significant underachievement in reading used the ROSS reading program, which was accompanied by one of two conditions. In the phonological awareness (PA) condition, students were helped to discover the articulatory gestures of different speech sounds and were taught phonological decoding. They spent time on the computer doing practice exercises focused on phonological awareness and then time with the ROSS reading program. In the comprehension strategies (CS) condition, the students spent time in small groups learning the comprehension strategies used in Reciprocal Teaching and then used these strategies in conjunction with the ROSS reading program. The students in the two conditions had about the same amount of computer time, but different amounts of time reading stories with ROSS support (8 hours for the PA group and 18 hours for the CS group).

The results showed that students in both conditions made significant gains in phonological awareness and decoding. However, there were no differences in reading comprehension performance on two different standardized tests. These results suggest that the CS group did not use the comprehension strategies they had worked on when they were reading the passages on the tests. It is possible that they would have benefited from more extensive opportunities to use the strategies in reading environments other than the stories presented on the computer, so that they became more accustomed to using them spontaneously during reading.

Comprehensive Programs with a Comprehension Component

Various models have been developed that include a variety of different reading components (e.g., phonics, practice reading natural texts, and comprehension instruction), and yet provide practice and engagement in reading activities for all students in the class, regardless of their reading proficiency.

One such system is PALS, which stands for Peer Assisted Learning Strategies (Fuchs, Fuchs, and Burish 2000; Fuchs et al. 1997). PALS is a classwide peer-tutoring program. PALS programs are typically carried out three times a week for about a half hour each time; thus, they are supplemental programs, not the students' only reading instruction. The PALS programs have been shown to be effective in teaching reading strategies for average readers and for low achieving readers with and without disabilities. Studies of PALS have shown that this is an effective way to deliver an integrated program (i.e., one that involves word reading, fluency, and comprehension components) to young low-achieving readers.

Although PALS has been used most often in second- through sixth-grade classrooms, it has been adapted for first graders as well, so it is a system that could be used throughout the elementary years. In one study that reported on first-grade PALS (Mathes et al. 1998), reading activities included phonological awareness, phonics, oral reading, retelling, and predicting. These last two are components intended to provide regular practice using comprehension strategies that other studies have found to be effective for poor readers.

First-grade PALS involved pairs of students (one strong and one weaker reader) who worked together on reading activities. Authentic texts were used to facilitate vocabulary and syntax development and to increase students' interest in reading. When the class engaged in PALS reading activities, each pair of students carried out the same routines. The first routine was called Sounds and Words, which included code-based activities. The second, Partner Read-Aloud, started with "pre-reading" activities: looking at the book (the title, the pictures) and predicting what the book would be about. Then there was oral reading, followed by retelling. To accomplish the retelling, the coach (the stronger reader) asked what his or her partner learned first, and then what he or she learned next, and so on. The coach supplied information or asked additional questions as necessary. In this version of PALS, performance on various tests showed that the low achieving students benefited overall more than the high achieving students (Mathes et al. 1998).

Many comprehensive programs require a greater time commitment and may, in fact, constitute the entire reading program. One program that offers a comprehensive approach to literacy instruction and assistance for diverse learners is Success for All (Slavin et al. 1994). This is an early intervention program that was designed to meet the needs of at-risk students in kindergarten through grade 6. The program combines mixed ability cooperative learning groups and same-ability reading groups to teach reading and writing skills. One major element of this program is one-to-one tutoring by teachers; the tutoring is provided for students in grades 1 thorough 3 who are failing to learn to read.

The program prescribes the format and instructional activities. Working in groups of 4 or 5, the children carry out a variety of reading activities, including reading aloud, identifying elements of study grammar, practicing word recognition and vocabulary, and writing responses to stories. They receive instruction in comprehension strategies and opportunities to practice these in their teams. One advantage of this program is that it provides a way for students from linguistically and culturally different backgrounds and students with disabilities to learn reading with their peers. One study showed that inner-city, at-risk children (with and without special needs) who participated in Success for All performed significantly better on word reading and word attack measures than their peers in control schools (that is, schools using a different reading program) (Chambers et al. 1998). However, critics of the program have raised the question of the criteria used to identify "exemplary programs"—programs that are likely to be adopted at considerable expense by school districts when children are still underachieving in reading despite having made statistically significant gains (e.g., Pogrow 1998).

Programs like Success for All are brought in, intact, from the outside; teachers are taught to use the program, and the implementation may be closely monitored. In contrast to programs of this type, a number of reading programs are being developed by teachers and administrators in local schools and school districts. "Home-grown" reading programs have the advantage of selecting among practices that are known to be effective in order to design a program that suits the teachers and the students in a particular school. Such efforts to improve reading have been reported to be effective (e.g., Jackson et al. 1999). Often, teachers are involved in developing and implementing the revised reading program, and the teachers' sense of empowerment and responsibility may be important to its success. Such programs are likely to provide goals for different grade levels and as a result may acknowledge the importance of development of both word reading and comprehension from kindergarten on. Some programs of this type have brought about significant improvement in reading achievement school-wide, even when the school has many students at-risk for reading difficulties (e.g., Taylor et al. 2000).

COMMONLY ASKED QUESTIONS

How should the class be organized for effective instruction in reading and reading comprehension?

In recent years, the practice of placing children in "reading groups" with children at a similar reading level has been frowned on. This practice was criticized because it was thought that the different kinds of instruction provided to the children in "high" and "low" groups would perpetuate gaps in reading achievement. In addition, ability groups had the potential of negatively affecting students' academic self-concept and their motivation for reading. However, to cope with groups of students with diverse capabilities (including those with disabilities), teachers have felt the need to understand how best to organize their classrooms for the purposes of reading instruction and practice. Furthermore, as the results of one study have indicated, whole-class instruction in reading may not lead to significant growth in reading for students with learning disabilities (Vaughn, Moody and Schumm 1998). Possible alternative arrangements that a teacher could use within an elementary classroom include small groups, pairs, and flexible grouping arrangements. Flexible grouping refers to situations in which students work in different formats at different times. This may mean that students are placed in ability groups for one part of a reading lesson, but then participate in a mixed-ability discussion group, based on reading interests, for another part of the reading period.

Elbaum et al. (1999) carried out an analysis of studies that have compared grouping practices to whole-class instruction. They found that students with learning disabilities who received reading instruction in one of these alternative grouping arrangements experienced greater growth in reading than students taught in a whole-class format. The general education students, similarly, made better progress in groups than in whole-class reading instruction. One follow-up question of interest to teachers is how to select peers to work in pairs. Elbaum et al. (1999) found that there were positive effects both when the students with disabilities were the tutees (the tutor being a stronger reader) and when the students with disabilities served as both tutor and tutee. Thus, the stronger reader need not always be the one in control of the reading activities.

Peer arrangements can be used to supplement other grouping arrangements for purposes of providing much needed practice in reading. Such arrangements assure us that all students, without regard for their reading ability, are provided with similar opportunities to acquire reading skill. Elbaum et al. (1999) also suggested that peer-mediated instructional practices might improve the social relationships among the children. This may be a valuable outcome for classes characterized by cultural and linguistic diversity. In short, various grouping arrangements appear to be preferable to whole-class reading instruction for students who struggle with reading.

How should independent reading be encouraged in the early elementary years?

For "free reading" time to be beneficial to children, they need to be able to read connected text. However, even children who are not yet able to read to themselves enjoy having time to look at books or to read them with others. For some first graders, therefore, teachers might want to have different options for their students—books to look through, taped books to listen to while watching the text, partners to read with. By second grade, when it is important for children to gain fluency in reading, time should be set aside for independent reading on a daily basis. Again, because children will vary in terms of their ability to read connected text independently, a variety of options similar to those suggested for the first grade may be needed.

Although there are benefits associated with "free reading" time, teachers should be aware that fostering interest in independent reading does not necessarily lead to improvements in reading skill. For example, Morrow and Weinstein (1986) found that setting up "library centers" within classes did result in greater voluntary interest in reading among second graders, but there was no effect on reading habits at home, attitudes toward reading, or reading achievement. Particularly for older elementary students, the amount of reading students do in school is related to gains in reading achievement. In one study (Taylor, Frye, and Maruyama 1990), fifth and sixth graders kept daily reading logs from January through May. The students who read the most at school were the ones who made the greatest improvement in reading achievement. In contrast, the amount of reading at home was not related to growth in reading. While these results suggest that time devoted to independent reading is beneficial for students, it is likely that the amount of reading in school was itself attributable to the students' reading proficiency. Thus, the less able readers read less and also gained less than their peers.

If students are going to benefit from independent reading, it is important that teachers help them select books that are at an appropriate reading level. Books that are either too hard or too easy will not provide an opportunity for students to acquire word and world knowledge or improve their reading skill. Students acquire valuable practice if they are able to read most of the words on any given page—in other words, the book is at their independent reading level. This can be estimated by asking the student to count the number of "hard words" on one full page of the book. One rule of thumb is that the book is too hard if the student finds more than five "hard" words when there are about 100 words on a page. However, other factors should be considered, too—for example, the nature of the discourse (e.g., Is the book predominantly dialogue? is there a lot of figurative language?) and the students' background knowledge.

Teachers also need to consider how to make free reading time meaningful for older non-readers (e.g., students with reading disabilities or students who are second language learners and not yet able to read in

English). Such students can listen to books on tape while watching the text. There are also computer programs and books on CD-ROM that present natural texts but also provide help for students by making available pronunciations and meanings of unfamiliar words. As Reinking and Schreiber (1985) found, interacting with text on a screen may be limited to some extent by the readers' ability to read conventional print, even when the computer program provides computer-mediated textual manipulations. For this reason, adult assistance should be available.

How should a teacher determine when a child needs special help in reading apart from that provided in the classroom?

As may be evident from the earlier discussion, it is better to provide all the help a child needs early on so as to prevent serious reading problems from developing, and also to prevent the development of a negative attitude toward reading. It may be a good idea to consult with a reading specialist and special educator to get advice about the severity of the problems the student is having with the classroom instruction and reading activities. In some cases, specialists can help design a classroom intervention focused on the child's needs. If the child's reading does not improve in a timely fashion, the teacher has a further indication that the nature of the child's reading problems should be more fully investigated, and, if appropriate, intensive individualized help should be provided in a one-to-one setting.

In one elementary reading program, Guided Reading (Fountas and Pinnell 1996), the teachers are given a series of options called "Safety Nets" that provide ways to deal with students' reading problems. In first grade, Safety Nets include Reading Recovery and additional classroom support whereas in second grade, they include Reading Recovery, additional classroom support, and special education services. In fact, special education services are really not recommended until third or fourth grade, and then such help is considered appropriate for students who require "long-term support." In contrast, others recommend evaluation of the students' learning capabilities (including language and cognitive development when children appear to be at risk for reading difficulties), as this should help the teacher and the specialists in the school provide assistance in a timely fashion (Vellutino, Scanlon, and Lyon 2000). If the child does not make steady progress with classroom support or Reading Recovery, there are no advantages to withholding special education assistance, even if the child is only in first or second grade. The teacher should not view referral of a child for special education as a sign of his or her failure as a teacher of reading.

REFERENCES

Anderson, R. C., Nguyen-Jahuel, K., McMurlen, B., Archodidou, A., Kim, S., Reznitskaya, A., Tillmanns, M., and Gilbert, L. 2001. The snowball phenomenon: Spread of ways of talking and ways of thinking across groups of children. *Cognition and Instruction*, 19:1–46.

Baumann, J. F., Hoffman, J. V., Duffy-Hester, A. O., and Ro, J. M. 2000. The First R yester-day and today: US elementary reading instruction practices reported by teachers and administrators. *Reading Research Quarterly*, 35:338–77.

Beck, I. L., and McKeown, M. G. Hamilton, R. L., and Kucan, L. (Eds.) 1997. *Questioning the Author: An Approach for Enhancing Student Engagement with Text.* Newark, DE: International Reading Association.

Beck I. L., and McKeown, M. G. 2001. Text talk: Capturing the benefits of read-aloud experiences for young children. *The Reading Teacher*, 55:10–20.

Bowey, J. A. 1994. Grammatical awareness and learning to read: A critique. In *Literacy Acquisition and Social Context*, E. Assink (Ed.), (pp. 122–49). London: Harvester Wheatsheaf/Prentice Hall.

Brown, I. S., and Felton, R. H. 1990. Effects of instruction on beginning reading skills in children at risk for reading disability. *Reading and Writing: An Interdisciplinary Journal*, 2:223–41.

Brown, R., Pressley, M., Van Meter, P., and Schuder, T. 1996. A quasi-experimental validation of transactional strategies instruction with low-achieving second-grade readers. *Journal of Educational Psychology*, 88:18–37.

Bruner, J. S. 1983. *Actual Minds, Possible Worlds.* Cambridge, MA: Harvard University Press.

Catts, H. W., Fey, M. E., Zhang, X., and Tomblin, J. B. 1999. Language basis of reading and reading disabilities: Evidence from a longitudinal investigation. *Scientific Studies of Reading*, 3:331–61.

Center, Y., Wheldall, K., Freeman, L., Outhred, L., and McNaught, M. 1995. An evaluation of Reading Recovery. *Reading Research Quarterly*, 30:240–63.

Chambers, B., Abrami, P. C., Massue, F. M., and Morrison, S. 1998. Success for All: Evaluating an early intervention program for children at-risk of school failure. *Canadian Journal of Education*, 23:357–72.

Chinn, C. A., Anderson, R. C., and Waggoner, M. A. 2001. Patterns of discourse in two kinds of literature discussion. *Reading Research Quarterly*, 36:378–411.

Clark, D. B., and Uhry, J. K. 1995. *Dyslexia: Theory and Practice of Remedial Instruction*, (2nd ed.) Baltimore: York Press.

Dickinson, D. K., and Smith, M. W. 1994. Long-term effects of preschool teachers' book readings on low-income children's vocabulary and story comprehension. *Reading Research Quarterly*, 29:105–22.

Dickinson, D. K., and Tabors, P. O. 2001. *Beginning literacy with language: Young children learning at home and school.* Baltimore: Brookes Publishing Co.

Duke, N. K. 2000. 3.6 minutes per day: The scarcity of informational texts in first grade. *Reading Research Quarterly*, 35:202–24.

Duke, N. K., and Kays, J. 1998. "Can I say 'once upon a time'?": Kindergarten children developing knowledge of information book language. *Early Childhood Research Quarterly*, 13:295–318.

Elbaum, B., Vaughn, S., Hughes, M., and Moody, S. W. 1999. Grouping practices and reading outcomes for students with disabilities. *Exceptional Children*, 65:399–415.

Elley, W. B. 1989. Vocabulary acquisition from listening to stories. *Reading Research Quarterly*, 24:174–87.

Foorman, B. R., Francis, D. J., and Fletcher, J. M. 1998. The role of instruction in learning to read: Preventing reading failure in at-risk children. *Journal of Educational Psychology*, 90:37–55.

Fountas, I. C., and Pinnell, G. S. 1996. *Guided Reading: Good First Teaching for All Children.* Portsmouth, NH: Heinemann.

Fuchs, D., Fuchs, L. S., and Burish, P. 2000. Peer-Assisted Learning strategies: An evidence based practice to promote reading achievement. *Learning Disabilities Research and Practice*, 15:85–91.

Fuchs, D., Fuchs, L. S., Mathes, P. G., and Simmons, D. C. 1997. Peer-assisted strategies: Making classrooms more responsive to diversity. *American Educational Research Journal*, 34:174–206.

Goatley, V. J., Brock, C. H., and Raphael, T. E. 1995. Diverse learners participating in regular education "Book Clubs." *Reading Research Quarterly*, 30:352–80.

Halliday, M. A. K. 1987. Spoken and written modes of meaning. In *Comprehending Oral and Written Language*, R. Horowitz and S. J. Samuels (Eds.), (pp. 55–82). New York: Academic Press.

Hart, B., and Risley, T. R. 1995. Meaningful differences in the everyday experience of young American children. Baltimore: Paul H. Brookes Publishing Co.

Hiebert, E. H., and Taylor, B. M. 2000. Beginning reading instruction: Research on early interventions. In *Handbook of Reading Research*, Vol III, M. L. Kamil, P. B. Mosenthal, P. D. Pearson, and R. Barr (Eds.), (pp. 455–82). Mahwah, NJ: Lawrence Erlbaum.

Idol, L., and Croll, V. J. 1987. Story-mapping training as a means of improving reading comprehension. *Learning Disability Quarterly*, 10:214–29.

Jackson, J. B., Paratore, J. R., Chard, D. J., and Garnick, S. 1999. An early intervention supporting the literacy learning of children experiencing substantial difficulty. *Learning Disabilities Research and Practice*, 14:254–67.

Juel, C., 1988. Learning to read and write: a longitudinal study of 54 children from first through fourth grades. *Journal of Educational Psychology*, 80:437–47.

Lloyd, P. 1990. Children's communication, In *Understanding Children*, R. Grieve and M. Hughes (Eds.), (pp. 51–70). Cambridge, MA: Basil Blackwell Inc.

Mason, J. M. 1992. Reading stories to preliterate children: A proposed connection to reading. In *Reading Acquisition*, P. B. Gough, L. C. Ehri, and R. Treiman (Eds.), (pp. 215–41). Hillsdale, NJ: Lawrence Erlbaum.

Mathes, P. G., Howard, J. K., Allen, S. H., and Fuchs, D. 1998. Peer-assisted learning strategies for first-grade readers: Responding to the needs of diverse learners. *Reading Research Quarterly*, 33:62–94.

McGee, L. M., Courtney, L., and Lomax, R. G. 1994. Teachers' roles in first graders' grand conversations. In *Multidimensional Aspects of Literacy Research, Theory and Practice*, C. K. Kinzer, and D. J. Leu (Eds.), (pp. 517–26). Chicago: National Reading Conference.

Menyuk, P. 1999. *Reading and Linguistic Development.* Cambridge, MA: Brookline Books.

Montague, M., Maddux, C. D., and Dereshiwsky, M. I. 1990. Story grammar and comprehension and production of narrative prose by students with learning disabilities. *Journal of Learning Disabilities*, 23:190–97.

Morrow, L. M. 1990. Assessing children's understanding of story through their construction and reconstruction of narrative. In *Assessment for Instruction in Early Literacy*, L. M. Morrow and J. K. Smith (Eds.), (pp. 110–34). Englewood Cliffs, NJ: Prentice Hall.

Morrow, L. M., and Weinstein, C. S. 1986. Encouraging voluntary reading: The impact of a literature program on children's use of library centers. *Reading Research Quarterly*, 21:330–46.

Nagy, W. E., and Anderson, R. C. 1999. Metalinguistic awareness and literacy acquisition in different languages. In *Literacy: An International Handbook*, D. A. Wagner, R. L.Venezky, and B. V. Street (Eds.), (pp. 155–60). Oxford: Westview Press.

National Reading Panel. 2000. *Teaching children to read: An evidence-based assessment of the scientific research literature on reading and its implications for reading instruction.* Retrieved from: http://www.nichd.nih.gov/publications/nrp/report.htm

Oakhill, J., and Patel, S. 1991. Can imagery training help children who have comprehension problems? *Journal of Research in Reading*, 14:106–15.

Ogle, D. M. 1986. K-W-L: A teaching model that develops active reading of expository text. *The Reading Teacher*, 39:564–70.

Olson, R. K., Wise, B., Johnson, M. C., and Ring, J. 1997. The etiology and remediation of phonologically based word recognition and spelling disabilities: Are phonological deficits the "hole" story? In *Foundations of Reading Acquisition and Dyslexia: Implications for Early Intervention*, B. Blachman (Ed.), (pp. 305–26). Mahwah, NJ: Lawrence Erlbaum.

Pappas, C. C. 1993. Is narrative primary? Some insights from kindergarteners' pretend readings of stories and information books. *Journal of Reading Behavior*, 25:97–129.

Paris, S., G. and Oka, E. R. 1986. Self-regulated learning among exceptional children. *Exceptional Children*, 53:103–08.

Palincsar, A. S. 1991. Scaffolded instruction of listening comprehension with first graders at risk for academic difficulty. In *Toward the Practice of Theory-Based Instruction*, A. McKeough and J. L. Lupart (Eds.), (pp. 50–65). Hillsdale, NJ: Lawrence Erlbaum.

Palincsar, A. S., and Brown A. L. 1988. Teaching and practicing thinking skills to promote comprehension in the context of group problem-solving. *Remedial and Special Education*, 9:53–59.

Pinnell, G. S., Lyons, C. A., Deford, D. E., Bryk, A. S., and Seltzer, M. 1994. Comparing instructional models for the literacy education of high-risk first graders. *Reading Research Quarterly*, 29:8–39.

Pogrow, S. 1998. What is an exemplary program, and why should anyone care? A reaction to Slavin and Klein. *Educational Researcher*, 27:22–29.

Pressley, M. 2000. What should comprehension instruction be the instruction of? In *Handbook of Reading Research*, Vol 3., M. Kamil, P B. Mosenthal, P. D. Pearson, and R. Barr (Eds.). Mahwah, NJ: Lawrence Erlbaum.

Pressley, M., El-Dinary, P. B., Gaskins, I. W., Schuder, T., Bergman, J. L., Almasi, J., and Brown, R. 1992. Beyond direct explanation: Transactional instruction of reading comprehension strategies. *The Elementary School Journal*, 92:513–55.

Pressley, M., Johnson, C. J., Symons, S., McGoldrick, J. A., and Kurita, J. A. 1989. Strategies that improve children's memory and comprehension of text. *The Elementary School Journal*, 90:3–32.

Raphael, T., Florio-Runae, S., and George, M. 2001. *Book Club Plus: A Conceptual Framework to Organize Literacy Instruction.* University of Michigan: Center for the Improvement of Early Reading Achievement, Report #3-015.

Raphael, T.E., and McMahon, S.I. 1994. Book Clubs: An alternative framework for reading instruction. *The Reading Teacher*, 48:102–16.

Rankin-Erickson, J. L., and Pressley, M. 2000. A survey of instructional practices of special education teachers nominated as effective teachers of literacy. *Learning Disabilities Research and Practice*, 15:206–25.

Reinking, D., and Schreiner, R. 1985. The effects of computer-mediated text on measures of reading comprehension and reading behavior. *Reading Research Quarterly*, 20:536–52.

Rubin, H. 1988. Morphological knowledge and early writing ability. *Language and Speech*, 31:337–55.

Scanlon, D. M., and Vellutino, F. R. 1997. A comparison of the instructional backgrounds and cognitive profiles of poor, average, and good readers who were initially identified as at risk for reading failure. *Scientific Studies of Reading*, 1:191–215.

Scarborough, H. S. 2001. Connecting early language and literacy to later reading (dis)abilities: Evidence, theory, and practice. In *Handbook of Early Literacy Research*, S. B. Neuman and D. K. Dickinson (Eds.), (pp. 97–110). New York: Guilford Press.

Scarborough, H. S., Dobrich, W., and Hager, M. 1991. Preschool literacy experience and later reading achievement. *Journal of Learning Disabilities*, 24:508–11.

Shanahan, T., and Barr, R. 1995. Reading Recovery: An independent evaluation of the effects of an early instructional intervention for at-risk learners. *Reading Research Quarterly*, 30:958–96.

Slavin, R. E., Karweit, N. L., Wasik, B. A., Madden, N. A., and Dolan, L. J. 1994. Success for All: A comprehensive approach to prevention and early intervention. In *Preventing Early School Failure*, R. E. Slavin, N. L. Karweit, and B. A. Wasik (Eds.), (pp. 175–205). Boston: Allyn and Bacon.

Snow, C. E., Burns, S., and Griffin, P. 1998. *Preventing Reading Difficulties in Young Children.* Washington, DC: National Academy Press.

Stanovich, K. E. 1994. Constructivism in reading education. *Journal of Special Education*, 28:259–74.

Swanson, H. L. 1999. Instructional components that predict treatment outcomes for students with learning disabilities: Support for a combined strategy and direct instruction model. *Learning Disabilities Research and Practice*, 13:129–40.

Tabors, P. O., Snow, C. E., and Dickinson, D. K. 2001. Homes and school together: Supporting language and literacy development. In *Beginning Literacy with Language*, D. K. Dickinson and P. O. Tabors (Eds.), (pp. 313–34). Baltimore: Paul H.Brookes.

Taylor, B. M., Frye, B. J., and Maruyama, G.M. 1990. Time spent reading and reading growth. *American Educational Research Journal*, 27:351–62.

Taylor, B. M., Pearson, P. D., Clark, K., and Walpole, S. 2000. Effective schools and accomplished teachers: Lessons about primary-grade reading instruction in low-income schools. *Elementary School Journal*, 101:121–65.

Torgesen, J. K., Wagner, R. K., and Rashotte, C. A. 1997. Approaches to prevention and remediation of phonologically based reading disabilities. In *Foundations of Reading Acquisition and Dyslexia*, B. Blachman (Ed.), (pp. 287–304). Mahwah, NJ: Lawrence Erlbaum.

Tunmer, W. E., Herriman, M. L., and Nesdale, A. R. 1988. Metalinguistic abilities and beginning reading. *Reading Research Quarterly*, 23:134–58.

Vaughn, S., Moody, S. W., and Schumm, J. S. 1998. Broken promises: Reading instruction in the resource room. *Exceptional Children*, 64:211–25.

Vellutino, F. R., Scanlon, D. M., and Lyon, G. R. 2000. Differentiating between difficult-to-remediate and readily remediated poor readers: More evidence against the IQ-achievement discrepancy. *Journal of Learning Disabilities*, 33:223–38.

Wallach, G. P., and Butler, K. G. 1994. Creating communication, literacy, and classroom success. In *Language Learning Disabilities in School-Age Children and Adolescents*, G. P. Wallach and K. A. Butler (Eds.) (pp. 2–26). Boston: Allyn and Bacon.

Watson, R. 2001. Literacy and oral language: Implications for early literacy acquisition. In *Handbook of Early Literacy Research*, S. B. Neuman and D. K. Dickinson (Eds.), (pp. 43–53). New York: Guilford Press.

Whitehurst, G. J., and Lonigan, C. J. 2001. Emergent literacy: Development from prereaders to readers. In *Handbook of Early Literacy Research*, S. B. Neuman and D. K. Dickinson (Eds.), (pp. 11–29). New York: Guilford Press.

Wilkinson, L. C., and Silliman, E. R. 2000. Classroom language and literacy learning. In *Handbook of Reading Research*, Vol III, M. L. Kamil, P. B. Mosenthal, P. D. Pearson, and R. Barr (Eds.), (pp. 337–60). Mahwah, NJ: Lawrence Erlbaum.

Wise, B. W., and Olson, R. K. 1995. Computer-based phonological awareness and reading instruction. *Annals of Dyslexia*, 45:99–122.

9

Comprehension Instruction in Content Areas

GETTING STARTED

✓ What kinds of difficulties might students experience with content area reading in middle and high school?
✓ What are some reasons for including reading instruction in content classes?
✓ How can content area teachers effectively address reading while ensuring that students learn content information?
✓ What kinds of accommodations are appropriate for very poor readers?

STRUGGLING READERS IN THE CLASSROOM

Students with reading disabilities often reach middle school without adequate literacy skills to handle reading assignments in science, social studies, and literature classes. Since the IDEA 1997 requirement that special education students have access to the standard curriculum, students with mild disabilities are more likely to be included in regular classes and less likely to receive reading instruction outside the regular classroom. It is incumbent upon content area teachers to help these students (as well as other poor readers who do not have a special education label) manage the reading requirments in their classes.

Poor readers are often on the margins of a class, literally and figuratively. By adolescence, many have developed a repertoire of coping strategies that enable them to avoid exposing their inadequacies (Brozo 1990). For instance, they may engage in disruptive behavior, avoid eye contact with teachers, "forget" to bring materials to class, rely on the help of friends, and so on. Such "survival" strategies are, in fact, quite effective in deflecting teachers' attention from the difficulties students have with reading. Research suggests that teachers rarely call on these students to answer questions or read aloud. They may seat them (or allow them to seat themselves) further from the front of the room and generally expect less of them than they do of other students (e.g., Johnston and Winograd 1985). However, as Brozo (1990) noted, strategies that enable poor readers to "hide out" in the classroom are self-defeating in the long run, for they limit opportunities for reading practice and further development of literacy skills. Ultimately, such avoidance behavior may lead to a lifetime of dodging situations in which reading is expected.

In spite of their face-saving actions, however, many poor readers would like to acquire the skills necessary to succeed in school. In a series of interviews of middle school students with severe reading disabilities, McCray, Vaughn, and Neal (2001) found that most such students had a desire to learn to read. They understood the connection between reading and later employment opportunities and said that they would not mind doing remedial work if the result would be improved reading skills. Unfortunately—as is often the case once students reach middle school—high quality instruction with the potential to result in meaningful improvement in reading was not typically available to them.

Undoubtedly, most teachers would agree with Brozo's (1990) assertion that we have an ethical obligation to prevent poor readers from fading into the woodwork, yet they are often not sure how they can help. A high school teacher often has 100 or more students, each with unique strengths and weaknesses, interests and experiences. Getting to know all of them and designing instruction to meet individual learning needs is a daunting task, especially in the case of students who habitually avoid contact with teachers. In this chapter, we provide some recommendations for helping struggling readers gain competence and confidence.

THE NATURE OF CONTENT-AREA READING

By the time they reach middle school, most students are reasonably adept at comprehending simple narratives. Many have had instruction in "story grammar" (see Chapters 7 and 8), and most can understand the plots of stories and novels written for young readers. However, throughout the middle and secondary grades, the literature introduced in language arts classes grows increasingly complex. Plots may not follow familiar forms, language may differ markedly from contemporary English, and more information may need to be inferred by the reader (Gardill and Jitendra 1999). Students are exposed to works representing a variety of literary genres. Moreover, they are expected to learn to analyze literature on multiple levels. Poor readers, as well as average-achievers, often lack strategies for reading and evaluating complex stories, poetry, and drama.

Expository text poses even greater challenges for many struggling readers in the middle and secondary grades than does narrative text (e.g., Armbruster, Anderson, and Meyer 1991). Compounding the problem is the fact that expository text is more likely to be encountered in science and social studies classes than in the language arts classes where middle and secondary students typically receive most of their reading instruction. Because science and social studies teachers are not likely to provide reading instruction, students often do not receive the same degree of support in their efforts to read expository text as they do in their reading of literature.

Textbooks are the most common reading material in science and social studies classes. In fact, textbooks, along with accompanying teachers' guides, often provide the basis for what is taught and how the information is presented. However, it is uncertain to what degree teachers actually expect students to read and learn from textbooks. DiGisi and Willett (1995) explored use of textbooks in high school science classes. Whereas at higher academic levels (Honors and Advanced Placement classes), teachers *did* expect students to learn independently from textbooks, in lower-track classes, textbooks were regarded more as a "reference," "reinforcement," or "supplement." Teachers of lower-track classes assigned less reading and provided most of the course content in class through alternative means. Even when reading was assigned, students generally had no real need to comprehend or learn from their books. DiGisi and Willett expressed concern about the lack of emphasis on learning how to construct new knowledge through reading. Other researchers have echoed this concern. For instance, Adams, Carnine, and Gersten (1982) warned that the tendency of teachers to provide all necessary information may promote passive reading and study habits:

> Students can often learn important information when the teacher guides the learning with lectures, drills, study guides, and the like. But without teacher guidance, at least some students will not develop many strategies for independently extracting information from the text and systematically learning and rehearsing this information (p. 29).

McCray, Vaughn, and Neal (2001) interviewed a poor reader at the middle school level who also voiced this concern:

> We don't read our science textbook because the teacher said [that] he never liked reading his science textbook when he was little, so he would just tell us to remember certain facts and information that he gave us in class. We don't have a social studies book either. I feel that I could be learning so much more if I had homework and read more for myself (p. 27).

Nonetheless, in their decisions about how (or if) to use textbooks, teachers may be responding to the very real difficulties their students have in comprehending them. Cawley, Miller, and Carr (1990) explored the question of whether students with learning disabilities (LD) and other low achievers ages 12 to 15 could read and comprehend passages from elementary-level science textbooks (grades 1–6). Only about a third of the students with LD met the researchers' criteria for adequate independent reading at ANY grade level. "Slow learners" and students with mild mental retardation fared even worse. The authors concluded that for students with LD and other low achievers, textbooks are not likely to be an effective way of conveying science knowledge.

Reading and comprehending textbooks may, in fact, be challenging even for average achievers. The structure of expository text may be unfamiliar to them (see Chapter 7), and they may be unaware of how to use organizational guides (headings, subheadings, bold-face print, etc.) or interpret the graphics. Many students are not as engaged by content-area subject matter as they are by fictional stories and may not be as motivated to put effort into comprehending textbooks. Furthermore, textbooks are often not particularly well written or "reader friendly." McKeown et al. (1992) describe the results of a study in which they analyzed several popular social studies series. They concluded that social studies texts are often poorly organized and lack textual coherence. As a result, readers were required to make many inferences connecting ideas and events (see Chapters 6 and 7 for a more complete discussion of this issue). Moreover, McKeown et al. (1992) argued that textbook authors often assume an unrealistic degree of background knowledge on the part of their intended readers. Similarly, Nicholson (1984) concluded that there is often a mismatch between students' "everyday" knowledge and the "expert" knowledge assumed by textbook authors. Science texts tend to be particularly difficult for many readers because they are often densely packed with concepts (many of which are very abstract), have high prior knowledge demands, and introduce tremendous numbers of new and specialized vocabulary words (Craig and Yore 1996). In fact, in an analysis of grade 6 to 9 science texts, Hurd et al. (1981, cited in Musheno and Lawson 1999) found that there were roughly twice as many new terms introduced than in foreign-language texts designed for the same grade levels!

Research suggests that at least until the later years of high school, many students are ill-prepared to read textbooks, especially science texts. Craig and Yore (1996) found that when encountering difficulties in reading science text, the typical middle school student used social strategies (i.e., asking for help) or relatively superficial text-based strategies (e.g., rereading, reading more slowly). They seemed unaware of strategies for integrating their own prior knowledge with text for active construction of meaning. Moreover, many middle school and secondary students have difficulty monitoring their comprehension of science text and often lack awareness of when they do not understand. Otero and Cambanario (1990) documented growth between the 10th and 12th grades in students' abilities to monitor their understanding and identify useful strategies for improving comprehension. The younger students often had an "illusion of understanding" when they really did not. The authors argued that metacognitive strategy instruction, including comprehension monitoring, should be a part of content-area classes throughout the secondary grades.

Clearly there is a need for instruction in reading and study strategies in content-area classes, not only for poor readers but for all students, and not only in language arts classes but in all classes. Whether or not a teacher considers the textbook itself appropriate, students of all ability levels could benefit from instruction in effective strategies for learning from text.

Of course, this recommendation is not new. Content-area teachers have long been advised to introduce techniques that foster active engagement in the reading and studying processes. One of the best known of these is SQ3R (Robinson 1941, cited in Adams, Carnine, and Gersten 1982). Designed to help students learn *how* to learn from textbooks, SQ3R involves five steps:

SURVEY:	Read through chapter headings.
QUESTION:	Generate questions based on the headings.
READ:	Read each chapter section to answer questions.
RECITE:	Recite or take notes on the highlights of each section.
REVIEW:	After reading the whole chapter, review main points.

Although SQ3R is often advocated as a useful comprehension strategy for poor readers, research on the technique over the years, most of which involved college students, has yielded mixed results (reviewed in Adams, Carnine, and Gersten 1982). In some studies, students showed improvement in reading rate and comprehension as a result of SQ3R, but in others they did not, including most studies involving younger students (reviewed in Schumaker et al. 1982). Further, because virtually all the studies focused on normally achieving readers, it is not clear whether SQ3R is effective for students with serious comprehension problems.

We know from other research on strategy instruction that poor readers often need specific guidance on *how* to formulate good questions, *how* to identify key information, and so on (see Chapter 4). Unless such instruction accompanies the introduction of SQ3R, it may not be of much use to poor readers. With this in mind, Schumaker et al. (1982) developed a technique called MULTIPASS, based on SQ3R, in which students are taught to make several "passes" over a textbook passage. Their innovation was not so much the technique itself as their teaching method (see Chapter 4 for a discussion of the University of Kansas strategies instruction method). Instruction was very explicit and intense. Students first practiced on controlled materials before applying the strategy to grade-level text. Under these training conditions, there was clear improvement for adolescents with learning disabilities. These findings suggest that for poor readers, the secret may not be so much in the particular strategy or set of strategies as in how they are taught. As we noted in Chapter 4, for maximum benefits, instruction needs to be systematic and sustained over time, with many opportunities to practice and to extend the use of a strategy to other situations.

Of course, all of this takes time. Teachers are often concerned about the amount of time required for reading instruction (Bakken, Mastropieri, and Scruggs 1997). They are worried about "covering the content" (often in order to prepare their students for state assessments) and may find it difficult to justify taking the time to teach reading strategies. If strategy instruction is going to be effective, the time factor must certainly be acknowledged and planned for (Lauterbach and Bender 1994). However, we contend that *both* content and strategic knowledge can be taught. In fact, there may well be a false dichotomy between the two: strategy instruction may not only improve comprehension but also enhance learning and memory (Bos and Anders 1992).

Another typical concern is how to address the needs of all students in a mixed-ability classroom. Teachers often wonder whether average and above-average achievers will also benefit from techniques designed to help lower achieving students. They worry that taking the time to teach and reinforce reading strategies will prevent them from providing meaningful instruction to the more capable students.

In the next section of this chapter, we present a variety of research-supported means of addressing reading comprehension in the content-area classroom at the middle and secondary levels. Some of the techniques we discuss may also be appropriate for children in the upper elementary grades. We have especially targeted methods that have been shown to foster long-term learning and memory as well as comprehension, and we include ideas for differentiating instruction according to student needs. We would like to refer the reader to Chapter 4 for a discussion of issues related to learning, maintenance, and generalization of strategies and to Chapter 7 for a discussion of text structure, as these chapters provide background for the current discussion. Our emphasis here is on expository text because it often poses the greatest challenges for struggling readers, but we also include some ideas for helping students cope with the more difficult literature encountered at the middle and secondary grades. We conclude the chapter with ideas for alternative means of organizing instruction, including means of making content information accessible for students who are unable to read with any degree of proficiency.

INSTRUCTIONAL OPTIONS IN THE CONTENT CLASSROOM

In this section, we present a variety of instructional options. In deciding which to use, teachers should consider not only the characteristics of individual learners, but also the nature of the texts and tasks, and how instruction is to be organized. For instance, some of the techniques we discuss are "packages" of strategies that involve specific pre-reading and post-reading activities as well as strategies applied during reading. Some teachers may consider these impractical because they are too inflexible or not well suited to their particular content area or preferred means of organizing instruction. Such teachers may prefer to design their own sets of "before, during, and after" activities that reinforce strategic reading behavior.

As noted earlier, familiarity with basic narrative structure may not prepare students for reading expository text, which is generally organized around a hierarchical structure of ideas rather than around a sequence of causally connected events. The challenges for a reader of expository text are twofold: detecting the author's organizational plan in order to make *internal* connections among ideas in the text, and linking ideas in the text to prior knowledge and experiences to make *external* connections to other sources of information (Mayer 1987). Effective content-area reading instruction helps students meet these challenges.

"Packaged" Strategies

MULTIPASS: Earlier we briefly mentioned MULTIPASS (Schumaker et al. 1982) as an example of a strategy package that has the potential to help students with reading disabilities extract important information from textbook chapters. Although based on SQ3R, MULTIPASS involves much more explicit instruction in how to use headings and chapter questions to identify and remember central concepts. The strategy requires the student to make three "passes" over the chapter. During the first pass, the "Survey" pass, the student reads the title and introductory and summary sections, examines the illustrations, reads headings to see how the chapter is organized, examines the table of contents to see the chapter's relationship to adjacent chapters, and finally paraphrases information gleaned from this procedure. During the second pass, the "Size-Up" pass, the student uses questions at the end of the chapter, headings, and italicized words as indicators of what the key concepts in the chapter are. He or she generates questions based on these clues and answers them by reading relevant portions of the text. The student then paraphrases important facts and ideas from the chapter. During the final pass, the "Sort-out" pass, the student reinforces his or her understanding by answering the questions at the end of the chapter. MULTIPASS allows poor readers to extract central information from the textbook without actually reading the entire chapter. As noted earlier, when the MULTIPASS strategies were taught explicitly and students were given sufficient opportunities to practice and generalize, the system proved to be quite effective for poor readers at the high school level (Schumaker et al. 1982).

POSSE: Another example of a strategy "package" that has proven to be helpful for learning disabled students in the upper elementary and middle grades is POSSE (Englert and Mariage 1991). POSSE is similar to Reciprocal Teaching (see Chapter 4) in that students work in small collaborative groups in which they take turns leading a dialogue about a section of a chapter. However, POSSE also involves additional steps in which students activate their prior knowledge and map the structure of the text using a graphic organizer. Students are taught to apply the following steps:

PREDICT: Based on the title, headings, and illustrations, students brainstorm a list of predictions about what information might be in the chapter and generate questions that they hope will be answered.

ORGANIZE: Students use a semantic map to organize the ideas they brainstormed. The purpose of this step is to encourage them to think about organization as they read and to speculate about what categories of information the author might include.

SEARCH: Students search for the author's structure as they read and create a semantic map representing this structure.

SUMMARIZE: Students summarize the main ideas and ask one another questions that a teacher might ask.

EVALUATE: Students compare their predictions with the actual ideas in the text, clarify portions of the text that they found confusing, and predict the content of the next section of text.

Englert and Mariage (1991) recommended that the teacher serve as a "scribe," recording the students' ideas on the graphic organizer to eliminate the need for a great deal of writing on their part. The teacher may also wish to create and provide the students with copies of a form for recording ideas (see figure 9.1 for an example).

The advantages of both MULTIPASS and POSSE are that they give students a set of procedures to apply before, during, and after reading that aid comprehension and improve memory for what they read. However, there are many other options that may be equally effective and that provide greater flexibility for the teacher. We recommend teaching and reinforcing strategy use at each stage: before students read a selection, while they are reading, and after they read.

POSSE

<u>P</u>redict what ideas are in the story.

people disappear
ships and planes disappear
near Florida
in a different country
stories about it not all true
not exactly a triangle
instruments do not work
5 fighter planes disappeared
stories on TV about it

rescue planes used
some ships/planes make it through
magnetic force
fighter planes disappeared

Student Questions:
What does it look like?
Why do things disappear?
Who discovered it?

<u>O</u>rganize <u>your</u> thoughts.

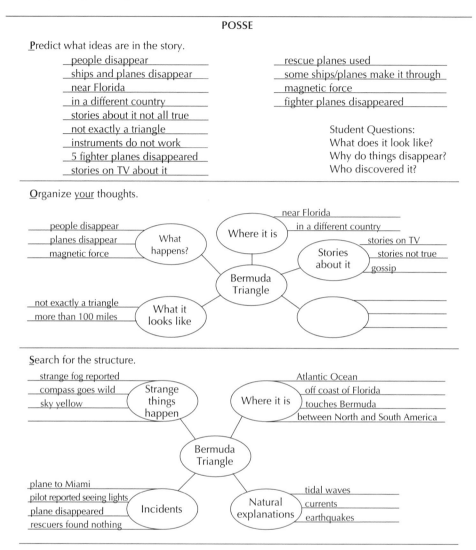

<u>S</u>earch for the structure.

<u>S</u>ummarize. Summarize the Main Idea in your own words. Ask a "Teacher"
       Question about the Main Idea.

<u>E</u>valuate. Compare. Clarify. Predict.

Figure 9.1   Partially completed POSSE strategy sheet. From Englert, C. S., and Marriage, T. V. 1991. Making students partners in the comprehension process: Organizing the reading "POSSE." Learning Disability Quarterly, 14:123–38. Reprinted with permission of Learning Disability Quarterly.

Before Reading

According to Cibrowski (1995), the pre-reading stage is the most important phase of instruction for poor readers. Such students tend to approach reading tasks with little enthusiasm and no clear goals. Further, as Bos and Anders (1992) pointed out, in elementary school poor readers often spend time in the resource room during content instruction. Thus, they may not have an adequate body of domain-specific content knowledge upon which to draw as they read, a limitation that compounds the difficulty they have with comprehending informational text. Cibrowski (1995) argued that pre-reading activities should address three main goals: (1) helping students think about what they already know, (2) focusing their attention on the purpose for reading (which should be well-defined), and (3) sparking their interest and curiosity. Cibrowski suggested that teachers survey students about their interests, their strengths and weaknesses, and significant experiences they have had. A teacher can use this information to engage students and help them link new information to old. This allows students to approach reading with greater confidence and—we hope—enthusiasm.

The K-W-L technique (see Chapter 4), which is often advocated for use in the elementary grades, is equally appropriate for older students. Teachers may wish to provide forms on which students can record what they already know about a topic, what they hope to learn, and later—after they have read—what they learned. Another option is to give students a list of questions to answer about central concepts and vocabulary in the upcoming reading to assess what they already know (Cibrowski 1995). In this way, a teacher can anticipate the parts of a chapter that are likely to be particularly challenging for students and, if necessary, supply students with key background information in advance.

In addition to helping students activate background knowledge, these techniques can alert teachers to misconceptions that their students may have about the topic. As many researchers have observed (e.g, Lipson 1982; Maria and MacGinitie 1982; Walraven and Reitsma 1993), prior knowledge can be a "double-edged sword." To learn effectively, students must be able to relate new information to what they already know. However, when background knowledge is irrelevant or inaccurate, it can divert attention from central concepts and interfere with comprehension. Students may have difficulty modifying cherished misconceptions, even when information in the text contradicts what they believe to be true.

Over the years, many researchers have found that presenting students with a graphic representation of text information before they read enhances comprehension and memory (e.g., Alverman 1988; Armbruster, Anderson, and Meyer 1991; Sinatra, Stahl-Gemake, and Berg 1984). Instructional graphics have been given a variety of labels (e.g., "concept maps," "semantic maps," "graphic organizers," "thematic maps," "frames"). They have proven to be powerful learning tools for students of all ability levels. When presented to students before reading, such "advance organizers" alert students to the central concepts, draw their attention to the author's organizational plan, and highlight the relationships among ideas. Additionally, they provide a written record of text information that can be used as a study aid. See figure 9.2 for an example (from Sinatra, Stahl-Gemake, and Berg 1984). Different types of maps can correspond to different organizational systems. See figure 9.3 for a variety of examples (from Calfee and Chambliss 1988).

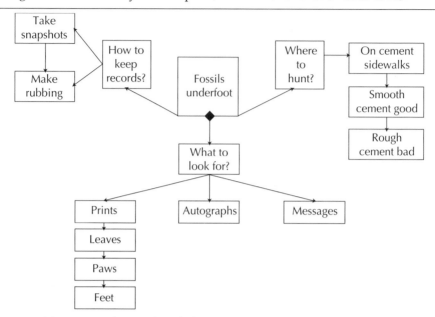

Figure 9.2   Thematic map for "Fossils Underfoot." From Sinatra, Richard, Stahl-Gemake, Josephine, and Berg, David N. 1983, October. Improving reading comprehension of disabled readers through semantic mapping. The Reading Teacher 38 (1):p. 26. Reprinted with permission of Richard Sinatra and the International Reading Association. All rights reserved.

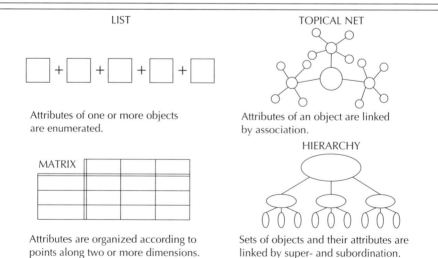

Figure 9.3   Structural models for descriptive expository writing. Reprinted from Calfee, R., and Chambliss, M. 1988. Beyond decoding: Pictures of expository prose. Annals of Dyslexia 38:243–57, with permission of the International Dyslexia Association, granted on January 4, 2002.

Another option is to present students with a partially complete or blank graphic and ask them fill it in as they read (e.g., Armbruster, Anderson, and Meyer 1991) or have them construct their own graphic representations of text content. Berkowitz (1986) found that for normally achieving sixth graders, graphic organizers were more effective comprehension aids when the students constructed them. However, this may be too much to expect of younger students and poor readers, at least initially. Alvermann and Boothby (1986) found that even high-achieving fourth graders needed extensive instruction before they were able to create their own graphics. However, some research indicates that teacher-constructed graphics may work well. Armbruster, Anderson, and Meyer (1991), for instance, found that for fourth and fifth graders, teacher-generated graphics were as effective in enhancing comprehension and memory as blank graphics filled in by the students. Teachers might want to consider differentiating instruction by expecting different levels of independence from different groups of students. Some students might be asked to create graphic representations of the text entirely on their own. Others could fill in a blank or partially completed graphic. Those who need it could be given the completed graphic to use as a guide while reading. As students grow more proficient at using and creating graphics, greater independence can be expected.

Cibrowski (1995) recommended that in constructing graphics, teachers avoid the temptation to include too many details. She argued that an effective map is not a mere outline of a chapter, but a representation of key concepts and important details. Teachers may want to ask themselves what is really crucial that students learn from their reading and create graphics that will help them focus on this information.

Other researchers (e.g., McCormick 1989) have found that supplying students with a written preview of an upcoming reading assignment, either by itself or as an adjunct to a graphic organizer, can be effective. In McCormick's study, the previews included questions that were designed to prompt discussion, arouse interest, and activate background knowledge; a synopsis of the passage; and a list of potentially difficult vocabulary. Before the students read the passage, the teacher led them in a discussion of the questions, read the synopsis aloud to them, and supplied pronunciations and definitions of the vocabulary words. Both skilled and less skilled readers benefited from this preparatory technique.

Another pre-reading technique that can be extremely powerful is to introduce new concepts with analogies (Cibrowski 1995; Glynn, Duit, and Thiele 1995; Risco and Alvarez 1986). Risco and Alvarez (1986) observed that the use of analogies in this way was helpful for both normally achieving students and poor readers in the upper elementary grades. Analogies can help students relate ideas within the text to one another and to make connections to relevant background knowledge. This may be particularly helpful in science, which is laden with highly abstract concepts. For instance, carbohydrate molecules, which consist of long chains of simple sugars bonded together, could be compared to a freight train made up of boxcars linked together. A drug overdose could be compared to a situation in which water is running into a sink at a faster rate than it is draining. According to Glynn, Duit, and Thiele (1995),

Ideally, an analogy effectively drawn between two concepts will help students transfer their existing knowledge to the understanding, organizing, and visualizing of new knowledge. The result is often a higher order, relational understanding; that is, students see how the features of a concept fit together and how the concept in question relates to other concepts (p. 255).[6]

It is also helpful to teach students to recognize analogies that authors have provided in the text.

During Reading

A common practice in middle and secondary classrooms is to assign reading for homework. However, as Cibrowski (1995) noted, poor readers are typically not very successful with independent silent reading of lengthy passages. Because of slow, effortful decoding, they may quickly become bored and inattentive. When working independently, they are less motivated to try to apply strategies and tend to view a reading assignment as a burdensome task to finish rather than an opportunity to learn. In fact, it is quite likely that many relatively good readers share these attitudes toward textbook reading assignments. For these reasons, we recommend that teachers devote more in-class time to reading. Time devoted to teaching and guided practice of reading strategies may be very well spent, for ultimately it may enable students of all ability levels to become more independent learners.

Content-area teachers may be particularly interested in helping students learn to apply "organizational" strategies—techniques that help them recognize the author's organizational plan and distinguish central ideas from details (see Chapters 4 and 7 for more detailed discussions). One very useful strategy is to teach students to attend carefully to headings and subheadings, a central component of SQ3R and MULTIPASS. However, though these features are common in textbooks, not all expository texts have headings. Students who are learning to read informational texts may benefit from explicit instruction in text structure. There are several patterns that are common in expository text, especially enumeration (list), time order, comparison/contrast, cause-effect, and problem-solution (Meyer 1985). Some practitioners have questioned the value of teaching students to recognize text structures on the grounds that real texts are too "messy." It is certainly true that a text may contain a variety of structures, and that few natural texts conform perfectly to models. However, basic structures *are* identifiable in expository text, and research suggests that it is helpful to teach students to recognize them (e.g., Armbruster, Anderson, and Ostertag 1987; Bakken, Mastropieri, and Scruggs 1997).

---

[6]Glynn, Duit, and Thiele (1995) offered several cautions about teaching with analogies. First they recommended that teachers keep in mind that no analogy is perfect. Since the concepts being compared are similar but *not* identical, all analogies "break down" at some point, which may lead to misconceptions. Teachers may need to point out how the two concepts are *not* alike or ask students to identify both similarities and differences. Secondly, an analogy is not useful if a student does not understand the supposedly familiar concept. For instance, the human heart is often compared to a pump. However, most students probably do not really understand how a pump works.

In a recent study specifically focusing on poor readers, Bakken, Mastropieri, and Scruggs (1997) assigned 54 eighth graders with LD to one of three treatment conditions: text structure training, paraphrasing training, and the traditional approach of reading and answering questions. The students in the text structure group were taught to recognize several structures that are common in science texts. During the course of three 30-minute training sessions, they practiced identifying main ideas, locating supporting details, and labeling the text structures. Their attention was drawn to similarities and differences in the various text structures. The students in this group had better recall of text information both immediately and a day later than the students in either of the control groups. Bakken, Mastropieri, and Scruggs (1997) pointed out that students in the study were able to learn to apply this text structure strategy in a relatively short period of time. However, these researchers did not address the issue of long-term maintenance of the strategy; it is likely that many poor readers would need more extensive practice in order to fully make it a part of their repertoire of strategies.

In addition to their role in alerting students to key concepts before they read, graphic organizers are a useful way of representing the text structure visually. As noted earlier, students can be given a partially completed graphic that highlights central ideas and general organization before they read. Instead of an outline form, however, teachers may wish to give students a graphic that represents the broader conceptual structure of a text. For instance, Armbruster, Anderson, and Ostertag (1987) taught fifth graders to recognize problem/solution patterns, a common structure in social studies text. The students used a general conceptual map to record information related to problems and their solutions (see Figure 9.4). Rather than being tied to a specific text, such a graphic can help students attend to commonalities in structure across texts. It may also reinforce students' understanding of the "big ideas" in a given discipline. For instance, the study of history involves a cycle of causes and effects: actions, usually undertaken to solve a problem, have certain consequences, which in turn lead to further actions. Ellis (1997) argued that understanding such broad conceptual frameworks—instead of recall of lots of specific facts and details—should be the focus of instruction for students with learning disabilities at the secondary level.

Ehlinger and Pritchard (1994) suggested a procedure for teaching students to identify text structures. They recommended that teachers begin with passages a single paragraph in length, and then proceed to longer passages that have the same predominant organizational structure as the paragraphs. Initially students should work with model texts that conform to the pattern before moving to natural text, which may have several secondary patterns embedded within a predominant structure. Ehlinger and Pritchard (1994) suggested teaching students to use clues provided in the topic sentence and "signal words" to predict structure. For instance, *first*, *next*, and *finally* usually indicate a list; *however, on the other hand*, and *similarly* often indicate comparison or contrast. Many poor readers will probably need extensive practice before they have mastered this strategy. Ehlinger and Pritchard suggested having students work in pairs on practice passages, taking turns in the roles of "thinker" and "listener/recorder." The thinker talks aloud as the students read through the passage, making and confirming

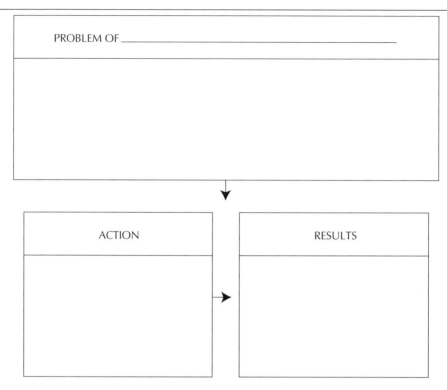

PROBLEM = something bad; a situation that people would like to change
ACTION   = what people *do* to try to solve the problem
RESULTS   = what happens as a result of the action; the effect or outcome of
                 trying to solve the problem

Figure 9.4   Problem/solution frame. Armbruster, Bonnie B., Anderson, Thomas, H., and Ostertag, Joyce. 1987. Does text structure/summarization instruction facilitate learning from expository text? Reading Research Quarterly 22 (3):p. 335. Reprinted with permission of Bonnie B. Armbruster and the International Reading Association. All rights reserved.

predictions about the text structure. The listener makes notes or fills in a graphic organizer.

Application of reading strategies in pairs or in small groups is an instructional technique that has promise for the content area classroom. A number of researchers have examined the effectiveness of collaborative reading strategies in the regular classroom (Anderson and Roit 1993; Bos and Anders 1992; Gallego 1992; King and Parent Johnson 1999; Lederer 2000; Miller, Miller, and Rosen 1988). The results have been quite positive on the whole. For instance, Miller, Miller, and Rosen (1988) reported better comprehension text scores, lengthier summaries, better grades, and better behavior for seventh graders who used Reciprocal Teaching in their social studies classes relative to students who received traditional instruction. More recently King and Parent Johnson (1999) observed improvement on both informal and standardized reading assessments for students in heterogeneous classrooms who used Reciprocal Teaching. However, neither of these research teams specifically examined the impact of Reciprocal Teaching on the achievement of poor readers. Other researchers have focused more directly on struggling readers. In a series of studies conducted over the course of three years, Bos and Anders (1992) found that for bilingual students and those with LD in the upper elementary and middle grades strategy instruction in cooperative learning groups was more effective than traditional instruction in helping students learn content area concepts. Lederer (2000) found similar effects for students with LD integrated into mixed ability classrooms.

Lederer (2000) also sought to answer a logistical question about the implementation of Reciprocal Teaching in classrooms: Is the technique still effective when the teacher does not continuously participate in the group? As originally conceptualized, Reciprocal Teaching and related techniques such as POSSE (Englert and Mariage 1991) and Collaborative Strategic Reading (Vaughn and Klingner 1999) require that the teacher be a member of the group to model strategies and offer encouragement. While this may work well in a resource setting, it is obviously not feasible in a class of 30 students. Unlike some of the other researchers investigating Reciprocal Teaching in the classroom, Lederer (2000) sought to test the technique under realistic classroom conditions. Instruction was provided entirely by the single researcher with the assistance of a classroom aide. They rotated among the groups, giving equal time to each group. The groups were asked to appoint a discussion leader and were given a worksheet to structure the process. The students with LD who participated in the collaborative reading groups had significantly better scores on reading comprehension measures and produced better summaries than students with LD receiving traditional instruction.

Vaughn, Klingner, and Bryant (2001) also developed a systematic procedure for using Collaborative Strategic Reading, a technique similar to Reciprocal Teaching, in the larger classroom. During the first few days of instruction, the teacher presents four strategies (predicting, monitoring, identifying main ideas, and summarizing) to the entire class and models their use. Selected students are then asked to model the use of the strategies for the class. Finally, the teacher and a small group of students demonstrate the group reading process. After the students have become proficient in applying the strategies in full-class activities, the teacher divides the class into small groups or pairs in which each student is assigned a specific role. In the small groups, students collaboratively apply the strategies to reading assignments. With this degree of initial preparation, students seem to be capable of working with relative independence (Vaughn, Klingner, and Bryant 2001).

Another promising technique—described in detail in Chapter 8—is PALS (Peer Assisted Learning Strategies). Students read in pairs, with each dyad consisting of a higher and a lower achieving student, to apply a specific set of comprehension strategies. This technique has been documented as effective in elementary grade classrooms. Fuchs et al. (2001) have recently demonstrated its effectiveness for high school students with reading disabilities, with slight modifications in the procedure used in elementary school.

Thus far, we have focused exclusively on the text itself. However, most textbooks also contain numerous illustrations, diagrams, graphs, maps, and charts that may be beneficial to poor readers. A common assumption is that students who have difficulty reading a textbook can get a good bit of the information through the illustrations. However, this may be more myth than reality unless they are given instruction in how to use the illustrations. Research indicates that illustrations most effectively support learning when pictures are integrated with the text and when pictures and text are processed concurrently (Levin and Mayer 1993; Mayer et al. 1995). In most diagrams, however, information is compressed, and many details are omitted (Nicholson 1984). Readers must fill in the "gaps" by integrating textual information with pictorial information. Many textbook illustrations lack captions and are not cross-referenced with the text (Woodward 1993).[7] In these cases, the link between pictures and text is ambiguous and must be inferred, a task that often requires sophisticated reasoning skills (Hannus and Hyönä 1999). Teachers may wish to draw students' attention to particular textbook graphics that *are* instructionally useful. Students may benefit from explicit instruction in how to integrate textual information with pictorial information and how to interpret various kinds of graphics. In collaborative reading groups, students might be encouraged to discuss the relationship between the text and the illustrations.

After Reading

It is beneficial for all students, and particularly for poor readers, to follow a reading assignment with post-reading activities that encourage them to review newly acquired knowledge and "extend what they learn in their textbooks to their personal world" (Cibrowski 1995, p. 99).

For starters, students should be encouraged to complete the K-W-L process by considering what they learned from their reading and relating it to prior knowledge (K) and to the questions they generated about the topic (W). At this point, students may also be asked to consider what further questions they have about a topic (Ogle 1986). In a recent intervention study that was conducted during the course of an entire school year, Cantrell, Fusaro, and Dougherty (2000) taught students in seventh grade social studies classrooms to use K-W-L to structure journal responses. Compared to students in a control group who were taught to use their reading journals to summarize what they had read, students in the K-W-L group learned and retained significantly more content knowledge. The authors attribute the difference to the use of journals throughout the reading process rather than after reading only. It also seems likely that the K-W-L procedure encourages students to personalize knowledge in a way that summarization alone does not. However, the authors did not specifically comment on the performance of poor readers in their sample. Although it is likely that such students would benefit from this technique, poor readers often struggle with writing and

---

[7]Woodward (1993) pointed out that illustrations are included in modern textbooks largely to enhance their marketability. Beautifully illustrated books with full-color photographs on every page grab the attention of selection committees and are more likely to be chosen. The tendency is to "equate attractive layout and stunning photographs with instructional quality" (p. 123), which is not necessarily the case.

may have difficulty producing extensive journal entries. Such students might be encouraged to structure their responses in the form of a list or fill in a K-W-L graphic (see Chapter 4).

Students can also be encouraged to add information to concepts maps or create new ones. Such graphics can be designed to emphasize interpretations and conclusions rather than merely a review of the material. Idol (1987) used this approach with poor readers in a high school social studies class. During the course of the intervention, students were taught to consider other viewpoints, draw their own conclusions, and relate historical issues to today's world. They recorded their responses on a "Critical Thinking Map" (see figure 9.5).

Comprehension of Literature

Many of the procedures we describe in this chapter can be applied to reading of literature as well as expository texts. However, the specific questions that students are asked to pose may differ. As noted earlier, the literature to which students are exposed in the middle and secondary grades is more complex than that encountered in elementary school. More information must be inferred, there are often multiple problems, complications, and "twists," and students are expected to identify such components as theme and mood and recognize a variety of literary devices. Gardill and Jitendra (1999) sought to extend the work of Idol and Croll (1987) by applying the concept of a story map to more sophisticated literature. Middle school students with LD were taught to complete an "advanced story map" on which they recorded detailed character information (e.g., "clues" to characters' personalities, their reactions to events, etc.); sources of conflict; unexpected plot twists; and the theme. The students demonstrated better comprehension of short stories, generalization of the strategy to longer works of fiction, and maintenance of the strategy over time. Gurney et al. (1990) devised a similar technique for high school students with learning disabilities. Students in their study were explicitly taught strategies for identifying sources of conflict, clues about characterization, plot twists, and theme. This was followed by a guided practice phase in which teachers provided encouragement and feedback; however, the students were required to apply the strategies on their own and use a graphic organizer to take notes. After this instruction, the researchers observed improvements in the students' ability to answer questions about story components in classic short stories that are often included in high school literature analogies (e.g., De Maupassant's "The Necklace" and Hawthorne's "The Birthmark"). However, they were less successful at answering detail-oriented multiple choice questions taken from basal readers.

Gurney et al. (1990) noted that theme was the most difficult component to teach, requiring more extensive teacher modeling and explanation that the plot-based components. Williams (1993) also found that adolescents with learning disabilities had particular difficulty identifying the themes of stories, relative both to their peers and to younger students without disabilities. As Gersten et al. (2001) noted, the concept of theme is highly abstract. With the exception of fables, in which the "moral" typically appears at the end, the themes of works of literature

Name _____   Chap. _____ Part _____

Date _____   Phase _____

Important Events, Points, or Steps

```
[                                                              ]
```

Main Idea/Lesson

```
[                                                              ]
```

Other Viewpoints/Opinions

```
[                                                              ]
```

Reader's Conclusion

```
[                                                              ]
```

Relevance to Today

```
[                                                              ]
```

Figure 9.5   A map for critical thinking. From "A critical thinking map to improve content area comprehension of poor readers" by L. Idol, 1987, Remedial and Special Education 8:28–40. Copyright (1987) by PRO-ED, Inc. Reprinted with permission.

are seldom stated explicitly. Rather, the reader must integrate plot-level information in order to recognize a general pattern in story events. Williams and her colleagues developed a method of instruction that was specifically designed to help middle-school students learn to identify themes in stories and apply the themes to real life (Williams et al. 1994). The researchers began by teaching story grammar components, then used additional sets of guiding questions to teach theme identification and generalization to life situations. Students who received the training were successful at comprehending the concept of theme and at recognizing, in different stories, the themes that had been discussed during instruction. Applying a theme to real-life situations and recognizing themes that had *not* been previously discussed proved more difficult, especially for students with severe LD. Nonetheless the authors concluded that students with LD and other poor readers are likely to profit from explicit instruction in "higher-order" comprehension skills.

Instruction Organized Around Problem-Solving

Teachers may wish to have students complete post-reading activities collaboratively in small groups. Application of newly acquired knowledge to such activities as science experiments (Palincsar, Anderson, and David 1993) can strengthen students' understanding of concepts and increase the likelihood of long-term retention. An alternative is to make problem-solving the focus of instruction. Thus far in our discussion, we have assumed the traditional lecture-based means of organizing content instruction. Although this continues to be the instructional model that is most frequently used in content area classes, it is becoming increasingly popular for teachers to organize instruction around real-life problems as an alternative to lecture-based presentation. Unlike traditional instruction, in which all the information needed to solve problems is provided to students in advance, in problem-based learning, students learn concepts and information through their efforts to solve the problem (Greenwald 2000). The teacher serves as a "guide" or "coach," offering suggestions and raising questions to challenge students' thinking, but *not* supplying the answers. In fact, there is usually no single right answer or specific strategy for solving the problem.

　　Proponents of problem-based learning argue that this approach serves as an "apprenticeship for real-life problem-solving" (Stepien and Gallagher 1993, p. 26), in that students are asked to "assume the roles of scientists, doctors, historians, or others who might have a real stake in the proposed problem" (p. 26). For instance, in a high school biology class, students might be given a stack of patient files and be asked to take the role of public health officials seeking to discover the cause of an outbreak of Legionnaires' disease. In a history class studying Nazi Germany, students might be assigned the role of directors of an art gallery who have been asked to discard any paintings with themes that are counter to the government's vision. In order to tackle such a problem, the students must conduct research on the Nazi Party that goes well beyond what is likely to be included in most high school textbooks. According to Stepien and Gallagher (1993), the nature of the questions can change in the course of solving the problem. For instance, once the students have identified a set of "suspect" paintings in their gallery's collection, they might ask themselves what the penalty might be if they do not destroy the art and whether or not they could negotiate with the Nazis. Answering these questions would lead to further research. In making a final decision about their course of action, they might debate whether or not saving the paintings is worth the personal risk.

Organizing instruction around such problems allows students to "personalize" learning in a way that typically does not occur with lecture-based presentation. They learn research skills, they learn to work collaboratively with others, they gain insight into the complexity of the "real-world," and their long-term memory for information learned though the experience will probably be greater (Greenwald 2000; Stepien and Gallagher 1993). Problems can be judiciously selected so that the teacher's instructional goals are incorporated. Obviously such an approach to instruction differs radically from the traditional textbook and lecture format, and it requires both the teacher and the students to conceptualize their respective roles in different ways. For a variety of reasons, problem-based instruction has the potential to benefit greatly struggling readers in content classes; however, it also poses additional challenges for these students.

An obvious advantage of problem-based learning for poor readers is that, by its very nature, it has the potential to draw reluctant students in by stimulating their interest and curiosity. As a result, they may work harder and more persistently, gaining much-needed practice with academic skills. In problem-based learning activities, students are usually asked to work collaboratively in small groups, sharing the workload by assuming responsibility for different aspects of the research and the consolidation of information. Hence, poor readers can take charge of tasks that they can manage. For instance, the teacher can direct these students to a set of easier books on a given topic. In fact, sources of information need not be limited to books. Documentary films, Internet sites, and various types of multi-media presentations that integrate pictures, movies, and text can be valuable sources of information. In some instances, students may gather information relevant to the problem through interviews or surveys. Poor readers can be assigned the task of investigating these sources, while more capable readers tackle complex texts. When the better readers then share what they have learned with the group, poor readers gain access to this information without having to read the material themselves.

On the other hand, teachers will need to think carefully about how to structure problem-based learning experiences for less-capable students. Difficulty retaining information and transferring knowledge to new situations is a particular problem for students with LD (see Chapter 4). It may not be enough to merely provide such students with the *opportunity* to solve complex problems. Unless there is sufficient structure, research suggests that students with LD may not profit from opportunities to learn through experience (reviewed in Gersten and Baker 1998). They often have difficulty in retrieving and organizing information and in formulating hypotheses, two key skills needed in problem-solving activities (Gersten and Baker 1998). Moreover, because of past failures, many such students have a tendency to withdraw from challenging situations. Gersten and Baker argued that there is a great "need for classroom strategies that will improve the ability of students with learning disabilities to apply knowledge and skills to real-world situations" (p. 23). While these students definitely need experience with problem-solving activities, in order to benefit from these experiences, they also need explicit instruction in the higher-order reasoning processes involved (Swanson 2001). Gersten and Baker (1998) recommended that teachers provide explicit instruction in the concepts necessary to solve problems through extensive modeling of reasoning processes and active coaching. Materials such as graphic organizers and semantic maps may be helpful, as well as written reminders of options, strategies, and questions. With such supports, students may be more successful at transferring what they have learned from one problem-solving experience to another. Finally, as Gersten and Baker (1998) observed, it is important to provide students with multiple opportunities to solve complex problems in order for transfer of learning to occur.

COMMONLY ASKED QUESTIONS

What can teachers do to assist students whose reading skills are so low that they are essentially nonreaders?

In a recent large-scale intervention study, Bryant et al. (1999) examined the effect of several research-supported practices on the reading achievement of middle school students in mixed-ability classrooms. Of particular interest was whether or not students of all ability levels would profit from intensive, multi-component reading instruction that was sustained for a substantial amount of time (4 months) and reinforced in all of the students' classes. Teachers trained by the researchers provided instruction in word recognition, fluency, and comprehension using a number of the techniques we have described in this book. Comprehension, for instance, was addressed through collaborative, small-group strategy training. On the whole, the approach was very successful. Most students made significant gains in all three areas. However, the researchers identified a small group of extremely poor readers who made little or no improvement during the course of the intervention.

Bryant et al. (1999) concluded that very poor readers need intensive one-to-one or small group instruction in addition to what can reasonably be provided in the regular classroom. They need additional time to learn to apply reading strategies and sufficient practice with easier materials before applying strategies to grade-level text. We recommend that whenever possible, content area teachers collaborate with special education teachers to design a coherent, consistent reading program for these students. Cibrowski (1995) suggested that regular and special educators decide who will be responsible for teaching which strategies and how what is taught in one setting will be reinforced in other settings. For example, a student might learn and practice a strategy in the resource room that will be used in one or more of the student's content area classes. The role of the content area teacher will be to assist the student in applying the strategy to reading assignments in his or her class.

Students with some degree of reading proficiency may benefit from having access to easier reading material. Content area teachers may want to build a collection of materials in which key concepts are addressed at more manageable reading levels. In literature classes, materials such as Cliff's Notes and plot summaries may be of assistance to students who are unable to handle the reading.

Other students may benefit from alternatives to traditional text. One possibility is to package the most important information from the text in graphic form. A number of researchers (Darch and Carnine 1986; Darch and Eaves 1986; Mastropieri and Peters 1987) found that very poor readers who are simply not able to derive any meaning from textbooks benefited from visual displays such as that depicted in figure 9.6 (from Darch and Carnine 1986).

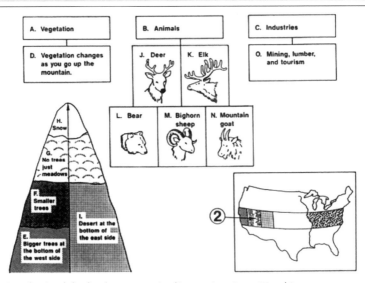

Figure 9.6   Sample visual display from one unit of instruction. From "Teaching content area material to learning disabled students" by C. Darch and D. Carnine, 1986, Exceptional Children 53:240–46. Copyright (1986) by The Council for Exceptional Children. Reprinted with permission.

Unlike the instructional graphics we described earlier, which serve as reading guides, these graphics are intended to be substitutes for reading. They may give very poor readers access to key information and serve as study aids. However, constructing them may require more time and effort than most teachers can spare. An alternative might be to draw students attention to selected graphics in the textbook in which information is consolidated (though see above discussion of textbook illustrations.)

Another popular option is to use recorded texts as an alternative to reading. For *some* students and for *some* types of text, this may be helpful. Sawyer and Kosoff (1981) explored the effectiveness of recorded texts for five adolescent boys with dyslexia. For these students, the auditory presentation was a viable alternative to reading. Sawyer and Kosoff concluded that their subjects possessed adequate levels of vocabulary and linguistic knowledge to comprehend grade-level content area material. However, this is probably not the case for a good many poor readers, who often have difficulty with listening comprehension as well as reading comprehension. Ganschow and Weber (1987) found that for students of all ability levels in the 4th-6th grades, reading alone or reading and listening simultaneously was more effective than listening alone. Carlisle (1993) compared reading and listening to science texts in a sample of 4th and 6th graders. Like Ganschow and Weber, she found weaker performance in listening than in reading at both grade levels, for normally achieving students as well as those with learning disabilities. In fact, no learning disabled student in her sample was significantly better at listening than reading. Carlisle speculated that the density of concepts in science texts might make them particularly difficult to comprehend through an auditory presentation. Other types of text—most notably works of fiction—are probably more easily processed auditorily. To summarize, *if* students have adequate receptive language abilities and *if* a text is comprehensible through listening, recorded books may be useful.

Other media such as films, CD-ROMs, and Internet sites designed for young readers may be valuable tools for granting nonreaders access to content information. Research on the effectiveness of such materials is limited at this point. Though they are unlikely to be a complete panacea for the difficulties poor readers encounter, they may well be helpful.

What criteria can teachers use to decide if a textbook is appropriate for their students?

When passages in textbooks were examined, global coherence (i.e., the overall organization is readily identifiable) and local coherence (i.e., ideas within the passages are clearly connected to one another) affected the extent to which students find textbooks "readable" (Anderson and Armbruster 1986). Where a particular textbook must be used but is judged to be "inconsiderate," given the students' needs, several different measures to change texts have been recommended with the goal of making them more accessible to the students with reading problems. Conte, Menyuk, and Bashir (1994) explored two types of alterations of social studies texts for middle-school students with language disorders. One was simplified vocabulary and syntax, and the other involved rewriting expository passages to make them narratives. They found that the students benefited from both types of changes. Beck and her colleagues (1984) studied changes in stories that might improve their potential to support students' learning. The coherence of the texts was improved by making connections within the text more evident, by filling potential knowledge gaps, and by clarifying events. A comparison of comprehension of the original and the revised texts showed that both skilled and less skilled readers performed better on the revised text. The comprehension of the less skilled readers on the revised text was brought up to the level of the skilled readers on the commercial version.

However, suggestions for improving texts in textbooks are probably more useful to textbook publishers than teachers. Correcting the problems of poorly developed textbooks requires more work and time than teachers have to devote to the effort! A more realistic solution is to provide supports for the linguistic and structural demands of learning from the textbook. Suggestions for activities before, during, and after reading from this chapter should help students understand and integrate information presented in textbook passages. Another solution is to find ways to use other available texts to support students' learning in the content area. This may mean group and individual projects in the library, exploration of resources through the Internet, and so on. Problem-based learning may lead teachers to create their own texts—or to rely on students to develop texts that support others' learning. There are many options, so that teachers need not feel that they have to put up with textbooks that truly do not support and foster content-area learning.

The committee that recommends the adoption of textbooks in districts and schools plays an important role. Teachers are advised to volunteer to serve on textbook adoption committees, when possible, so that their views are considered in the decision-making process. We recommend that teachers and school administrators study the textbook adoption process so that it runs smoothly. Articles are available that give advice about such matters as choosing committee members and establishing timelines (see, for instance, Stein et al. 2001).

Some factors to consider when evaluating textbooks are listed in figure 9.7:

(1) *Content:* What is the scope of the content and the depth of treatment of different topics? Does the content match the goals of the curriculum?

(2) *Lay-Out:* Consider the font and the visual presentation of the pages. Are headings in bold? Are key words presented in bold? Is the textbook text-rich (substantive treatment of topics) or text-poor (fragmented texts with little development of ideas and information)? Are there numerous "boxed" items that contain irrelevant information and are in fact potentially distracting?

(3) *Structural support and organization:* Examine the coherence of the text in several parts of the textbook. Consider both global and local coherence. Are the sections related to one another in a logical fashion? Are the relations within and across sections made explicit?

(4) Pictures, diagrams, visual displays: Are these relevant to the text? Do they support learning of concepts and information?

(5) *Linguistic complexity:* Consider the vocabulary and the complexity of sentences. Is some effort made to preview words that students need to know to understand the text? Is signaling used to show relations of ideas within and across sentences?

(6) *Pre-reading and post-reading activities:* Are the recommended activities before and after reading appropriate to support student's understanding of central concepts, principles, and facts?

Figure 9.7   Some points to consider in textbook evaluation and selection.

REFERENCES

Adams, A., Carnine, D., and Gersten, R. 1982. Instructional strategies for studying content area texts in the intermediate grades. *Reading Research Quarterly*, 18:27–55.

Alvermann, D. E. 1988. Effects of spontaneous and induced lookbacks on self-perceived high- and low-ability comprehenders. *Journal of Educational Research*, 81:325–31.

Alvermann, D. E., and Boothby, P. R. 1986. Children's transfer of graphic organizer instruction. *Reading Psychology*, 7:87–100.

Anderson, T. H., and Armbruster, B. B. 1986. Readable textbooks, or selecting a textbook is not like buying a pair of shoes. In *Reading Comprehension: From Research to Practice*, J. Orsanu (Ed.), (pp. 151–62). Hillsdale, NJ: Lawrence Erlbaum.

Anderson, V., and Roit, M. 1993. Planning and implementing collaborative strategy instruction for delayed readers in grades 6-10. *The Elementary School Journal*, 94:121–37.

Armbruster, B. B., Anderson, T. H., and Meyer, J. L. 1991. Improving content-area reading using instructional graphics. *Reading Research Quarterly*, 26:393–416.

Armbruster, B. B., Anderson, T. H., and Ostertag, J. 1987. Does text structure/summarization instruction facilitate learning from expository text? *Reading Research Quarterly*, 22:331–46.

Bakken, J. P., Mastropieri, M. A., and Scruggs, T. E. 1997. Reading comprehension of expository science material and students with learning disabilities: A comparison of strategies. *The Journal of Special Education*, 31:300–24.

Beck, I. L., McKeown, M. G., Omanson, R. C., and Pople, M. T. 1984. Improving the comprehensibility of stories: The effects of revisions that improve coherence. *Reading Research Quarterly*, 19:263–77.

Berkowitz, S. J. 1986. Effects of instruction in text organization on sixth-grade students' memory for expository reading. *Reading Research Quarterly*, 21:161–78.

Bos, C. S., and Anders, P. L. 1992. Using interactive teaching and learning strategies to promote text comprehension and content learning for students with learning disabilities. *International Journal of Disability, Development, and Education*, 39:25–38.

Brozo, W. G. 1990. Hiding out in secondary content classrooms: Coping strategies of unsuccessful readers. *Journal of Reading*, 33:324–28.

Bryant, D. P., Vaughn, S., Linan-Thompson, S., Ugel, N., Hamff, A., and Hougen, M. 1999. Reading outcomes for students with and without reading disabilities in general education middle-school content area classes. *Learning Disability Quarterly*, 23:238–52.

Calfee, R., and Chambliss, M. 1988. Beyond decoding: Pictures of expository prose. *Annals of Dyslexia*, 38:243–57.

Cantrell, R. J., Fusaro, J. A., and Dougherty, E. A. 2000. Exploring the effectiveness of journal writing on learning social studies: A comparative study. *Reading Psychology*, 21:1–11.

Carlisle, J. F. 1993. Understanding passages in science textbooks: A comparison of students with and without learning disabilities. D. J. Leu and C. K. Kinzer (Eds.). *42nd Yearbook of the National Reading Conference*, 42:235–42.

Cawley, J. F., Miller, J. H., and Carr, S. C. 1990. An examination of the reading performance of students with mild educational handicaps or learning disabilities. *Journal of Learning Disabilities*, 23:284–90.

Cibrowski, J. 1995. Using textbooks with students who cannot read them. *Remedial and Special Education*, 16:90–101.

Conte, B., Menyuk, P., and Bashir, A. 1994. Facilitating reading comprehension in middle school students with language disorders. *International Journal of Psycholinguistics*, 10:273–80.

Craig, M. T., and Yore, L. D. 1996. Middle school students' awareness of strategies for resolving comprehension difficulties in science reading. *Journal of Research and Development in Education*, 29:226–38.

Darch, C., and Carnine, D. 1986. Teaching content area material to learning disabled students. *Exceptional Children*, 53:240–46.

Darch, C., and Eaves, R. C. 1986. Visual displays to increase comprehension of high school learning-disabled students. *The Journal of Special Education*, 20:309–18.

DiGisi, L. L., and Willett, J. B. 1995. What high school biology teachers say about their textbook use: A descriptive study. *Journal of Research in Science Teaching*, 32:123–42.

Ehlinger, J., and Pritchard, R. 1994. Using think alongs in secondary content areas. *Research and Instruction*, 33:187–206.

Ellis, E. S. 1997. Watering up the curriculum for adolescents with learning disabilities. *Remedial and Special Education*, 18:326–46.

Englert, C. S., and Mariage, T. V. 1991. Making students partners in the comprehension process: Organizing the reading "POSSE." *Learning Disability Quarterly*, 14:123–38.

Fuchs, D., Fuchs, L. S., Thompson, A., Svenson, E., Yen, L., Al Otaiba, S., et al. 2001. Peer-assisted learning strategies in reading: Extensions for kindergarten, first grade, and high school. *Remedial and Special Education*, 22:15–21.

Ganschow, L., and Weber, D. B. 1987. Effects of mode of presentation on comprehension of below average, average, and above average readers. *Perceptual and Motor Skills*, 64:899–905.

Gallego, M. A. 1992. Collaborative instruction for reading comprehension: The role of discourse and discussion. In *Promoting Academic Competence and Literacy in School*, M. Pressley, K. R. Harris, and J. T. Guthrie (Eds.), (pp. 223–42). New York: Academic Press, Inc.

Gardill, M. C., and Jitendra, A. K. 1999. Advanced story map instruction: Effects on the reading comprehension of students with learning disabilities. *Journal of Special Education*, 33:2–17.

Gersten, R., and Baker, S. 1998. Real world use of scientific concepts: Integrating situated cognition with explicit instruction. *Exceptional Children*, 65:23–35.

Gersten, R., Fuchs, L., Williams, J. P., and Baker, S. 2001. Teaching reading comprehension strategies to students with learning disabilities: A review of the research. *Review of Educational Research*, 71:279–320.

Glynn, S. M., Duit, R., and Thiele, R. B. 1995. Teaching science with analogies: A strategy for constructing knowledge. In *Learning Science in the Schools: Research Reforming Practice*, S. M. Glynn and R. Duit (Eds.), (pp. 247–73). Mahwah, NJ: Lawrence Erlbaum.

Greenwald, N. L. 2000. Learning from problems. *The Science Teacher*, 67(4):28–32.

Gurney, D., Gersten, R., Dimino, J., and Carnine, D. 1990. Story grammar: Effective literature instruction for high school students with learning disabilities. *Journal of Learning Disabilities*, 23:335–48.

Hannus, M., and Hyönä, J. 1999. Utilization of illustrations during learning of science textbook passages among low- and high-ability children. *Contemporary Educational Psychology*, 24:95–123.

Idol, L. 1987. A critical thinking map to improve content area comprehension of poor readers. *Remedial and Special Education*, 8(4):28–40.

Idol, L., and Croll, V. J. 1987. Story-mapping training as a means of improving reading comprehension. *Learning Disability Quarterly*, 10:214–29.

Johnston, P., and Winograd, P. 1985. Passive failure in reading. *Journal of Reading Behavior*, 17:279–301.

King, C. M., and Parent Johnson, L. M. 1999. Constructing meaning via reciprocal teaching. *Reading Research and Instruction*, 38:169–86.

Lauterbach, S. L., and Bender, W. N. 1994. The inclusion of students with mild disabilities in content areas classes: Cognitive instructional modifications. *The High School Journal*, 77:261–65.

Lederer, J. M. 2000. Reciprocal teaching of social studies in inclusive elementary classrooms. *Journal of Learning Disabilities*, 33:91–106.

Levin, J. R., and Mayer, R. E. 1993. Understanding illustrations in text. In *Learning from Textbooks: Theory and Practice*, B. K. Britton, A. Woodward, and M. Binkley (Eds.), (pp. 95–113). Hillsdale, NJ: Lawrence Erlbaum.

Lipson, M. Y. 1982. Learning new information from text: The role of prior knowledge and reading ability. *Journal of Reading Behavior*, 14:243–61.

Maria, K. and MacGinitie, W. 1982. Reading comprehension disabilities: Knowledge structures and non-accommodating text processing strategies. *Annals of Dyslexia*, 32:33–59.

Mastropieri, M. A., and Peters, E. E. 1987. Increasing prose recall of learning disabled and reading disabled students via spatial organizers. *Journal of Educational Research*, 80:272–76.

Mayer, R. E. 1987. Instructional variables that influence cognitive processes during read-ing. In *Executive Control Processes in Reading*, B. K. Britton, and S. M. Glynn (Eds.), (pp. 201–16). Hillsdale, NJ: Lawrence Erlbaum.

Mayer, R. E., Steinhoff, K., Bower, G., and Mars, R. 1995. A generative theory of textbook design: Using annotated illustrations to foster meaningful learning of science text. *Educational Technology Research and Development*, 43:31–43.

McCormick, S. 1989. Effects of previews on more skilled and less skilled readers' compre-hension of expository text. *Journal of Reading Behavior*, 21:219–39.

McCray, A. D., Vaughn, S., and Neal, L. I. 2001. Not all students learn to read by third grade: Middle school students speak out about their reading disabilities. *The Journal of Special Education*, 35:17–30.

McKeown, M. G., Beck, I. L., Sinatra, G. M., and Loxterman, J. A. 1992. The contribution of prior knowledge and coherent text to comprehension. *Reading Research Quarterly*, 27:79–93.

Meyer, B. J. F. 1985. Prose analysis: Purposes, procedures, and problems. In *Understanding Expository Text*, B. K. Britton and B. J. Back (Eds.), (pp. 11–64). Hillsdale, NJ: Lawrence Erlbaum.

Miller, C. D., Miller, L. F., and Rosen, L. A. 1988. Modified reciprocal teaching in a regular classroom. *Journal of Experimental Education*, 56:183–86.

Musheno, B. V., and Lawson, A. E. 1999. Effects of learning cycle and traditional text on comprehension of science concepts by students at differing reasoning levels. *Journal of Research in Science Teaching*, 36:23–37.

Nicholson, T. 1984. Experts and novices: A study of reading in the high school classroom. *Reading Research Quarterly*, 19:436–51.

Ogle, D. 1986. K-W-L: A teaching model that develops active reading of expository text. *The Reading Teacher*, 39:564–70.

Otero, J. C., and Campanario, J. M. 1990. Comprehension evaluation and regulation in learning from science texts. *Journal of Research in Science Teaching*, 27:447–60.

Palincsar, A. S., Anderson, C., and David, Y. M. 1993. Pursuing scientific literacy in the middle grades through collaborative problem solving. *The Elementary School Journal*, 93:643–58.

Risco, V. J., and Alvarez, M. C. 1986. An investigation of poor readers' use of a thematic strategy to comprehend text. *Reading Research Quarterly*, 21:298–315.

Sawyer, D. J., and Kosoff, T. O. 1981. Accommodating the learning needs of reading dis-abled adolescents: A language-processing issue. *Learning Disability Quarterly*, 4:61–68.

Schumaker, J. B., Deshler, D. D., Alley, G. R., Warner, M. M., and Denton, P. H. 1982. MULTIPASS: A learning strategy for improving reading comprehension. *Learning Disability Quarterly*, 5:295–304.

Sinatra, R. C., Stahl-Gemake, J., and Berg, D. N. 1984. Improving reading comprehension of disabled readers through semantic mapping. *The Reading Teacher*, 38:22–29.

Stein, M., Stuen, C., Carnine, D., and Long, R. M. 2001. Textbook evaluation and adoption practices. *Reading and Writing Quarterly*, 17:5–23.

Stepien, W., and Gallagher, S. 1993. Problem-based learning: As authentic as it gets. *Educational Leadership*, 50(7):25–28.

Swanson, H. L. 2001. Research on interventions for adolescents with learning disabilities: A meta-analysis of outcomes related to higher-order processing. *Elementary School Journal*, 101:331–48.

Vaughn, S. and Klingner, J. K. 1999. Teaching reading comprehension through collaborative strategic reading. *Intervention in School and Clinic*, 34:284–92.

Vaughn, S., Klingner, J. K., and Bryant, D. P. 2001. Collaborative strategic reading as a means to enhance peer-mediated instruction for reading comprehension and content learning. *Remedial and Special Education*, 22:66–74.

Walraven, M., and Reitsma, P. 1993. The effect of teaching strategies for reading comprehension to poor readers and the possible surplus effect of activating prior knowledge. In *42nd Yearbook of the National Reading Conference*, D. J. Leu and C. K. Kinzer (Eds.), 42:243–50.

Williams, J. P. 1993. Comprehension of students with and without learning disabilities: Identification of narrative themes and idiosyncratic text representations. *Journal of Educational Psychology*, 85:631–41.

Williams, J. P., Brown, L. G., Silverstein, A. K., and deCani, J. S. 1994. An instructional program in comprehension of narrative themes for adolescents with learning disabilities. *Learning Disability Quarterly*, 17:205–21.

Woodward, A. 1993. Do illustrations serve an instructional purpose in U.S. textbooks? In *Learning from Textbooks: Theory and Practice*, B. K. Britton, A. Woodward, and M. Binkley (Eds.), (pp. 115–34). Hillsdale, NJ: Lawrence Erlbaum.

10

Assessment of Reading Comprehension

GETTING STARTED

✓ What are the most common purposes of assessing reading achievement?
✓ What issues should teachers keep in mind when reading assessment is used to identify students who have significant problems with reading comprehension?
✓ How can we distinguish students with word reading problems that affect comprehension from students with specific comprehension problems?
✓ How can we estimate the risk of later reading comprehension difficulties among kindergartners and first graders?
✓ Are students with significant reading problems required to take state and district achievement tests? How are decisions about testing accommodations made?

PURPOSES OF ASSESSMENT

Assessments are means of taking stock. Educational assessments are used to evaluate reading from a number of different perspectives. Some assessments of reading achievement are used to monitor students' learning and to fine-tune instructional programs. Teachers usually choose, administer, and interpret the results of such assessments. Other assessments of reading are used to compare reading achievement in different classrooms, schools, districts or states. Such assessments are usually designed by experts at the state level, or they are published tests used nationwide. District, state, and national educational agencies may use the results of such tests to set policies and evaluate the effectiveness of schools. It is important to consider the purpose of a given reading assessment to avoid misinterpretation of the results or inappropriate uses of test results. This is true whether our interest is reading comprehension or any other area of school achievement.

223

In this chapter, we will discuss four common purposes for reading assessments. One purpose is identification of children with special needs. This primarily involves determining whether a child qualifies for special education services, given federal, state and local regulations concerning eligibility criteria. Such assessments must comply with established procedures and must take into account the identification criteria for such categories of exceptionality as specific learning disabilities. A second purpose is identification of children at risk for significant learning problems, with the goal of providing appropriate services soon enough to forestall serious difficulties acquiring literacy and concomitant social, emotional, and academic problems (Catts et al. 2001). Often considered a means of initiating preventative measures, identification of children at risk for reading disabilities can be carried out quite effectively as early as kindergarten (O'Connor and Jenkins 1999). A third purpose is accountability. School administrators, as well as state and national educational agencies, are interested in making sure that teachers, schools, school districts, and states are successful in their efforts to teach children to read. A fourth purpose is monitoring the progress of children in their classroom reading programs. Teachers need this information to evaluate and modify reading instruction and learning activities for the whole class and for individual children within the class.

Each of these purposes is aligned with specific views about appropriate assessment measures. The best known measures of reading comprehension are standardized tests that are group administered. They provide a way to compare the performance of a given child to that of other children of the same age or grade level. Such tests are not developed to determine how much progress the student is making in the reading curriculum of his or her school. Curriculum-based measures, on the other hand, are one way to compare different students' response to instruction, given the content of the curriculum. These measures also provide a way to examine students' improvement in reading on a regular basis. However, they are not suitable for comparing students' reading in classrooms using different instructional methods or materials. Informal measures of comprehension include informal reading inventories (published or teacher-made), analyses of students' oral reading accuracy and speed, or performance measures. In general, performance measures require students to use information or knowledge, whether this involves applications or simply explanations (Elliott 1998). Performance measures vary on a dimension called "authenticity." Authentic measures reflect students' responses to reading and related activities in the context of their school courses. Authentic assessments might reflect students' interest in and feelings about books they have read, for example. Perhaps the most commonly used form of authentic reading assessment is the portfolio, which when used to assess progress in reading might include book reports a student has written, excerpts from a reading journal, and so on.

Experts generally agree that measures of reading comprehension should be valid and reliable so that they can help us determine whether the students are learning what we hope and expect that they are learning. The same experts do not agree on the characteristics of tests that make them valid, however. For example, a common method for assessing passage comprehension involves asking students to read a short passage and then pick answers to multiple-choice questions. This activity may not reflect teachers' views of what reading comprehension is all about. For instance, to teachers who expect students to read books in order to learn course content, the task could seem artificial. To them, it is important that readers understand and remember information from the text, but this task does not tap long-term memory. Rather, it indicates whether they can find answers to questions in the text, make inferences about information presented in the text, and the like.

Finding valid means of assessing comprehension of written texts has been a concern for decades. At present, there is no single measure that will appropriately assess all aspects of reading comprehension that teachers and policy makers wish to know about. Researchers continue to search for forms of assessment that reflect the dynamic nature of reading comprehension and engagement with natural texts and that are sensitive to developmental changes in comprehension capabilities. There is a need for assessments that reflect knowledge acquired from reading, engagement with reading, and application of information and ideas drawn from reading (Valencia and Wixson 2000). There also is a need for assessments that tell us about the processes by which students construct meaning from texts, as well as assessments that provide insights into the outcomes of reading—what the reader retains after reading and how he or she thinks about what has been read. Clearly, there are no simple solutions to the many challenges of designing effective assessments of reading comprehension. Because teachers are responsible for selecting or designing classroom assessments, as well as interpreting the results of state assessments, they need to be well informed about current practices in the assessment of reading comprehension.

ASSESSMENT AT THE DISTRICT AND STATE LEVELS

In general, assessments designed and implemented at the district and state levels are used for broad purposes of educational planning and evaluation. Information about the performance of elementary students in reading, for example, might be gathered using a published, standardized reading achievement test or a reading test developed and mandated by the state. At the district level, the results might help the school administration evaluate such organizational and educational matters as the effects of different reading programs, the way classes are constituted, or changing demographics within the school district. The results of such reading tests are typically shared with parents, so that they have an opportunity to learn how their child performs in reading (and other areas) in comparison to other children in the same school or district.

Our current educational climate has fostered considerable interest in school reform—specifically, fostering changes in educational programs, instructional methods and materials, and assessment systems in an effort to improve the reading achievement of all children, but in particular to improve the reading achievement of the least able children. School reform efforts typically involve integrating curriculum, instruction and assessment (Simmons et al. 2000). Simmons et al. (2000) recommended that, in formulating plans for assessment of reading, schools establish mechanisms for teachers to keep track of the performances of children on a regular basis, so that progress can be monitored and changes made in educational programs on a timely basis. Somewhat similarly, a study of effective schools found that students' reading achievement was significantly related to regular classroom assessment of pupil progress, home-school links, and collaborative efforts among teachers (Taylor et al. 1999). School reform has made many teachers and administrators aware of the importance of coordinating assessment and instruction. Not surprisingly, current questions focus on the most useful types of reading assessments for purposes of improving school-wide instruction.

Because a national goal is that every child can read by third grade, state agencies may choose to use the scores from the state achievement test to determine how successful schools and teachers are at meeting this goal. Most states have developed their own reading assessment instruments. According to Elliott et al. (2000), in 1995–1996, all but four states had a state assessment in place. Although the state instruments vary widely in content and task, they often attempt to link the assessment of reading to state standards for reading achievement. These standards articulate the goals of the reading or literacy curriculum at each grade level. State standards vary widely in specificity, content, and the extent to which they have been translated into particular systems of curriculum, instruction, and assessment (Wixson and Dutro 1998). Because state standards and the assessment instruments have assumed such importance in determining how successful schools are at teaching children to read, it is a good idea for teachers to be well informed about them. However, state reading tests are probably not going to tell teachers all they want to know about their students' growth in reading. As noted earlier, such test scores provide a narrow window into the child's world of reading, as it were.

Prior to 1997, many states excused students with disabilities from participation in state assessments. However, with the reauthorization of the Individuals with Disabilities Education Act in 1997, special education funding was made contingent on the participation of students with disabilities in state assessments (Elliott et al. 2000). The law requires that an alternate assessment be developed for students who are judged unable to participate in the regular state assessment (Kleinert et al. 2000; Ysseldyke and Olsen 1999). In addition, schools must make decisions about providing appropriate accommodations for students with disabilities who do participate in the regular assessments. The term accommodations refers to adjustments in the conditions of taking the tests that make it possible for individuals with special needs to demonstrate their reading skill and knowledge. These include changes in the setting, timing, or method of taking a test. For example, a visually impaired student might take a comprehension test with a text published with large-print or in Braille.

Policies concerning accommodations vary by state. The team that developed the student's Individualized Educational Program is usually given primary responsibility for making the decision about participation in testing and determination of accommodations (Thurlow et al. 2000). However, states do not all allow the same accommodations. For example, in some states test questions can be read aloud to the student (most often, in content area courses), whereas in other states, no oral reading of the test questions is permitted.

Although it may seem unfair to require students with severe reading disabilities to take tests that require lots of reading, there are reasons that it is important to have information on state assessments about all children, regardless of their skill levels. Thurlow and her colleagues (2000) explain some of the negative consequences of excluding students from the tests. One is that such exclusion results in students' not being required to follow the school's curriculum. Exclusion also leads to increases in retention, increases in rate of referral to special education, and spurious comparisons across schools. Allington and McGill-Franzen (1992) recalculated data from high achieving schools to include students who had been retained or placed in special education and found that the gains reported by such schools largely disappeared. Schools "look better" if they can exclude their poorest readers from the assessments, but to do so, they have to have a convincing reason, such as keeping them back a grade or placing them in more restrictive special education settings. Such actions may not be in the best interests of the students.

Accommodations can be thought of as falling into several categories (Thurlow et al. 2000). One is the *presentation format*. An example is using Braille or large-print text for students who are visually impaired. A second is the *response format*, which refers to the manner in which students respond. For example, they might be allowed to point to an answer or use a computer to respond. A third is *the setting of the test*. For example, a student might be allowed to take the test at home or in the resource room. The fourth is *the timing of the test*. For example, a student might be allowed extended time to take the test or given additional breaks during the test. Of these, students with reading disabilities are most likely to be given timing accommodations, particularly extended time to take the test.

A study of the effectiveness of accommodations (Fuchs et al. 2000) has shown that students with LD benefited from some accommodations more than others, but overall they benefited more than students without LD who were given the same accommodations. Students with and without LD were given tests with and without accommodations of extended time, large print, or reading aloud. When their performances on parallel tests were compared, the results showed that the accommodations gave the students with LD a greater boost than they gave students without LD. As a group, students with LD profited from reading aloud but not from extended time or large print. One concern that is raised by this study is that the teachers' decisions about what were appropriate accommodations for their students did not correspond to the benefits the students derived from these accommodations. The results suggest that objective information (e.g., diagnostic tests) about students' special needs might provide a better basis for selecting accommodations.

Alternate forms of assessment are most needed for students with severe cognitive deficits or multiple disabilities, as these students can not benefit sufficiently from the types of test accommodations described above (Ysseldyke and Olson 1999). Such students are typically not working toward a regular high school diploma. As a result, the content and the form of achievement tests are justifiably altered. Alternative assessments may involve observational assessments of the development of their life skills. An example in the area of reading might be assessment of functional reading skills (e.g., reading environmental signs). The option of alternate forms of assessment is typically not appropriate for students with learning or reading disabilities.

ASSESSMENT FOR IDENTIFICATION OF A READING DISABILITY

The second purpose of assessment of reading is to identify those children who have sufficiently severe problems with reading that they qualify for special education services. Because our focus is on reading comprehension, a natural question to ask is whether there is such a thing as a specific disability in reading comprehension. As we noted in Chapter 2, there is, but students with specific problems with comprehension are less common than those who either have problems *only* with word reading or have combined problems with word reading and listening comprehension (Aaron, Joshi and Williams 1999). Put another way, only a small percent of students who are found to have problems understanding what they read will have problems with reading comprehension *but not* decoding (Shankweiler et al. 1999). As we noted in our discussion of the nature of reading problems, many researchers consider deficits in phonological processes, which lead to poor skills in decoding, to be the defining characteristic of a reading disability (Stanovich 1991; Torgesen and Wagner 1998). We should keep in mind that poor comprehension is often the result of poor decoding problems. As we saw in Chapter 3, if the student cannot read a text accurately and fluently, he or she will have trouble understanding it.

Patterns of Difficulties with Reading Comprehension

So that appropriate educational programs can be devised, we need to distinguish three different patterns of severe reading problems. To do so, we need to use three types of measures: word reading (or, as some prefer, decoding), reading comprehension, and listening comprehension. Two of the patterns of students' performance on these tests involve word-reading problems that are or are not accompanied by language comprehension problems. In the flow chart of figure 10.1, these patterns are shown at the far left and far right.

For both patterns, the students have significant word-reading problems, as well as very low reading comprehension scores. However, some of these students show comprehension problems only when they read, not when they listen to passages of equivalent difficulty. That is, their comprehension problems in reading stem from their word reading difficulties. The way to distinguish students with language comprehension difficulties from those with specific reading comprehension problems is to assess both listening and reading comprehension (Carlisle 1989; Carlisle and Felbinger 1991). Students with language comprehension problems can be identified because they perform less well than their peers on a test of comprehension, both when passages are read aloud to them and when they read to themselves.

Comparing listening and reading comprehension is a fairly straightforward process when standardized tests are used, because both listening and reading

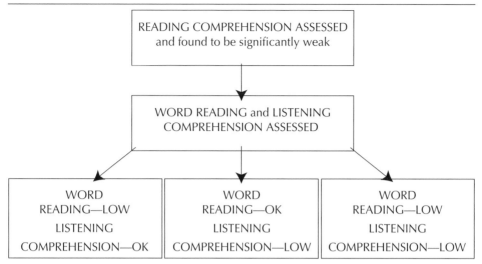

Figure 10.1   A process to identify patterns of difficulties in reading comprehension

measures will have been normed for the age group. If a test is standardized, it means that we can determine what is normal for students of different grades or ages. Thus, students who perform significantly below average on both tests of listening and reading comprehension would be likely to have general difficulties with language comprehension—difficulties that are not specific to reading.

However, if teachers are comparing listening and reading informally (e.g., using an Informal Reading Inventory), they need to interpret the results with an understanding of developmental expectations. Overviews of listening and reading comprehension, such as the one written by Sticht and James (1984), are helpful resources for teachers. Although this topic was discussed in Chapter 2, a brief explanation is needed here so our readers can get a sense of developmental changes as they relate to assessment. First graders usually demonstrate better comprehension after listening than after reading a text, in large part because they are just learning to read words, and their small reading vocabulary places a limit on the difficulty of text they can understand when reading on their own. By about fifth grade, however, students typically can understand passages they read and listen to that are equivalent in difficulty. This is because their word reading skills are sufficiently automatic so that they do not stand in the way of comprehension. By eighth grade, students often perform better on comprehension tests following reading than following listening. One reason is that the reader can proceed at his or her own pace in making sense of a difficult passage; the text is permanent and can be reread as needed in part or whole. In contrast, texts presented for listening are delivered at a pace selected by the speaker and offer no opportunities to revisit the text in order to make sense of it.

Unlike the two patterns discussed so far, the third pattern that results in significant difficulties in reading comprehension involves students whose word reading is not significantly weak. Instead, their specific weakness is language comprehension and verbal reasoning. Their difficulties understanding language are apparent following both reading and listening to passages. Of the three patterns, this one is the least common among school-age children. Most students with language comprehension problems have word reading problems as well (Aaron et al. 1999; Catts et al. 1999).

As figure 10.1 shows, it is possible to identify students with these three patterns of reading difficulties using listening and reading discrepancy scores and a word reading measure (Aaron 1991; Spring and French 1990). As the flow chart shows, the first step involves identifying students with significant weaknesses in reading comprehension. Once these students are given a word reading and a listening comprehension test, the teacher (perhaps with the help of an educational consultant in the school) can determine which of the three patterns best represents the nature of the student's reading problems.

As noted earlier, one reason for determining the nature of reading comprehension problems is that this information is crucial in order to design an appropriate educational program for a student. Students with significant weaknesses in word reading will need an instructional program in letter-sound correspondences, phonics, decoding strategies, and the like. Students with both listening and reading comprehension weaknesses will need an instructional program in comprehension strategies, components of language (vocabulary, grammar), and the like. The students with weaknesses in both word reading and reading comprehension will, of course, need comprehensive programs that include both types of instruction. Finally, regardless of the pattern of strengths and weaknesses, students with reading comprehension problems would benefit from exposure to literature and expository texts, whether they listen to books on tape or listen to a parent or classmate reading aloud. While they are receiving special instruction in reading, they should not fall behind their peers in text comprehension because they are not gathering experience with written texts.

Some students with weaknesses in both listening and reading comprehension may have more significant problems with reading than with listening comprehension. Their oral language comprehension is not so much weaker than that of their peers that they could be described as having a language disability. Primary among their traits is likely to be a difficulty making inferences while reading (Cain and Oakhill 1999; Oakhill and Yuill 1996). Other aspects of verbal reasoning and metacognition may also be affected, so that these poor readers might particularly benefit from instruction in comprehension strategies and methods of comprehension monitoring.

Identification Criteria for Reading Disabilities

We have argued that we should attempt to identify different patterns of poor comprehension so that we can design appropriate educational programs. However, it is important to consider criteria that are used to determine whether students with these three patterns of poor comprehension will qualify for special services in reading in today's schools. First, by "special services" we do not mean extra reading instruction and practice that takes place within the classroom or pull-out programs designed to "jump-start" students who are having problems learning to read in first grade (e.g., Reading Recovery).

Older students with severe reading problems are often several grade levels below their peers. Typically, their reading problems have been evident from the time they started to learn to read, and efforts to provide help in the classroom have not been adequate to solve the problem. Under these circumstances, students are typically referred for an assessment to determine whether the reading problem is such that it fits the criteria for a specific learning disability (LD). As we noted in Chapter 2, a reading disability is typically regarded as one manifestation of a specific LD. Students with specific LD are eligible for special education services, which may include instruction in reading from a specialist.

The operational criteria for identifying specific learning disability are part of federal law (USOE 1977). These criteria specify that the student should be underachieving in one or more areas of language and academic functioning (e.g., oral expression, reading)—that is, performing significantly below expectations for their age or grade level. There should also be a severe discrepancy between the student's learning potential (usually interpreted as intelligence) and his or her achievement in one or more areas that involve understanding and use of language, spoken or written. There are exclusionary criteria as well; to qualify as having a specific learning disability, the student's learning problems cannot be primarily due to mental retardation, sensory impairment, emotional or behavioral disabilities, or cultural or economic disadvantage. For students with reading problems, underachievement is usually evident not just from significant problems on standardized tests but also from difficulties completing reading assignments in class. Students who are severely impaired in their reading ability are likely to be struggling academically in any of their courses that involve reading.

The most hotly debated aspect of the identification criteria is what is called the "discrepancy" requirement. The debate has focused on whether it is enough to identify reading disabilities on the basis of significant underachievement in reading, given grade-level expectations, or whether reading achievement must be significantly lower than intelligence (Siegel 1992; Stanovich 1991). Siegel (1992) has argued that discrepancy should not be the basis for identification of students who need help with reading. She has shown that students with significant word-reading problems but different levels of IQ have similar profiles in terms of phonological processes, working memory, and other reading-related characteristics. Whether students show significant discrepancies between reading and intelligence or not, her argument is that all students with severe word-reading problems need considerable help learning to read.

An important point is that when a "discrepancy" system is used, on average, students are not identified as have a reading disability until age 10 (Fletcher et al. 1998). This is partly because in the early elementary years, given the lack of sensitivity of standardized measures, students with reading problems often do not show the significant discrepancy needed to qualify for special education services. Several years may pass before their problems are severe, and they qualify for the LD label. The down side to late diagnosis of a severe reading problem is that the older the students are, the harder it is to treat their reading problems effectively.

Strag found that "when the diagnosis of dyslexia was made in the first two grades of school nearly 82% of the students could be brought up to their normal classroom work, whereas only 46% of the dyslexic problems idenitified in the third grade were remediated and only 10 to 15% of those observed in grades five to seven could be helped when the diagnosis of learning problems was made at those grade levels" (in Fletcher et al. 1998, p. 52).

Finding a solution to the debate over the discrepancy requirement is extremely important because the students who qualify as having a specific learning disability will vary, depending on which of these systems is used (Fletcher et al. 1998; Torgesen and Wagner 1998). If the criterion is very low achievement on achievement tests, students who are very bright will not be identified as having learning disabilities in reading, even if their reading is much lower than would be expected, given their intelligence. If the criterion is a significant discrepancy between reading and IQ, students with mild problems in reading, relative to their IQ, will not qualify for special services in reading, even if their reading achievement is considerably below grade level. Both systems, used alone, have a number of theoretical and practical implications. For example, if the federal definition of reading disabilities specified significant underachievement in reading, without regard for IQ, then a large portion of the school-age population (about 16%) would be found to have specific learning disabilities and would require special education services. This might seem to be an unnecessary inflation of the number of students who qualify for learning disability services. One suggestion for getting rid of the problematic use of IQ to establish a discrepancy is to identify specific reading disabilities by a significant discrepancy between listening and reading comprehension (e.g., Badian 1999). However, this would mean that students who are weak in both listening and reading comprehension would not qualify for services in the learning disabilities category. Elimination of students with general problems in comprehension would not be a theoretically sound change.

Another point of debate is the possibility that students with significant word-reading problems but different IQ levels respond differently to reading instruction (Torgesen and Wagner 1998). To date, this issue has remained a difficult one on which to reach consensus. However, even if brighter students with significant reading problems do respond readily to special instruction, this factor probably should not dictate identification criteria. It seems unlikely that anyone wants to reserve the LD label for either those students whose problems are readily solved by special reading instruction or those students whose problems are particularly recalcitrant.

All professionals in the field of learning disabilities should consider the implications of the two systems for identifying reading disabilities—underachievement and discrepancy from ability—and participate in the debate as they see fit. Because our focus is on reading comprehension, it is important to think about this debate with comprehension in mind. In the general population, intelligence is significantly related to reading comprehension. Not surprisingly, therefore, for many students with reading problems, we do not find a gap between verbal ability and reading comprehension. If such a gap were necessary for a student to receive special education services, there would be under-identification of children with severe comprehension problems. This might be particularly the case for students with language-learning problems, as they would be likely to perform at a similar below-average level on tests of verbal ability and reading comprehension.

ASSESSMENT TO IDENTIFY CHILDREN AT RISK FOR READING DISABILITIES

A third purpose for an assessment of reading is to identify those young children who are at risk for reading disabilities. There are several compelling arguments for carrying out such assessments. One is that it is far easier to prevent serious reading problems than to correct them once they are established. As early as first grade, children who struggle with reading are likely to lose interest in reading, to see themselves as less able students than their peers, and to begin to engage in avoidance behaviors (McKenna, Kear, and Ellsworth 1995).

Assessment in kindergarten and first grade often does not entail designation of a reading disability or learning disability. Sometimes the purpose is to identify children "at risk" for language and literacy problems. If we can identify those children with the beginning "symptoms" of difficulties learning to read, corrective measures can be taken early on. For example, we might want to identify children who are eligible for reading programs designed to catch and correct initial problems learning to read (e.g., Reading Recovery). The focus of such assessments is not specifically comprehension. In fact, if comprehension is assessed at all, it is done with oral language measures, sometimes focused on component skills, such as vocabulary knowledge. Even in first grade, children have very limited reading comprehension capabilities.

Two types of assessments designed to predict those students at risk for reading difficulties are in general use. One type is screening tests to identify children who appear to lack the prerequisite capabilities to acquire word-reading skills. The other type is batteries designed to identify children with a broader profile of language-learning problems that place them at risk for failure in learning to read. This would include potential problems with both word reading and comprehension.

Effective screening batteries are those that have good "hit" rates in prediction studies. This means that most of the children predicted to have reading problems one or two years later actually do. A screening battery that effectively identifies the children who are going to have trouble learning to read prevents the dual problems of providing unnecessary instruction for children who did not need it or not providing instruction for children who really did need it, despite their performance on the screening test. An example of a kindergarten screening test is one developed by Muter, Hulme, and Snowling (in Muter 2000); it is made up of measures of phonological awareness, a speech rate test (time repeating "buttercup," which serves as a measure of phonological memory), and a test of letter knowledge.

Because short screening batteries are efficient and practical for schools, researchers have worked to identify screening tests with a small number of measures that still are quite effective at identifying the children who turn out to have serious difficulties learning word reading a year or so later. O'Connor and Jenkins (1999) found that the time point of administration of the screening test affects the extent to which children's performances on the screening battery correctly predict reading disability. Their screening battery given at the start of first grade had greater predictive accuracy than the battery given in the spring of kindergarten, which in turn had greater predictive accuracy than a battery given in the fall of kindergarten. In addition, of the three best predictive measures, one changed over this time period. Speed of letter naming and phonemic segmentation were strong predictors, overall. Syllable deletion was useful when included in the early kindergarten battery but not useful in the late kindergarten battery; at this point, a task called sound repetition provided greater discrimination than syllable deletion did. At both of these screening points, three tasks identified most of the students who turned out to have significant word reading problems at the end of grade 1. Specifically, in April, rapid letter naming, phoneme segmentation, and sound repetition identified all but one first grader who subsequently showed serious problems acquiring word reading skill.

Some batteries assess a broader range of language-related capabilities. A compilation of the measures commonly used to predict reading difficulties at school entry can be found in Snow, Burns and Griffin (1998, p. 110); these measures include a variety of language and early literacy measures. The most common language measures are verbal memory for stories or sentences, receptive vocabulary, rapid serial naming, expressive language, and phonological awareness; the most common early literacy measures are reading readiness and letter identification. When researchers use multiple predictors, they typically use an index of early print skills (e.g., letter identification), phonological awareness, and IQ. Even with these measures, a number of children who later develop reading difficulties do not perform poorly enough to earn an at-risk designation (Snow, Burns, and Griffin 1998). In all likelihood, adding language measures to the battery would improve the ability to identify children at risk for reading comprehension problems.

Other screening batteries have been developed with the purpose of identifying persistent reading problems (i.e., those that do not respond to common interventions in school). Badian (2000) found that, of the measures given to the students when they were in preschool, three were most effective at discriminating good and poor readers at grade 2—sentence memory, orthographic processing and color naming. (Orthographic processing required the child to point to one of four stimuli that matched the item at the far left of the row; the items were made up of numbers, letter strings, and words; foils involved spatial and sequencing errors.) Overall, 92% of one cohort and 87% of a second cohort were accurately identified as good or poor readers. Further analyses to identify the measures that discriminated children with persistent reading problems showed that in grade 7, sentence memory, letter naming, and orthographic processing classified most of the students with enduring reading problems.

For teachers and clinicians who are working with children with possible speech and language disabilities, the more comprehensive screening batteries may provide more information about the various areas of language learning that would need to be addressed in children's school setting or in their language therapy (Catts et al. 2001). As Catts and his colleagues (1999) have pointed out, "early recognition of these children's risks for future reading difficulties should result in broad-based language intervention programs that target literacy as well as oral language impairments" (p. 38). Comprehensive language instruction is important for such children; school programs offering instruction in phonological awareness and basic phonics will not be sufficient. They will help with access to the code, but not access to ideas and information, which is dependent on improvement of their vocabulary, grammar, and ability to construct meaning while reading.

Many teachers are understandably confused by the differences in early literacy screening batteries. Several principles to keep in mind are these: (a) the more language traits that are measured, the wider the net that is cast to capture potentially struggling readers (but remember that the more comprehensive batteries take time and personnel to administer) and (b) the danger of screening in a narrow way is that students with problems not tapped by the screening battery will obviously not be identified as needing help. For example, although the three measures used by O'Connor and Jenkins do not take much time to administer, only students who are likely to have word-reading problems will be identified. Teachers will not be forewarned about the needs of children with limited oral language development—that is, those children at risk for specific reading comprehension problems.

Some teachers and schools resist recommendations to use preschool screening batteries, believing that too much testing is a waste of time. They prefer a "wait and watch" approach, in which they identify children at risk for reading difficulties by their slow progress in acquiring early literacy skills, such as alphabet and phonological awareness in kindergarten and first grade. As noted earlier, the danger of waiting until the end of first grade to identify children in need of more extended or intensive instruction is that it becomes difficult to offset the problems of initial reading failure. Quite a few early reading problems can be effectively addressed with timely intervention in kindergarten and first grade; however, some children's reading problems are persistent and require continued intervention (Vellutino, Scanlon, and Lyon 2000).

Again, most screening instruments focus on oral language and initial indices of print awareness, not on reading comprehension. Screening instruments that are restricted to measures of phonological awareness and alphabet knowledge may predict early word reading achievement, and this in turn indicates whether students can use written texts to access ideas and information. That is, children cannot understand texts they cannot read. However, screening instruments of this type fall short of helping us identify the students who are already having trouble with comprehension (e.g., comprehension of stories others read to them).

Recently, efforts have been made to find more satisfactory ways to assess emergent reading comprehension capabilities in kindergarten and first grade. One promising method is using storybook retelling. In one project (Paris and Paris 2001), kindergartners, first graders, and second graders were given tasks to assess their understanding of wordless storybooks. First the children completed a "picture walk," which meant that they talked about what they saw as they turned the pages of the storybook. Then they were asked to retell the story. This measure of retelling was scored using elements of story grammar, such as identification of the characters and the initiating event. Finally, they were asked comprehension questions that focused on their ability to infer causes of events or motives of characters (e.g., "why-?" questions). Collectively, the three measures were sensitive to developmental changes in comprehension between kindergarten and second grade. Furthermore, they provided insights into children's awareness of story structure and the depth of their understanding of the story told implicitly through the pictures. For children who are not able to read at all or whose reading is at a primer level, storybook comprehension may be as valid a measure of reading comprehension as we can get.

ASSESSMENT FOR INSTRUCTION

A fourth purpose for assessing reading is to monitor students' progress in reading. The term formative assessment is appropriately used here, because the purpose is to collect data on students' progress toward particular short-term educational goals. Summative data collection, in contrast, involves assessment of students' progress toward long-term goals, as would be the case with most standardized tests of reading comprehension. In general, assessment of students' progress in the curriculum gives teachers a way to monitor their response to instruction. With this information, they have the opportunity to fine-tune what and how they are teaching. In some cases, teachers want to gather information about students' engagement in literacy activities (writing as well as reading) so that they have a picture of student learning that is richer and more naturalistic than the one provided by performance on standardized tests of reading. Approaches to assessment that serve these purposes include some quantitative and some qualitative methods.

Curriculum-Based Measures

In terms of methods that provide quantitative measures of children's response to instruction in the classroom, curriculum-based measures (CBM) have been shown to be valid and reliable tools for teachers. In general, CBM employs tasks of measurable reading behaviors, such as oral reading accuracy and fluency. Passages are taken from the course readings so that the teacher can assess students' performance on materials they are currently working on (Espin and Foegen 1996; Shin, Deno, and Espin 2000). Curriculum-based measures can be administered to individuals or groups. Even if CBM tasks measure isolated reading behaviors, performance on these measures tends to correspond with students' performance on more general tests of reading achievement. It is also related to learning and remembering content-area information (Espin and Deno 1993; Espin and Foegen 1996). For example, in a study of tenth graders' performance on an oral reading measure, Espin and Deno (1993) found that performance was significantly related to their grade point average and achievement test performance. A thought-provoking finding from this study is that reading aloud was more strongly related to academic success for students at the lower end of the grade-point distribution than those at the higher end. This raises the possibility that an oral reading measure could be useful in estimating the comprehension of students with reading problems in content-area textbooks.

An oral reading CBM is typically carried out by asking the student to read aloud a passage at an appropriate level of difficulty (for example, an excerpt from a book that student is reading in class). The teacher records errors, marks the passage at the completion of one minute, and calculates the number of words read accurately in that time. One problem with this method is that oral reading lacks face validity as a test of comprehension. Teachers do not get information about such comprehension skills as recalling main ideas. Therefore, oral reading measures are not seen as useful for evaluating and planning instruction in reading comprehension, in comparison to other measures of comprehension. However, oral reading measures can help teachers make judgments about the extent to which students can work effectively in texts of different levels of difficulty. While oral reading measures tend to be significantly correlated with measures of comprehension, there are several other CBMs that may seem to be more closely related to reading comprehension (Fuchs, Fuchs, and Maxwell 1988). These include measures of oral or written recall (retelling the information in a passage) and a technique called the maze task.

Oral and written recall measures, like oral reading measures, have been found to relate significantly to standardized reading achievement for students with disabilities (Fuchs, Fuchs, and Maxwell 1988). Recall measures show the amount of information the child retains after reading a passage; they also provide insights about how this information is organized in the student's memory. Scoring these measures may pose a challenge for teachers. The most superficial way is to use a simple word count. The problem with this measure is that the number of words may not be a good reflection of the number of ideas from the passage included in the retelling. A second scoring method is to count the number of content words in the retelling. This gives a better picture of the readers' grasp of information in the passage than a single word count does. A third method entails analysis of the idea units in the passage and use of this analysis as a template for scoring the ideas in the students' written or oral retelling. The second and third methods require quite a bit of work on the teacher's part, but the result may be a more detailed picture of the reader's comprehension and recall of the passage.

Another form of CBM is the maze task. It is more ostensibly focused on word and passage comprehension (Shin, Deno, and Espin 2000). A maze task is constructed by deleting every seventh word in a passage and replacing it with three multiple-choice alternatives (one correct and two alternatives). Part of a sample maze passage, given in Shin, Deno, and Espin 2000, is as follows: "My mother always likes to go home. She was born on a nice (farm/big/soon) in a valley. Her father started (home/the/sat) farm before she was born. When (red/she/told) was a little girl they lived (to/fun/in) a very old log house on (call/date/the) farm" (p. 166). Students are given three minutes to read the passage and select words among the alternatives, so speed of making decisions about correct words is a significant factor. The maze task has the advantage of being an efficiently administered measure of reading performance; it can be administered to groups, and it can be administered by computer. Recent studies have shown that the maze task is a valid and useful tool for assessing reading growth in the classroom (Espin and Foegen 1996).

In short, CBMs are useful to monitor the progress of children in reading and in content-area learning from reading. Information about the progress children are making in reading allows teachers to make instructional adjustments that they might not have made, based on the test data they ordinarily have about their students' reading (e.g., standardized test scores). A study of special education teachers' use of the CBM test results of their students in mathematics showed that teachers did make instructional adjustments based on CBM data. In addition, students whose instruction was adjusted because of their CBM performance made greater gains on global achievement tests than peers whose instruction was not adjusted in this way (Stecker and Fuchs 2000). It is possible similar results would be found for teachers' use of CBM test results in reading.

Performance Assessments

Many teachers prefer to assess children's progress by taking into account a broader range of students' traits and instructional variables than are measured by CBM or by traditional reading comprehension tests. They may want to use methods that are student-centered, reflecting, for example, students' motivation and interest. One form such an assessment might take would be a written response to a story that included feelings and experiences inspired by the text. Alternatively, they may want to understand the reasoning processes students use to arrive at an understanding of a text. One form such an assessment might take is a verbal protocol, in which the student is asked to verbalize or "talk aloud" about his or her understanding of a text at points during the reading of it (Pressley and Afflerbach 1995).

Measures of comprehension such as those described above are types of performance assessments. Performance assessment involves testing methods that require students to create an answer or a product that demonstrates their knowledge or skills (Elliott 1998). Performance measures are considered authentic when they reflect the conditions in which students have constructed meaning of the text, including group discussions, individual projects, or specific assignments the teacher has used to foster thinking about a given text. Authentic assessments are valued because they tap natural uses of reading and provide indices of complex interactions with texts (Valencia, Hiebert, and Afflerbach 1994). Other examples of authentic assessments are excerpts from students' reading journals, written responses to open-ended questions, and videotapes of plays read by students and acted out in class.

Performance measures differ from traditional tests in a number of ways. First, they are criterion-referenced, not norm-referenced. This means that the student is evaluated on criteria developed from an analysis of the content the test is covering. In contrast, norm-referenced measures evaluate a student's performance by comparison to that of other students. Second, performance measures test knowledge of material that is taught in the classroom, whereas traditional comprehension tests sample knowledge in the content domain, regardless of the content of that particular course.

One popular type of authentic assessment is the portfolio. A portfolio may be assembled based on criteria set up ahead of time by the teacher, or it may include the students' choice of work products that they would like others to use to evaluate their reading and learning (Stowell and Tierney 1995; Valencia, Hiebert, and Afflerbach 1994). Portfolios are valuable because they reflect work done over a period of time. They may reveal changes in students' responses to instruction and may contain substantive indices of students' accomplishment.

There is little written about the use of performance assessments specifically with students who are struggling to learn to read. In one study (Boerum 2000), sixth graders with LD engaged in authentic learning experiences, reflection, goal-setting and self-assessment. They also kept portfolios so that they could document their growth as learners to an outside audience. The results suggest that when given the opportunity to engage in authentic learning experiences and assessment, students with LD can clarify their strengths and weaknesses as learners and begin to set reasonable goals for improvement.

Because portfolios provide an insight into students' learning in relation to their course work and personal experiences, reading experts have tried to find ways to determine whether they can be used as outcome measures or achievement tests as well as measures of students' progress in the curriculum. That is, are they suitable for purposes of evaluation not only of instruction and learning within a given classroom, but also for purposes of comparing students' learning in different classrooms and schools? For portfolios to be useful across classrooms, there need to be criteria for evaluating the contents of the portfolio that are systematic—a scoring rubric, for instance, that could be used reliably by different teachers in different schools. Valencia and Wixson (2000) reported that, despite efforts to find ways to evaluate students' reading portfolios, the scoring rubrics developed for this purpose have not been as reliable and valid as they should be if they are to be used to compare student performance in different classrooms or schools. Experts in measurement are finding statewide performance tests that require a variety of types of responses promising (Goldberg and Roswell 2001), but there is much still to be learned about the usefulness of multi-measure tests for both teachers and policy-makers.

The information gained from a portfolio might complement information gained from traditional achievement tests. Wiig (2000) has argued that we must find ways to identify students whose learning difficulties are due to neuropsychological deficits in language and literacy in order to distinguish these students from others whose limited language and literacy development has other causes (e.g., limited motivation or opportunities to learn). Because different types of assessments have both limitations and advantages, she concluded that multidimensional and multi-perspective assessments should be used. These might include not only traditional measures but also behavioral rating scales, portfolio assessment, and self-evaluation. She argued that it is only through using both formal and informal measures that the causes for low achievement in literacy and language can be determined.

In some studies of reading instruction designed for diverse learners, assessment methods have included a variety of qualitative indices of growth and motivation, as well as test scores from a range of different literacy activities (e.g., written compositions as well as oral reading performance) (Raphael, Brock, and Wallace 1997). A comprehensive or multi-layered approach helps us acquire a rich understanding of the experiences and progress of students who are struggling readers in different models of classroom reading instruction. Among other findings, such studies tend to suggest that attention to students' interest and involvement in evaluating their own literacy experiences may be valuable ways to gain information to aid them in their learning.

COMMONLY ASKED QUESTIONS

Is there a single best task to rely on as a measure of reading comprehension?

No, there is not. Different tasks yield different pictures of students' comprehension capabilities. This is because different tasks place different requirements on the reader. Tasks such as multiple-choice questions or cloze procedures tend to be moderately correlated with one another, but the fact that they are not highly correlated suggests that they are measuring somewhat different reading behaviors or processes. Multiple-choice questions and cloze procedure tasks are typically used on standardized tests as ways to assess understanding of short passages. Comprehension tests that use multiple-choice questions are efficient to administer and score. They can help us understand students' ability to answer different kinds of questions (e.g., understanding of main ideas versus details). However, because the passage is available for the student's use while answering questions, memory for passage information is not an issue. The test becomes one of interpretation of text, not the ability to construct a mental representation of the text while reading.

Somewhat different processing requirements are placed on students when the cloze procedure is used to assess reading comprehension. Cloze refers to omitting words systematically (e.g., every 9th word). On group tests, the student is given several possible answers and picks the best word to complete the sentence. On tests that are administered individually, the student tells the examiner the word that might best fill the empty slot in the sentence or passage. An excerpt from Salvia and Hughes (1990), illustrates one form of a cloze test:

> Jack and Jill climbed Goose Hill to get some water from the spring in the pine grove at the top. They each carried two _____ containers that clanked as _____ climbed. When they reached _____ grove and found the _____ they filled their pails _____ drank their fill. Then _____ back down (p. 146).

Cloze tests tend to assess what we call "local" comprehension, which refers to sensitivity to the grammatical and semantic constraints on meaning. Cloze is not ideal if one wants to assess understanding and recall of ideas and information in natural passages.

Individualized tests of reading (particularly informal reading inventories) may use retelling as a way to assess comprehension (Leslie and Caldwell 2000). When the student is asked to tell the examiner about what he or she read, the task is often called free recall. Recent revisions of some individually administered achievement batteries include a subtest that uses free recall as a way to assess comprehension. Free recall tasks require students to organize information that they have taken in while reading in order to tell it to someone else. As a result, performance on free recall tasks reflects the students' memory for passage information, expressive language capabilities, and metacognitive capabilities. Students with LD may perform relatively poorly on such tasks because they require coordination of different processes. More specifically, although students with LD perform less well than their peers on various comprehension tasks, the gap between normally achieving and LD readers is more pronounced when the task is one of retelling (Carlisle 1999). Even so, teachers may find recall a helpful way to monitor the progress their students are making in reading (Fuchs, Fuchs, and Hamlett 1989).

Because the students' retelling must somehow be analyzed for its content and structure, scoring free recall tests is more challenging than scoring multiple-choice question tests or cloze tests. Nonetheless, the richness of information that is likely to be gathered from retellings may be worth the time it takes to analyze the students' retellings.

One other task used to assess reading comprehension is sentence verification. The sentence verification technique (SVT), developed by Royer and his colleagues (Royer et al. 1986), presents students with a series of sentences after they have read or listened to a passage. The students indicate whether a given sentence gives ideas and information that was in the passage. Those that give passage information are marked "old" and those that do not are marked "new." There are four sentence types: originals (sentences taken directly from the passage), paraphrases (lexical or word order shifts that do not change the basic ideas), meaning changes (shifts of one or two words that change the meaning), and distractors (sentences with information not in the passage). The following excerpt adapted from Salvia and Hughes (1990, p. 143), shows sample SVT test items.

Excerpt from the passage:

Jack and Jill climbed Goose Hill to get some water from the spring in the pine grove at the top. They each carried two empty containers that clanked as they climbed. When they reached the grove and found the spring, they filled their pails and drank their fill. Then they headed back down . . .

Directions: I want you to read each sentence below. Write old if there was a sentence in the passage that meant the same thing. Old sentences may use different words but they will mean the same thing. Write new if the information was not in the paragraph.

Test Items:

_____ Jack and Jill went up the hill to bring back some water. (paraphrase)
_____ They filled their pails and drank their fill. (original)
_____ The water was cool, and they were refreshed. (distractor)
_____ It was hot and Jack decided to roll down the hill. (meaning change)

The SVT has been found to be a valid measure of students' understanding of short passages (typically 12 to 16 sentences). Sentence verification technique tests are moderately strongly related to other types of comprehension tests, and they are sensitive to students' reading capabilities (Carlisle and Felbinger 1991). One particular value is that it offers a way to compare listening and reading comprehension (Royer et al. 1986). Because the passage is not present when students judge the test items after reading, as is also true after listening, performance in the two modalities can be directly compared. Another advantage to the SVT is that it is a good way to assess understanding of passage information without tapping expressive language capabilities. Finally, performances on SVT are sensitive to students' memory for text information and understanding of text structures. Although sentence verification offers many advantages, it is not currently used in published tests of comprehension for group or individual administration.

There is one other task used to assess reading comprehension in some standardized tests. This involves selecting a picture from a set of four that best represents the meaning of a sentence or short passage. Like SVT, picture selection does not require expressive language. It also does not require receptive language for processing the response options. However, one major limitation is that it can be used to assess only those sentences or passages that provide information that can be displayed in a single picture. It is very difficult to assess comprehension of abstract ideas or relations among ideas by use of pictorial representations.

To return to the question, different tasks are used to assess reading comprehension because they provide different insights into students' reading processes, and because they have different advantages and limitations as forms of measurement. When teachers are given information about their students' performance in reading, an understanding of the nature of the test will help them interpret the results.

What methods might teachers of content-area courses use to assess their students' ability to read and learn from the textbook?

Methods used to assess reading and learning from texts should be selected on the basis of the goals and content of the instruction. No one method is ideal for all situations. One method to track changes in the ability to read and understand texts would be to use curriculum-based measures (CBM), including oral reading and a maze test. These were described earlier, and more can be learned about the construction of such tests from Shin, Deno, and Espin (2000), Espin and Deno (1993), and Salvia and Hughes (1990). One advantage to using CBM is that follow-up testing could be carried out after measures have been put in place to help students improve their comprehension of content-area textbooks. See Chapter 9 for further discussion of content-area textbooks.

Another solution would be to use performance assessment, including (for example) free recall and written or oral reports. The tasks, content, or activities that make up the measure should reflect the curriculum and the goals and instructional methods of the teacher. For example, if a science teacher has taught students to use graphic organizers (e.g., concept maps) to aid in comprehension and recall of texts, he or she might ask the students to read a selection in the text book and make a concept map as a way to assess their learning "tools" in science.

Various options for carrying out performance assessment are currently being explored because they offer more sensitive tools for assessing the learning of students from culturally and linguistically different backgrounds and students with learning disabilities than are available through standardized tests (Elliott 1998). "Hands-on" activities used for such assessments are more commonly found in studies of math and writing, but can be used for reading as well. Comprehension assessment might include writing a sequel to a story, re-enacting an historical event, making a panorama that displays the setting and mood of a story, and so on. In designing a performance assessment, the teacher needs to make decisions about the extent to which the test is an authentic measure of classroom learning but also about reliable ways to score students' performance on such tests. Is it fair to give individual students scores on a measure that is based on a group project? Is it possible to reliably score students' re-enactment of scenes from a Shakespeare play? Performance tests may help us gather insights into students' reactions to reading activities, but they offer many challenges in terms of devising fair and systematic methods of evaluation!

Are there ways to distinguish students with significant learning disabilities in the area of reading comprehension that do not involve standardized tests?

It is difficult to determine whether a student's reading problems constitute a reading disability without norm-referenced measures of reading and related areas. However, Fuchs and Fuchs (1998) have suggested that teachers can use response to instruction as a way to make such a determination. They recommend using CBMs that have good technical characteristics (i.e., reliability and validity). With such instruments, teachers should be able to distinguish between ineffective teaching and unacceptable learning by one or more students in a class. The CBM tests, administered on a regular basis to all classes at a given grade level in a school or district, could show whether the growth rate of all students in a class was similar across teachers. The group mean and the amount of variation in each class would be important variables. Where there is a lot of variation in student response to instruction in a class, we would suspect that there are a few students with a slower rate of learning than is typical for that class. In contrast, where the class is making slow progress, relative to other classes at that grade level, but with relatively little variation in the class, one might suspect that there was a general lack of responsiveness on the part of the students.

Identifying students and classes that are making slow progress is, of course, the first step in taking corrective action. Where students whose rate of learning is below that of the group are given special help, performance on subsequent CBMs should show whether these students responded to the classroom intervention. If they did not, it might be time to consider a referral for a more thorough assessment of the students' learning capabilities. If, on the other hand, a student responds to the classroom intervention, it might be that his or her learning needs fall short of the severity and pervasiveness that are characteristic of learning disabilities or other categories of exceptionality. Teachers interested in this method of identifying students with significant comprehension problems would be well-advised to read about methods to implement a CBM in a school system that could be used for such purposes (e.g., Fuchs and Fuchs 1998; Self et al. 1991).

What should teachers do when they have trouble understanding diagnostic reports or reading assessments of their students?

Psychologists' reports are often written with specialized language, making it difficult for teachers to understand the nature of the students' problems and the recommendations for appropriate action. It may be impractical for classroom teachers to attempt to cope with the jargon in such reports on their own. Instead, a sensible approach is to take advantage of and indeed foster collaborative relations with the special services staff in the school. Regular educators have responsibilities in the process of working with students with special needs. These include carrying out pre-referral interventions, submitting a referral for evaluation, participating on the case study team, and monitoring the students' progress in their classes. In particular, teachers should take an active role in case study meetings where Individualized Educational Plans are devised for students in their classes.

Special and regular educators can learn a lot from one another about the children under their care if they talk regularly. Specialists (i.e., special education teachers or the school psychologist) can interpret diagnostic reports for teachers and help them understand ways to address the specific problems a student is experiencing. At the same time, by discussing the student's progress in the regular classroom, special services staff get a chance to evaluate their instructional recommendations. Collaboration of educators characterizes schools that have effective reading programs (Taylor et al. 1999).

REFERENCES

Aaron, P. G. 1991. Can reading disabilities be diagnosed without using intelligence tests? *Journal of Learning Disabilities*, 24:178–86, 191.

Aaron, P. G., Joshi, M., and Williams, K. A. 1999. Not all reading disabilities are alike. *Journal of Learning Disabilities*, 32:120–37.

Allington, R., and McGill-Franzen, A. 1992. Unintended effects of reform in New York. *Educational Policy*, 6:397–414.

Badian, N. A. 1999. Reading disability defined as a discrepancy between listening and reading comprehension: A longitudinal study of stability, gender differences, and prevalence. *Journal of Learning Disabilities*, 32:138–48.

Boerum, L. J. 2000. Developing portfolios with learning disabled students. *Reading and Writing Quarterly*, 16:211–38.

Cain, K., and Oakhill, J. V. 1999. Inference making ability and its relation to comprehension failure in young children. *Reading and Writing: An Interdisciplinary Journal*, 11:489–503.

Carlisle, J. F. 1989. Diagnosing comprehension deficits through listening and reading. *Annals of Dyslexia*, 39:159–76.

Carlisle, J. F., and Felbinger, L. 1991. Profiles of listening and reading comprehension. *Journal of Educational Research*, 84:345–54.

Carlisle, J. F. 1999. Free recall as a test of reading comprehension for students with learning disabilities. *Learning Disability Quarterly*, 22:11–22.

Catts, H. W., Fey, M. E., Zhang, X., and Tomblin, J.B. 1999. Language basis of reading and reading disabilities: Evidence from a longitudinal investigation. *Scientific Studies of Reading*, 3:331–61.

Catts, H. W., Fey, M. E., Zhang, X., and Tomblin, J. B. 2001. Estimating the risk of future difficulties in kindergarten children: A research-based model and its clinical implementation. *Language, Speech, and Hearing Services in Schools*, 32:38–50.

Elliott, J. L., Erickson, R.N., Thurlow, M.L., and Shriner, J.G. 2000. State-level accountability for the performance of students with disabilities. *Journal of Special Education*, 34:39–47.

Elliott, S. N. 1998. Performance assessment of students' achievement: Research and practice. *Learning Disabilities Research and Practice*, 13:233–41.

Espin, C. A., and Deno, S. L. 1993. Performance in reading from content-area texts as an indicator of achievement. *Remedial and Special Education*, 14:47–59.

Espin, C. A., and Foegen, A. 1996. Validity of general outcome measures for predicting secondary students' performance on content-area tasks. *Exceptional Children*, 62:497–514.

Fletcher, J. M., Francis, D. J., Shaywitz, S. E., Lyon, G. R., Foorman, B. R., Stuebing, K. K., and Shaywitz, B. A. 1998. Intelligence testing and the discrepancy model for children, with learning disabilities. *Learning Disabilities Research and Practice*, 13:186–203.

Fuchs, L. S., and Fuchs, D. 1998. Treatment validity: A unifying concept for reconceptualizing the identification of learning disabilities. *Learning Disabilities Research and Practice*, 13:204–19.

Fuchs, L. S., Fuchs, D., and Hamlett, C. L. 1989. Monitoring reading growth using student recalls: Effects of two teacher feedback systems. *Journal of Educational Research*, 83:103–10.

Fuchs, L. S., Fuchs, D., Eaton, S. B., Hamlett, C., Binkley, E., and Crouch, R. 2000. Using objective data sources to enhance teacher judgments about test accommodations. *Exceptional Children*, 67:67–81.

Fuchs, L. S., Fuchs, D., and Maxwell, L. 1988. The validity of informal reading comprehension measures. *Remedial and Special Education*, 9:20–28.

Goldberg, G. L., and Roswell, B. S. 2001. Are multiple measures meaningful? Lessons from a statewide performance assessment. *Applied Measurement in Education*, 14:125–50.

Kleinert, H. L., Haig, J., Kearns, J. F., and Kennedy, S. 2000. Alternate assessments: Lessons learned and roads to be taken. *Exceptional Children*, 67:51–66.

Leslie, L., and Caldwell, J. 2000. *Qualitative Reading Inventory III*. NY: Harper Collins.

McKenna, M. C., Kear, D. J., and Ellsworth, R. A. 1995. Children's attitude toward reading: A national survey. *Reading Research Quarterly*, 30:934–56.

Muter, V. 2000. Screening for early reading failure. In *Prediction and Prevention of Reading Failure*, N. Badian (Ed.), (pp. 1–29). Baltimore: York Press.

Oakhill, J., and Yuill, N. 1996. Higher order factors in comprehension disability: Processes and remediation. In *Reading Comprehension Difficulties: Processes and Intervention*, C. Cornoldi and J. Oakhill (Eds.), (pp. 69–92). Mahwah, NJ: Lawrence Erlbaum.

O'Connor, R. E., and Jenkins, J. R. 1999. Prediction of reading disabilities in kindergarten and first grade. *Scientific Studies of Reading*, 3:159–97.

Paris, S. and Paris, A. 2001. Children's comprehension of narrative picture books. *Center for the Improvement of Early Reading Achievement Report #3-102*. Ann Arbor: University of Michigan.

Pressley, M., and Afflerbach, P. 1995. *Verbal Protocols of Reading*. Hillsdale, NJ: Lawrence Erlbaum.

Raphael, T. E., Brock, C. H., and Wallace, S. 1997. Encouraging quality peer talk with diverse students in mainstream classrooms: Learning from and with teachers. In *Peer Talk in the Classroom: Learning From Research*, J. R. Paratore and T. McCormick (Eds.), (pp. 176–206). Newark, DE: International Reading Association.

Royer, J., Kulhavy, R., Lee, S., and Peterson, S. 1986. The relationship between reading and listening comprehension. *Educational and Psychological Research*, 6:299–314.

Salvia, J., and Hughes, C. 1990. *Curriculum-based Assessment: Testing What is Taught*. New York: Macmillan Publishing Co.

Self, H., Benning, A., Marston, D., and Magnusson, D. 1991. Cooperative teacher project: A model for students at risk. *Exceptional Children*, 58:26–35.

Shankweiler, D., Lundquist, E., Katz, L., Steubing, K. K., Fletcher, J. M., Brady, S., Fowler, A., Dreyer, L. G., Marchione, K. E., Shaywitz, S. E., and Shaywitz, B. A. 1999, Comprehension and decoding: Patterns of association in children with reading difficulties. *Scientific Studies of Reading*, 3:69–94.

Shin, J., Deno, S. L., and Espin, C. 2000. Technical adequacy of the maze task for curriculum-based measurement of reading growth. *Journal of Special Education*, 34:164–72.

Siegel, L. S. 1992. An evaluation of the discrepancy definition of dyslexia. *Journal of Learning Disabilities*, 25:618–29.

Simmons, D. C., Kuykendall, K., King, K., Cornachione, C., and Kame'enui, E. J. 2000. Implementation of a schoolwide reading improvement model: "No one ever told us it would be this hard!" *Learning Disabilities Research and Practice*, 15:92–100.

Snow, C. E., Burns, S., and Griffin, P. 1998. *Preventing Reading Difficulties in Young Children*. Washington, DC: National Academy Press.

Spring, C., and French, L. 1990. Identifying children with specific reading disabilities from listening and reading discrepancy scores. *Journal of Learning Disabilities*, 23:53–58.

Stanovich, K. E. 1991. Reading disability: Assessment issues. In *Handbook on the Assessment of Learning Disabilities: Theory, Research, and Practice*, H. L. Swanson (Ed.), (pp. 147–75). Austin, TX: PRO-ED.

Sticht, T. H., and James, H. J. 1984. Listening and reading. In *Handbook of Reading Research*, P. D. Pearson (Ed.), (pp. 293–17). New York: Longman.

Stecker, P. M., and Fuchs, L. S. 2000. Effecting superior achievement using curriculum-based measurement: The importance of individual progress monitoring. *Learning Disabilities Research and Practice*, 15:128–34.

Stowell, L. P., and Tierney, R. J. 1995. Portfolios in the classroom: What happens when teachers and students negotiate assessment? In *No Quick Fix: Rethinking Literacy Lessons in America's Elementary Schools*, R. Allington and S. Walmsley (Eds.), (pp. 78–94). New York: Teachers College Press.

Taylor, B. M., Pearson, P. D., Clark, K. F., and Walpole, S. 1999. Effective schools/ Accomplished teachers. *The Reading Teacher*, 53:156–59.

Thurlow, M. L., House, A. L., Scott, D. L., and Ysseldyke, J. F. 2000. Students with disabilities in large-scale assessments: State participation and accommodation policies. *Journal of Special Education*, 34:154–63.

Torgesen, J. K., and Wagner, R. K. 1998. Alternative diagnostic approaches for specific developmental reading disabilities. *Learning Disabilities Research and Practice*, 13:220–32.

United States Office of Education (USOE). 1977. Assistance to states for education of handicapped children: Procedures for evaluating specific learning disabilities. *Federal Register*, 42, G1082-G1085.

Valencia, S. W., Hiebert, E. H., and Afflerbach, P. P. (Eds.). 1994. *Authentic Reading Assessment: Practices and Possibilities*. Newark, DE: International Reading Association.

Valencia, S. W., and Wixson, K. 2000. Policy-oriented research on literacy standards and assessment. In *Handbook of Reading Research*, Vol. III, M. Kamil, P. B. Mosenthal, P. D. Pearson, and R. Barr (Eds.), (pp. 909-935). Mahwah, NJ: Lawrence Erlbaum.

Vellutino, F., Scanlon, D. M., and Lyon, G. R. 2000. Differentiating between difficult-to-remediate and readily remediated poor readers: More evidence against the IQ-achievement discrepancy definition of reading disability. *Journal of Learning Disabilities*, 33:223–38.

Wiig, E. H. 2000. Authentic and other assessments of language disabilities: When is fair fair? *Reading and Writing Quarterly*, 16:179–210.

Wixson, K. K., and Dutro, E. 1998. *Standards for primary-grade reading: An analysis of state frameworks*. Ann Arbor: University of Michigan, Center for the Improvement of Early Reading Achievement Report # 2-001.

Ysseldyke, J., and Olsen, K. 1999. Putting alternate assessments into practice: What to measures and possible sources of data. *Exceptional Children*, 65:175–85.

11

Implementation of Effective Practices in the Schools

GETTING STARTED

✓ What general conclusions can be drawn from the research on reading comprehension?
✓ What are some barriers to effective translation of research to classroom practice?
✓ What are some characteristics of effective professional development programs?

WHAT WORKS?

After examining multiple aspects of reading comprehension throughout this book, it is reasonable to ask if there are any general conclusions we can draw about effective comprehension instruction for poor readers. In recent years, a number of researchers have sought to answer this question through large-scale "meta-analyses" of the research literature on comprehension instruction for students with learning disabilities (e.g., Gersten et al. 1998; Mastropieri et al. 1996; Swanson 1999a). These researchers collected all of the studies of comprehension instruction involving students with learning disabilities (LD) that were conducted over the course of many years. For instance, Swanson and his colleagues (Swanson 1999a) included research conducted between 1963 and 1997, while Mastropieri et al. (1996) examined a similar set of studies conducted between 1976 and 1996. The researchers applied a set of statistical procedures to the data from these studies, which allowed them to determine the magnitude of the treatment effect across *all* of the studies. One of the most encouraging findings from this work was a large overall effect size for reading comprehension instruction. This finding clearly indicates that research-based comprehension interventions do indeed improve the reading of students with learning disabilities.

In addition to looking at overall effect sizes, Swanson and his colleagues identified particular instructional components that most strongly contributed to improvement in comprehension. They began with a long list of instructional components that might possibly have a positive impact on performance. Of these, only a few proved to be significantly predictive of positive intervention outcomes. The instructional components that had a significant impact on reading comprehension (Swanson 1999a) are summarized in table 11.1.

Findings from the other meta-analyses are generally consistent with Swanson's (1999a) results. Mastropieri et al. (1996) categorized the studies according to the nature of the intervention. They found the largest effects for instructional techniques that involved "self-questioning." This category included such practices as summarizing key points in paragraphs, asking questions to activate relevant background knowledge, making predictions, and self-monitoring of comprehension. Gersten et al. (1998) found that the most effective interventions involved strategies for self-monitoring (i.e., teaching students to monitor their comprehension and apply a variety of "repair" strategies when they realize they are not understanding) and text structuring (i.e., teaching students ways of asking themselves about what they read).

Swanson, Hoskyn, and Lee (1999) published the results of a "super" meta-analysis, compressing data from *all* studies of interventions for students with LD across content areas (see also Swanson 1999a; Swanson 1999b). When results of the overall meta-analysis were examined, the researchers were able to identify three aspects of instruction that made the most difference for students with LD, regardless of the type of intervention or the specific content being taught:

- Control of task difficulty
- Instruction in small interactive groups of six students or fewer
- Procedures that promote self-questioning and "thinking aloud"

Clearly, many of the teaching techniques we have recommended throughout this book incorporate the instructional components that these large-scale analyses of the research literature indicate are most effective. The component that Swanson, Hoskyn, and Lee (1999) termed "control of task difficulty" has much in common with the constructivist concept of "scaffolding." Examples and problems are carefully sequenced and sufficient support is provided to maintain high levels of student success. As the student's competence grows, support is gradually withdrawn and the difficulty level is increased. Continued use of strategies and generalization to new tasks is often a problem for students with learning disabilities (Gersten et al. 2001; Gersten et al. 1998). Carefully structured support and gradual increase in the degree of challenge are likely to help students effectively transfer what they have learned to new reading experiences. There is abundant research support for providing reading instruction in small interactive groups or pairs (e.g., Elbaum et al. 1999; Fuchs et al. 2001; Schumm, Moody, and Vaughn 2000) through collaborative reading practices such as Reciprocal Teaching and PALS. Not only is this means of organizing instruction likely to improve academic performance, but it may also have a positive impact on self-concept (Schumm, Moody, and Vaughn 2000) and increase the likelihood that students will persevere on challenging tasks (Vaughn, Gersten, and Chard 2000). Finally, through the use of "thinking aloud" approaches, a teacher can demonstrate the application of

Table 11.1   Best Instructional Practices in Reading Comprehension for Students with Learning Disabilities (adapted from Swanson 1999a)

Instructional Component	Description
Directed Response/Questioning	The teacher directs the students to ask question, the teacher and students or students engage in dialogue, or the teacher asks questions.
Control of Task Difficulty	The level of task difficulty is controlled—either through the degree of assistance provided by the teacher or through the sequencing of tasks from easy to more challenging.
Elaboration	The teacher provides additional information or explanation of concepts, procedures, and steps.
Teacher Modeling	The teacher provides modeling or demonstrations of the processes or procedures the students are to follow.
Small Group Instruction	Instruction occurs in the context of a small group and/or students interact verbally in a small group by themselves or with the teacher.
Strategy Cues	The teacher reminds students to use strategies, provides verbal reminders of strategy procedures, encourages students to "think aloud" as they apply strategies, or describes the benefits of strategy use.

strategies and procedures for solving problems that students may well not think of on their own. According to Harris and Pressley (1991), explicit teaching and modeling of strategies provides students with "their culture's best-kept secret about how to attain academic success" (p. 395). Moreover, asking students to make their own thought processes overt enables teachers and peers to provide them with feedback that serves to guide their learning and correct misperceptions (Vaughn, Gersten, and Chard 2000).

Teachers may ask the question of whether these instructional practices are only useful for students with LD or whether they have broader applicability. Research suggests that effective instruction for students with LD is, in fact, equally effective for other students. Based on several meta-analyses of the LD research, Vaughn, Gersten, and Chard (2000) concluded: "In all cases where interventions have demonstrated significant positive effects for students with LD, they have resulted in at least as high (and most often higher) effect sizes for all other students, including average and high achieving students" (p. 108). Moreover, these components of quality instruction for students with LD are remarkably similar to practices that characterize effective instruction in high-poverty schools. Taylor et al. (2000) found that relative to less effective teachers in these settings, the most effective teachers (1) devoted more time to small-group instruction, (2) "coached" children as opposed to telling them information, (3) asked higher level questions in the course of discussions, and (4) fostered high levels of on-task behavior.

THE GAP BETWEEN RESEARCH AND PRACTICE

Findings from the accumulated body of research on effective comprehension instruction seem quite clear. Unfortunately, however, many of the instructional practices that have the most potential to make a meaningful difference for students with LD and other poor readers are seldom employed. Currently, whole-class, undifferentiated instruction seems to be the norm in both general education (Schumm et al. 2000) and resource settings (Moody et al. 2000). Moreover, when strategy instruction and cooperative learning are incorporated, the quality of the instruction is often poor (Gersten et al. 1997). Implementation tends to be erratic rather than systematic, and essential elements (such as active participation of students with LD) are often omitted. Taylor and Pearson (2001a) reported on findings from their observations of 130 teachers in K–6 classrooms in nine high-poverty schools across the United States. None of the teaching practices associated with high achievement (see above) were very often implemented. They observed whole-group instruction 60% to 70% of the time. There was very little high-level questioning, telling (as opposed to coaching) was the primary interaction style of most teachers, and students were more often passive recipients of instruction than active participants.

Why is there so little transfer of research-supported teaching practices to the typical classroom? According to Vaughn, Klingner, and Hughes (2000), the reasons most frequently offered tend to fall in one of two categories: "blame the teachers" or "blame the researchers." Teachers are often characterized as being resistant to change, lacking in knowledge, and determined to choose comfortable, familiar practices over those that are less familiar but more effective. Researchers, on the other hand, are accused of not respecting teachers, of not understanding classroom reality, and of underestimating teachers' need for concreteness and specificity (Gersten et al. 1997). Although there are probably some grains of truth in these claims, this is certainly an overly simplistic view of the issue.

We know, for instance, from focus groups with teachers (Gersten, Chard, and Baker 2000) that teachers are eager to learn about and implement innovative practices, especially those that research has shown to be effective for all students, both normal-achievers and those with learning difficulties. For their part, many researchers have, in recent years, made a concerted effort to involve teachers in the process of developing instructional techniques and adapting them for classroom use (e.g., Englert and Tarrant 1995; Fuchs et al. 2001; Schumm and Vaughn 1995).

However, knowledge of teaching techniques and experience in implementing them are not, by themselves, necessarily sufficient to result in sustained use of the techniques. Even intensive, lengthy professional development programs involving collaboration between teachers and researchers do not always lead to long-term change in teaching practices (Gersten et al. 1997; Klingner, Vaughn, and Hughes 1999). Changes in classroom practice have been compared to lifestyle changes prescribed by a physician following an event such as a heart attack or a diagnosis of hypertension or high cholesterol (Vaughn, Klingner, and

Hughes 2000). In such cases, it is common for patients to practice new health reg-imens temporarily, but eventually return to old habits. Moreover, some people turn to fad treatments unsubstantiated by research rather than continue the pre-scribed intervention. This lack of follow-through in making medically warranted changes in diet, exercise, and medication—a situation in which the stakes are very high and very personal—illustrates the difficulty human beings have with long-term change. In fact, Vaughn, Klingner, and Hughes (2000) argued that there are good reasons to expect even less sustained implementation of research-based teaching practices. The consequences are less personal than they are in the case of medical treatment, the results are often not immediately obvious to teach-ers, and the new teaching methods are replacing techniques that teachers usually believe are at least reasonably effective for most students.

Factors Affecting Sustained Use of New Teaching Practices

A critical factor in whether or not teachers will implement a technique on a long-term basis is what Gersten et al. (1997) dubbed "the reality principle." As these authors observed, "Instructional interventions that are effective only in tightly controlled settings and are implemented with resources or class sizes that do not represent the realities of the classroom setting may provide important guidelines for the development of interventions, but they hold little promise for directly im-proving classroom practice" (p. 469). Unless techniques are adapted for the class-room and unless teachers receive concrete examples and specific procedures for implementing them, the chances of anything more than superficial and erratic ex-perimentation are low.

Klingner, Vaughn, and Hughes (1999) interviewed teachers who had partici-pated in an intensive, year-long professional development program three years earlier about their continued use of three research-based reading interventions. Many of the factors the teachers mentioned that either promoted or deterred sus-tained use of the techniques had to do with practicality in the face of classroom realities. Easy access to necessary materials, the freedom to adapt or modify a technique, adequate time for implementing the techniques, and compatibility of the techniques with personal teaching style were all factors the teachers felt con-tributed to sustained use of the practices. Conversely, when asked about barriers to long-term implementation, the teachers mentioned lack of planning or instruc-tional time, lack of access to materials, overly large class sizes, and the diverse in-structional needs of students.

This final point highlights the recurrent finding across many studies that teaching practices designed to help students with disabilities are most likely to be sustained by classroom teachers when the teachers perceive them to be effec-tive for normally achieving students as well (reviewed in Gersten et al. 1997; Vaughn, Klingner, and Hughes 2000). As Gersten et al. (1997) bluntly pointed out, "Instructional practices that are designed exclusively to meet the needs of a particular student [are] typically ignored" (p. 469). Given the many demands on teachers' time and the wide range of diverse learning needs in today's class-rooms, it is crucial that teaching techniques be beneficial for students of all ability levels. Teachers need ideas for adapting instructional practices to meet diverse needs as well as practical guidelines for handling day-to-day issues, such as classroom management and scheduling, when they are using a new technique.

Research also suggests that the magnitude of change affects the extent to which teachers will continue a practice on a long-term basis (reviewed in Gersten, Chard, and Baker 2000). Neither small, seemingly trivial changes nor broad, sweeping changes are likely to be sustained over time. Rather, innovations that have the best chance of being implemented are those that teachers perceive as adding to their repertoire of techniques and that do not require radical shifts in their current teaching practices or conceptual understanding of the nature of teaching and learning.

Broader-scale changes often require that teachers rethink what they do and why. As Gersten, Chard, and Baker (2000) noted, "There is a growing sense of the importance of integrating the underlying concepts that drive instruction with the practice or craft knowledge that teachers bring to bear as they work to implement innovative instructional practices" (p. 450). For instance, Pressley and El-Dinary (1997) noted that, in their experience, teachers are often uneasy about the prospect of teaching reading comprehension strategies, in part because doing so means "letting go" of some old patterns of thinking and behaving. Effective comprehension strategies instruction involves giving up some teacher control in service of the goal of producing autonomous, self-sufficient readers. As Pressley and El-Dinary observed, "This can be very difficult for teachers who have believed for much of their career that they should be in control of their students" (p. 487).

Learning something new often involves some degree of personal risk. Research suggests that teachers who are more likely to adopt new methods are those with greater confidence in their abilities, or "self-efficacy" (summarized in Gersten, Chard, and Baker 2000; Wong 1997). Teachers who doubt the ability of their low-achieving students to learn are often equally doubtful of their own ability to make a difference or to implement new practices effectively. Such teachers are less likely to try a new approach than those with assurance in their ability to succeed in mastering a new practice. Not surprisingly, teacher self-efficacy has been linked to positive student outcomes (see Gersten, Chard, and Baker 2000).

Supporting Teachers' Efforts

In order to learn new techniques and take the risks needed to make meaningful changes in practice, teachers need support from a variety of sources including outside consultants, colleagues, and administrators. In most cases, a one-time professional development seminar is unlikely to be sufficient for teachers to fully understand and learn to implement a new practice. They might experiment briefly with a technique, but quickly abandon it unless there is on-going support during the process of learning the new practice and figuring out how to implement it in a given classroom. This can take a considerable amount of time, often a year or more (Englert and Tarrant 1995; Klingner, Vaughn, and Hughes 1999).

In a study of effective professional development programs, Birman et al. (2000) identified three factors that were related to success: the intensity and duration of the professional development; techniques that were both relevant and research-based; and opportunities for the teachers themselves to engage in active learning through role playing, joint planning sessions, critiques of lessons, and the like. Such a process gives teachers the opportunity to internalize the approach. Several of the teachers that Klingner, Vaughn, and Hughes (1999) interviewed observed that forgetting how to implement a technique or never fully understanding it in the first place is a deterrent to sustained use of the practice. Moreover, when teachers do use a method for an extended period of time, with guidance and support, chances are greater that they will see its beneficial effects on student learning. In fact, one of the strongest incentives for teachers to continue using an approach is witnessing improvements in learning that can be attributed to the instructional innovation (Englert and Tarrant 1995; Klingner, Vaughn, and Hughes 1999). Moreover, changes in teachers' conceptual beliefs about teaching and the nature of student learning often follow successful changes in practice (Gersten and Dimino 2001).

In addition to support from outside consultants or members of the research community, teachers who are attempting to make changes in their teaching practices greatly benefit from having colleagues to whom they can turn for support. The teachers that Klingner, Vaughn, and Hughes (1999) interviewed said that having the support of colleagues who were also implementing the approaches was an important factor in their long-term use of research-based teaching practices. Such a support network provides teachers with opportunities to share ideas and collaboratively solve problems that arise as they seek to implement new practices. Teachers with particular experience or expertise can share this knowledge with their peers. Gersten, Chard, and Baker (2000) observed that such sharing might occur in a "more collegial, practical, and useful fashion than in a brief visit from an outside consultant" with similar expertise (p. 451). However, support networks outside of school are valuable, too. Research (reviewed in Gersten, Chard, and Baker 2000) indicates that active involvement in some sort of strong "professional community"—whether at the local, district, state, or national level—enhances teachers' sense of competence and their ability to sustain innovative teaching practices.

Several of the teachers interviewed by Klingner, Vaughn, and Hughes (1999) mentioned administrative support as a key factor in sustained use of techniques. Administrators can play a substantial role in creating a "school culture" that supports innovation and change. Without such support, teachers seeking to implement new methods can be placed in the uncomfortable position of having to justify their practices to administrators and parents before they themselves are convinced of their effectiveness (Ball 1995).

Outside Forces and Political Factors

Of course, there are forces beyond the level of individual classrooms and schools that play a role in the research-practice gap. One of these is the current emphasis on high stakes testing in the name of "accountability." A number of the teachers in the Klingner, Vaughn, and Hughes (1999) study felt that high stakes achievement testing and pressure to cover certain content placed constraints on their use of innovative teaching methods. Because the teachers perceived that their performance was being evaluated along with that of their students, they were reluctant to experiment with new approaches. They were frank about their choice to sacrifice possible long-term gains in, for instance, reading comprehension that might come about through their use of a collaborative strategy instruction method in favor of practices (e.g., the use of test preparation materials) that they knew would enable their students to perform adequately on the tests. Similarly, a fourth–grade teacher quoted by Vaughn, Klingner, and Hughes (2000) explained why he seldom used a process writing approach:

> There is no question that the kids like it, but I am held accountable in the spring for the writing test, and they have to learn to do particular things in a particular way or they will not make the score. So I must continue to teach writing the way I know will get the students to make passing marks (p. 168).

Carnine (1997) considered the research-practice gap from a broader perspective. He argued that the real "influence producers" in education, most notably curriculum "experts" in educational organizations and publishing companies, tend to promote popular educational innovations before they have been substantiated by research. The influence producers tend to have far greater sway over publishers, practitioners, state legislatures, and departments of education than do researchers. As Stanovich and Stanovich (1997) observed, researchers are often hesitant to make firm claims about the effectiveness of instructional technique. From the perspective of the social scientist, there are very good reasons for this. Inherent in even the best-designed study are limitations of research methodologies and questions about whether or not results generalize to populations other than the research sample. No article published in a scholarly journal would be complete without a frank discussion of the limitations of the study. However, other voices fill the void that researchers leave, and the result is that teachers and administrators are confronted with a barrage of information from a variety of sources about instructional methods and materials, some of which may be based on research and some of which may be unsubstantiated fads. Lacking knowledge of criteria for evaluating the credibility of competing claims, those responsible for selecting among the vast array of choices may be drawn to the glitziest ads or the most compelling personal testimony. The tentative conclusions of researchers may lead teachers to think that there is little consensus among researchers and, therefore, that there is no real reason to change instructional practices (Vaughn, Klingner, and Hughes 2000).

Obviously, there are many hurdles to overcome in the task of translating research into classroom practice. Although there are no easy solutions to the dilemma, one way schools and the research community collectively can effect change is to develop models of professional development that meet established criteria for effectiveness: sufficient intensity and duration; relevant and research-based techniques; and active involvement of teachers (Birman et al. 2000).

PROMISING MODELS OF PROFESSIONAL DEVELOPMENT

The traditional professional development method of providing brief workshops has not lead to meaningful changes in classroom implementation, nor has the "top down" model with researchers identifying the problems, crafting solutions, and expecting teachers to implement them as prescribed. In recent years, researchers and school personnel have looked for other solutions. Research on how best to bring about lasting change is still in its infancy (Gersten, Chard, and Baker 2000); however, several alternative models have been developed that show promise. In this section, we briefly describe some of these newer models of professional development.

Teacher-Researcher Collaboration

In recent years, there have been numerous experiments with direct collaboration between teachers and researchers in designing and implementing instructional innovations (e.g., Abbott et al. 1999; Englert and Tarrant 1995; Schumm and Vaughn 1995). Such projects ideally involve weaving together the "external" knowledge supplied by the researchers with the personal knowledge of the teachers (Schumm and Vaughn 1995).

Englert and Tarrant (1995) began with five "guiding principles" based on a socio-cultural perspective of learning and teaching. These included embedding instruction in meaningful activities, guiding students toward self-regulated learning, involving students in dialogue, and building "learning communities" in the classroom. These general principles provided a theoretical basis for teachers' decisions about instruction for less skilled readers. The university research team did not provide all the answers, as this was considered to lead to dependence on outsiders for answers. Rather, the researchers asked a group of nine teachers to help develop a curriculum for special education students in the elementary grades—with the five principles in mind. The teachers and researchers worked closely together over the course of three years, meeting and sharing expertise. Englert and Tarrant (1995) observed that the accumulated wisdom of the members of the community was greater than that of the researchers or the individual teachers. The team collaboratively solved problems that emerged and determined how best to adapt techniques to fit specific classroom contexts. The group provided support as teachers took risks and altered their approaches. Moving from the structure of a very quiet classroom where students worked in seats to a more active, dialogue-based classroom was initially a source of discomfort for many of the teachers. Englert and Tarrant noted the group discussed both failures and successes, and these were seen as a natural part of the inquiry process.

Englert and Tarrant (1995) reported increasing interest in and "ownership" of the theoretical principles on which the instruction was based. Many of the teachers expressed surprise and excitement about the positive effect on student learning, which led to increased interest. Over time, there was a "ripple effect" as the original teachers involved in the project mentored others, gave presentations at conferences, and opened their classrooms to serve as demonstration sites.

Englert and Tarrant noted that the collaborative efforts resulted in more profound changes than they had initially anticipated, changes that endured well beyond the time frame of the original project.

We agree with Bos (1995) that the success of such projects has been encouraging. However, there are a number of factors that may limit the feasibility of the model. First, the approach can be very time-intensive on the part of the researchers. Abbott et al. (1999), for instance, reported that members of their research team spent approximately 50% of each day in the schools over the course of several years. Moreover, as Carnine (1995) noted, there are not nearly enough researchers to collaborate in such a fashion with every school district in the United States! Other models may have more potential for bringing about widespread change.

The "Homegrown" Approach

The "homegrown" approach, a term coined by Stringfield, Milsap, and Herman (1997), is sometimes used to describe change processes that schools take on by themselves, perhaps with the aid of a facilitator, in which they select programs and adapt them to fit their unique needs. Gersten and Dimino (2001) described one such project that was designed to help classroom teachers meet the needs of special education students in their classes. Unlike the collaborative projects described above, in this case, the researchers deliberately played a "behind the scenes" role, with school district staff assuming primary responsibility for designing and sustaining use of the program. A facilitator who was employed by both the school district and the research institution served as an intermediary.

The first stage of the project involved a district-wide needs assessment involving general and special educators and administrators. Based on this assessment, district staff concluded that their greatest areas of concern were early literacy in kindergarten and first grade and reading comprehension at the middle school level. Programs to meet these needs were selected. A phonemic awareness program was adopted for kindergarten and Peer Assisted Learning Strategies (PALS, Fuchs et al. 1997) at the middle school level. The programs were adapted to meet the unique needs of the particular schools. These decisions were made by a team of school personnel with input from the facilitator. For instance, at the middle school level, a group of language arts teachers worked with the principal and the facilitator to determine the particular approach that would be used. The facilitator and a mentor teacher, who had experience with PALS, provided the initial training and remained available for support. As part of the project, some of the teachers collaborated with the researchers in an action research project examining the effects of PALS on fluency and comprehension. This provided solid evidence of students' growth. The teacher involvement in the process of data collection and analysis demonstrated to the teachers the effectiveness of the program and introduced them to the research process.

Schoolwide Reading Improvement Model

A more structured model for professional development is the Schoolwide Reading Improvement Model (SRIM, Kame'enui, Simmons, and Coyne 2000), a program specifically designed to prevent early reading difficulties. Again, the scope extends beyond individual teachers; efforts are coordinated schoolwide. However, the reading instruction provided is tailored to the unique needs of individual schools.

The program is divided into five stages. The first of these involves a "big picture" analysis of school goals, instructional priorities, teacher philosophies, and current practices. A planning and evaluation guide has been developed by the researchers to aid school personnel in this process. Another aspect of the first stage is deciding how to identify those children who are at risk for reading disabilities or delay. Kame'enui, Simmons, and Coyne (2000) suggest using either norms on locally developed achievement tests or performance on tasks associated with early reading achievement (phonemic segmentation, letter naming, etc.).

The second stage involves grouping children according to their instructional needs. Kame'enui et al. suggest three classifications: Intensive, Strategic, and Benchmark. The Intensive students are those who are seriously at risk, who perform well below expected levels on all measures. The Strategic students are those with less severe needs, but who need monitoring and more carefully designed instruction than is typical in most classrooms. Finally, the Benchmark students are those who are meeting or exceeding expectations on critical literacy skills, those who are not at risk for reading failure. Instruction is provided in small, homogenous groups with frequent monitoring to adjust the groups based on current needs. In other words, in this model, a given child is not destined to remain in the "low" group permanently.

In the third stage, a collaborative team constructs or customizes an intervention program to fit the needs of the school. A school can select an intervention program from a "menu" of research-validated options. Decisions are made about such factors as which curriculum materials will be adopted, how time for reading instruction will be scheduled, and what kind of progress-monitoring system will be used. The fourth stage involves setting goals and monitoring children's progress toward meeting them. Kame'enui, Simmons, and Coyne (2000) suggest that collaborative teams meet every two weeks to discuss instructional issues. The fifth stage involves evaluating the effectiveness of the intervention program and making adjustments accordingly.

School Change Project

Like the other professional development approaches we have profiled here, the School Change Project (Taylor et al. 2001) operates from the philosophy that school personnel should be involved in constructing programs that are appropriate for their settings, but that, in contrast to the "homegrown" approach, they should not have to start from scratch. Taylor and Pearson (2001b) offer a framework for school personnel to use in making decisions about how to create a reading program.

An innovative feature of the School Change Project is the use of technology to dispense information. Through an internet-based multimedia program, Taylor and her colleagues have provided summaries of relevant research, recommended readings, videoclips of effective practice in action, and planning activities. There are six key components to the program, based on factors found to distinguish exceptionally effective schools in high-poverty communities (Taylor et al. 2000). These are classroom practice, schoolwide reading programs, reading interventions for low-achievers, school-home-community relations, and professional development. There is a degree of choice in how each component will be implemented. They recommend that a school team consisting of teachers, the principal, and an external facilitator review the material and make decisions. At least 75% of the teachers in a given school must agree to participate. To assess the effectiveness of the program, randomly selected teachers are observed periodically and given feedback. Target students representing the high, middle, and low thirds of these teachers' classes are assessed over time.

Twelve schools participated in the project during the 2000–2001 school year. They represented diverse regions of the nation, from a small town in North Carolina to urban schools in Minneapolis/St. Paul and Los Angeles. Preliminary results are documenting the success of the project. In the area of reading comprehension, practices such as asking questions after reading, working on comprehension skills and strategies, and engaging students in small-group instruction were found to be positively correlated with growth in comprehension (Taylor et al. 2001).

The four models we have profiled here are a few examples of current efforts to transfer research-based instructional techniques to classroom practice. They are by no means the only options. When designing a professional development program in reading instruction, it might be helpful to consider a list of characteristics of quality inservice teacher education that Anders, Hoffman, and Duffy (2000) extracted from a review of the literature:

- Intensive commitment and concentrated effort
- Ongoing monitoring and support in the context of classroom practice
- Opportunities for teachers to reflect systematically on their practices as they implement new methods
- Opportunities for conversation, discussion, and negotiation
- Voluntary participation
- Collaboration

To be effective, the process of change clearly involves an on-going commitment on the part of everyone involved—administrators, teachers, and outside consultants. However, beyond that, it appears to be very important that teachers' input is valued and that they have opportunities to share their ideas and experiences with others. Professional development models that incorporate these elements—when implemented on a widespread basis—have the potential to help bridge the gulf between research and classroom practice.

PRESERVICE TEACHER TRAINING

Most of the research on effective professional development programs has focused on practicing teachers. Less is known about how to prepare new teachers to implement research-based practices effectively. Research indicates that teacher education programs *do* have an effect on the practices of recent graduates (reviewed in Anders, Hoffman, and Duffy 2000). Findings from several studies suggest that practicum and student teaching experiences have a particularly strong impact. Some researchers, however, have found that once teachers are in the field, there is not a great deal of transfer of techniques introduced in undergraduate methods classes to classroom practice, especially at the secondary level (reviewed in Bean 2000). This may be due in part to a lack of effective modeling on the part of cooperating teachers during the student teaching experience (Bean 2000). A cooperating teacher's more traditional style, as well as the classroom realities we discussed above (high stakes assessment, time limitations, behavior management, etc.) can exert a powerful effect on a new teacher's beliefs about the feasibility of such practices as strategies instruction, use of graphic organizers, and interactive reading approaches.

Huberman (1995) theorized that teachers go through several developmental stages as their careers progress. The first three years of teaching are characterized as a "survival" stage. New teachers often feel very vulnerable and seek out techniques that they think will help them feel more in control. If this is true, it is easy to see the appeal of more traditional, teacher-directed practices, such as lecture and full class instruction, over techniques such as strategy instruction or small-group collaborative reading approaches that require a teacher to relinquish some control in order to foster greater self-sufficiency in the students.

Given the potential impact of field-based experiences, perhaps one solution is to rethink traditional models of student teaching. Banaszak, Wilson, and McClelland (1995) proposed one model in which the roles of campus student teaching supervisor and cooperating teacher are assigned to a single individual, a "master teacher" who possesses a Master's degree, at least five years of teaching experience, and supervisory experience, and who has taken part in a summer training program. As appealing as this idea may be, it seems unlikely that there are sufficient numbers of teachers with the necessary credentials who would be willing to devote the time to mentoring student teachers. Another increasingly popular option is designating certain schools as "professional development sites" in which university staff work closely with the teachers to provide carefully crafted experiences for pre-service teachers.

Another issue is the knowledge base provided to pre-service teachers as part of their undergraduate course work. For instance, Moats (1995) observed that a "missing foundation" in many teacher education programs is training in the structure of the English language needed to effectively teach students to process phonological, syntactic, and morphological "building blocks" as they learn to read and write. Stanovich and Stanovich (1997) argued that it is important to give teachers a system for evaluating the credibility of the claims of "experts." They suggested three criteria: publication of findings in peer reviewed journals, the replication of results by multiple researchers, and a consensus in the research community that sufficient work has been done to validate a given approach. Such knowledge, they noted, is "a useful inoculation against passing fads and fashions" (p. 479). Other researchers have focused on the knowledge, beliefs, and attitudes of preservice teachers, with an emphasis on how these factors affect classroom practice (Anders, Hoffman, and Duffy 2000). Although this research is intriguing, it has thus far led to few firm conclusions about the best way to structure teacher education programs. Moreover, as Anders, Hoffman, and Duffy noted, we do not know how undergraduate experiences shape *long-term* practices and career development. Preservice teacher education is clearly an area in which more research is needed.

CONCLUSIONS

Gersten, Chard, and Baker (2000) observed that "sustaining implementation in classrooms is infinitely more complicated than telling teachers and others that there is a knowledge base on effective practices and they should be using it" (p. 454). Nonetheless, we would argue that the first step in meaningful change *is* becoming aware of the body of knowledge on effective instruction for struggling readers. What we have sought to do in this book is to provide an introduction to that knowledge base with suggestions for classroom implementation. We hope that our readers will find this information useful, and that it may spur discussion within the community of educators about effective comprehension practices, how to transfer them to the classroom, and how to foster a "school culture" that is supportive of innovation.

Such discussions, we believe, are timely and relevant, given the emergence of a significant national movement toward effective reading comprehension instruction. In a recently released report of the RAND Reading Study Group (2002), the authors argued that our current challenge is to improve the reading comprehension of the nation's children. This will require awareness on the part of researchers, educators, and policy makers that the goal of ensuring that all children are reading on grade level by the third grade is only a first step. Beyond that, most children need well-designed instruction in reading comprehension in order to reach the levels of reading achievement necessary to meet the demands of life in our technological society. Meeting this new and challenging goal will require teachers who are able to orchestrate knowledge about readers, texts, tasks, and instructional context to foster competence, critical thinking, and motivation in their students (RAND Reading Study Group 2002). We hope that our book will be one tool that will help prepare teachers for this task.

REFERENCES

Abbott, M., Walton, C., Tapia, Y., and Greenwood, C. R. 1999. Research to practice: A "blueprint" for closing the gap in local schools. *Exceptional Children*, 65:339–52.

Anders, P. L., Hoffman, J. V., and Duffy, G. G. 2000. Teaching teachers to teach reading: Paradigm shifts, persistent, problems, and challenges. In *Handbook of Reading Research*, Vol. III, M. L. Kamil, P. B. Mosenthal, P. D. Pearson, and R. Barr (Eds.), (pp. 719–42). Mahwah, NJ: Lawrence Erlbaum.

Ball, D. L. 1995. Blurring the boundaries of research and practice. *Remedial and Special Education*, 16:354–63.

Banaszak, R. A., Wilson, E. K., and McClelland, S. M. 1995. Redefining the student teaching triad. *Teacher Education Research and Practice*, 11:50–59.

Bean, T. W. 2000. Reading in the content areas: Social constructivist dimensions. In *Handbook of Reading Research*, Vol. III, M. L. Kamil, P. B. Mosenthal, P. D. Pearson, and R. Barr (Eds.), (pp. 629–44). Mahwah, NJ: Lawrence Erlbaum.

Birman, B. F., Desimone, L., Porter, A. C., and Garet, M. S. 2000. Designing professional development that works. *Educational Leadership*, 57(8):28–33.

Bos, C. S. 1995. Professional development and teacher change: Encouraging news from the trenches. *Remedial and Special Education*, 16:379–82.

Carnine, D. 1995. The professional context for collaboration and collaborative research. *Remedial and Special Education*, 16:368–71.

Carnine, D. 1997. Bridging the research-to-practice gap. *Exceptional Children*, 63:513–21.

Elbaum, B., Vaughn, S., Hughes, M., and Moody, S. W. 1999. Grouping practices and reading outcomes for students with disabilities. *Exceptional Children*, 65:399–415.

Englert, C. S., and Tarrant, K. L. 1995. Creating collaborative cultures for educational change. *Remedial and Special Education*, 16:325–36.

Fuchs, D., Fuchs, L. S., Mathes, P. H., and Simmons, D. C. 1997. Peer-assisted strategies: Making classrooms more responsive to diversity. *American Educational Research Journal*, 34:174–206.

Fuchs, D., Fuchs, L. S., Thompson, A., Svenson, E., Yen, L., Al Otaiba, S., et al. 2001. Peer-assisted learning strategies in reading: Extensions for kindergarten, first grade, and high school. *Remedial and Special Education*, 22:15–21.

Gersten, R., Chard, D., and Baker, S. 2000. Factors enhancing sustained use of research-based instructional practices. *Journal of Learning Disabilities*, 33:445–57.

Gersten, R., and Dimino, J. 2001. The realities of translating research into classroom practice. *Learning Disabilities Research and Practice*, 16:120–30.

Gersten, R., Fuchs, L., Williams, J. P., and Baker, S. 2001. Teaching reading comprehension strategies to students with learning disabilities: A review of the research. *Review of Educational Research*, 71:279–320.

Gersten, R., Vaughn, S., Deshler, D., and Schiller, E. 1997. What we know about using research findings: Implications for improving special education practice. *Journal of Learning Disabilities*, 30:466–76.

Gersten, R., Williams, J., Fuchs, L., and Baker, S. 1998. *Improving reading comprehension for children with disabilities: A review of the research* (Final Report: Section 1, U.S. Department of Education Contract HS 921700). Washington, DC: U.S. Department of Education.

Harris, K. R., and Pressley, M. 1991. The nature of cognitive strategy instruction. Interactive strategy construction. *Exceptional Children*, 57:392–404.

Huberman, M. 1995. Professional careers and professional development: Some intersections. In *Professional Development in Education: New Paradigms and Practices*, T. R. Guskey and M. Huberman (Eds.), (pp. 193–224). New York: Teachers College Press, Columbia University.

Kame'enui, E. J., Simmons, D. C., and Coyne, M. D. 2000. Schools as host environments: Toward a schoolwide reading improvement model. *Annals of Dyslexia*, 50:33–51.

Klingner, J. K., Vaughn, S., and Hughes, M. T. 1999. Sustaining research-based practices in reading: A 3-year follow-up. *Remedial and Special Education*, 20:263–74.

Mastropieri, M. A., Scruggs, T. E., Bakken, J. P., and Whedon, C. 1996. Reading comprehension: A synthesis of research in learning disabilities. In *Advances in Learning and Behavioral Disabilities*, T. E. Scruggs and M. A. Mastropieri (Eds.), (Vol. 10, Part B, pp. 201–23). Greenwich, CT: JAI Press.

Moats, L. C. 1995. The missing foundation in teacher education. *American Educator*, 19(2):9, 43–51.

Moody, S. W., Vaughn, S., Hughes, M. T., and Fischer, M. 2000. Reading instruction in the resource room: Set up for failure. *Exceptional Children*, 66:305–16.

Pressley, M., and El-Dinary, P. B. 1997. What we know about translating comprehension-strategies instruction research into practice. *Journal of Learning Disabilities*, 30:486–89.

RAND Reading Study Group 2002. *Reading for understanding: Toward a research and development program in reading comprehension.* Retrieved January 4, 2002, from http://www.rand.org/multi/achievementforall/reading/readreport.html

Schumm, J. S., Moody, S. W., and Vaughn, S. 2000. Grouping for reading instruction: Does one size fit all? *Journal of Learning Disabilities*, 33:477–88.

Schumm, J. S., and Vaughn, S. 1995. Meaningful professional development in accommodating students with disabilities: Lessons learned. *Remedial and Special Education*, 16:344–53.

Stanovich, P. J., and Stanovich, K. E. 1997. Research into practice in special education. *Journal of Learning Disabilities*, 30:477–81.

Stringfield, S., Milsap, M. A., and Herman, R. 1997. *Urban and suburban/rural strategies for educating disadvantaged children.* Washington, DC: Planning and Evaluation Service, U.S. Department of Education.

Swanson, H. L. 1999a. Reading research for students with LD: A meta-analysis of intervention outcomes. *Journal of Learning Disabilities*, 32:504–32.

Swanson, H. L. 1999b. Instructional components that predict treatment outcomes for students with learning disabilities: Support for a combined strategy and direct instruction model. *Learning Disabilities Research and Practice*, 13:129–40.

Swanson, H. L., Hoskyn, M., and Lee, C. 1999. *Interventions for Students with Learning Disabilities: A Meta-analysis of Treatment Outcomes.* New York: Guilford.

Taylor, B. M., and Pearson, P. D. 2001a. *The CIERA school change classroom observation scheme.* Retrieved November 20, 2001, from http://education.umn.edu/ci/taylor/taylor1.html

Taylor, B. M., and Pearson, P. D. 2001b. *The CIERA school change project: Translating research on effective reading instruction and school reform into practice in high-poverty elementary schools.* Retrieved November 20, 2001, from http://education.umn.edu/ci/taylor/taylor1.html

Taylor, B. M., Pearson, P. D., Clark, K., and Walpole, S. 2000. Effective schools and accomplished teachers: Lessons about primary grade reading instruction in low-income schools. *The Elementary School Journal*, 101:121–65.

Taylor, B. M., Peterson, D., Pearson, D., Jaynes, C., Knezek, S., Bender, P., et al. 2001. School reform in high-poverty schools. Paper presented at the annual meeting of the American Educational Research Association, Seattle, April, 2001.

Vaughn, S., Gersten, R., Chard, D. J. 2000. The underlying message in LD intervention research: Findings from research syntheses. *Exceptional Children*, 67:99–114.

Vaughn, S., Klingner, J., and Hughes, M. 2000. Sustainability of research-based practices. *Exceptional Children*, 66:163–71.

Wong, B. Y. L. 1997. Clearing hurdles in teacher adoption and sustained use of research-based instruction. *Journal of Learning Disabilities*, 30:482–85.

Grappling with Decisions about Reading Instruction for Struggling Readers

In the same way that we have recommended that teachers give thought to the tasks they asked students to perform after reading, we have pondered how best to close our discussion of reading comprehension instruction for students who are struggling readers. We decided to offer the following vignettes to enrich the educational experiences of individuals who are reading and learning from this book. These are intended to provide "real-life" situations, problems that teachers, administrators, parents, and students are likely to face. We hope the vignettes will help readers review and integrate the knowledge they have acquired from the different chapters.

We also encourage readers to use the vignettes for group discussion, as they all focus on complex problems that do not lend themselves to easy solutions. They involve difficult decisions about such issues as revising a reading curriculum for elementary children in a school where many are not reading on grade level, or considering how to best serve students with poor comprehension skills in content–area courses. Collaborative problem solving is a powerful way to bring about improvements in teaching reading in today's schools. We encourage our readers to apply what they have learned about reading comprehension to improve the teaching of reading and to understand and address the needs of students who struggle with reading.

NINTH-GRADE STUDENTS STUDY FOR A SCIENCE TEST

The Teacher's Perspective

Ms. Shinn likes to teach her ninth-grade biology students through activity-based learning, but she has come to realize that the students do best on the projects when they have a fair amount of background knowledge on the topic or topics that are involved. As a result, she typically asks the students to read the relevant chapter or chapters in the biology textbook recommended by the school's science department. She tells the students which of the topics they need to study and then tests them on their learning. Then she starts the class on projects or hands-on activities. At present, the students are working on a chapter on the frog, focused particularly on the various systems within the body (circulatory, digestive, etc). Once the students have taken their test on this information, they will be working in pairs to dissect a frog. They will write up joint lab reports, and they will be asked to compare the frog's systems with those in the human being.

Ms. Shinn tells her students that she is not a good reader, and she is very supportive of the students for whom reading the textbook is difficult. However, she leaves it to them to figure out what they need to do to meet her expectations. They are free to come to her for advice, and when asked, she has several favorite study techniques she suggests to them (e.g., make visual aids or use mnemonic clues).

Three Students' Perspectives

Here are verbal pictures of three of Ms. Shinn's students as they prepare for the science test.

Jimmy.   For the third time, Jimmy is reading through the assigned chapter in his biology book, sitting in the study hall. He has ten more minutes before the bell will ring and he must go take the test on the chapter. The chapter is on the frog, and he understands (or thinks he understands) all of the general ideas. However, the class is going to be dissecting frogs in lab the following week, so the teacher wants the students to learn the parts of the frog and describe their functions. Although very bright, Jimmy reads at a sixth-grade level. He received services through Special Education all the way through elementary school, but since then he has been working on his own, with the help of his parents. He has come a long way (he could not read at all until third grade), but he still has trouble pronouncing the multi-syllable words. He also cannot remember their spelling. He is pretty sure he will not pass the test.

Maria.   Maria is also in study hall, and she too is taking the biology test in a few minutes. However, after she read the chapter once, she gave up. She felt overwhelmed by all of the information and did not understand a lot of what she was reading. Maria's family came to the United States when she was in 6th grade. As a ninth grader, she no longer gets ESL help. She is in all of the basic-level ninth-grade required courses at the high school. Maria also reads at a sixth–grade level, but her word recognition skills are excellent. With a bit of study, she can also memorize spellings of science words. Her problem is that she does not understand words and sentences in the textbook. Mr. Phillips, the after-school study skills instructor, suggested that she take notes as she read the chapter, but this did not help Maria pass the last test, and she has not gone back to talk to this teacher. She also has not completed her reading for her literature class, so she puts the biology book away and spends the last ten minutes reading the story by Hawthorne the class is discussing today.

Rene.   Rene is getting ready for her Biology test next period by working with a peer in the Learning Center. Rene has had a diagnosed language disorder and learning disability for years. The biology course is very hard for her, but she likes her class and her teachers, and also she likes working with her tutor and the "learning buddy" her teacher and tutor assigned her. She is completing a semantic feature analysis with her buddy, Terese. They have placed lots of the words that they need to learn in the chart, and they are talking about how the parts differ in function from the human being—how the eyes are different, how the lungs are different. She thinks the discussion is helping her. Rene is wondering what the frog sees under water; perhaps it looks like swimming underwater with goggles on, an experience she is familiar with.

Discussion Points:

1.   The students are faced with the same task, and they are reading and studying the same text. Consider the learners, the situations in which they are currently reading and studying, and the tasks they are using to facilitate their reading and learning about the topic at hand. As you examine these situations:
   ✓ Write down questions or concerns that come to mind.
   ✓ Think over your reading and/or go back to the appropriate chapters in this book to refresh your memory for relevant information on students' characteristics, instructional methods for content area courses, and guidelines for instruction from these and other parts of the book.
   ✓ Write alternative solutions to your questions and concerns. If possible, discuss your thoughts with others.
2.   Consider how these students might fare when they take the test; consider also how they might do on the project that follows the test.
3.   Put yourself in the shoes of this teacher:
   ✓ If you were the teacher, would you consider the test a good measure of the knowledge the students have of the science topic?
   ✓ How might you figure out whether the students gained valuable background knowledge through this system?
   ✓ What are some alternative ways to assess the students' learning from the textbook—and learning from the science projects as well?

SUCCUMBING TO THE PRESSURES OF HIGH-STAKES TESTS?

Lucy Roberts is a fourth-grade teacher at an elementary school in a mid-sized city. Her school has not been designated as "low-performing" based on student performance on state assessments, nor has it received an "exemplary" rating. Lucy's principal has made it clear to both the teachers and the students that he expects them to strive for this recognition. If an "exemplary" rating is earned, it will mean some additional funding from the state. Moreover, it will elevate the status of the school in the eyes of the public, since the ratings that area schools receive are published in the local newspaper. Lucy's own salary increase for next year is tied to how well her students perform on the end-of-grade assessments.

Lucy, like most of her colleagues, is finding herself spending more and more time on "drill and practice" activities in preparation for the test. She gives frequent practice tests, and every six weeks she administers a state-mandated criterion referenced assessment to determine whether or not her students are meeting interim "benchmarks." "It seems as if all I do is test," she complained to a friend.

The majority of the children at Lucy's school come from middle class families. However, about a quarter of the students qualify for free or reduced lunches, and there is a growing population of Hispanic students, most of whom are in the process of learning English. She has one ESL student, Miguel, who is proficient in English at a conversational level, but who struggles with the more complex vocabulary and syntax of academic language. There are three special education students in Lucy's class who receive assistance in the resource room for one or two hours each day. Several other students in the group have notable difficulty, but do not qualify for special education services. Lucy tries to spend extra time with these lower-achieving students, sometimes working with them in a group while the other students are engaged in "seatwork." However, most of her time is spent in full-class instruction.

Lucy feels that her students are learning some valuable reading comprehension skills. In preparation for the tests, she has spent a lot of time teaching them strategies for reading short passages and answering multiple-choice questions. They are getting better at recognizing components of a narrative, identifying main ideas, and selecting the best title for a passage. However, she worries about what they are *not* getting. She suspects that few, if any, of her students think to apply the same strategies when they read independently, and she questions how useful some of these strategies really are outside of a test-taking context. She wishes there were more time for content area instruction. Because fourth graders are not assessed on their knowledge of science and social studies, Lucy and her colleagues have been discouraged from spending much time on these subjects. Lucy tries to devote about 45 minutes twice a week to science or social studies, but often she finds that, for a variety of reasons, this time is cut short.

Lucy would like to experiment with different teaching methods and different ways of organizing instruction in her classroom, but she is afraid of abandoning methods that she feels are most likely to result in good test scores. She would like to incorporate more small group work, more meaningful reading and writing activities, and more content area instruction yet still ensure that her students perform well on the state assessments. She would like to more effectively differentiate instruction for students of differing abilities; however, she worries about the effects of ability grouping on the self-esteem of lower achieving students. Most of all, she is hesitant to "go against the grain" in a school climate in which the emphasis is on a direct connection between what is taught and what is measured by state assessments. Lucy likes her principal very much personally and realizes that he is under tremendous pressure to foster high achievement; however, she wishes he were more supportive of innovation and experimentation.

Discussion Questions

- ✓ What do you think Lucy can do to provide more varied instruction without sacrificing performance on state assessments?
- ✓ How might Lucy teach test-relevant skills through reading and writing activities in the content areas?
- ✓ How might Lucy orchestrate small-group instruction in reading comprehension? Would you recommend that she group the students randomly, by ability, or in some other way?
- ✓ How might Lucy go about creating a support-network for herself as she learns about and implements alternative teaching methods?

MATCHING TEACHING METHODS TO STUDENT NEEDS: CHANGES CONTEMPLATED BY A HISTORY TEACHER

Dan Kaiser has been teaching eleventh–grade American History for 15 years. In that time he has altered his teaching methods very little. As he describes it: "I talk, the students write down what I say, and every couple of weeks I test them on what I said." He gives reading assignments from the textbook for homework, but he never holds his students accountable for the material. He says, "I assign reading, but I know most of my students don't do it. A lot of them can't. It's pretty dry stuff to sixteen-year-olds. I never test them on material I haven't covered in class."

Dan specializes in teaching the average and lower track classes. He feels that he has the ability to relate well to his students. He observes, "The kids like me, and I like the kids. I'm a pretty entertaining lecturer. I keep 'em awake. They enjoy my jokes, and maybe they leave my class having learned a few facts about history." Dan frequently supplements his lectures by showing videotapes. For his lower track students, most of whom have difficulty reading and taking notes, he provides study aids such as outlines, summaries of key information, and definitions of important terms.

Several things have happened recently that have made Dan rethink some of his teaching methods. His school recently got a new principal who has a special education background and who hopes to raise levels of reading achievement by encouraging all teachers to emphasize reading instruction. She organized a professional development workshop on ways to incorporate comprehension strategy instruction into content area classes. Dan had never thought of himself as a teacher of reading. Like many of his colleagues, he had always assumed that the important thing was the information his students learned. Another request that the new principal made was that teachers spend some of their free periods observing colleagues' classes and sharing ideas about instruction. Dan observed a friend of his teaching an honors section of American History and was impressed with the use of problem-based learning. The students were exploring the decision to drop the atomic bomb on Hiroshima and Nagasaki by debating the issue from the perspectives of a Japanese citizen, an American military strategist, a nuclear physicist, and an advisor to President Truman (Ettzevoglou-Hoyer, Hammond, and Mueller 1999). Dan was impressed with the students' motivation, the eagerness with which they engaged in research (which included reading some difficult original documents obtained through the Internet), and the complexity of their thinking. "But there's no way my kids can do that," he thought. "It's like comparing apples and oranges." Still, he was intrigued by this means of immersing students in the drama of historical events.

In optimistic moments, Dan is thinking seriously about making some radical changes in his teaching methods. He would like to make a concerted effort to help his students become more effective readers by teaching them comprehension strategies explicitly. He likes the idea of small-group collaborative strategy instruction, but he wonders whether or not it will work in his classes. He thinks that his success at managing student behavior is due in large part to his teacher-directed style that allows him to maintain tight control over the class as a whole. He worries that breaking the students into small groups will be asking for trouble. "Some of my kids are pretty tough customers," he says. "You have to stay on top of them every minute or they act up." He is concerned that some of the very poor readers will feel uncomfortable reading aloud in groups with other students and worries that they will be made fun of.

After reflecting further on his visit to the honors class, he thinks that problem-based learning might be a way for his students to have more meaningful learning experiences. He thinks that many of his students would be motivated by assuming the roles of real players in historical events, but he is not sure they can handle open-ended problems that require independent thinking and research. He realizes that for most of his students, the assignment will need to be much more structured than what he witnessed in his friend's class, and he is not sure how to provide the structure. He wonders how he can effectively involve extremely poor readers in the process. Finally, Dan is concerned that comprehension strategies and problem-solving activities will absorb more time than he can afford to spend, given his obligation to cover American history, from colonization to the present.

Discussion Questions

✓ What method(s) of comprehension strategy instruction do you think would work best in Dan's classes? Why?

✓ How might Dan structure problem-based or experiential learning to make it accessible for his lower-achieving students?

✓ Should Dan decide to provide instruction in small groups, what do you think he will need to do to help the students stay "on task"? What might he do to minimize the potential for misbehavior?

✓ What types of texts might Dan make use of in addition to or instead of the textbook? Where might he turn for resources for the very poor readers in his classes who cannot read the textbook? How can he make use of the Internet and other multi-media resources?

✓ What do you think of the dramatic changes in teaching methods that Dan is contemplating? What are the potential benefits to his students? What problems do you think might arise?

DEBATING THE PROS AND CONS OF READING INSTRUCTION IN PULL-IN AND PULL-OUT SETTINGS

Sarah Stuart is a special education teacher who works primarily with fourth and fifth graders in a resource room setting. In recent years, she has become frustrated by the increasing numbers of students for whom she is expected to provide "individualized" services. This year, she has no fewer than nine children at a time, and there are twelve in one of her fourth-grade groups. She has Mr. Tompkins, a paraprofessional, working with her. He takes responsibility for working with some of the children, following her directions. Still, Sarah feels that the numbers are too high for her to provide quality instruction. The children with more severe disabilities consume much of her time, and she worries that students with milder learning disabilities, who are capable of working more independently, do not get enough individual attention.

To help alleviate this problem, Sarah has been trying to group the students according to reading level, so that she can provide small-group reading instruction to children with similar needs. She has noticed that many of her students have difficulty with reading comprehension, in spite of improved decoding. She has been using Reciprocal Teaching to help them read more strategically. Sarah has observed significant progress in many of her students. She worries, though, that they are not getting enough practice with strategy use outside of the resource setting to really internalize the strategies. Sarah has talked with the classroom teachers about trying to reinforce the strategies the students are learning when they are completing reading assignments in the regular class; however, she suspects that this does not happen on a systematic basis, given the number of students and competing demands on teachers' time.

The district special education coordinator has also become concerned about the overcrowded conditions in resource rooms. She has recommended that students with relatively mild reading or learning disabilities receive services in the general classroom whenever possible, reserving resource room instruction for children with more severe difficulties. According to this model, the special educator would serve as a consultant to the classroom teacher and also would provide services in the classroom, in collaboration with the classroom teacher. Sarah has mixed feelings about this change. She certainly agrees that there are too many children in the resource room at a given time, and she believes that the students might be more successful at generalizing what they have learned to other reading tasks if they are taught in a single setting. She also knows that there are other students in the general classroom who could benefit from the same kind of instruction she provides in the resource room. She is not sure, however, that she and the general education teachers will be able to reach agreement on the methods that should be used.

Sarah is becoming convinced that the advantages of the collaboration/ consultation model outweigh the disadvantages. The district coordinator has made it clear that she would like someone to take her suggestions seriously, and Sarah feels the time has come to look at a new way to meet the needs of the students with learning disabilities. She has begun conversations with the two fifth-grade teachers, both of whom she gets along with. These teachers have expressed interest in beginning discussions that might lead to collaboration and team teaching. One of the two is particularly concerned about the reading comprehension of a number of students in her class. She would like to discuss Sarah's ideas for implementing comprehension strategy instruction on a class-wide basis. Before beginning, however, all three teachers feel the need to learn more about how to implement techniques they have read about but never seen demonstrated. And they need to get the support of the administration and perhaps the parents of children with learning disabilities as well. Sarah is certain there are other problems they need to address, and she is worried that the group will move forward without having thought out all the ramifications of this drastic change.

Discussion Questions

✓ What do you see as the pros and cons of providing services for special education students in the resource room as opposed to the regular classroom? Which skills might be better addressed in the resource room? Which in the regular classroom?

✓ What can special educators and classroom teachers do to help students generalize what they have learned in one context to the other context?

✓ Based on what you have read, what approaches to comprehension instruction would you recommend that Sarah and her colleagues take? Where can they turn for help in learning how to implement these approaches?

✓ How would you recommend that Sarah and her colleagues orchestrate the co-teaching arrangement?

✓ What should these teachers expect by way of support from the school administration, the special education staff, and the parents of students with special needs?

SCHOOL AND COMMUNITY LINKS: USING VOLUNTEERS AS READING COACHES

In an effort to improve the reading achievement of students at the "low performing" elementary schools in the district, the local school board has decided to recruit tutors to work individually with children who need extra help. The program is being publicized through ads in the newspaper and public service announcements on local radio and television stations. The ads are aimed at retired citizens, high school and college students, and working adults who can spare a few hours a week. A special effort is being made to recruit people who speak Spanish to work with students who are learning English as a second language. The people who have signed on so far are a diverse group. A few are retired teachers; others are college students majoring in education. Most, however, have had very little experience working with children who have learning difficulties. The tutors are enthusiastic and eager to help, but they will need training in effective methods of reading instruction.

The school board decided to leave it up to administrators and faculty at each school to determine how to make use of the tutors in their particular setting. A committee from each school must submit a written proposal before tutors will be assigned to them. The principal of Andrews Elementary School, one of the target schools, appointed a committee of two special education teachers, three classroom teachers, and the ESL teacher to write their proposal. Andrews has a very diverse student body. About 50% of the students are African American. Twenty-five percent are White. The remaining 25% are primarily Hispanic, though in recent years, the Asian population in the community has been growing. The vast majority of the students come from low-income families, and many are considered "at risk" for academic difficulties.

At its first meeting, the committee generated the following questions:

1. How should children be selected to participate in the tutoring program?
2. How should the tutors be trained, and who should provide the training? Which methods of reading instruction should they be taught?
3. Should the tutors be supplied with lesson plans, or be expected to create their own?
4. Should the tutors work with the children outside of the classroom, or would it be more helpful for them to assume responsibility for working with specific children in their classes?
5. How can the tutors best assist the ESL students?
6. Who will supervise the tutors and provide feedback to them?
7. How can we assess the success of the tutoring program?

Discussion Questions

✓ What, if any, additional questions to you think it is important for the committee to consider?
✓ What would you recommend that the committee include in their proposal to the school board?

HOW TO REVITALIZE AN ELEMENTARY READING PROGRAM?

Pete Chase and Rae Dixon have worked together at the same elementary school district for 15 years. Both started out as classroom teachers, but for the last four years Pete has been the Language Arts Coordinator and Rae the Reading

Specialist. The school district is in a small city not far from a large mid-western city. Many of the children come from low-income homes. The school population is linguistically and ethnically diverse. In the last five years, these two colleagues have made a concerted effort to improve the reading of the children in the primary years, concerned because of the school's low performance overall on state reading assessments. They brought in Guided Reading (Fountas and Pinnelll 1996) and made sure the teachers knew how to keep running records and through this method to keep track of the progress of individual children in their class. They also bought a basal system that advocated a balanced literacy approach. They made sure that the teachers were familiar with the state standards for reading achievement at the early and upper elementary levels. They also offered the teachers many opportunities to design the reading program that they used so that it reflected their best professional judgment of ways to meet the needs of their children.

As a result of these efforts, the district's reading scores for third graders have improved somewhat, but over 50% of the children are still not at an "acceptable" level on the state reading assessment. A careful analysis of the state test results also showed that there was a lot of variation in the children's reading performance across classrooms.

Over the summer, Pete and Rae have had several meetings at which they evaluated the situation and together came to the conclusion that although they had brought about some positive changes, they had a long way to go to meet their goals. They are concerned about a new flood of referrals for learning disabilities evaluations at the third- and fourth-grade levels, and they realize that there are more children in the bottom quartile on the state reading tests than there were in the past. Why was it that their children could not read and understand the seemingly simple passages on the state test? At the end of the last meeting, they started to develop an action plan. The first step involved brainstorming measures that might be "steps forward." These included:

Bring in a program of explicit instruction in phonological awareness and phonics?

Provide the children with more direct instruction in comprehension?

Take away the teachers' opportunities to craft their own programs?

Reorganize the classes at each grade level (1–3) so that there were homogeneous groups during all or part of the two-hour literacy block?

Add time for instruction in language, including vocabulary?

Talk with outside consultants about packaged reading programs (e.g., Success for All)?

Pete and Rae are not entirely sure where to go from here, but they already know that the district administration will be taking a close look at the steps they take to revitalize the reading curriculum.

Discussion Questions

✓   What do you think about the list of ideas Pete and Rae came up with? Are there any of their ideas you would take off the list? Are there other measures you would add to the list?

✓ Why might there be an increase in referrals for evaluation of learning disabilities? Is there information they should be collecting about the students that would help them improve their reading curriculum?

✓ If you were a teacher working in this district, what might make your job of teaching reading to diverse learners easier than it currently is?

THE STUDENT'S PERSPECTIVE
A STRUGGLING READER IN HIGH SCHOOL

Michael, age 14, is a freshman in high school. He is a sociable teenager who plays the trumpet in the school's jazz band. Michael had difficulty learning to read as a young child. In the second grade, he was labeled learning disabled, and he began going to the resource room an hour a day to work on reading and writing. Eventually, Michael became more proficient at decoding words; however, throughout elementary school, he continued to have difficulty with fluency. By the time he had read a passage with several unfamiliar words, Michael often could not remember the meaning of what he had read. In spite of his reading difficulties, Michael had many interests and learned easily through listening.

School became markedly more difficult for Michael in middle school, when he changed classes and dealt with the expectations of several teachers. The special educator suggested that Michael's teachers try peer tutoring or cooperative learning groups, so that he could hear some of the information being shared orally, and thus not be so dependent on reading. These strategies were not consistently implemented, however, and Michael struggled to make Cs. His parents were somewhat confused over his reading difficulty, since, at this point, Michael did not seem to have too much difficulty with word identification, although his reading remained slow and he could not seem to remember what he read. Michael became frustrated, and he began to lose interest in school.

Now Michael is in high school. Psychoeducational testing indicates that he has an above average IQ, and several of his middle school teachers indicated that the grades he earned in their classes probably did not reflect his capabilities. In high school he has been placed in regular classes. Members of his IEP team felt that he could handle the standard workload. He does, however, spend one period a day getting extra help in the resource room. However, he is feeling overwhelmed by the expectations of his teachers. The reading assigned by his English teacher, Ms. Myers, is lengthy and difficult. At the moment, his class is reading *Romeo and Juliet*, and he finds the Shakespearean English impossible to decipher. His teacher sometimes gives "pop quizzes" to make sure the students have done their reading. Michael usually fails these. Mr. Olsen, his history teacher, uses a difficult textbook and some supplemental reading assignments. Most of the information is delivered through lectures. Though Mr. Olsen spent some time at the beginning of the year teaching the class how to take notes, Michael never mastered this skill. Michael has always enjoyed science, but he's having a hard time in biology with heavy reading assignments and tests that require a great deal of memorization. Michael has never before had serious difficulty with math, yet he failed the last test in algebra, which involved solving word problems.

For the first time, Michael is being tested on information from the reading as well as material from class lectures and discussions. He does not know how he can possibly complete all of the reading he is assigned. The writing assignments are also problematic for him. His teachers tell him that he has good ideas, but they are often poorly organized and under-developed. In addition, he makes many mistakes with grammar, spelling, and punctuation, even though he uses the spelling and grammar checkers on his word processor. He does get assistance with reading and writing in the resource room, but there is not time to address everything. When he concentrates on getting caught up in one class, he falls behind in all the others.

Band is Michael's refuge. There he feels confident and competent. He wishes that he could be equally sure of himself in all of his courses. Michael hopes to go to college and major in music. He has thought he might like to be a high school music teacher and band director. He knows he will have to improve his reading to get into college and succeed. However, right now he is wondering if he will even make it through high school. Michael avoids talking with his teachers about the difficulties he is having. They give him extra time on tests and overlook some of the errors in his writing. He is not sure what else they would be willing or able to do to help. Besides, he does not want to be treated differently from the other students or have his teachers do anything that would draw his classmates' attention to his reading difficulties.

Discussion Questions

- ✓ How would you characterize the difficulties Michael continues to have with reading comprehension? On the basis of what you have read, what are the underlying difficulties that have contributed to his present underachievement in reading?
- ✓ Given your answer to the first question, in what aspects of reading does Michael need to make progress in order to meet his goal of becoming a better reader?
- ✓ Can you suggest ways for Michael to approach his teachers? Is he right that there is not much more that they can do for him? Is Michael doing all that he can to help himself out?
- ✓ What might be the role of the special education teacher or other support services staff members at the school?
- ✓ Prepare a comprehensive plan to address Michaels' difficulties with his academic work. Your plan should include (but not be limited to) recommended changes in the organization of instruction in their classes and possible accommodations or modifications.
- ✓ Do you think high school teachers should feel obligated to teach reading? Why or why not?

REFERENCES

Ettzevoglou-Hoyer, N., Hammond, H., and Mueller, T. 1999. *The decision to drop the bomb.* Retrieved January 11, 2002, from http://www.richmond.edu/academics/ a&s/ education/projects/webquests/wwii/bomb.html

Fountas, I. C., and Pinnell, G. S. 1996. *Guided Reading: Good First Teaching for All Children.* Portsmouth, NH: Heinemann.

Index

Page numbers in italic represent material that appears in tables or figures; n represents footnote.

Words (*continued*)
   individual sounds in, 19; instruction in learning new, 98–107; key
   word method to learn new,
   104–105; in a list vs. in a text, 46–47,
   54; learning to decode individual,
   19; mnemonic methods of learning
   new, 104–105; number learned per
   year, 96; requiring students to
   learn too many new, 109; sensitivity to sound structure of, 20;
   sentences from scrambled, 126–27;
strategies to recognize, 42; to be
taught from reading materials, 102.
See also Vocabulary
Working memory, 124; deficits in syntactic skills and, 118; working with
   students with limitations in, 80. *See
   also* Verbal working memory
Writing disabilities, reading and, 35
Written language, syntax of, 118–19

Zigmond, N., 8